Managing Technology Integration for Human Resources in Industry 5.0

Naman Sharma
Indian Institute of Foreign Trade, India

Kumar Shalender
Chitkara University, India

IGI Global
PUBLISHER of TIMELY KNOWLEDGE

A volume in the Advances in Human Resources Management and Organizational Development (AHRMOD) Book Series

Published in the United States of America by
IGI Global
Business Science Reference (an imprint of IGI Global)
701 E. Chocolate Avenue
Hershey PA, USA 17033
Tel: 717-533-8845
Fax: 717-533-8661
E-mail: cust@igi-global.com
Web site: http://www.igi-global.com

Library of Congress Cataloging-in-Publication Data

Names: Sharma, Naman, 1986- editor. | Shalender, Kumar, 1984- editor.
Title: Managing technology integration for human resources in industry 5.0 / editors, Naman Sharma and Kumar Shalender.
Description: Hershey, PA : Business Science Reference, [2023] | Includes bibliographical references and index. | Summary: "Managing Technology Integration for Human Resources in Industry 5.0 provides insights into the impact of industrial revolution 4.0 in human resources. It provides insights for both industry and academia to assist them in teaching and training the next generation leaders through universities and corporate training. Covering topics such as business performance, human technology integration, and digitalization, this premier reference source is an essential resource for human resource managers, IT managers, organizational executives and leaders, entrepreneurs, students and educators of higher education, librarians, researchers, and academicians"-- Provided by publisher.
Identifiers: LCCN 2022043715 (print) | LCCN 2022043716 (ebook) | ISBN 9781668467459 (hardcover) | ISBN 9781668467466 (paperback) | ISBN 9781668467473 (ebook)
Subjects: LCSH: Human capital--Management. | Management--Technological innovations. | Personnel management.
Classification: LCC HD4904.7 .M326 2023 (print) | LCC HD4904.7 (ebook) | DDC 658.3--dc23/eng/20220929
LC record available at https://lccn.loc.gov/2022043715
LC ebook record available at https://lccn.loc.gov/2022043716

This book is published in the IGI Global book series Advances in Human Resources Management and Organizational Development (AHRMOD) (ISSN: 2327-3372; eISSN: 2327-3380)

British Cataloguing in Publication Data
A Cataloguing in Publication record for this book is available from the British Library.

Advances in Human Resources Management and Organizational Development (AHRMOD) Book Series

Patricia Ordóñez de Pablos
Universidad de Oviedo, Spain

ISSN:2327-3372
EISSN:2327-3380

Mission

A solid foundation is essential to the development and success of any organization and can be accomplished through the effective and careful management of an organization's human capital. Research in human resources management and organizational development is necessary in providing business leaders with the tools and methodologies which will assist in the development and maintenance of their organizational structure.

The **Advances in Human Resources Management and Organizational Development (AHRMOD) Book Series** aims to publish the latest research on all aspects of human resources as well as the latest methodologies, tools, and theories regarding organizational development and sustainability. The **AHRMOD Book Series** intends to provide business professionals, managers, researchers, and students with the necessary resources to effectively develop and implement organizational strategies.

Coverage

- Upward Feedback
- Disputes Resolution
- Work-Life Balance
- Organizational Behavior
- Organizational Learning
- Employment and Labor Laws
- Entrepreneurialism
- Employee Benefits
- Workplace Culture
- Worker Behavior and Engagement

IGI Global is currently accepting manuscripts for publication within this series. To submit a proposal for a volume in this series, please contact our Acquisition Editors at Acquisitions@igi-global.com or visit: http://www.igi-global.com/publish/.

The Advances in Human Resources Management and Organizational Development (AHRMOD) Book Series (ISSN 2327-3372) is published by IGI Global, 701 E. Chocolate Avenue, Hershey, PA 17033-1240, USA, www.igi-global.com. This series is composed of titles available for purchase individually; each title is edited to be contextually exclusive from any other title within the series. For pricing and ordering information please visit http://www.igi-global.com/book-series/advances-human-resources-management-organizational/73670. Postmaster: Send all address changes to above address.

Titles in this Series

For a list of additional titles in this series, please visit: www.igi-global.com/book-series/advances-human-resources-management-organizational/73670

Examining the Aging Workforce and Its Impact on Economic and Social Development
Bruno de Sousa Lopes (University of Aveiro, Portugal) Maria Céu Lamas (School of Health, Polytechnic of Porto, Portugal) Vanessa Amorim (Porto Accounting and Business School, Polytechnic of Porto, Portugal) and Orlando Lima Rua (Porto Accounting and Business School, Polytechnic of Porto, Portugal)
Business Science Reference • © 2023 • 215pp • H/C (ISBN: 9781668463512) • US $225.00

The Experiences of Black Women Diversity Practitioners in Historically White Institutions
Tristen Brenaé Johnson (Moffitt Cancer Center, USA)
Information Science Reference • © 2023 • 330pp • H/C (ISBN: 9781668435649) • US $215.00

Handbook of Research on Acceleration Programs for SMEs
Inês Lisboa (Politechnic Institute of Leiria, Portugal) Nuno Teixeira (Politechnic Institute of Setúbal, Portugal) Liliane Segura (Presbiteriano Mackenzie Institute, Brazil) Tomáš Krulický (Institute of Technology and Business, České Budějovice, Czech Republic) and Veronika Machová (Institute of Technology and Business, České Budějovice, Czech Republic)
Business Science Reference • © 2023 • 575pp • H/C (ISBN: 9781668456668) • US $360.00

Leadership Perspectives on Effective Intergenerational Communication and Management
Fatma Ince (Mersin University, Turkey)
Business Science Reference • © 2023 • 320pp • H/C (ISBN: 9781668461402) • US $230.00

Developing Diversity, Equity, and Inclusion Policies for Promoting Employee Sustainability and Well-Being
Sónia P. Gonçalves (ISCSP-ULisboa, Portugal) Paula Cristina Nunes Figueiredo (Universidade Lusófona, Portugal) Eduardo Luis Soares Tomé (ULHT - Universidade Lusófona, Portugal) and José Baptista (ISCSP-ULisboa, Portugal)
Business Science Reference • © 2023 • 330pp • H/C (ISBN: 9781668441817) • US $240.00

Global Citizenship and Its Impact on Multiculturalism in the Workplace
Randa Diab-Bahman (Kuwait College of Science and Technology, Kuwait) and Abrar Al-Enzi (Gulf University for Science and Technology, Kuwait)
Business Science Reference • © 2023 • 300pp • H/C (ISBN: 9781668454367) • US $240.00

IGI Global
PUBLISHER of TIMELY KNOWLEDGE

701 East Chocolate Avenue, Hershey, PA 17033, USA
Tel: 717-533-8845 x100 • Fax: 717-533-8661
E-Mail: cust@igi-global.com • www.igi-global.com

Editorial Advisory Board

Table of Contents

Detailed Table of Contents

success of AI depends on a number of important factors being combined. The authors found that the use of artificial intelligence has helped the organizations in enhancing their performance and assists in gaining competitive advantage.

HR analytics is a paradigm shift from a traditional and intuitive-based approach to an evidence-based approach for aiding decision-making processes to enhance employee as well as organizational performance and profitability. This chapter discusses the concept of HR analytics, followed by its application to three HR functions: recruitment, employee engagement, and employee retention. Two case studies for each of these three HR functions are also succinctly discussed. Some relevant statistics regarding the current state of implementation of HR analytics in organizations is also briefly discussed. Key issues related to the HR analytics implementation process, moderating factors to implement HR analytics, and challenges of implementation are also discussed in this chapter. The chapter concludes with a discussion on the future of HR analytics. Considering the scope of the book, technical details like regression models or machine learning algorithms are not discussed in this chapter.

With the growing digitalization, the use of machine learning and artificial intelligence has increased in businesses. Humans have gotten smarter while using and collaborating with such machines and integrated to the invention of Industry 5.0. A company like Tesla also depends on humans to create efficient work from robotic devices. Industry 5.0 objects to creating a balance between the use of machinery and human with the promotional use of technologies. Business owners must transform their strategies to attract customers, suppliers, and global markets. This chapter aims to identify the critical factors that Industry 4.0 lacked and were identified and transited to Industry 5.0. With artificial intelligence, the internet of things, machine learning, and nascent technologies, the human pace of work will subsequently be the essential constituent of the future workplace. Thus, India consists of many small and medium-sized companies and start-ups, and the latest technologies and adoption of Industry 5.0 is essential for Indian business owners.

Businesses benefit from supply chain management because it enables the compatibility, integration,

means in the process from the development of the industrial revolution to the present day has also led to an increase in international labor migration. Although labor migration is among the most criticized issues, it is actually an important criterion in providing the workforce to meet the change needs of companies in the process called the new normal after the COVİD-19 pandemic. Undoubtedly, different ideas and talents coming from the workforce from different countries come to the fore in the success of multinational companies that have increased in recent years. Under the title of diversity, equality, and inclusiveness practice, senior managers in companies should adopt the corporate culture that gathers employees of different races, languages, colors, religions, and beliefs under one roof and pay attention to ensuring equal rights.

Preface

As we will advance towards Industry 5.0, characterized by the convergence of emerging technologies such as artificial intelligence, the internet of things, and robotics, organizations must carefully consider how they can effectively integrate these technologies into their operations. This is especially true for human resources departments, which play a key role in managing the workforce and ensuring that employees have the skills and competencies needed to thrive in the digital age. Our book attempts to address the issues and possibilities that may play a vital role in the integration of technology and human workforce in organizations during Industry 5.0.

One key aspect of managing technology integration in human resources for Industry 5.0 is understanding the impact that new technologies will have on the workforce. This includes assessing the skills and competencies that will be required to effectively use these technologies, as well as identifying any potential challenges or obstacles that may arise during the integration process. For example, an organization may need to invest in training programs to help employees learn how to use new software or hardware, or may need to provide support to employees as they adapt to new ways of working. Leadership also plays an important role in making these decisions related to technological integrations for the workforce. The first two chapters of the book, 'Embedding Technology in Human Resource Management' and 'Emerging Challenges and Opportunities for Leaders in Industry-5.0: A Roadmap Through Literature Review', attempt to highlight and discuss these concerns and requirements.

Further, an important aspect of managing technology integration in human resources is ensuring that there is a clear strategy in place for how the new technologies will be adopted and implemented. This may involve creating a timeline for rolling out the technologies, establishing goals and benchmarks for measuring success, and developing a plan for training and onboarding employees to use the new technologies. It is also important to ensure that employees are involved in the process, as they will be the ones using the new technologies daily. By involving employees in the planning and implementation process, organizations can gain valuable insights into how the technologies can best be used to support their needs and goals. Chapters 5 and 6 of our book, 'The Role of Human Centricity in the Transition From Industry 4.0 to Industry 5.0: An Integrative Literature Review' and 'Towards an Automated, Vigilant, and Strategic HRM Function in Industry 5.0', make sincere efforts to study these aspects and provide the readers with an insight into these issues.

Another important aspect of managing technology integration in human resources for Industry 5.0 is staying up to date with the latest technologies and trends. This may involve attending industry conferences and events, reading relevant research and articles, and staying in touch with key stakeholders in the technology and HR fields. By staying informed and engaged, organizations can ensure that they are making the most of the latest technologies to support their workforce and drive business success. The book chapters 'Human Technology Integration: Augmenting Human Abilities With Intelligent Technologies and Pervasive Computing Emerging Trends', 'Integrating Human and Artificial Intelligence Within Organizations: A Conceptual Framework Based on Artistry and Scientific HR Elements', 'How Does the Use of AI in HRM Contribute to Improved Business Performance? A Systematic Review', and 'Information and Communication Technologies in Logistics and Supply Chain Management in Turkey: Human Resource Practices and New Challenges', provide key insights on these trends and hopefully will keep readers interested in future of HR Tech.

Chapter 1 discusses that technology-driven human resource management is the order of the day. The knowledge of available technologies and their implications in some HRM functions is critical for today's managers. The focus of the chapter is to discuss the challenges and issues in traditional HRM and the impact of the integration of technologies in some of the HRM functions like human resource planning, candidate tracking, workforce management, talent acquisition & recruitment, career management, employee relationship management, compensation, training, succession planning, retention, and others. The chapter also provides a list of software tools available for various HRM functions and their purpose, Information Technologies in Industry 5.0.

Chapter 2 talks about the way the industry has developed over a period of time. Industry 1.0 had a different scenario than inustry 5.0. The revolution of industries transformed the economy of the country which was based on agriculture and handicrafts at an earlier time. With this revolution, Leaders also required necessary qualities which are demanding and leading in the future.In the world of a fast-growing business, the transformation of leadership has become an important topic to be discussed. It has become necessary to analyze new leadership techniques and skill sets required to form the organizational structure which will be best suitable for new-age leadership. This article is focusing on the changes in leadership practices from industry-1.0 to industry 5.0. Moreover, this article also highlights the challenges, opportunities, and required skill sets for leaders in Industry-5.0.

In Chapter 3, the advent of Internet of Things (IoT) and cloud computing coupled with several breakthroughs in the field of Artificial Intelligence, have made ambient intelligence possible which incorporate pervasive computing, human computer interaction, artificial intelligence and IoT. Whose objective is to tune the environment to understand human needs and seamless integration of technology with life. Which is the bedrock for human technology integration; where artificial systems and miniaturized nanotechnology devices are embodied or implanted in human body which can either function as replacement for human body parts or the extension of human capabilities. This chapter will investigate the trends and advancement in human computer integration. Find out, how human augmentation technologies can be used to replicate, supplement and exceed human abilities? Also verify the impact of human technology augmentation on Industry 5.0 and the challenges that contend with human technology integration.

Chapter 4 discusses how artificial intelligence (AI) and human resources (HR) are often presented as a dichotomy by researchers. Rhetoric at present posit AI as a potential threat to HR. AI is seen as the ability of a machine to perform cognitive tasks, such as perceiving, reasoning and problem solving which we often associate with human minds. However, studies have also found that emotions, tacit knowledge, ethics, common-sense and pro-social behavior are fine human virtues that cannot be replaced by any intelligent machine. Thus, this study opines that organizations cannot achieve desired effectiveness by putting AI and people at the extreme ends of a continuum. The literature has many cases of specific human-AI proposals that widely address several organizational needs. The reverse case is less common, to use specific organizational needs as a basis for formulating general human-AI proposals. This chapter is a nascent attempt to propose a conceptual framework of human capabilities (artistry/soft and scientific/hard) that are used to characterize the required human-AI intervention.

Chapter 5, presents the 2021 European Commission report "Industry 5.0: Towards Sustainable, Human-Centric and Resilient European Industry." However, there is no clarity in the literature on the concept of human-centricity and there is a lack of clear definitions and intercurrent relationships are not identified. The paper aims to assess, critique and synthesize literature on the topic to enable a firm foundation for advancing knowledge and facilitating theory development. The study answers three research questions: RQ1 – What are the concepts that identify the human-centric approach in firms' management? RQ2 – What are the main definitions of the concepts and their gaps, overlaps, similarities or contrasts? RQ3 – What are the intervening relationships between the concepts and definitions that guide the implementation of human-centric Industry 4.0 or 5.0? The chapter implements an integrative literature review and contributes to the literature through the creation of a conceptual framework, useful for the promotion and application of a human-centric approach in Industry 4.0 and 5.0.

Chapter 6 references technological applications' advancements in the HRM function and suggests the revised HRM function in industry 5.0. In the first part a brief background has been given on the technological advancements in the function followed by an extensive literature review of the ongoing and probable application areas of technologies in HRM function. Subsequently, the author develops certain models of operations that the HRs will have to follow which will help in imbibing the technological practices of machine learning, artificial intelligence, blockchain while adhering to the data privacy practices. Thus, this approach makes the HRM function more automated but vigilant and strategic simultaneously so that HRs can monitor and control the cobots in Industry 5.0.

Chapter 7 discusses human resource management (HRM) in organizations is rapidly being transformed by information technologies. The COVID-19 pandemic has intensified the pace of digitalization of HR processes, which has become particularly important in the context of the digital transformation of human resource activities. Those organizations that take advantage of digital HRM technologies are better positioned than those that pay less attention to them. Additionally, organizations have had to adapt to new work models such as hybrid or remote work. This chapter describes how digitization is reshaping human resources by introducing digital HR transformation in different activities, comparing digital recruitment to traditional recruitment, focusing on the role of applicant tracking systems in recruitment and selection, and examining digital trends and work models. Finally, several practical implications will be discussed.

Chapter 8 aims to review the usage of Artificial Intelligence in human resource management (HRM) to enhance the organizational performance. The current study is a conceptual effort that integrates several streams of literature to give critical review of the interaction between AI and HRM in modern organizations. The present review enables industrialists to think of AI as a collection or combination of numerous IT configurations in the many company business areas rather than as a single technology because the success of AI depends on a number of important factors being combined. We found that the use of Artificial Intelligence has helped the organizations in enhancing their performance and assist in gaining competitive advantage.

In Chapter 9, HR analytics is a paradigm shift from traditional and intuitive-based approach to an evidence-based approach for aiding decision-making process to enhance employees' as well as organization's performance and profitability. This chapter discusses the concept of HR Analytics, followed by its application to three HR functions: recruitment, employee engagement and employee retention. Two case studies for each of these three HR functions are also succinctly discussed. Some relevant statistics regarding the current state of implementation of HR Analytics in organizations is also briefly discussed.

Key issues related to the HR Analytics implementation process, moderating factors to implement HR Analytics and challenges of implementation are also discussed in this chapter. The chapter concludes with a discussion on the future of HR Analytics. Considering the scope of the book, technical details like regression models or machine learning algorithms are not discussed in this chapter.

With the growing digitalization, the use of machine learning and artificial intelligence has increased in businesses. Humans have got smatter while using and collaborating with such machines and integrated to the invention of Industry 5.0. A company like Tesla also depends on humans to create efficient work from robotic devices. Industry 5.0 objects to creating a balance between the use of machinery and human with the promotional use of technologies. Business owners must transform their strategies to attract customers, suppliers and global markets. Chapter 10 aims to identify the critical factors that industry 4.0 lacked and identify and transited by Industry 5.0. With artificial intelligence, the internet of things, machine learning, and nascent technologies, the human pace of work will subsequently be the essential constituent of the future workplace. Thus, India consists of many small and medium-sized companies and start-ups, and the latest technologies and adoption of Industry 5.0 is essential for Indian business owners.

Businesses benefit from supply chain management because it enables the compatibility, integration, and high performance of applications, as well as the development of competitive qualities such as pricing, quality and innovation. Today, businesses use information technology to compete and achieve their goals. Industry 4.0 is a new situation that has emerged as informatics, communication, internet, sensors, automation, artificial intelligence, and robotic technologies greatly affect and change production processes. As a result of Industry 4.0, information and automation technologies have caused the supply chain to adapt by digitizing it. On the other hand, with Industry 5.0 studies, it is aimed to reveal great innovations in logistics and supply chain management. In Chapter 11, the information and communication technologies used in the logistics and supply chain sector will be examined, Industry 5.0 applications will be discussed, and the current situation of Turkey will be evaluated.

The objective of Chapter 12 is to study the effect of big data marketing and human resources management on the performance of companies and to find in return a relevant solutions. This study of review is based on the selection of 22 recent articles. This literature search designates the causal relationship between marketing theory and big data, while indicating the specificities of big data marketing. Then, this study indicates the opportunities and constraints found with the following of this type of integration. After that, it indicates the importance of the correlation between big data and human resources and also the necessity of performance. Finally, this research specifies the effects of big data marketing and human resources management on the performance of companies. The contribution of this study is justified by previous studies that point this gap based on the consideration of marketing and management literature.

Chapter 13 focuses on the critical observable determinants reflecting the benefits of e-working for academicians. It highlights the four core constructs viz Work-life balance, job effectiveness or performance, flexibility, employee relationship, and trust with the organization, which is of prime importance for a fruitful remote working in the current scenario. Empirical testing of the proposed research model was done by collecting data through online questionnaires from 230 academicians involved in online teaching. The study showed that in an e-working scenario, there is indeed a healthier work-life balance, and increased e-working results in improved efficiency or work productivity. The e-working model is quite new for the education sector, and the current study will help colleges and universities to understand and support the well-being of academicians working remotely and will also help the stakeholders of the education sector to frame the strategies keeping in mind the requirement of academicians.

Chapter 14 discusses the acceleration of globalization in the world as a result of the development of technology and transportation means in the process from the development of the industrial revolution to the present day has also led to an increase in international labor migration. Although labor migration is among the most critized issues, it is actually an important criterion in providing the workforce to meet the change needs of companies in the process called the new normal after the COVID-19 pandemic. Undoubtedly, different ideas and talents coming from the workforce from different countries come to the fore in the success of multinational companies that have increased in recent years. Under the title of diversity, equality and inclusiveness practice, senior managers in companies should adopt the corporate culture that gathers employees of different races, languages, colors, religions and beliefs under one roof and pay attention to ensuring equal rights.

Overall, managing technology integration for human resources in Industry 5.0 requires a thoughtful and strategic approach. By understanding the impact of new technologies on the workforce, developing a clear plan for adoption and implementation, and staying informed about the latest trends, organizations can effectively integrate these technologies and support the needs of their employees in the digital age. Hopefully, this book will help both researchers as well as practitioners to take a stock of current HR tech and also prepare their respective courses for the future in this tremendously fascinating space of tech integration with human resources in organizations.

Naman Sharma
Indian Institute of Foreign Trade, India

Kumar Shalender
Chitkara University, India

Acknowledgment

We are honored to present to you the latest publication *Managing Technology Integration for Human Resources in Industry 5.0*. It has been our pleasure to work with the esteemed authors of this book and see their vision come to fruition.

As the editor of this book, we acknowledge the efforts of our team of reviewers. They took it as their responsibility to guide the authors through the review process and ensure that their message is conveyed in the clearest and most impactful way possible. We are proud to say that this book is the result of tireless effort and collaboration between the authors, editors, and our team of reviewers.

In the end, we are truly grateful to our families for their understanding and never-dying support to us in completion of this book on time. We hope that you enjoy reading this book as much as we enjoyed working on it.

Chapter 1
Embedding Technology in Human Resource Management

Bhanumathi P.
M.S. Ramaiah Institute of Management, India

Jeevitha R.
M.S. Ramaiah Institute of Management, India

Rema V.
M.S. Ramaiah Institute of Management, India

ABSTRACT

Technology-driven human resource management is the order of the day. The knowledge of available technologies and their implications in some HRM functions is critical for today's managers. The focus of the chapter is to discuss the challenges and issues in traditional HRM, and the impact of the integration of technologies in some of the HRM functions like human resource planning, candidate tracking, workforce management, talent acquisition and recruitment, career management, employee relationship management, compensation, training, succession planning, retention, and others. The chapter also provides a list of software tools available for various HRM functions and their purpose, information technologies in Industry 5.0

INTRODUCTION

Human beings hardly live and work in isolation. They tend to plan, develop relations, and manage the activities or work consciously and unconsciously. Every person from childhood acquires knowledge and experience to understand others and behave in a particular situation in life. Similarly, it is applicable in the workplace. The concept of Human Resource Management works based on managing relations in the workplace. HRM gained importance in academic and other commercial spaces in the mid-1980s.

It is multidisciplinary that encapsulates theories and ideas from several fields, such as management, economics, sociology, psychology, etc. Men, money, material, and machinery are the various resources

DOI: 10.4018/978-1-6684-6745-9.ch001

collected, coordinated, and utilized only with the help of people. There is no single rule to manage people effectively, as people's needs are different and alike. The effectiveness of HRM depends on the prevailing conditions in the organizational space. The three essential components of any organization: are people, purpose, and structure. Employees are considered an asset to any organization, and competency will not guarantee the firm's competitiveness. They ought to perform all kinds of organizational activities.

An organization can grow and diversify when employees are talented, qualified, competent, placed in an appropriate position, trained, committed, and managed effectively for a firm's success. Human resource management's focal point is to get maximum contributions from employees to achieve individual and organizational, functional, and societal objectives; their effective utilization is necessary.

The primary human resource activities are personnel policies, legal policies, job descriptions, recruitment process, selection, training, and development of employees, employee compensation and benefit system, career progression and management, employee coordination & relations, performance appraisal and management, termination, KPIs, etc. It involves both quantitative and qualitative information. Collecting data depends on the time, type, and target audience size.

CHALLENGES AND ISSUES IN TRADITIONAL HRM

Present-day HRM is under constant pressure to perform in changing conditions and performance demands. Some of the pressure points in today's HRM are; Increasing globalization, Rapid technological changes, Tougher competition, Acquisitions, alliances, and mergers, changing structures, and hierarchical levels, New ways of delegation of authority and work, Diverse workforce, Delivering economic value to both employees and customers, Growing need for flexibility and creativity, Downsizing and Consolidations, Job rotations and so on. Apart from all these, the various functions of HRM have many challenges, which are discussed below:

Increased Unconscious Human Bias in HRM

Human bias tends to unconsciously develop behaviors to deal with critical or decision-making situations (Haselton, Nettle, & Murray, 2015). Human bias would happen outside our conscious mind's awareness and may result in erroneous decision-making. They may also force us to consider poor options and infer wrong insights. Human likes or dislikes and personal experiences do not have enough scientific theory to prove, according to Baer, T., 2019. Cognitive bias study is a prominent research area in social psychology, taking a new dimension due to the increased use of information technologies and the availability of a large amount of human behavioral data. Cognitive bias could limit human rational thinking capabilities (Oberai, & Anand, 2018).

One of today's manager's desirable characteristics is to deal with these biases, infer the outcome of thinking styles, and avoid future negative impacts (Dalton & Villagran, 2018). These biases come in many types: projection bias, confirmation bias, negativity bias, self-enhancement bias, spill-over effects, blind spots, fundamental attribution error, recency bias, etc.

In human resource management, unconscious bias negatively affects recruitment, retention, performance management, promotion, client relations, and work schedule. Table 2 highlights workplace biases and their impacts (Dvorsky, 2013) (Thomas, 2018).

Table 1. Various functions of HRM

HRP (Human Resource Planning)	After globalization, human resource roles have taken a paradigm shift. This HRP acts as a differentiator in its business operation. The HR manager has to maintain the right kind of talent in terms of soft and hard skills to optimize the organization's day-to-day functioning.
Candidate Tracking System	The traditional method leads to poor staffing, harming the organization's day-to-day activities. By integrating with technology, an organization can minimize traditional paper-based processes of tracking challenges.
Workforce Management	Organizations today have a heterogeneous workforce with diverse minds and cultural backgrounds that will guide them to new creations & ideas. The culture of any workplace is its root, hence HR managers' efforts to develop a thriving culture in an organization.
Talent Acquisition & Recruitment	The reasons could be a lack of understanding of the job profile, fewer applications due to poor reach, and limited access to diversity & talent that exist. The other reasons could be the reactive approach to hiring, less visibility in the outside world, duration of the hiring process, unconscious decision-making biases, etc.
Career Development	A lack of self-confidence and self-esteem misses out on many opportunities and career-related advancement on the personal front. Globalization and the pandemic have brought many changes in technological requirements for better sustainability, innovation, creativeness, and adapting themselves to disruptive technologies coming the way of the organization's functioning.
Relationship Management	Establishing operating procedures in hiring, training, career development, compensation, and employee-centric benefits are vital in implementing ERM as a strategic goal.
Compensation	Managing desirable compensation plans and communicating the same to every employee requires a lot of data crunching, effort, and time. The other challenges could be internal equity, pay transparency, the gap in employee expectations, poor design of incentive schemes, etc.
Optimizing Workflow	In the era of technology, workflow automation software eases manual work, which is time-consuming and increased person-hours. The aid of technology supports HR by handling the functions seamlessly.
Employee Retention	The employee work profile is one of the big data sources companies can leverage to retain the employee by sensing the chances of leaving the organization. Some implicit biases influencing employee retention include guilt-by-association, in-group favoritism, prince syndrome, sloppy sentimentalism, and the one-mistake rule (Parkhurst, J., 2017).
Training	• Content limitations - lags content freshness • No personalization -single size fits all strategy • Not User-friendly - poor quality of experience • Lack of metrics to measure ROI - improper assessments • Training program for employees takes place in an organized, quiet environment; thus, the pressures of work and the hullaballoo of the working space are absent. • Training can be tough to schedule for employees who are working unconventional shifts. • The employees cannot take training at any time they wish

HR executives need to deal with their strengths and weaknesses. HR managers have some desirable characteristics to overcome unconscious bias (McCormick, H., 2016).

1. Introspection of biases and collect feedback from peers and people around you.

Table 2. Types of Bias. Source: Bhanumathi,2020

Types of Bias	Description	Effect
Affinity Bias	Sharing similar qualities when compared to others	It will reduce the diversity and creativity of people
Attribution Bias	Attributing the success to an individual and failures to other external factors	Wrong conclusions on successes and failures of people involved
Beauty Bias	Attractiveness	Judging by the physical attributes of a person
Confirmation Bias	Evidence to suit individual viewpoints leads to favoritism of information which strengthens personal beliefs	Neglecting details that are against one's beliefs, no objective analysis of the situation
Gender Bias	Gender roles and stereotypic	Gender takes preference over qualities
Halo effect Bias	Look, everything is impressive	Neglecting details and overconfidence
Horns effect	Focus on the negative side	Wrong judgments
Anchoring	Fixing on initial information, e.g., salary negotiations on initial numbers	Blinded by first impressions
Overconfidence	Far too optimistic	Wrong decisions
Framing	Influenced by the problem formulation	Not linked with the solution
Availability	Dependent on readily available knowledge	Lack of scope for alternatives
Self-serving	Taking personal credit for success and others for failures	Self-centeredness

2. Overcome immediate reactions to situations and be proactive in understanding the possible impact of problems.
3. Work in diversified teams; do not be a stereotypical worker.
4. Overcome the negativity in thinking and start any assignments with optimism to achieve.
5. Develop the ability to separate experiences from current facts.
6. Be tech-savvy, explore the opportunities to integrate technologies in HR functions, and enrich decisions with data and facts.
7. Create monitors for your own unconscious biases.
8. Develop the ability to analyze the data statistically and scientifically, do not make decisions based only on your gut feelings.
9. Use premortems to imagine a future failure and explain the cause; this exercise develops optimism and encourages the realistic assessment of risks. Also, the team should prepare backup plans.
10. In a think-twice approach, the team can make two possible forecasts and take the average result; this approach makes the team think about the problem from a different perspective.

Motivations for Integrating Technology in HRM

The evolving market and pandemic conditions and threats have challenged small and big organizations to stay competitive through expansion, operational efficiency, etc. Changing times require a modern operation and dissemination of information, and HR takes a strategic role. The organization should focus

Figure 1. Industry-wise integration of HR Analytics. Source: Based on the primary research conducted by Noack, B

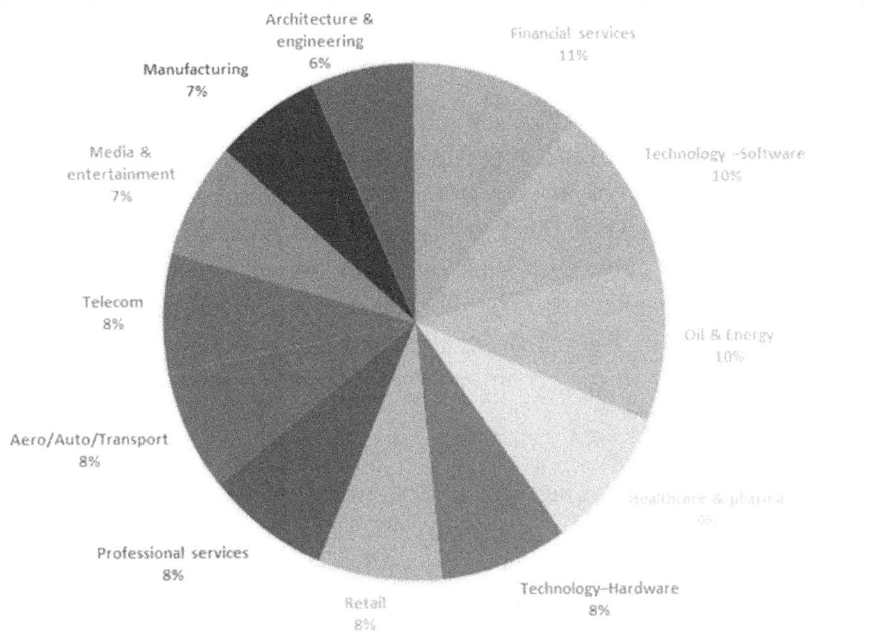

on the Agile HR model to facilitate and improve the fast-changing market and technology demands and upgrade the system to maintain compliance.

Paychex Pulse 2020 HR Survey states that 85% and above HR professionals opined that technology had strengthened their contribution to any organization.80% and above reported that it would allow them to uphold or raise their headcount and upsurge employee productivity.HR department and technology have become essential assets in accomplishing the associated tasks. Technology has changed how we think and do almost everything, including work. Professional life counts on the internet and multiple applications designed to help us outperform our job effectively and efficiently. Human resources management is no exception

The HR process of small and big organizations requires sophisticated technologies from hiring to firing employees and everything else. The requirement of technology-based activities is for various reasons, such as streamlining HR processes of the organization, reducing administrative tasks, reducing compliance costs associated, improving service, competing effectively, ease of work, raising productivity, managing diverse groups, and providing real-time data and metrics to managers for better decision making.

Technology Enablement for HRM Functions

The integration of analytics can be observed across industries, including financial services, oil& energy, Healthcare, and Pharma, across the HR functions (refer to Figure1).

Technology enablement discussions are in the areas of workforce management, candidate tracking system, Performance analytics, administration, succession planning, recruitment, talent acquisition, relationship management, compensation, optimizing workflow, employee retention, data security, unconscious human bias, online training, etc.,

HRP (Human Resource Planning)

Some of the forecasting techniques of HRP are job analysis, trend analysis, online surveys, and scatter plots. These techniques will help the planning process be more accessible and save time. The ERP (Enterprise resource planning) is used to track employees' time, effort, attendance, PF, ESI, etc., Thereby improving employee data management. The automation of HRP processes eliminates paperwork, speeds up many tasks, and contributes to better performance. Technology changes how HR departments approach and contact employees, store employee data in files, and analyze employee performance. Artificial intelligence, cloud-based HR, and people analytics will help enhance the effectiveness of HRP.

Candidate Tracking System

The candidate tracking software helps manage the recruitment process right from the potential candidate reading the job post, applying, and setting up an interview. The most popular approaches adopted to source and match the best fit are key-based and questionnaire-based. Compared to others, the former process identifies employees' initial fit based on the words and phrases found throughout their resumes, cover letters, and other correspondence. The latter approach automatically ranks the best candidate based on responses given by the candidate for questions. It includes behavioral questions which will pre-screen loyal applicants vs. applicants who may be inclined to job-jumping. Technology-enabled tracking system reduces the hiring time and attracts the growing number of millennials, reducing the attrition rate of millennials immediately after 6months.

The integration of an applicant tracking system (ATS) in an organization will help in sourcing candidates (LinkedIn and through other platforms), scheduling interviews, rewards and referrals, talent pool management, and also services like video proctoring, job offer management, feedback, generating reports and analytics, candidate management, etc.,

Workforce Management (WFM)

Workforce management is a commonly used tool of HR technology in today's workforce. According to the work trend index, seventy percent of workers prefer flexible remote work options to continue, and 65 percent crave more in-person time with their teams. A report by Microsoft says that 66% of industry leaders consider redesigning their workplace for hybrid work (Refer to fig 2). Hybrid work is inevitable.

Investing in a sound workforce management system helps to spend less time looking at spreadsheets and searching through email chains and more time interacting with the company's employees. Sarvseh et al. 2021, emphasized the various technology and digitally enabled employee tracking and monitoring systems for the supervisors and managers to keep an eye on remotely working employees and have real-time data for evaluating their performances.

The digitally enabled employee tracking system will crop up a few issues, like employee engagement and loyalty in a dynamic working space. The company should focus on pulse surveys and employee assistance programs and keep the human touch alive (Dave Ulrich).

Figure 2. Work trend index. Source: https://www.microsoft.com/en-us/worklab/work-trend-index/hybrid-work

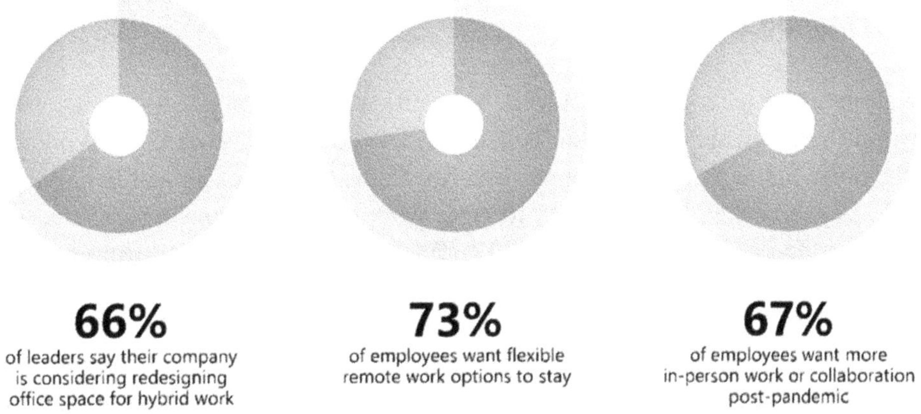

Talent Acquisition and Recruitment

Integrating technology and predictive analytics in recruitment has become a game-changer in the data-driven era. The Human Resources Information System (HRIS) consists of a tremendous amount of data which, if leveraged through analytics, gives better outcomes and aids decision-making. A significant study (Schmidt et al., 2016) exploring the practical relevance of 100 years of research assessments regarding selection techniques emphasizes that past work experience is relevant to predicting job performance by 16%. Personality traits and a candidate's cognitive ability constitute 78% of job performance. Thus, the requirement of Predictive hiring software can combine several variables that will determine the hiring of a prospective candidate. Such software uses the robust employee data pool and facilitates by recommendation of appropriate candidates for a specified profile. Candidate Relationship Management (CRM) software such as Yello, Beamery- a London-based start-up, and Avature-an enterprise SaaS Global Talent Acquisition platforms are trending, simplifying the hiring process with faster scheduling, integration with ATS and high-power automation. Leading brands like Toyota, Walgreens, Tableau, Adobe, and Energy Transfer use Yello to optimize hiring timelines and enhance the employer's brand. 17% of Avature's clients are from Fortune 500 companies. It demonstrates the spike in the adoption of technology in recruitment.

Career Development

Technology can enable conversations between managers and employees, including support for regular discussions between staff and supervisors across the career management process. Technology can foster multidirectional career progression by building talent pools that help identify the right roles for employees. Technology can support career development by introducing Learning management systems (LMS) to create knowledge pathways that track career goals. LMS eases the document's creation and administers career development goals and achievements. Technology also helps publicize openings internally and conduct a search within groups of high-potential employees. Encourage employees to develop careers using technological tools, which help them create an online profile showcasing their expertise and broader potential skill set.

Relationship Management

Employee relations (ER) technology has played a significant role along two dimensions- workflow efficiency within the HR teams and seamless handling of the diverse workforce. Work From Home has become the norm in the current pandemic scenario, and remote management in employee engagement is needed. As part of the ER technology, Remote Workforce Management software, such as Zoho People's remote workforce management, Scoro, YouTrack, Fleep, and ProWorkflow, are among a few software to handle agile teams' track and drive performance during such unprecedented times. It is for sure that an investment in ER technology translates into more significant benefits for an organization. A well-established ER mechanism generates intangible benefits regarding a happier, engaged, productive workforce that will likely contribute to positive branding, making an organization sought-after.

Compensation

Adopting digital technologies by organizations such as Total Rewards Statement (TRS) creates a sense of personal bonding as it communicates monetary and non-monetary perks obtained by an employee. Such a transparent mechanism fosters employee morale and ensures retention. Forward-thinking organizations are also expanding the company's ownership to the employees through stock options contributing to a dynamic workforce ecosystem. Companies use technology platforms to manage compensation that is employee-specific. Skill-based compensation models have gained greater importance in attracting and retaining talent. Some of the trending compensation management software in the year 2022 are Decusoft Compose- a tool for flexible compensation management, Xactly -for quota-based work, Balanced Comp -primarily used for the finance industry, Payfactors – an AI-powered compensation tool, Workday- a tool for data integrations across different organizational functions, etc.

Optimizing Workflow

In the digital transformation era, technology has penetrated all organizational elements, with HR no exception. Camunda's The State of Process Automation Report 2020 shows that 36% of global organizations have implemented technologies to automate workflows, and 29% are planning to do so shortly. Technology eases the administrative tasks of HR. Technology that brings workflow automation saves time, reduces manual tasks and paperwork, facilitates smooth onboarding, and optimizes the organization's overall workflow.

Employee Retention

Human Resources technology helps improve employee retention and advance human resource development for any business. It will enhance efficiency and create a more cordial work system for employees of the organization. The research from Oracle in 2022 shows that 88% of workers feel the meaning of success has changed; now, priority has moved to work-life balance, mental health, and workplace flexibility. The recruitment software helps organizations find suitable candidates with the required skills for specific jobs more successfully. Software such as JAZZHR, BreezyHR, Recruiterbox, Cornerstone On Demand, and many more do all the challenging tasks like comparison, conflicting skills, communication, background verification, and candidates' goals in onboarding the candidates. They are more willing to stay around. Technology helps the organization connect and communicate with employees, schedule important meetings, assign tasks, work remotely, and carry out daily tasks more efficiently. It's time for all organizations to invest in new HR technologies that make employees feel a sense of belongingness, increase efficiency and productivity, and increase retention. Every organization must adopt novel and latest ways to satisfy its people; this will further help control the turnover rate (Henson, 2007).

Artificial Intelligence is integrated into many ways to handle this situation; some of them are listed below;

1. They are identifying the employees who are having poor workplace engagement. Highly engaged employees are 87% less likely to change their jobs.
2. Advanced sentiment analytics may also reveal reasons to classify employee sentiments concerning their manager behaviors and identify biased managers (Yi, J., Nasukawa, T., Bunescu, R., & Niblack, W., 2003).
3. AI-enabled conversation bots can be employed to make the employees voice their opinions with due anonymization; these conversations will provide the platform for employees to raise their grievances to their managerial staff.
4. Understand employee personality, perspectives, and desires and how far these deviate from organizational culture.
5. AI can also give input to managers about critical points employees might be ready for new challenges and roles.

As per the definition given by (Liddy, E. D., 2001), Natural language processing (NLP) is a field in AI comprising a set of techniques for deriving meaningful insights from naturally occurring texts using linguistic analysis. There are quite a few efforts to apply NLP in handling human bias by processing the textual and audio data captured from human-to-human interactions. An HR DSS with NLP takes inputs from various sources such as appraisals, 360-degree feedback, social media interactions, employee counseling sessions, surveys, employee competencies, etc. Further, an NLP algorithm for sentiment analysis, classifications, hypothesis creation, discovering topic and concept connections, inferencing conversations, and knowledge discovery.

NLP techniques help identify subconscious bias in the following ways.

1. Tagging diversities will help increase the diversity of candidates while recruiting (Ranjan, P., & Basu, H. V. S. S. A., 2003).
2. Measures can provide essential feedback and counseling for the employees to overcome inherent bias (Croskerry, P., Singhal, G., & Mamede, S., 2013).
3. To analyze comments to understand the theme of discussions out of the words, e.g., opinion on leadership, interpersonal communications, and attaching the probabilities for over 70 different themes available in the study.

Training:

During the 1980s, organizations adopted technology-based approaches to training employees. IBM in the 1980s used technology for training employees, which was less than 5%; during 1990, the technology-based delivery in training raised to 30%, and now it is expected to reach 75% usage of technology in all training and development programs of the organization.

Technologies-enabled tools such as web-based training, mobile learning, video-based training, avatars, simulations, virtual environment, HTML 5 and responsive design, automation and adaptive learning, big data, etc., are used for online and offline training. Most organizations rely on online activity to monitor employee performance through LMS (Learning Management System). Organizations utilize technology-based approaches to reach out and train multiple employees at a cost-effective and easily accessible time.

Succession Planning:

Artificial intelligence (AI), machine learning, and other data-driven emerging technologies can identify the potential successor for any vacant position in any organization. Succession planning software helps assess the present and future behavioral, cognitive, and technical assessments. It seamlessly provides 360-degree feedback about an employee's best fit for the vacant position.

Tools and Technologies for HRM

Hr system survey depicts organizations that successfully implement sophisticated HR technology tools outpace those that do not (2009-2010 HR Systems Survey) (Refer to table 3).

INDUSTRY 5.0

Industry 5.0 confers the people working with robots, big data, the internet of things, and more intelligent machines, which help humans work better and faster by leveraging these advanced technologies. This industry 5.0 augments a personal human touch to industry 4.0, which focuses on automation and efficiency. Industry 5.0 applies to every sector and every organization and has three key pillars: human-centric, resilient, and sustainable business. Industry 5.0 brings many benefits to enterprises, employees, and society which focuses on empowering employees that augment the competitiveness of industry interns and attract the best talents. It is suitable for the planet, favoring circular production models, and supports technologies that focus on sharing, leasing, reusing, repairing, refurbishing, and recycling existing materials and products as long as possible.

Human-centric: "promotes talents, diversity, and empowerment."

Resilient strategy: "agile and resilient with flexible and adaptable technologies."

Sustainable strategy: "leads action on sustainability and respects planetary boundaries."

Industry -4.0 Vs. Industry-5.0

The top 10 in-demand skills by 2025, as per the "future of job report "(2016,2020), are (Gugerçin,2021), Analytical thinking and innovation, Active learning strategies, Complex problem-solving, Critical think-

Figure 3. HR Tech trends.
Source: Gartner's report on HR emerging trends

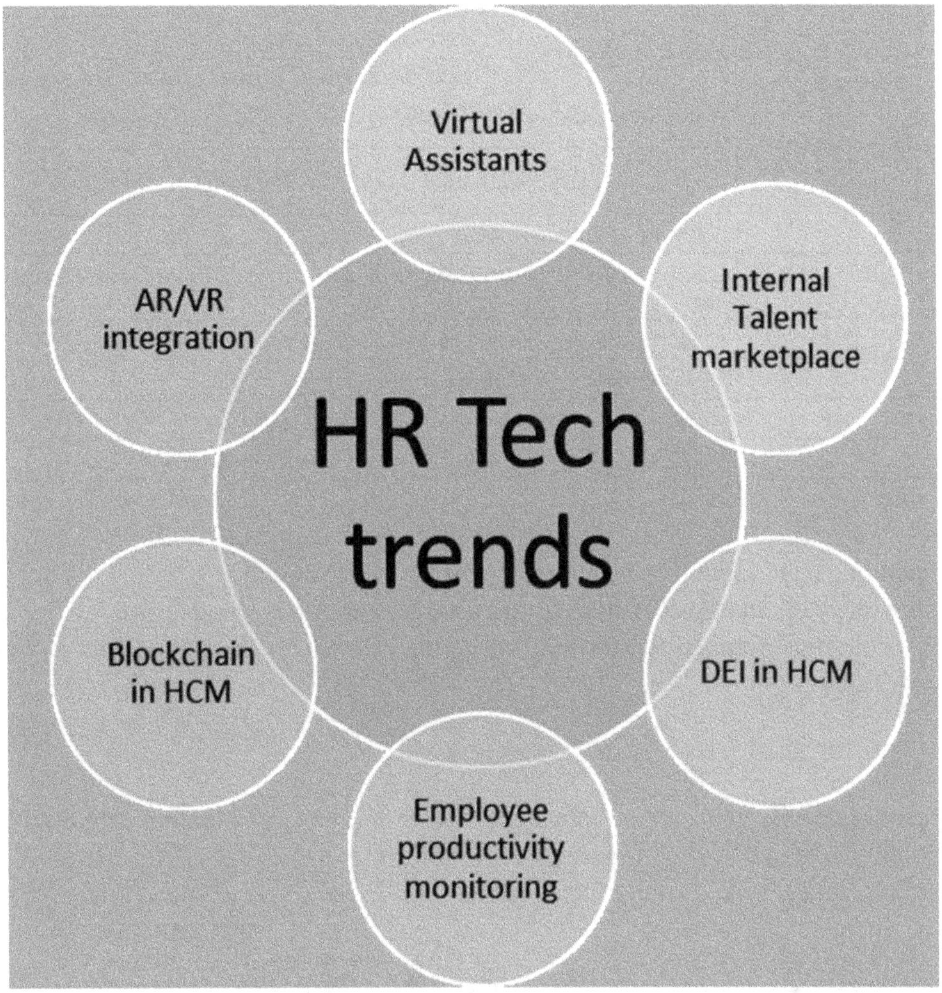

ing and analysis, Creativity, originality, and initiative, Leadership and social influence, Technology use, monitoring, and control, Technology design and programming, Resilience, stress tolerance, and flexibility and Reasoning, problem-solving, and creativity.

Opportunities of Industry 5.0

- Manufacturing provides incredible options for customization.
- It offers an opportunity for creative employees which optimizes their efficiency.
- Generate employment positively.
- Help the client digitally manage repeated follow-up assignments (Haleem & Javaid, 2019).
- Operator within the production cell gets more engaged in the planning method than in the more or less automated manufacturing method (Rossi, 2018).
- It emphasizes design to function, allowing for more tailor-made products.

Table 3. Software tools and technologies for HRM

Product	Purpose
X.ai https://x.ai	Scheduling Interviews
ClearFit https://clearfit.com	Automatically finding and ranking candidates
AirCTO https://aircto.com/	Automate the candidate screening process
Textio	Creation job postings
Entelo	Handling unconscious bias. It is possible to anonymize candidate data which may lead to human bias.
Everwise	Identification of employee skill gaps and plans pathways for employee learning
GoHire	Interview scheduling, recruiting, and chatbots.
Workday	Workday analysis of employees to identify employee potential
Ascendify Aspire	Visualizing employee growth opportunities by using Career assistant software

- Manufacturing methods will be better with real-time information.
- Increased safety of employees with COBOTs used for hazardous works.
- More excellent opportunities for start-ups and entrepreneurs for new products and services associated with industry 5.0.

Figure 4. Source:https://www.frost.com/frost-perspectives/industry-5-0-bringing-empowered-humans-back-to-the-shop-floor/

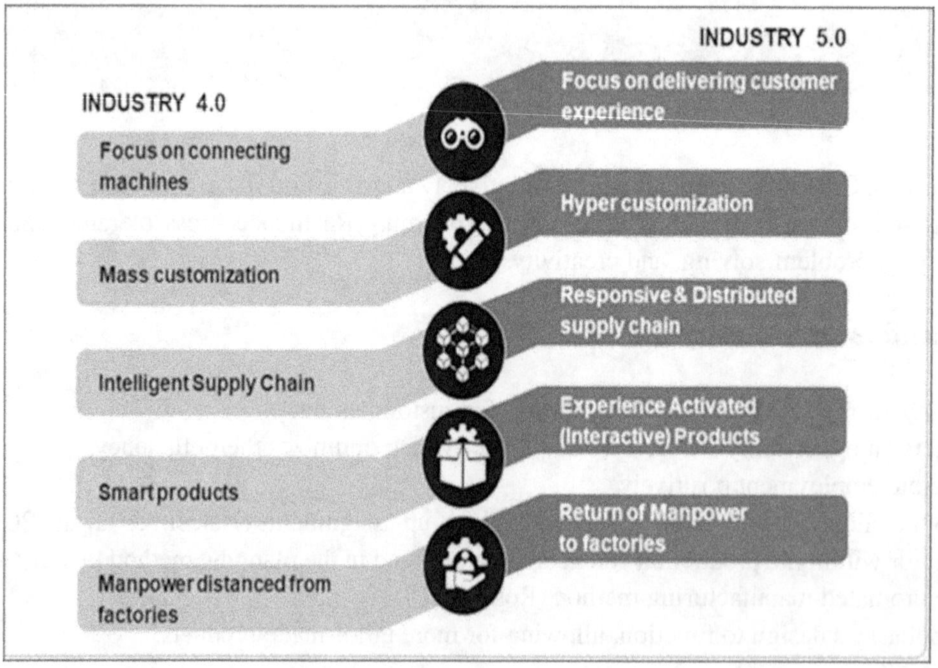

- Industry 5.0 provides increased importance to human-machine interaction, research, and development in the respective domain.
- Robots can offer quality services to remote locations with the help of industry 5.0, particularly in healthcare.

Challenges of Industry 5.0

- Increases work polarization where employees split into two communities: extraordinarily trained and qualified, low-paid and unqualified.
- Training employees to adopt cutting-edge technologies requires behavioral change.
- Intelligent manufacturing systems demand higher autonomy in industry 5.0.
- Acquiring high-quality and integrity data from manufacturing systems is challenging and complex to accommodate diverse data repositories (Thoben, 2017).
- Increased cyber security threat in manufacturing lines in industry 5.0 because of increased connectivity application of communications protocols.
- It demands high investment to fully capitalize on its pillars which are human-centric, resilient, and sustainable businesses, especially SMEs.
- It offers tremendous potential in healthcare, but a high degree of accuracy and precision is expected, which requires huge investments and infrastructure.

INDUSTRY 5.0 TECHNOLOGIES AND HRM

This section gives a brief overview of some essential information technologies that play a critical role in industry 5.0 with relevance to HRM.

Artificial Intelligence (AI) and Industry 5.0

AI is entering the new normal in industry 5.0 compared to its application in industry 4.0. The new normal includes using AI to create intelligent machines, replacing many earlier tasks through human cognitive intelligence with machines embedded with cognitive intelligence. Mainly, those applications demand inferencing during complex situations where humans score better than machines because of their superior Intelligent Quotients and common-sense abilities. AI would transform from narrow intelligence to generalized intelligence where the higher levels of intelligent algorithms can be seen in action both in the manufacturing and service industries; thereby, there is an increased scope for transfer learning. The motive of transfer learning is to apply the knowledge acquired from a situation 'A' to another situation 'B,' thereby reducing the efforts involved in training artificially intelligent machines.

AI in HRM of Industry 5.0

In industry 5.0, we can witness artificially intelligent machines working side-by-side with humans, providing workplace augmentation and learning by doing. This would promote collaborative work environments where humans and machines work collaboratively on tasks that demand intellectual capabilities. As human is good at applying common sense and rational thinking abilities, machines would be good at using the vast experience obtained during training. AI would play a critical role in Industry 5.0 are collaborative robots, intelligent healthcare, supply chain management, cloud manufacturing, the Internet of everything, digital twins, edge computing, edge intelligence, automotive, augmented and virtual reality, 3D printing, and so on.

Predictive Analytics and Industry 5.0

With increased computational power, AI-based memory systems, extensive data availability, technology availability, and affordability, organizations are heavily leveraging the power of analytics in the functionalities. Harnessing the power of big data is done extensively by organizations today to improve design, processes, and system efficiencies.

Predictive Analytics in HRM of Industry 5.0

Human Resource Predictive Analytics (HRPA) is an evolving application of predictive analytics in HRM. Predictive analytics relies on current and historical data to assess future patterns that can support decision-making. Today, Human Resource Information Systems consist of robust talent pool data that needs to be utilized to make better decisions. Some of the evolving applications of Predictive Analytics are in the area of Talent predictions, Risk modeling, Retention Modelling, and Response Modelling, among others (Mishra. et al.,2016). Analysis of the Continuous performance of employees, satisfaction levels, and intentions to exit prematurely are in the ambit of risk modeling, which can help make proactive decisions and retain the right talent. Regression, clustering, classification, association, and anomaly detection are among the predictive algorithms widely used in People Analytics. Companies like Nielson, Google, and HP have integrated the power of predictive analytics into HR functions. Time to hire, recruitment cost to hire, engagement rating, early turnover, performance and potential metric, cost of HR per employee, and absenteeism are among the HR metrics whose projections and future estimates are likely to optimize HR functions.

Cobots and Industry 5.0

The current trends in automation have seen the rapid development of Collaborative robots or Cobots. Cobots are embedded with high-powered sensors with increased capabilities of detecting human presence and enhancing human capabilities (Maddikunta,2022). The integration of Industry 5.0 involves a human-centric approach with the integration of Cobots in the functionalities.

Cobots in HRM of Industry 5.0

Cobots support the ease of manual tasks done by the workforce, increase process efficiency, and aid time optimization. The human workforce executes critical thinking tasks. Cobots can be used in work profile analysis, effectively reducing the tedious manual tasks of HR personnel in screening candidate profiles. Maintaining an extensive database of employees' interests, experience, past performance, and other critical details with an AI-integrated memory can help plan customized employee training and development initiatives. With enhanced capabilities, cobots can analyze human behavior, vital to building employee-employer relationships in a work setting (Saxena, 2021). The unified approach of a human-cobot work setting in a manufacturing setting can be very significant in creating safe -workspaces where the cobot could replace the human being in routine tasks. This kind of collaborative setting is the way forward. Trans-disciplinary research is imperative to make this kind of human-robot integration a successful reality. The paradigm of machines replacing humans is no longer the trend; the road ahead should be seamless and co-functioning for both entities to enhance organizational productivity (Mara et al.,2021). Recruiting the right talent is a critical function involving cost to a firm. A projection with reasonable estimates of a potential candidate's tenure in the organization based on a past candidate's profile can ensure the right hire.

Blockchain and Industry 5.0:

Blockchains are designed to provide security and trust-worthy infrastructure for business transactions, leveraging popular technologies like cloud computing, cryptography, distributed infrastructure services, peer-to-peer networking architectures, etc. The technology removes the dependency on the central entity or main server where complete knowledge is situated and advocates a shared model for transaction processing. The main objective of blockchain is to establish a trusted, transparent and effective mechanism for Peer-to-Peer systems for collaborative business processes which involves online transactions.

Blockchain in HRM of Industry 5.0

- Building a blockchain system for tracking and authenticating education details, skills details, training details, workplace performance details, etc. This would serve as a trustworthy data source for potential employers and apply data analytics over blockchain for talent acquisition and promotions.
- Applicants can write all their employment history and achievements onto a blockchain, which can be referred to by prospective employers. Data blocks of resumes are used to store permanent resume blockchains, thereby reducing fraud due to resume falsification.
- Past employers could write onto a blockchain about why an employee is promoted, achievements, strengths, weaknesses, reasons for leaving the job, etc. Therefore, blockchain works as a reflector of both successes and failures.
- Blockchain technology can be leveraged to track individuals' income and expenditures. These recordings would reduce book-keeping activities to a maximum extent, thereby helping the dynamic taxing system practiced in some parts of the world.
- Blockchains can be used to implement an intelligent/smart contracts system, which is used to track progress made, adherence to terms and conditions, minimize oversight negligence, and so on. Smart contract management plays a vital role in intellectual property management on a worldwide scale. Smart contracts also bring transparency into the system so that every stakeholder knows the complete process and context.
- As freelancing is trending, any company would prefer recruiting contingent employees for short-term requirements. Blockchains would become prominent lookouts for such requirements, where skills, expertise, and relevant experience in freelancing are readily available.
- Blockchains are opening up avenues to enroll students to enroll for digital diploma courses. This will ensure transcript Genuity of transcripts and avoids data manipulation.

Digital Twinning and Industry 5.0

A real-world physical object, process, or service can be cloned to create a digital twin in the virtual world. Digital twinned models can be used to develop simulations to analyze performance and derive business insights from the process. The result of digital twinning can be later used in the real world to get the production output. A digital twin can help HR to move beyond data and analytics into a more visual and collaborative world.

Digital Twinning in HRM of Industry 5.0

- HRM can use digital twins of employees to predict which employee may be prone to offers from competitors.
- With digital twin technology, organizations can monitor employees' workloads and plan for employee enrichment programs and training programs.
- Using twin systems, organizations can create destressing and fitness activities for employees.

CONCLUSION

Industry 5.0 is bringing up many new opportunities for 20th-century managers to leverage various technologies and services for efficiently implementing various managerial functions. Especially the human resource management function can use the best tools and applications developed around this ecosystem to provide the best-performing human resource to the organization. This will cut down the cost of business operations in terms of human resource optimization, tracking, acquisition, performance management, and so on.

REFERENCES

Baer, T. (2019). Bias in Human Decision-Making. *Understand, Manage, and Prevent Algorithmic Bias*, 9–20. doi:10.1007/978-1-4842-4885-0_2

Bendick, M. Jr, & Nunes, A. P. (2013). Developing the research basis for controlling bias in hiring. *The Journal of Social Issues*, *68*, 238–262.

Bhanumathi P. (2020). Unconscious Human Bias in HR Functions and Mitigation using Artificial Intelligence. *Journal of Arts, Humanities and Social Sciences, 7*(28).

Black, S. L., Washington, M. L., & Schmidt, G. B. (2016). *How to stay current in social media to be competitive in recruitment and selection. Social Media in Employee Selection and Recruitment*. Springer.

Croskerry, P., Singhal, G., & Mamede, S. (2013). Cognitive debiasing 1: Origins of bias and theory of debiasing. *BMJ Quality & Safety*, *22*(Suppl 2), ii58–ii64.

Dalton, S., & Villagran, M. (2018). Minimizing and addressing implicit bias in the workplace: Be proactive, part one. *College & Research Libraries News*, *79*(9), 478. doi:10.5860/crln.79.9.478

Dijk, R. (2022). 5 Advanced Data Analysis Techniques Applied to People Analytics. *Academy to Innovate HR*. https://www.aihr.com/blog/advanced-data-analysis-techniques-applied-to-people-analytics/.

Dvorsky, G. (2013). The 12 cognitive biases that prevent you from being rational. *Gizmodo.*

Gartner. (2022). *Six Emerging HR Technology Trends.* Gartner. https://www.gartner.com/en/human-resources/trends/emerging-hr-technology

Gillenson, M. L., & Sanders, T. C. (2005). Employee relationship management: Applying the concept of personalization to U.S. Navy sailors. *Information Systems Research, 22*(1), 45–50.

Gould-Williams, J. (2003). The importance of HR practices and workplace trust in achieving superior performance: A study of public-sector organizations. *International Journal of Human Resource Management, 14*(1), 28–54.

Gugerçin, S., & Gugerçin, U. (2021). How Employees Survive In The Industry 5.0 Era: In-Demand Skills Of The Near Future. *International Journal of Disciplines Economics & Administrative Sciences Studies, 7*(31), 524-533

Haselton, M. G., Nettle, D., & Murray, D. R. (2015). The Evolution of Cognitive Bias, 1–20. The Handbook of Evolutionary Psychology. Wiley. doi:10.1002/9781119125563.evpsych241

International Journal of Academic Research in Business and Social Sciences. (2017). *International Journal of Academic Research in Business and Social Sciences, 7*(3).

Liddy, E. D. (2001). *Natural language processing*. Syracuse University.

Maddikunta, P. K. R., Pham, Q. V., Prabadevi, B., Deepa, N., Dev, K., Gadekallu, T. R., & Liyanage, M. (2022). Industry 5.0: A survey on enabling technologies and potential applications. *Journal of Industrial Information Integration, 26*, 100257.

Mara, M., Meyer, K., Heiml, M., Pichler, H., Haring, R., Krenn, B., & Layer-Wagner, T. (2021). *CoBot studio VR: A virtual reality game environment for transdisciplinary research on interpretability and trust in human-robot collaboration*. Springer.

McCormick, H. (2016). *The Real Effects of Unconscious Bias in the Workplace.* University of North Carolina Chapel Hill Executive Development.

Miller, J. S., & Cardy, R. L. (2000). Technology and managing people. *Journal of Labor Research, 21*(3), 447–461.

Mishra, S. N., Lama, D. R., & Pal, Y. (2016). Human Resource Predictive Analytics (HRPA) for HR management in organizations. *International Journal of Scientific & Technology Research, 5*(5), 33–35.

Mondal, S. (2021). AI for Recruiting: News, Tips, and Trends- The 25 Top Recruiting Software Tools Of 02021. *Ideal.* https://ideal.com/top-recruiting-software/.

Mordor Intelligence. (2022). Workflow Automation Market – Growt, Trends, Covid-19 Impact, And Forecasts (2022 – 2027). Mordor Intelligence. https://www.mordorintelligence.com/industry-reports/workflow-automation-market.

Moumita & Bhanumathi, P. (2021). A Study On Integration Of Artificial Intelligence In Human Resources Management. *Utkal Historical Research Journal, 34*(XXIII).

Noack, B. (2019). Big data analytics in human resource management: Automated decision-making processes, predictive hiring algorithms, and cutting-edge workplace surveillance technologies. *Psycho-sociological Issues in Human Resource Management*, *7*(2), 37–42.

Oberai, H., & Anand, I. M. (2018). Unconscious bias: Thinking without thinking. *Human Resource Management International Digest*, *26*(6), 14–17. doi:10.1108/hrmid-05-2018-0102

Parkhurst, C. A. L. (2017). *Presentation Design and Retention* [Doctoral dissertation, Old Dominion University].

Praveen, S., & Karuppasamy, R. (2017). Competency-based compensation system: As a strategic HR technique with special reference to Coimbatore. *International Journal of Economic Policy in Emerging Economies*, *10*(1), 116–128.

Ranjan, P., & Basu, H. V. S. S. A. (2003). *Part of speech tagging and local word grouping techniques for natural language parsing in Hindi*. In Proceedings of the 1st International Conference on Natural Language Processing (ICON 2003). Semantic Scholar.

Reitsma, T. (2022). Ten Best Employee Compensation Management Software In. *People Managing People.* https://peoplemanagingpeople.com/tools/best-compensation-management-software/.

Sarvesh, K. R., & Bhanumathi, P. (2022). A study on the Technology-driven employee monitoring trend during COVID-19. *Journal of Fundamental & Comparative Research*, *12*(7).

Saxena, A., Saxena, A., Sharma, R., & Parashar, M. (2021). *Emergence of Futuristic HRM in Perspective of Human-Cobot's Collaborative Functionality.* Research Gate.

Schmidt, F. L., Oh, I. S., & Shaffer, J. A. (2016). The validity and utility of selection methods in personnel psychology: Practical and theoretical implications of 100 years. *Fox School of Business Research Paper*, 1-74.

Senyucel, Z. (2009). *Managing the Human Resources in the 21st century.* Zorlu.

Shaw, J. D., Gupta, N., & Delery, J. E. (2001). Congruence between technology and compensation systems: Implications for strategy implementation. *Strategic Management Journal*, *22*(4), 379–386.

Soll, J.B., Katherine, L.M., & Payne, J.W. (2015). Outsmart your own biases. *Harward Business Review*.

Specht, M. (n.d.). *2009-2010 HR Systems Survey*, (12th ed.). Cedar Crestone .

Srinivasan, M. (2022). *Recent Trends in Compensation & Benefits.* LinkedIn. https://www.linkedin.com/pulse/recent-trends-compensation-benefits-mridhula-srinivasan

Strohmeier, S. (2013). Employee relationship management—Realizing competitive advantage through information technology? *Human Resource Management Review*, *23*(1), 93–104.

Thoben, K. D., Wiesner, S., & Wuest, T. (2017). Industrie 4.0 and smart manufacturing-a review of research issues and application examples. *International Journal of automation technology, 11*(1), 4-16.

Thomas, O. (2018). Two decades of cognitive bias research in entrepreneurship: What do we know and where do we go from here? *Management Review Quarterly, 68*(2), 107–143. doi:10.100711301-018-0135-9

Ulrich, D. (2022). *How HR Innovation Is Driving The Future Of Work?* Sage.

Veena, V., & Bhanumathi, P. (2021). Inclusion of AI in improving employee retention among millennials: A case study of select IT firms. *PIMT Journal of Research UGC approved (Care List), 13*(4).

Work Management. (2022). 23 Remote Team Management Tools & Software. *Scoro.* https://www.scoro.com/blog/remote-employee-management-tools/.

Yi, J., Nasukawa, T., Bunescu, R., & Niblack, W. (2003). Sentiment analyzer: Extracting sentiments about a given topic using natural language processing techniques. In *Third IEEE international conference on data mining* (pp. 427-434). IEEE.

Chapter 2
Emerging Challenges and Opportunities for Leaders in Industry 5.0:
A Roadmap Through Literature Review

Shraddha Rathod
Vishwakarma University, India

Pooja Agrawal
https://orcid.org/0000-0003-0971-5451
Vishwakarma University, India

ABSTRACT

The industry has developed over a period of time. Industry 1.0 had a different scenario than Industry 5.0. The revolution of industries transformed the economy of the country which was based on agriculture and handicrafts at an earlier time. With this revolution, leaders also required necessary qualities which are demanding and leading in the future. In the world of a fast-growing business, the transformation of leadership has become an important topic to be discussed. It has become necessary to analyze new leadership techniques and skill sets required to form the organizational structure which will be best suitable for new-age leadership. This chapter is focusing on the changes in leadership practices from Industry 1.0 to Industry 5.0. Moreover, this chapter also highlights the challenges, opportunities, and required skill sets for leaders in Industry 5.0.

INTRODUCTION

The industry has developed over a while and with up-gradation in the environment. Industry 1.0 had a different scenario than industry 5.0. The industrial revolution transformed the country's economy, which was based on agriculture and handicrafts at an earlier time (Sigit R Lukito et. al., 2019). With this revolution, leaders also required necessary qualities which are demanding and leading in the future. The

DOI: 10.4018/978-1-6684-6745-9.ch002

earlier leaders were controlling, autocratic, and dictatorial in their leadership but in the 21st century, the leadership practices have changed with time and requirements. In this modern era, classical leadership techniques and management theories are vanishing due to their restricted organisational culture and ineffective working environment. With this digitalization, leadership is also transformed from a traditional approach to a modern approach. This transformation demands different characteristics of today's leaders like quick decision-making, effective leadership and team-building spirit (Sigit R Lukito et. al., 2019).

The current situation has become more competitive, complex, volatile and changeable. With the changing scenario, leadership has also changed regarding required qualities, abilities and skill-set. In recent years, the leader and employees relationship has become more collaborative, allowing employees to decide the best approach to fulfilling the responsibility (Jakubik et. al., 2018).

In the world of a fast-growing business, leadership transformation has become an important topic to be discussed. It has become necessary to analyse new leadership techniques and skill sets required to form the organisational structure which will be best suitable for new-age leadership. This article focuses on the leadership practices changes from industry-1.0 to industry 5.0. Moreover, this article is also highlighting the challenges, opportunities and required skill-sets for leaders in Industry-5.0.

LITERATURE REVIEW

To understand the current complexity of leadership we need to understand how the leader has transformed their leadership approaches, the four historical approaches are dogmatic, humanistic, pragmatic and holistic approach (Jakubik et. al., 2018). The dogmatic approach was more focused on the economy rather than people. People were assumed as "rational economic animals" this was between the mid-1840s to 1940s. The humanistic approach to be seen between the 1930s to 1940s were humans assumed as "social animals" and leaders in this approach worked for better human relations, which resulted in improved people's performance. The pragmatic approach can be understood as an approach for the leaders as the way democratic leadership approaches which were held during the 1950s talk more about creativity and efficiency. After the 1950s the holistic approach evolved this approach focuses on humans, technology and the environment and relationships between leaders and employees.The leadership in industry 1.0 was completely different compared to industry 5.0. The role of leaders has changed over time, and with the growing industry, leadership has also changed.

In IR1.0 and IR 2.0, the leaders were not interested in opening up the decision-making process to the employees. After the 1980s the leadership was more focused on the connection and communication within an organisation with the motto of smooth industry growth and knowledge for the organisation's sustainability (Jakubik et. al., 2018). Under such kind of leadership employees used to feel undervalued due to limited recognition of their contributions. As time evolved the leadership also changed in IR 4.0 and IR 5.0. In industrial revolutions in the digital era, the leadership allows members to succeed or fail based completely on their skills.

Zulkifli et. al., (2021) argued that the leaders in Industry 1.0 mainly were associated with controls, directives, pre-decided processes and restrictions, which were quite conflicting with a new approach to experiment and adopted new procedures, as time evolved IR 4.0 and IR 5.0 the new point opinions were welcomed. Freedom of thought and free hands to experiment with new ideas cheered. IR 5.0 the new style and methods were enlarged to motivate others, work more collaboratively, and achieve and lead the organisation towards its final goals. In industry 5.0 leadership is more about collaborating and co-create. The leaders need to change and challenge the longstanding point of view of a leader's character as a commanding. Leaders need to be more cooperative, engaging and focused approach towards the growth of an organisation (Kazim 2019; Cahyadi et. al., 2021)

IR 5.0 is a set of rising and congregating tools like virtual reality, augmented reality, cloud computing, and system integration. Industry 5.0 is all about using artificial intelligence, autonomous robots collaboratively working with robots. The traditional leadership style has transformed into a rapidly growing technological era where leaders must practice and implement innovative digital environments to succeed. IR 5.0 has opened a new path inthe working and learning environment to create new employee opportunities.

In a digitally competitive era, future leaders need to improve fitting knowledge and skills to develop into digital leaders (Zulkifli et. al., 2021).It has become necessary to analyse new leadership techniques and skill sets required to form the organisational structure which will be best suitable for new-age leadership. In this digital era leader's visionary and futuristic approach can lead an organisation towards achieving its goal (Jibrail et. al., 2001).

Zulkifli et. al., (2021) argued that the traditional leadership and features have become outdated and are not well matched with the technological era and it does not match the requirement of humans and technology. To embrace the challenges of the transformation of IR 5.0 the leadership needs to come out of its comfort zones to lead an organisation with a strong self-awareness of the current trend of leadership approaches. The IR-5.0 brings considerable challenges where leaders need to adjust their way of working with new technology, structure and strategies.

OBJECTIVES

1. To understand the transformation in leadership from industry-1.0 to industry 5.0.
2. To diagnose the skills set required by the leader in industry 5.0.
3. To explore the challenges and opportunities for leaders in industry 5.0.

RESEARCH METHODOLOGY

The current research work is qualitative, and findings are based on secondary data. A huge amount of literature was collected and thoroughly studied to analyse the challenges and opportunities required by leaders in industry-5.0. The research papers were collected from various sources like Google Scholar, Google, Academia, Research Gate and others.

FINDINGS

Table 1.

Leadership in the Industrial Revolution	Findings
Leadership in IR 1.0	In the 18th century, when the first industrial revolution began, leaders followed the hierarchical system. The organisation also followed the same system, resulting in a more controlled and autocratic working organisation. Leadership in IR 1.0 was more self-centric and didn't consider employees' points of view. They were not interested in a group decision-making process. The IR 1.0 was more of a dogmatic approach. It was more focused on the economy rather than people. People were assumed as "rational economic animals". Zulkifli et. al., (2021) elaborated that the leadership in industry 1.0 was mostly associated with controls, directives, and pre-decided processes that conflicted with a new approach to experiment and adopt new procedures.
Leadership in IR 2.0	Leaders of IR 1.0 didn't take any employees' consideration and decisions taken by leaders only. Lack of communication was the biggest issue faced by leaders in IR 2.0 Another biggest issue in IR 2.0 was the lack of employees' encouragement and support, resulting in an unsatisfied working force. In IR 2.0 sometimes leaders might have been ready to listen to your ideas and suggestions as leadership was going through major changes in the industry.
Leadership in IR 3.0	The 3rd IR in 20th century leadership was more focused on the connection and communication within an organisation The IR 3.0's motto was a smooth growth of the industry and knowledge for the sustainability of the organisation. Leadership in IR3.0 was a pragmatic approach where leaders believed in democratic leadership approaches. After the 1980s the concept of leadership shifted to the concept of visionary leadership and charismatic and inspirational leadership.
Leadership in IR 4.0	As time evolved, the leadership skill requirements have also changed. The leadership in IR4.0 talks more about the holistic approach, which focuses on humans, technology, the environment and the relationships between leaders and employees. The 4th IR is characterised by applying information and communication technologies to industry. Leaders were doing "all they could" to create a workforce for IR 4.0
Leadership in IR 5.0	The leadership in IR 5.0 is more about collaborative working. Leaders are giving employees more freedom of thought and free hands to experiment with new ideas. Leaders welcome the new point of opinion. IR 5.0 the new style and methods were enlarged to motivate others, work more collaboratively, Technically advanced knowledge is also becoming a part of leaders in industry-5.0.

CHALLENGES

The various challenges faced by leaders in Industry-5.0 can be list out as follows-

1- Environment complexity

Change management and leadership are interrelated. Change is a standardized process of shifting one working practice to another. New technology has disturbed old working practices. Changes are rapidly happening on a large scale as we are already witnessed the technological transformation of industries. Industry 4.0 and 5.0 have become more complex and challenging due to rapid changes in the use of technology. Adopting the new change and technology in its best way might be difficult sometimes for leaders in the current and future challenges. Leaders need to accept the change and complexity of the situation. Challenges can be complicated, but leaders need to find the causes and solutions.

2- Lack of vision

The most common challenge is the lack in creative power of a leader. The leadership need to be more forward-thinking and long-range planned. As technologies are changing, its impact on the organisation is easily visible and leaders need to be more visionary to handle it. A lack of vision can cost an organisation's current and future strategies and operations. This may also include the possibility of leader acknowledging positively deviant employees (Sharma 2019; Sharma, 2021). A leader's lack of vision can negatively affect and push back its growth for years. For the sustainability of an organisation, leaders need to have a clear and achievable vision.

3- Technological Advancement

Leaders in IR 5.0 remain challenged to adoption of new technology. Sometimes, leaders face difficulties adopting rapid change and understanding all the new technology-driven opportunities. According to Deloitte's report "technology will become the universal language of business". In recent times, the industry has experienced many changes and development where leaders feel pressured to keep themselves updated in the rapidly changing technological world. Leaders are adopting more and more advanced technologies to for the sustainability of business but leaders are facing an increasing array of new technology where more and more technologies are innovated every day. Many leaders are now focusing more on using more and more advanced technologies to sustain their organisations' position in a competitive market.

4- Lack of skilled talent

The skills set required in industry 5.0 has become clearer. According to Deloitte's annual millennial survey, many leaders are aware of the current education system which are inadequate to meet the required skill sets to face challenges. Lack in the most need skills leaders and employees can slow down the process in business.

5- Lack of Communication

To lead a team effectively, leaders must have excellent communication skills but unfortunately, many leaders lack this. Maintaining consistency in communication with every employee is somewhat difficult in a larger organisation. Two-way communication between leaders and team members is a practice that will help to know each other's expected work and the outcome. Another factor in the communication gap is not being transparent. Being transparent can help leaders to have clear commination, less secretiveness and less confusionamong the team members.

6- Changes in requirement of skill sets

Reflecting on the changes in the industrial revolution, leaders need to be more complex thinkers, more creative, must be risk takers and able to resolve conflicts. Easy adaptability to new changes e.g. policy change, and new practices proposed within an organisation. Leaders must need to have strategic thinking abilities demanded in industries 5.0.

7- Lack of conflict management

Conflict-resolving abilities are very much important for leaders a workplace can become toxic when leaders allow conflicts to foster rather than stepping in to resolve them. Practices like active listening and empathy with employees can help leaders make impartial decisions. Leaders need to be impartial to manage internal politics within organisations.

8- Lack of growth opportunities

A good leader never grows alone he lifts others also. Providing growth opportunities to employees is one of the common and important challenges faced by leaders. Most leaders focus on organisational goals and growth; the employee's individual goal is less important.

9- Lack of Motivation

A leadership position comes with lots of hardships and responsibilities. Keeping everyone motivated within an organisation has become a major challenge for leaders. Every employee's attitude is not the same managing can be difficult sometimes. In the 21st century, the workforce faces different issues than employees of the previous industrial revolution. With changing time, stress and anxiety has become part of employees' lifestyle. To cope with such problems, leaders need to assist and motivate employees to overcome their stress and anxiety.

OPPORTUNITIES

1- Productivity improvement

Effective leadership involves getting the best out of the people and bringing diverse skills and personalities to achieve a common goal. In this competitive business, world leaders need to work on employee retention and bring out the best and bright employees not only by motto but also to save money and help in increasing productivity.

2- Better communication

Communication must not be one way, for better and more effective there should be two-way communication. It can affect the overall success of an organisation. It is an effective technique which can lead engagement and satisfaction among employees. Conducting one-on-one meetings between leaders and employees will be very helpful in building a better rapport between leaders and employees.

3- Boost morale of employees

At the time of change, the leadership must build a strong relationship with employees' morale. A highly motivated employee with high morale always performs their best.

4- More Creativity

Leaders need to have qualities like innovation, ambition and problem-solving with innovative ideas. A creative leader always finds a new path to achieve their organisational goal more effectively. They can easily map the path to achieve a new level of success.

5- Positive working environment

Leadership is not just about top-down making policy but it is more than this. A positive working environment can be an incredible advantage for any organisation. In industry-5.0, leaders are still struggling to create and maintain a positive working environment at a workplace. To create and maintain a positive workplace environment, leaders need to be more committed, open, and communicate better.

6- Better teamwork

A great leader demonstrates respect for team members in several ways, but being engaged with the team and working with different employees with different personalities, experiences, talents, and skills in a team enable and empowers a team to achieve organisational and individual goals effortlessly.

LEADERSHIP SKILLS

Personal communication

Leaders feel confident when their communication strengthens, which can boost their effects on others. Command over communication skills can help leaders to share his/her ideas in the best possible way with co-workers. They need to be good listeners as well.

Empathy, Positivity, Confidence, Vision, and Transparency

The leader needs to understand employees' wants, needs, and concerns. They need to be more empathic while dealing with employee-related problems. Empathy with an employee not only helps employees but will also help create a harmonious working environment. Displaying empathy will help build trust and respect from a colleague. Boosting the morals of employees is the biggest task for leaders. A positive environment makes working place happier to work. A visionary leader can semblance of a vision for the organisation's future. Leaders need to be truthful to employees and transparent in delivered information.

Critical Thinker

Leading a business towards accomplishing its final goals is very challenging for leaders. To achieve this goal sometimes leaders, need to take tough decisions and hard calls. Critical thinking is required before making any tough decisions. Leaders must have qualities like being extremely analytical and visionary in decision-making decisions. Critical thinkers are always intellectual decision-makers as they ensure that all possible outcomes are assessed and the best action to take is chosen.

Problem Solver

Being an effective leader doesn't mean doing everything by the leader himself. Whenever it needs, leaders must seek advice from the expertise of others. They should welcome and appreciate each member's input, and employees decide on the best approach to succeed or fail.

Agile Teams and Quick Decision Making

Leadership opens the door for employees to participate in the decision-making process, where employees' points of view and their creative ideas were considered. Employees must be always welcome to share their ideas and suggestions. Much is needed to work collaboratively in the workplace, which can open up vast knowledge and ideas.

SUGGESTIONS_

- Leaders need to adopt innovative practices for a sustainable organisation in the era of globalisation and digitalisation.
- Leaders should be more futuristic and realistic to overcome challenges.
- The leaders should adopt the strategy which have effectiveness for longer period of time and have a positive impact on the process.
- To overcome the skill set gaps leaders should implement and adopt the change management strategy. The strategies need to be easy to implement and aligned with the organizational environment in every situation.
- To fill the skills gap required the leaders should be provided with training programs in dealing with the change.
- Creating a positive working environment begins with the leaders, yet many are still struggling to create and maintain a positive working environment.
- In creating a positive and satisfied working environment, leaders must focus on their policies.

RECOMMENDATION_

- The industrial revolution 5.0 is underway in bringing many changes to industries. For the change, leaders need to be prepared for change if they don't want to feel left behind hand in the era of the industrial revolution.
- The following things that are needed to be taken into consideration for better and effective leadership
    - a) Need to have a basic ability to be a leader
    - b) Need to be a quick decision maker
    - c) Leaders should be more open to change and experiments
    - d) Leaders need to be more passionate and eager to adopt the technology

CONCLUSION

Industry 5.0 and its continuous demand for innovations encourage leaders to transform their leadership styles. It determined that some leaders resisted the change and found it difficult to embrace leadership transformation. Leadership and the workplace are experiencing transformation for better and more sustainable business. Globalisation and digitalisation influenced the leadership practices which shifts egocentric leadership into collaborative or allocentric leadership. Leadership in industry 5.0 demands more skills ever than required. To overcome challenges new age leadership paradigm needs to focus on new learning, communications, conflict resolution, creativity, innovations and more collaborative participation. Leadership in Industry 5.0 is more about connecting people rather than controlling and commanding.

The skill set required for effective leadership is continuously changing. As going through the industrial revolutions it was observed that the skill set and qualities required to be good leaders are changing than ever. Digitalisation and globalisation demand more and more skill sets. This chapter contributed in highlighting the transformation of leadership from industry 1.0 to industry 5.0. This chapter gives an overview of the challenges, opportunities and required skill set in the industry-5.0. Furthermore, this chapter will also be helpful for leaders to understand how effective strategies and policies can be implemented based on the challenges and opportunities described in the chapter.

IMPLICATIONS

This research article provides insight to modern leaders to adopt new practices and strategies for effective leadership in industry-5.0. Furthermore, leaders of industry-5.0 can understand the importance of a conducive work environment by giving autonomy, teamspirit, sustainability, learning and automation. This will provide a base for academicians and researchers for future research to diagnose the role of a leader and paradigm shift from industry-1.0 to 5.0. For leaders in industry 5.0, it's a great opportunity to improve the relationship between leaders and employees by discovering new opportunities for effectiveness. Industry 5.0 is more about digital transformation where companies are witnessing higher profits; there is wider scope and opportunities in digital transformation which will help in the improvement of the effectiveness and efficiency of an organization.

REFERENCES

Alessio, P., & Giustiniano, L. (2018). *Industry 4.0 and the emerging challenges to leadership*. Academic Press.

Baltezarevic, V., Baltezarevic, R., & Jovanovic, D. (2016). *Challenges Of Modern Leadership*. Academic Press.

Bass, B. M. (2000). The future of leadership in learning organizations. *The Journal of Leadership Studies*, *7*(3), 18–40. doi:10.1177/107179190000700302

Cahyadi, A., & Magda, R. (2021). Digital Leadership in the Economies of the G20 Countries: A Secondary. *Research in Economics*, *9*(1), 32. doi:10.3390/economies9010032

Day, D. V. (2000). Leadership development: A review in context. *The Leadership Quarterly*, *11*(4), 581–613. doi:10.1016/S1048-9843(00)00061-8

Jakubik, M., & Berazhny, I. (2018). *Rethinking leadership and its practices in the digital era*. Academic Press.

Jibrail, W., Fry, R., & Liyana-Pathirana, R. (2001, August). A modified serial-search DS code-acquisition scheme. In *Proceedings of the Sixth International Symposium on Signal Processing and its Applications (Cat. No. 01EX467)* (Vol. 2, pp. 481-484). IEEE. 10.1109/ISSPA.2001.950185

Kazim, F. A. (2019). Digital transformation and leadership style: a multiple case study. *The ISM Journal of International Business, 3*(1), 24-33.

Korejan, M. M., & Shahbazi, H. (2016). An analysis of the transformational leadership theory. *Journal of Fundamental and Applied Sciences*, *8*(3), 452–461. doi:10.4314/jfas.v8i3s.192

Martin, W. (2018). *Leadership: Outdated theories and emerging non-traditional leadership* [Doctoral dissertation]. Northcentral University.

Petrie, N. (2011). Future trends in leadership development. *Center for Creative Leadership White Paper, 5*(5), 36.

Sharma, N. (Ed.). (2019). *Analyzing workplace deviance in modern organizations*. IGI Global.

Sharma, N. (2021). Using positive deviance to enhance employee engagement: An interpretive structural modelling approach. *The International Journal of Organizational Analysis, 30*(1), 84–98. doi:10.1108/IJOA-07-2020-2341

Stefan, T., & Nazarov, A. D. (2020, November). Challenges and competencies of leadership in Covid-19 Pandemic. In Research technologies of pandemic coronavirus impact (RTCOV 2020) (pp. 518-524). Atlantis Press. doi:10.2991/assehr.k.201105.092

Tulasi, D., Lukito, R., Wahyu, D., & Ellitan, L. (2019). *The Role of Leadership in Industrial Revolution 4.0*. Academic Press.

Verma, R., Bharti, U., & Tripathi, U. (2022). Digital Era And Its Impact On Leadership Transformation. *Sachetas*, *1*(2), 36–41. doi:10.55955/120003

World Economic Forum. (2019). https://www.weforum.org/agenda/2019/01/these-four-leadership-styles-are-key-to-success-in-the-fourth-industrial-revolution/

Zulkifli, S. L. A., Omar, S. S., Ariffin, Z. Z., Mahadi, N., & Yaakop, A. Y. (2021). A Review of Leadership Approaches in the Industrial Revolution of 4.0 Era. *Online Journal for TVET Practitioners*, *6*(2), 21–27.

Chapter 3
Human Abilities Augmentation with Intelligent Technologies and Pervasive Computing Emerging Trends

David Egbe Ola
https://orcid.org/0000-0003-1676-4315
Federal College of Education Technical, Omoku, Nigeria

Dagogo William Legg-Jack
Walter Sisulu University, South Africa

ABSTRACT

The advent of internet of things (IoT) and cloud computing coupled with several breakthroughs in the field of artificial intelligence have made ambient intelligence, which incorporates pervasive computing, human-computer interaction, artificial intelligence, and IoT, possible. Whose objective is to tune the environment to understand human needs and seamless integration of technology with life? Which is the bedrock for human technology integration where artificial systems and miniaturized nanotechnology devices are embodied or implanted in human body which can either function as replacement for human body parts or the extension of human capabilities? This chapter will investigate the trends and advancement in human-computer integration. How can human augmentation technologies be used to replicate, supplement, and exceed human abilities? Also the chapter verifies the impact of human technology augmentation on Industry 5.0 and the challenges that contend with human technology integration.

INTRODUCTION

The possibility of integrating intelligent and intuitive technology devices with the human body which are capable of responding adaptively to human needs is one of the technology breakthroughs that will change our way of life and alleviate certain human deficiencies. This transformational technology fuses

DOI: 10.4018/978-1-6684-6745-9.ch003

pervasive computing, artificial intelligence and moves human computer interaction further to the level of integration where you have a fusion of artificial sensory capability with bio-sensing to extend certain capabilities, Farooq and Grudin (2019) observed that "Integration extends but doesn't replace interaction. Not all technologies are in the same stage of maturation. Interaction may take precedence. Robots, virtual assistants, and connected devices and the Internet of Things, for instance, are largely focused on interaction but will eventually graduate to the other end of the interaction-integration continuum". Mullen (2011) defined human technology integration as the "replacement of human parts and extension of human capabilities with engineered devices and substrates. Its result is hybrid biological-artificial systems". The goal of this emerging technology is to either extend certain capabilities or augments for lack of those abilities. Mullen (2011) further emphasized that "Human-technology integration proceeds via the development of engineered systems that allow the extension of human senses and capacity to act into the environment. Such systems include (wearable) computing devices and pervasive computing environments, as well as products that substitute or modify aspects of human's existing organic structure, e.g., prosthetics and engineered tissues and organs". There is growing concern about the ethical implication of further research and breakthroughs in bioprinted technology which will engineer the creation of biosynthetic and artificial human beings.

Human technology integration, which relies largely on artificial intelligence that simulates the intellectual ability of the human mind for the operation of machines, has the capability to seamlessly integrate with the human body for enhanced performance. Thanks to unabated advancement in the field of Artificial Intelligence (AI) and machine learning that is merging the gap between technology and humans, making it possible for AI enabled systems to be integrated with the human body to carry out functions once thought of as only achievable by humans with added augmentation. Mueller et al. (2020) in agreement stated that "The mainframe era of one-machine-to-many-users shifted to the one-machine-to-one-user era of the personal computer, followed by the one-user-to-many-machines era of mobiles, to finally the many-machines-to-many-users era of today's ubiquitous computing era. Looking towards the future, however, it appears that the next era will not be described by such a ratio, but rather that its distinguishing feature will be the blurring of the boundary between human and computer where user and technology together form a closely coupled system within a wider physical, digital, and social context". This era of ubiquitous computing where intelligent programs become an intricate part of everything will move us from the era of Internet of Things (IoT) to Internet of Everything (IoE) with the implant of intelligent systems into human body which will enable the computers to adjust to human body and extend its capability which can interact with the environment and integrate naturally like human body parts.

In human technology interaction, robotic systems equipped with artificial intelligence were made to assist in carrying out routine tasks whether in the industry or in everyday assisted living. Xing (2016) categorized robots that assist in everyday living mostly for the elderly into "robots assisting with daily living activities (such as feeding and dressing), robots assisting with instrumental activities of daily living (such as housekeeping and preparing food), and robots assisting with enhanced activities of daily living (such as communication and engaging in hobbies)". In industry 5.0 the trend will be different instead of having intelligent systems assisting humans from the background, they will rather be fused into human body that will augment for what is lacking, for instance in the case of cognitive impairment instead of using external aids that simply magnify auditory sounds that pass into the ear canal, bone anchored hearing systems that are surgically implanted will be used (Victory, 2022). In addition to many biotechnology breakthroughs that will make the introduction to human blood stream nanomedicine, a form of nanobot that will intelligently get rid of certain ailment, rejuvenate dead and worn out cells. Which will improve the quality of life and enhance healthy longevity.

Closely interwoven with human technology integration is augmentation which according to Word Economic Forum (2022) can be defined as "the use of technologies to simultaneously support people's empowerment and engagement, increase productivity and drive excellence across operations and business processes. It aims to realize the most effective ways to support or amplify human abilities with technology". This will alter the way people engage with everyday realities thus paving way for more integrated lifelong learning and development of employees with applications such as virtual reality (VR) and augmented reality (AR). World Economic Forum (2022) also added that "One application of augmentation technology is as a training tool powered by an immersive, virtual learning platform, which will be used to make learning faster, more agile, more individualized and more entertaining" The main purpose of augmentation is to enhance cognitive functions and improve physical capability. Which is in line with Rodrigues (2019) submission that "Across the globe, engineers, entrepreneurs, and policymakers are rapidly exploring new and marketable applications for human augmentation technology. Most of them are being designed to help people fulfil their long-lived desire to be smarter, faster, stronger, tougher, and more attractive, and to build new abilities that not long ago seemed like science fiction".

The main focus of this chapter is to investigate the emerging trends in human technology integration. Find out, how human augmentation technologies can be used to replicate, supplement and exceed human abilities? And the impact of human computer integration; what consequence will such integration have and what if integration progresses to substitution of the entire human body and life with artificial and biosynthetic one? What will be the ethical implication of such replacement?

BACKGROUND

This chapter examines the growing trends in human technology integration, by x-raying their categories based on the part of the body where the integration takes place, while some of the devices are worn on the skin, others went beyond the epidermis and dermis for a deep implant. The emergent trend unveiled that bioprinting has experienced many breakthroughs that made 3D bioprinting of organs possible. Though, the technology is still at the exploration stage and needs further refinement to enable bioprinted body parts transplant possible but experimental body organs like liver and brain are already used to test certain drugs.

This chapter also looked at human augmentation, which is multidisciplinary in nature and relied heavily on artificial intelligence (AI) to harness human to machine intelligence to replicate, supplement and exceed human abilities. Its palpable gains are yielding increased productivity, smart and augmented workforce that drive excellence in business operations. Technology Integration has wrapped the entire society and industrial work space around augmentation and in industry 5.0 where intelligent systems will collaborate with human beings to have a more human tailored and centric society, will witness more of the convergence of the cyberspace influenced by artificial intelligence with the physical human space. This will not only increase and enhance productivity but will lead to a smarter society where known deficiencies are augmented with specialised custom-made technologies.

Lastly, we discussed some of the challenges and the ethical concerns of human enhancement technologies which are: human technology compatibility, social inequality issues, ethical concerns of human modification among others

METHODOLOGY

Secondary research materials from published journals, websites and blogs were used for this Chapter, the researchers survey information from those published materials and use the direction and dimension of human technology integration revealed in those research to predict and define trends in human technology integration as regard what has been achieved, and what will be potentially achieved in the near time.

The Emerging Trends in Human Technology Integration

The era of human computer integration which is thought of in the past as science fiction is fast becoming a reality, for instance 3D bioprinting of living human bones, skin tissues, blood vessels, organs etc. have become a reality, though still under development to enable the transplant of bioprinted body part into humans but, that actualization will be possible in no time. Wallace and Little (2022) revealed that "The artificial creation of human skin, tissue and internal organs may sound like a futuristic dream but, incredibly, much of it is happening right now, albeit still in the early stages. In research facilities and hospitals around the globe, advancements in 3D printing and, more particularly, bioprinting are providing new options for treatment and scientific study. Indeed, bioprinting has the potential to be the next big thing in health care and personalised medicine". Gaget (2018) added that "Some 3D bioprinted liver tissues have already been printed by researchers in Tokyo and can be used in the development and testing of drugs. Researchers from the Department of Mechanical Engineering at Imperial College London created brain-like tissues thanks to bioprinting. This impressive 3D structure is incredibly soft, similar to the brain texture". These technologies when fully integrated with human body will provide a new lease of life to in need organ transplant which is in short supply currently and some other human prevailing problems.

Types of Human Technology integration

Currently they are two types of human computer integration which are **fusion and symbiosis**: In **fusion**, the technology device is implanted to human body. Mueller et al. (2020) define fusion "as an integration in which devices extend the experienced human body or in which the human body extends devices. Fusion occurs on an individual level and often only affects a sub-part of the user, such as a limb or a sense". Mueller et al. (2020) also added to the concept of fusion that "Such integration occurs primarily at an individual level through sensory fusion, with computers providing information directly to human senses rather than through symbolic representations and understanding the user's implicit, precognitive needs through bio-sensing". In **symbiotic** integration humans and computer technology work together in complementary effort on certain task to achieve predefined goals. Devices that belong to this type of human technology integration are mainly worn on the skin such as wearable devices and exoskeletons that are capable of helping operators in logistic company in lifting metric tons of weight thus reliving operator of lifting strenuous weight. Bornet (2022) added that "technology becomes able to understand natural language and even anticipate your needs, making its own suggestions about tasks you might like it to do for you. Input and output devices become better integrated with software, streamlining automated processes and removing humans from the loop for routine operations, only requiring human supervision when something unexpected happens. Automation becomes intelligent automation". Human technology integration seeks to exploit the gains of intelligent systems that makes automation possible to alleviate human challenges through integration.

Table 1. Categories of human technology integration, devices used and application

Technology integration type	Part of body Integration	Types devices involved	Application
Epidermal technologies	Epidermis (worn on the skin)	DuoSkin, iSkin, Skintillates, e-Skin, Microfluidic, SkinMarks and the host of others	Epidermal devices function in providing additional functionalities that augment the use of the skin.
Transdermal technologies	Transend epidermis to dermis	Climara, Dermo-patch, Beauty patch (at R and D stages.	These devices open access through the epidermis to the dermis.
Subdermal technologies	Dermis	Microchips (RFID) devices, Micro-phones, Touch sensors	Provide access and interface to other electronic devices for communication. These devices serve as a medium of connecting people to Internet of Things (IoT)
Deep implanted technologies	Permanently implanted to human body using surgery	Pacemaker (implanted in the chest to regulate the heart functions), cochlear implants, artificial smart leg	Designed to coexist with human organs. Used to augment certain organ deficiency

Human technology integration can take place at different layer of human body, those that are worn on the skin are called **epidermal technologies**, these epidermal devices are simulated after human skin which can result in seamless human machine interface and an electronically interactive skin, which can be used to observe and monitor human important organs like heart for blood pressure. Steimle (2022) further described them as having "Embedded functional materials that create fully flexible electronic components for sensing, output, processing, and power in a micron-thin form factor that computationally augment the natural functions of our skin". Those integrated into the deeper layer of the skin are referred to as **Subdermal technologies**, while according to Mueller et al. (2020) "**Transdermal technologies** contain an epidermal and subdermal part, similar to a piercing. They combine several advantages of the previous technologies, i.e., they enable a deeper integration with the body while supporting easy access from outside to the body. Body parts that allow for piercing (e.g., the ear and the nose) can host electronics that are still easily removable. Transdermal objects, common in the body modification scene, open a path from the outside to the inside of the body but require constant care to avoid infections". Those whose integration are done using surgical procedure on a permanent basis are referred to as **Deep implanted technologies.** Lastly, the integrations that are done for a specific duration of time are called **pass through technology**. "The advantage of the pass-through technology is that devices under this group automatically exit the body or dissolve after a certain time. Examples include digested pills that are able to track body temperature" (Zhuying 2018). Sobot (2019) in summary of the above classification suggest that "A possible strictly engineering classification of general biomedical devices in relation to the human body is: a) wearable devices, b) implantable devices, and c) ingestible devices". The table I below give a detailed information about the part of the body these technology integrations take place, the types of devices integrated and the application.

Most of the human compatible technology devices mentioned above, are e-health devices that are implantable into human body to provide augmentation for deficiencies and remediation for lack of certain abilities. For instance **Brain-Computer Interface** (Brain to machine interface) which is a deep implant technology that can be used to control personal computers through transmitted brain signals as a result of the connection between the implant and the brain which function as an interface between the human mind and the computer to enable people with impairment in their speech and mobility to be able to use their mind to move robotic arms and interface with their personal computers to control the mouse to send messages, shop online and interact with the digital world. Deep Brain Simulation is another deep implant device that is used to treat movement disorder. Bionic arms and leg have been greatly improved on with the breakthroughs in brain to machine interface which has permitted the seamless integration of prosthetics into human body. The table II below give a detail of implantable technologies, number of users per year and average cost of procedure.

Table 2. Implantable Technology and rate of usage. Source (Sobot, 2019)

Technology Integration Device	User per year (millions)	Average cost of procedure ($1000)
Artificial Smart Leg	0.13	40
Artificial hips	0.25	45
Artificial knee	0.5	22
Cardiovascular (Pacemake) Defibrillator	0.4	20 – 40
Metal Hardware	1.0	2 – 25
Coronary Stents	0.5	15
Ventricular Assist	0.11	150
Breast implant	0.4	3 – 5
Cochlear Implant	-	30-40
Artificial Eye Lenses	2.6	3-5
Hearing Aid	2.0	1 – 4

REPLICATING, SUPPLEMENTING AND EXCEEDING HUMAN ABILITIES THROUGH AUGMENTATION

Human Augmentation is a term that is multidisciplinary in nature, it embraces every discipline that contributes to the enhancement of human abilities. Though augmented reality, virtual reality and artificial (AI) intelligence contribute immensely to human augmentation, they are just a fraction of the whole. Raisamo (2019) define human augmentation as "*an interdisciplinary field that addresses methods, technologies and their applications for enhancing sensing, action and/or cognitive abilities of a human. This is achieved through sensing and actuation technologies, fusion and fission of information, and artificial intelligence (AI) methods.* The role of augmentation according to Rodrigues (2019) "is to help people fulfil their long-lived desire to be smarter, faster, stronger, tougher, and more attractive, and to build new abilities that not long ago seemed like science fiction". The use of technology in augmenting human abilities and expertise has proven relevant in aiding analytical skills, intelligent decision-making, physical capabilities and knowledge acquisition which has open new possibilities for augmented workforce that has witness increased productivity, drive quality and excellence in workplace. This enhancement is guarantee by augmented intelligence where machines equipped with machine learning capability collaborate with human intelligence to deliver business solutions. Little wonder the demand for human augmentation products is high. According to human augmentation market indices (2022) "the market is estimated to be worth USD 131.7 billion in 2021 and is projected to reach USD 341.2 billion by 2026, at a CAGR of 21.0%. Growing demand for wearable human augmentation devices in healthcare sector, the recent advent of AI-powered wearable devices and rapid technological advancements such as availability of fast processing chipsets, miniaturization of sensors, use of brain-computer interfaces and evolution of nanotechnology are some of the major factors contributing to the market growth".

Human augmentation can be divided into three different categories as discussed below:

"**Augmented senses** (aka enhanced senses, extended senses) are achieved by interpreting available multisensory information and presenting content to the human through selected human senses. Sub-classes include augmented vision, hearing, haptic sensation, smell, and taste.

Augmented action is achieved by sensing human actions and mapping them to actions in local, remote or virtual environments. Sub-classes include motor augmentation, amplified force, and movement, speech input, gaze-based controls, teleoperation, remote presence, and others.

Augmented cognition (aka enhanced cognition) is achieved by detecting human cognitive state, using analytical tools to make a correct interpretation of it, and adapting computer's response to match the current and predictive needs of the user (e.g., providing stored or recorded information during natural interaction)". (Raisamo et al., 2019)

There are so many technologies that contributed to human augmentation and others which are emerging technologies that will impact tremendously on human technology augmentation as presented in the table III below:

Replicating Human Ability

This category of augmentation encompasses technologies that restore or re-establish abilities that are inactive or whose use are truncated as a result of bad health or damaged and missing body parts. A good illustration is a prosthetic arm or leg for amputees. Bruce (2022) added that "Replication also aids in providing equal opportunities for those who have experienced an accident or illness. Also, it helps those who were born with inadequacies and face daily challenges". Examples of devices used under this category are: eSight (that help the blind to see their environment), Artificial limbs, bioprinting (creating artificial human like tissue, organs from bio synthetic materials) and Cochlear implant (that work on the restoration of hearing loss), among others. Table IV below gave a detailed presentation of replication augmentation technology and application.

Supplementing Human Abilities

These devices are designed to enhance one's ability to do certain things. "For example, these could be devices that boost one's strength, improve one's vision. This also pushes them beyond their natural limits or devices that boost their intelligence. The human enhancement that strengthens our physical or mental limitations has revolutionary potential. It will also improve our culture and our prospects" (Bruce, 2022). Examples of these devices are plastron or exoskeleton (designed to amplify human strength), Mixed Reality Smart Glasses, Translation Tool and Neuralink. Table V below discussed these technologies and their application

Table 3. Technologies that foster human augmentation. Source (World Economic Forum, 2022) with modification from the author

Augmented reality (AR) Enhanced version of the physical world achieved by digital visual elements, sound or other stimuli	**Computer Vision** Area of artificial intelligence (AI) that enables systems to derive information from images, videos and other visual input	**Exoskeleton** External anatomical feature that supports and protects an operator's body during physical tasks
Industrial internet of thing (IIoT) Application of connected sensors and other devices to machinery and processes in industrial settings	**Intelligent decision-making support** System that helps facilitate decision-making, judgements and courses of action based on data	**Wearables (not exoskeletons)** Electronic devices that can be worn as accessories, e.g. embedded in protective work clothing
Virtual reality (VR) Computer-generated, immersive simulation of a three-dimensional image or environment	**Collaborative robots (cobots)** Machines capable of carrying out a complex series of actions semi-automatically in collaboration with operators	**Connected worker platforms** Digital tool designed for operators to improve communication and control in industrial settings
Mixed reality (MR) Merging of real and virtual worlds to generate environments in which physical and digital objects coexist and interact	**Mobile devices** Portable, electronic equipment that can connect to the internet	**Smart workstations** An area in which industrial work is carried out supported by technological means, e.g. task guidance
IoT precision Sensors are an essential part of monitoring the environment around the user to process data and critical control of performance. With the recent developments in precision sensors, they would be able to recognize changes in the human body. Furthermore, IoT devices could integrate with prosthetic body parts or exoskeletons and help the user navigate their environment safely.	**Edge Computing** is the workload transition from the cloud to the "edge." Edge in this context refers to local computations made by the device autonomously without referring back to the cloud.	**Quantum Computing –** Practical application of quantum computing would not only increase the speed of computing for human augmentation devices but also would affect the development of other products by solving complex scientific problems. As we mentioned in our previous article, quantum computing can provide artificial intelligence with a boost in terms of computation, allowing it to perform more complex tasks

Exceeding Human Abilities

"Exceeding refers to the technology that allows us to perform tasks beyond our physical capability. This also includes typical superhero abilities such as the ability to fly, flying is considered to be an add-on

Table 4. Replication Technologies and Application

Replication Augmentation Technology	Application
Prosthetic or bionic limbs	An artificial limb is used for the rehabilitation of mobility in the case of limbs amputation.
Sight correction (eSight)	Provide blind people with the ability to see their environment.
Hearing aid (Cochlear Implants)	Bioelectronic hearing aids are either worn close to the ear or implanted, as in the case of Neuroprosthetic devices like cochlear implants for the restoration of hearing.
Bioprinting	Used 3D bioprinting technology to create organic tissues that include bones, skin, organ etc. that can be used for transplant. Artificial corneas are created for sight problem like cataracts.
Sign language to speech translator (MotionSavvy)	It translates sign language to speech and speech to sign language for those with hearing loss or impairment.

Table 5. supplanting human ability augmentation technologies

Supplementing Human Ability Augmentation Technology	Application
Exoskeleton	Wearable devices that give special strength and ability to the users either in the industries, "the Sarcos Guardian is an example of an industrial exoskeleton that allows a human worker to lift up to 200 pounds, perform precise operations with heavy machinery, and handle repetitive motions without strain" (Rodrigues, 2019). Or for personal enhancement such a robotic exoskeleton that can help paralysed people walk.
Brain-machine interface devices (Sychron and Neuralink)	Sychron and Neuralink are the major players in the human computer interface devices whose goal is to control the computers through brain signals by implanting microchips into human brain. The technology can be used to treat neurological disorders. Though much of its potentials are under development.
Foreign Language translators: Real-time earbuds (Waverly Lab's earbuds)	An earbud can translate foreign language real time without the need of an interpreter.
Surgical Robots	An artificial intelligence (AI) powered robots work in collaboration with surgeon to carry out high precision neurosurgery. "These devices also have inbuilt optics for extra-sensory information while working". (Day One, 2021)
Virtual Reality Glasses (Oculus Quest 2, HTC Vive Cosmos) VR closed off the users view of the outside world and immersed them into the virtual world	Used for a more engaged training whether in educational sector or industrial training of employees. Relevant in virtual showrooms where 3D prototype designs of products can be explored.
Mixed Reality Smart Glasses (HoloLens 2, Magic Leap, Nreal Light, Think Reality A3) Mixed Reality Smart Glasses enables the user to interact with the virtual world and the physical world at the same time.	Mixed reality smart glasses have found many industrial applications such as interactive working. In product development, "you can design a 3D model and have colleagues or customers view the digital design through AR glasses. You get meaningful feedback and you don't even have to be in the same room to do it". It is also used in training employees in a mixed reality environment with 3D objects that enables workers to gain experience with just digital objects. (Aliger Augmented reality, n.d)

activity that transcends human ability. The ability to breathe underwater, the ability to detect chemicals through the nose, etc. This type of augmentation may be the most fascinating. But it is also the most distant and will take a long time to develop fully. Also, a significant part of its current applications finds a place in the military or specific industries". (Bruce, 2022) Examples of these technology with practical application are Artificial Blood Cell, Artificial Chip, Nanobot and Flyboard Air

Human Technology Augmentation and Industry 5.0

In industry 5.0, human expert will collaborate with smart machines to achieve high productivity and efficiency, the workforce will be highly augmented with intelligent and accurate machines to obtain a more resource efficient and human centric manufacturing that will deliver user defined and customized products. Tange et al. (2020) buttress that "Industry 5.0 is currently conceptualized to leverage the unique creativity of human experts to collaborate with powerful, smart and accurate machinery. Many technical visionaries believe that Industry 5.0 will bring back the human touch to the manufacturing industry". Instead of robots trying to replace the workforce they will rather collaborate and augment the workforce with a better synergy using human computer interface. "Industry 5.0 is a future evolution

Table 6. Augmentation technologies that exceed human abilities

Exceeding Human Ability Augmentation Technology	Application
Flying Flyboard Air (Zapata Flyboard Air)	It enables people to fly at a moderate altitude of 500 feet in the air.
Artificial Blood Cell	It performs the vital function of the blood by transporting oxygen and carbon dioxide to and out of the body but cannot carry out the other complementary function of the natural blood such fighting diseases. but, with so many other advantages such as prevention of complication associated with the natural blood, among others.
Nanobots	They can be used to deliver drug with precision to cells and tissues are carryout repair work. "Scientists have worked on developing nanobots that can precisely measure key cancer biomarkers at low concentration levels, enabling the early detection of multiple types of cancer and overcoming the limitations of currently available methods". (Moore, 2021) A final interesting development in nanobot research is "using nanotechnology to establish a 'global superbrain' where human thought, theoretically, could be transferred to an artificial interface, establishing a human 'brain-cloud interface'".
Synthetic Memory Chip	Though application is still at the conceptual stage, but neuroscientist believe that it is possible to install by implant a synthetic memory chip that will connect with the brain neurons to store and retrieve information. The concept is borne out of the fact that, computer hard drives are better at storing, retaining and retrieving information at great speed and accuracy.

designed to use the creativity of human experts working together with efficient, intelligent and accurate machines". Industry 5.0, human experts will be able to control robots with brain signals using human machine interface. "The fifth industrial revolution will likely push for more advanced human–machine interfaces using artificial intelligence (AI) algorithms. This will mean better integration, enabling faster, better automation combined with the power of human brains" (Aslam et al., 2020).

Virtual training using virtual and augmented reality devices without exposing the workforce to training hazards, at the same time delivering a cost-effective training will be an integral of workforce training in industry 5.0 thus, giving the HR more time to concentrate organisation growth, productivity and other administrative assignment. Forbes reported that "34% of HR leaders invest in workforce learning and retraining as part of their strategy to prepare for the future of work. And 5.0 will free HR teams from much of the day-to-day administration" (Eschbach, 2021). Learning new skills and lifelong learning by the employees will be assessible and faster thus removing the possibility of skill gap. According to World Economic Forum (2022) a training was conducted for more than "7,800 employees who were trained in first courses alone. Using Gemba's immersive learning platform, as well as state-of-the art hardware (Oculus Quest 2, Microsoft HoloLens 2), enabled Aptiv to convey knowledge at a much higher depth and breadth, with an 80% higher efficiency compared to real-world training".

Enabling Technologies for Human Technology Augmentation and Industry 5.0

There are several technologies that will play vital in the realization of the goals of human technology integration and industry 5.0 they are listed and briefly explained below:

1. Nanotechnology
2. Artificial intelligence (IA)
3. Highspeed 5G and 6G networks and beyond
4. Cloud/Edge and fog computing
5. Internet of everything (IOE)
6. Collaborative robots
7. Biotechnology empowered by AI
8. Digital twins' simulation
9. Blockchain Technology

NANOTECHNOLOGY

The fundamental goal of nanotechnology is engineering of materials and devices at nanometre scale that is creating things from the smallest element possible. One of the applications of nanotechnology is the development of nanorobots used for targeted drug delivery, cellular and tissue repair, diagnosis of cancer at early stage etc. The technology is also relevant in the miniaturisation of electronics, actuators, sensors and computing devices with enhanced capabilities. In computer science, for instance, "Integrating silicon nanophotonic components into CMOS integrated circuits. Provide a higher speed of data transmission between integrated circuits than is possible with electrical signals" (Ferreira and Filipe 2022). Nanotechnology has immense potentials for human technology integration, the nano systems can be used to reduce the size of human augmentation devices.

Artificial intelligence (IA)

Artificial intelligence is the science of developing machines that mimic human intelligence. The subset, which is called machine learning, enables the machine to learn and improve performance without being explicitly programmed, AI and machine learning has revolutionised the modern world. Human augmentation devices are equipped with artificial intelligence that enable them to make smart decisions and perform intelligent task. Deep learning which is a subset of machine learning, has imparted "robots and intelligent machines with reliable cognition and visualization capability, which is necessary in autonomous applications, including collaborative robots (cobots). Deep learning strategies are basically founded on artificial neural networks with a comparatively large number of layers in their structure". (Nahavandi, 2019).

Highspeed 5G and 6G Networks and beyond

The synchronisation and collaboration of heterogeneous device connected to the internet space required a high-speed internet like 5G for seamless operation. According to David (2019) "5G will support over 250 connected devices per square kilometre, with each device being able to support up to 1GHz in bandwidth. This will see sensors on any device being capable of interconnectivity regardless of wi-fi availability, leading to mobile devices having 24/7 access to bandwidth".

Edge and Fog Computing

According to Overheid (2022) "Edge computing is data computation that happens at the network's edge, in close proximity to the physical location creating the data. On the other hand, fog computing acts as a mediator between the edge and the cloud for various purposes, such as data filtering". Such that both technologies co-exist without the ability of one to replace the other. Salman et al. (2020) revealed that fog computing has addressed the challenge of augmented reality by lowing latency. "Augmented reality applications are computationally intensive and have latency requirements in the range of 15-20 milliseconds. Fog computing addresses these requirements by providing on-demand computing capacity and lower latency by bringing the computational resources closer to the augmented reality devices. "Augmented cognition can transform human capabilities but delivering its benefits in real time will require low-latency wireless access to powerful infrastructural resources by lightweight wearable devices. Edge computing is the only viable approach to meeting these stringent requirements.". (Satyanarayanan and Davies 2019)

Internet of Everything (IoE)

Industry 5.0 will extend the functionality of the internet of things (IoT) to the internet of everything where intelligent devices become a part of everyday life. "It is an ecosystem where everything is interconnected Thus, IoE is a wider concept that includes not only machine-to-machine communication (M2M) but also people to machine (P2M) and people to people (P2P) communication through technology". (Shinkarenko, 2020)

Collaborative Robots

Industry 5.0 will be anchored on the humans working in partnership with robotic systems and smart machines powered by innovative and enhanced technology. Robotic online marketing team (2020) emphasized that "Where Industry 4.0 was focused mainly on ensuring consistency of quality, flow, and data collection, Industry 5.0, while still focused on these goals, puts more attention on highly-skilled people and robots working side-by-side to create individualized products, from smartphones to cars, for the customer. In Industry 4.0, humans and robots worked independently. They may have worked on the same production line but there were clear delineations between where the robot worked and where the human worked. With Industry 5.0, that delineation gets hazier as humans and robots start to work side-by-side and even together. These types of robots are known as collaborative robots and will accomplish the required tasks of heavy lifting and ensuring consistency while the skilled human provides the cognitive skills of a craftsperson".

Biotechnology Empowered by AI

Biotechnology is the application of the knowledge of biological sciences to develop products that solve human problems. The merging of biotechnology with artificial intelligence which enable biotech devices operate with synthesize intelligence will revolutionize the health industry. For instance, DeepMind "create the most comprehensive map of proteins to date using artificial intelligence Before this breakthrough, determining the structure of a protein could only be done by a series of expensive and time-consuming experiments. However, DeepMind showed that relying on Alphafold, its AI software, it could produce accurate predictions of a protein's structure" (Brown, 2021).

Digital Twin Simulation

To meet the goal of delivering quality, personalised and custom-made products in industry 5.0, digital twin kind of simulation that can determine what will happen to a product in the real world when put to use will revolutionize production. Miskini (2018) added that "A Digital Twin interface is a simulation that is entirely based on the physical replica of the simulated object itself. The digital twin simulation can extrapolate how an object, product or a system will work in the future after all necessary structural changes are implemented". "Digital twins and simulation technologies optimise production, test products and processes and detect possible harmful effects" (Muller, 2020).

Blockchain Technology

Blockchain technology will be very vital in enhancing the security of technology devices in industry 5.0 because of its ability to deliver transparent and tamperproof solutions that are auditable. Though Permissionless blockchain is more accessible but due to its inherent scalability bottleneck it will not be suitable for internet of everything environment, permission blockchain will therefore be more suitable

Challenges with Human Technology Integration

In a bid to exploit the potentials of technologies that aid human technology integration, there are certain challenges to contend with for the full implementation, some of the most obvious challenges are discussed below:

Human Technology Compatibility

People's personalities differ, so their peculiarities, most human augmentation devices are not designed with that understanding, they are mostly one size fits all kinds of designs which can react differently when integrated with the human body. The rate at which these technologies are accepted and utilised will depend on how they can seamlessly integrate with the human body without a negative reaction.

Widened Gap of Social Inequality

Technology disadvantaged people will find it very difficult to compete with those who have augmentation technology at their disposal thus widening the gap of social inequality. For instance, if two industries are producing the same kind of product company A use augmented workforce and B due to limited resources couldn't afford a technology enhanced workforce, the B industry cannot compete favourably with A. Zicong (2021) buttress more that "social resources are limited and scarce to the needs of human development, so not everyone has the opportunity to enjoy the benefits of human augmentation technology. At this time, for those who have not been enhanced, the man-made difference might distinguish people with human augmentation technology from normal people when they are faced with the same competitions. Whether in sports competitions or in any other field, they are always in an unequal competitive environment and at a disadvantage compared with those who have been utilizing human augmentation technology".

The Ethical Concerns of irreversible Enhancement

Some biotechnology enhancements like genetic modification whose effects are irrevocable raised ethical concerns. It promotes infringement on the rights of new babies whose traits are genetically modified without their consent. This will also alter the natural make-up of the child and the ability to naturally compete in the child's environment. Zicong (2021) also added that "This modification is irreversible, which may partially increase the child's competitive advantages, but may also constrain the child's future choices and opportunities".

Privacy and Security Issues

Most of the augmentation devices in a bid to enable them deliver human centric services, the manufacturer needs to collect people's private information, though this may not be collected with the intention of spying on the users but to optimize the algorithm of the device to deliver a more enhanced service. Privacy issues should be considered early in the design and should not be a post design consideration. The Internet of Things IoT that interconnect billions of devices through the internet space could be a hotbed for cybercriminals. It is therefore important the security of the augmentation device should be considered right from the development stage.

CONCLUSION

In this chapter, we have discovered that the multidisciplinary field of human technology integration is impacting virtually every faucet of human life, thanks to research and new discoveries that are shaping the rapid expansion of this very essential field. Technology integration extends the potentials of human computer interaction but does not substitute it. Integration is more human centric, that is, it tends to customise technology to suit individuals and solve specific problems, judging from this reality we discovered that human technology integration will be the bedrock of industry 5.0.

In this investigation, we also discovered that human augmentation stretched the role of integration to replicate, supplement and even exceed certain human abilities that are dormant, deactivated as a result of illness or accident, it rekindled the hope of biotechnology organ transplant, nanomedicine and nanobots which are already helpful in solving health associated problems. In addition, we looked at some drawbacks to human technology augmentation.

REFERENCES

Aliger Augmented Reality. (n.d.). *Mixed Reality Glasses: work more efficiently thanks to AR visualisation*. Retrieved from https://alegerglobal.com/en/augmented-reality/smart-glasses/mixed-reality-glasses/

Aslam, F., Aimin, W., Li, M., & Ur Rehman, K. (2020). Innovation in the era of IoT and industry 5.0: Absolute innovation management (AIM) framework. *Information (Basel), 11*(2), 124. doi:10.3390/info11020124

Bornet, P. (2022). *The Symbiosis of People and Technology*. Forbes Technology Council. Retrieve from https://www.forbes.com/sites/ forbes techcouncil /2022 /01/12 /the- symbiosis- of- people-and -technology /?sh= 42433dd71 fe4

Brown, A. (2021). Artificial Intelligence Is Transforming Biotechnology, Especially When It Comes to Innovations In Nitric Oxide. *Forbes*. Retrieved on 02/09/2022 https://www.forbes.com/sites/anniebrown/2021/10/25/artificial-intelligence-is-transforming-biotechnology-especially-when -it-comes-to-innovations-in-nitric-oxide/?sh=d3e27797f00b

Bruce, D. (2022). *Human Augmentation Technology and its Real-Life Applications*. KnowledgeNile. https :// www. knowledgenile. com/ blogs/ human- augmentation- technology-and -its-real -life -applications/

Day One. (2021). *What is Human Augmentation? Will it become a megatrend in the future?* Retrieved from https://www.day1tech.com/what-is-human-augmentation-will-it-become-a-megatrend-in-the-future/

Eschbach, A. P. (2021). *These 9 sets of matching family Pajamas are on sale for Cyber Monday*. Retrieved August 28, 2022, from https://www.forbes.com/sites/forbes-personal-shopper/2021/11 /29/matching-family-pajamas/?sh=b8665353ba84

Farooq, U., & Grudin, J. (2019). *Human-Computer Integration. Microsoft Corporation Microsoft*. ACM.

Ferreira, A. M., & Filipe, J. A. (2022). *Nanotechnology Applications: The future arrived suddenly*. Retrieved from https://www. researchgate.net/ publication/357953395 _Nanotechnology _Applications _The_future_ arrived_suddenly

Gaget, L. (2018). *3D bioprinting: What can we achieve today with a 3D bioprinter?* https:// www. sculpteo.com / blog/ 2018/ 02/21/3d- bioprinti ng -what-can-we-achieve-today-with-a-3d-bioprinter/

Human Augmentation Market. (2022). *Human Augmentation Market by Product Type (Wearable Devices, Virtual Reality Devices, Augmented Reality Devices, Exoskeletons, Intelligent Virtual Assistants), Functionality, Application, & Geography (2021-2026)*. https:// www. Market sand markets.com/Market-Reports/human-augmentation-market-177215310.html

Maddikunta, K., Pham, Q., Prabadevi, B., Deepa, N., Kapal, D., Gadekallu, T., ... Liyanage, M. (2021). Industry 5.0: A survey on enabling technologies and potential applications. *Journal of Industrial Information Integration, 26*, 100257. Advance online publication. doi:10.1016/j.jii.2021.100257

Miskini, C. (2018). *Normal simulation models versus a digital twin-based simulation*. Challenge Advisory. https://www.challenge.org/insights/digital-twin-simulations/

Moore, S. (2021). *An Overview of Nanobots and the Most Recent Developments*. https://www.azonano.com/article.aspx?ArticleID=5761

Mueller, F., Lopes, P., Strohmeier, P., Wendy J., Seim, C., Weigel, M., Nanayakkara, S., Obrist M., … Maes, P. (2020). *Next Steps in Human-Computer Integration*. Association for Computing Machinery. doi:10.1145/3313831.3376242

Mullen, K. M. (2011). Human-technology Integration. In A. A. Minai, D. Braha, & Y. Bar-Yam (Eds.), *Unifying Themes in Complex Systems*. Springer. doi:10.1007/978-3-642-17635-7_31

Müller, J. (2020). *Enabling Technologies for Industry 5.0: Results of a workshop with Europe's technology leaders*. Publications Office of the European Union.

Nahavandi, S. (2019). Industry 5.0—A Human-Centric Solution. Institute for Intelligent Systems Research and Innovation, Deakin University.

Overheid, A. (2022, April 15). *Understanding Fog Computing vs Edge Computing*. https://www.onlogic.com/company/io-hub/fog-computing-vs-edge-computing/#:~:text=In%20a%20nutshell%2C%20edge%20computing,purposes%2C%20such%20as%20data%20filtering

Raisamo, R., Rakkolainen, I., Majaranta, P., Salminen, K., Rantala, J., & Farooq, A. (2019). Human Augmentation: Past, present and future. *International Journal of Human-Computer Studies*, *131*, 131–143. Advance online publication. doi:10.1016/j.ijhcs.2019.05.008

Robotics Online Marketing Team. (2020). *The Role of Collaborative Robots in Industry 5.0*. https://www.automate.org/blogs/the-role-of-collaborative-robots-in-industry-5-0

Rodrigues, J. (2019). *15 examples of human augmentation in everyday life*. https://www.freshconsulting.com/insights/blog/examples-of-human-augmentation/

Satyanarayanan, M., & Davies, N. (2019). Augmenting Cognition Through Edge Computing. *Augmenting Cognition Through Edge Computing. in Computer*, *52*(7), 37–46. doi:10.1109/MC.2019.2911878

Shinkarenko, A. (2020). *Internet of everything vs internet of things*. Retrieved from https:// www. Itransition.com/blog/ internet-of- everything-vs- internet-of- things

Sobot, R. (2019, November 30). Implantable Technology: History, Controversies, and Social Implications. *IEEE Technology and Society Magazine*. doi:10.1109/MTS.2018.2880167

Steimle, J. (2022). On-Skin Computing. *Communications of the Association for Computing Machinery (ACM)*. https://cacm.acm.org/magazines/2022/4/259400-on-skin-computing/fulltext

Tange, K., De Donno, M., Fafoutis, X., & Dragoni, N. (2020). A Systematic Survey of Industrial Internet of Things Security: Requirements and Fog Computing Opportunities. *IEEE Communications Surveys and Tutorials*, *22*(4), 2489–2520. doi:10.1109/COMST.2020.3011208

Victory, J. (2022). *Bone-anchored hearing systems*. https://www.healthyhearing.com/help/hearing-aids/bone-anchored

Wallace, G., & Little, M. (2022). *Printing the future: 3D bioprinters and their uses.* Retrieved from https://www.science.org.au/curious/people-medicine/bioprinting#~:text=Bioprinting%20is%20an%20extension%20of,medical%20procedures%2C%20training%20and%20testing

World Economic Forum. (2022). *Augmented Workforce: Empowering People, Transforming Manufacturing.* World Economic Forum and University of Cambridge.

Xing, B. (2016). Smart Robot Control via Novel Computational Intelligence Methods for Ambient Assisted Living. In Trends in Ambient Intelligent Systems: The Role of Computational Intelligence. Springer International Publishing. doi:10.1007/978-3-319-30184-6_2

Zhuying, L., Brandmueller, F., Greuter, & Mueller, F. (2018). The Guts Game: Designing Playful Experiences for Ingestible Devices. In *Extended Abstracts of the 2018 CHI Conference on Human Factors in Computing Systems (CHI EA '18).* ACM. 10.1145/3170427.3186604

Zicong, L. (2021). Ethical Problems Concerning Human Augmentation Technology and Its Future Aspects. *Advances in Social Science, Education and Humanities Research,* vol. 554. *Proceedings of the 7th International Conference on Humanities and Social Science Research.*

Chapter 4
Integrating Human and Artificial Intelligence Within Organizations:
A Conceptual Framework Based on Artistry and Scientific HR Elements

Ekta Sinha
https://orcid.org/0000-0003-3944-1199
S.P. Jain School of Global Management, India

ABSTRACT

Artificial intelligence (AI) and human resources (HR) are often presented as a dichotomy by researchers. Rhetoric at present posits AI as a potential threat to HR. AI is seen as the ability of a machine to perform cognitive tasks, such as perceiving, reasoning, and problem solving, which we often associate with human minds. However, studies have also found that emotions, tacit knowledge, ethics, common sense, and pro-social behavior are fine human virtues that cannot be replaced by any intelligent machine. Thus, this study opines that organizations cannot achieve desired effectiveness by putting AI and people at the extreme ends of a continuum. The literature has many cases of specific human-AI proposals that widely address several organizational needs. The reverse case, to use specific organizational needs as a basis for formulating general human-AI proposal, is less common. This chapter is a nascent attempt to propose a conceptual framework of human capabilities (artistry/soft and scientific/hard) that are used to characterize the required human-AI intervention.

INTRODUCTION

Human Resource (HR) is not known for introducing budding technologies and its functions has been seen as administrative and enabling function, rather than a strategic business function. But, Artificial Intelligence (AI) provides a terrific opportunity. The consumerization of HR processes and functions

DOI: 10.4018/978-1-6684-6745-9.ch004

has brought AI to the forefront of innovation in HR. From recruitment to employee learning, and performance management, AI has the potential to transform HR (Biswas, 2019). This is important as there is a rich profusion available of financial capital and economic assets to most businesses, their monetization or value unlocking has remained a challenge. To make good on this, there is a need for an HR to take responsibility and be the differentiator that delivers value to stakeholders (Srivastava, 2018). With careful integration of AI in managing HR functions this feat can be achieved. However, the popular view presents AI and HR in conflict with each other. Either they talk of eliminating jobs and people because of AI (e.g., Kalev, 2016) or they advocate automation of processes to achieve better organizational outcomes (e.g., Chelliah, 2017). Very few studies discuss about integrating these two very powerful assets- AI and humans- for organizations to remain competitive. It is important to understand that while, AI systems can "learn" from past data, recognise patterns and display human like capabilities" (Russell & Intelligence, 1995); peoples' commitment, work engagement and loyalty towards their organizations also play a very important role in organizational growth (Keenoy, 1994). While AI systems support an analytical decision-making approach, they are less capable of understanding "common-sense situations" (Guszcza et al., 2017). Compared to humans they are less viable in uncertain, dynamic and unpredictable environments, particularly outside of a predefined domain of knowledge (Brynjolfsson & McAfee, 2012). This can be better understood by looking at *"artistry/soft"* and *"scientific/hard"* elements of HR. A human intervention can be a differentiator in creating/unlocking organizational wealth. To develop 'human' as an asset for organization, it is important to understand the underlying *"artistry/soft"* and *"scientific/hard"* elements of HR. While scientific HR elements include aspects like, calculative and tough-minded; artistry HR elements place an emphasis on "human" (Storey, 1987) aspect. The scientific HR elements emphasise on the quantitative, calculative and business-strategic aspects of managing the "headcount"; the artistry HR elements focus on emotions, ethics, common-sense, trust and treating employees as valued assets and a source of competitive advantage through their commitment, adaptability and high-quality skill and performance (Legge, 1995). The cognitive capabilities of AI sync well with the scientific elements of HR. However, when it comes to understanding context, building trust, laying emotional support, i.e., artistry HR elements, AI is still in its nascent state (Kamar, 2016). Most of the existing work fail to recognise the importance of artistry elements of HR and focus only on scientific elements, hence they present a biased view and fail to see the economics of insightful and balanced AI-human intervention within organizations. To address this gap, this work presents a framework which develops an understanding of human-AI intervention within organizations for better HR management.

Probing Questions

- How can organizations ensure they are digitally transforming at the right pace without losing the all-important human touch?
- What are the barriers in human-AI integration?

METHODOLOGY

This paper, uses the method of 'typology' (Jaakkola, 2020), to develop a conceptual categorization that "explains the fuzzy nature of many subjects by logically and causally combining different constructs into a coherent and explanatory set of types" (Cornelissen 2017). When the extant knowledge relating to a particular domain is diffused and fragmented, this approach helps to differentiate and distinguish between the concepts to provide an answer to the questions undertaken (MacInnis, 2011). Such categorization helps to present "a more precise and nuanced understanding of a phenomenon or concept, pinpointing and justifying key dimensions that distinguish the variants" (Jaakkola, 2020). Fiss (2011), suggests that typologies/classification help to reduce complexities and provides an understanding of the underlying effects and concepts. To carry out this research, the author gathered the available knowledge of the focal topic and then systematized it to capture the variability of particular characteristics of the concept.

LITERATURE REVIEW

What comes naturally to people (e.g., emotions) can be tricky for machines, and what's effortless for machines (e.g., analyzing terabytes of data) remains almost impossible for humans (Wilson and Daugherty, 2018). For decades scholars are trying to understand that how human and machines facilitate or inhibit organizational decision making (Joseph & Gaba, 2019). Technology is not new in the organizational context and the idea of an intelligent machine is old, but serious work on the artiðcial intelligence started lately. We may regard the subject of artiðcial intelligence as beginning with Turing's article 'Computing Machinery and Intelligence' (Turing 1950) and with Shannon's (1950) discussion on how a machine might be programmed to play chess. AI refers to systems or machines that mimic human intelligence to perform tasks and can iteratively improve themselves based on the information they collect. AI manifests in a number of forms, like 'Chatbots' use AI to understand customer problems faster and provide more efficient answers or 'intelligent assistants' use AI to parse critical information from large free-text datasets to improve decision making (OCI, n.d.).

AI is much more about the process and the capability for superpowered thinking and data analysis than it is about any particular format or function. Although AI brings up images of high-functioning, human-like robots taking over the world, AI isn't a replacement of humans. It's intended to significantly enhance human capabilities and contributions. That makes it a very valuable business asset. With time the AI systems have evolved and by combining various technologies and methods they can produce desired results (Marr, 1976).

AI Classification

At present AI systems can be classified on three bases. First, on the basis of human resemblance; second, on the basis of business support; and third, on the basis of advancement in technology (Figure 1).

On the basis of Human Resemblance

Reactive machines are oldest form of AI and have limited capabilities. They emulate the human mind's ability to respond to different kinds of stimuli. But such machines do not have memory-based functionality. This means they cannot use previously gained experiences to inform their present actions, i.e., these machines do not have the ability to "learn" (Joshi, 2019). These machines could only be used for automatically responding to a limited set or combination of inputs. A popular example of a reactive AI machine is IBM's Deep Blue, a machine that beat chess Grandmaster Garry Kasparov in 1997. Limited memory AI, in addition to having the capabilities of emulating human actions can also learn from his-

Figure 1. Types of AI. Source: Adapted from, Joshi, 2019; Davenport and Ronanki (2018)

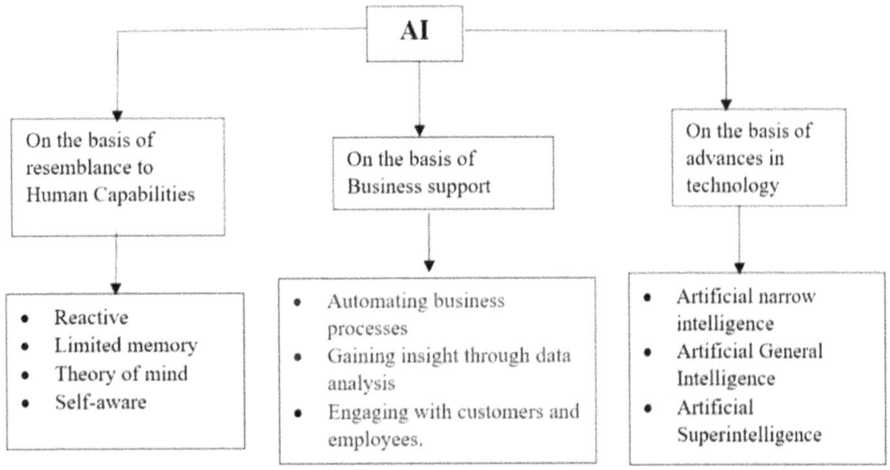

torical data to make decisions in the present (Joshi, 2019). Nearly all present-day machines fall under this category. Such machines learn through machine learning. Machine learning enables machines to learn from and make predictions based on data. The roots of machine learning are embedded in pattern recognition and the concept that algorithms can learn from recorded data without being programmed to do so (Biswas, 2019). For instance, an algorithm that needs to identify candidates' anomaly would rely on pattern of other suitable candidates to *teach itself* what an 'ideal candidate' should have. In this case, the end objective of the algorithm has been clearly defined – which is to identify a suitable candidate, but the steps to arrive at the objective is learned by the machine itself by training on data. Deep learning, unsupervised learning and reinforcement learning are constituents of machine learning (Jordan and Mitchell, 2015). AI which falls under the "Theory of mind" category and "Self-aware" is not found in abundance. These two are next level of AI systems and researcher are currently engaged in innovating such systems which would be able to better understand the entities, their needs, emotions, beliefs etc. (Joshi, 2019). At present such systems are lacking and the existing AI lacks real human insights.

On the basis of Business Support

The first category is automating business processes. This is the most common type. Such AI system deals with the automation of digital and physical tasks—typically back-office administrative and financial activities such as transferring data from e-mail and call-centre systems into systems of record and reaching into multiple systems to update records and handle customer communications (Davenport and Ronanki, 2018). This is the least expensive and easy to implement. Second in this category are AI systems which can gain insights through data analysis. It is used to detect patterns in vast volumes of data and interpret their meaning. Such cognitive insights are typically more data-intensive (e.g., images, visuals, speeches, documents etc.), detailed and their ability to use new data to make predictions improves over time (Davenport and Ronanki, 2018). For example, to predict what a particular customer is likely to buy and to identify credit fraud in real time and detect insurance claims fraud. Third type of

AI system in this category is "engaging with customers and employees". Such AI systems may include, intelligent agents that offer 24/7 customer service addressing a broad and growing array of issues from password requests to technical support questions—all in the customer's natural language; internal sites for answering employee questions on topics including IT, employee benefits, and HR policy etc. (Davenport and Ronanki, 2018).

On the basis of Advances in Technology

The first category is artificial narrow intelligence. This represents all the existing AI, including the most capable and complicated ones (Joshi, 2019). This category refers to AI systems that can only perform a specific task autonomously using human-like "scientific" capabilities. These systems correspond to all the "reactive" and "limited memory" AI, as discussed above. *Artificial general intelligence* and *Artificial superintelligence* AI systems are similar to "Theory of mind" and "Self-aware" category respectively (Figure 1) (as already discussed above), which are very sophisticated systems and are said to have a better understanding of the entities, their needs, emotions, beliefs etc. (Joshi, 2019). However, they are not available in abundance for organizational use.

While AI systems that exist in the present times are in their nascent stage, they can "learn" from past data, recognise patterns and can perform complex calculations (Russell & Intelligence, 1995). Organizations can adopt AI system(s) in managing their functions. Existing literature has well established the role of AI in computing complex data and making judgement based on objectivity (scientific HR elements) (Shrestha et al., 2019). However, the early conceptions of AI as "systems of knowing" that can display human-like capabilities such as, motivating and emotions (artistry HR elements) fell short of satisfying both scholars and practitioners (Desanctis & Jackson, 1993). While the extant literature shows that AI based systems have augmented the decision-making processes in various organizational functions such as, marketing and operations (e.g., Zheng et al., 2017), their role in handling human needs remains somewhat limited and thus under-explored. AI and automation are slowly finding their place into HR in many organizations around the world. For example, AI-based solutions now play important roles in Unilever's talent acquisition process (Marr, 2018). However, literature shows that routine operational tasks that machines could handle were separated from the complex managerial tasks reserved for humans (Raisch and Krakowski, in press). Thus, overlooking the opportunities and value creation that come by integrating the two. Consequently, AI was researched in computer science and operations research, whereas organization and management studies focused on humans (Rahwan et al., 2019). The ambiguity built around human-AI integration, leaves a room for an in-depth analysis considering both scientific and artistry HR elements. Today, businesses require both kinds of capabilities. Instead of designing AI systems that function alone, organizations should focus on integrating it with humans so that they can complement each other. This study explores the ways in which AI systems can resonate with HR functions without losing human touch to achieve shared goals and maximize stakeholders' wealth.

Scientific/Hard and Artistry/Soft HR Elements

HR is a discipline which encompasses both the worlds of science and arts (Gikopoulos, 2019). Scientific/hard elements of HR stress upon 'the quantitative, calculative and business-strategic aspects of managing the "headcount resources" in as "rational" a way as for any other factors of production' (Storey 1992, p. 29; Legge, 1995). The scientific aspect of HR adapts a view of *utilitarian-instrumentalism*, employees are treated as resources and factors of production and the focus is on minimizing the cost of this resource. Thus, it is mechanical in nature and very objective in approach. Whereas the artistry elements of HR stress upon building a 'high commitment work system' (Walton, 1985) through human relations where the 'behavior is primarily self-regulated rather than controlled by sanctions and relations within the organization are based on high levels of trust' (Wood 1996, p. 41). Artistry elements of HR adapts a *developmental-humanism* view, where employees are treated as human beings and are considered as valuable asset. The focus is on developing them and achieve the goal of commitment through self-direction (Truss et. al., 1997). Although scientific and artistry HR elements appear to be antagonistic and derived from very different intellectual traditions and assumptions, they both have been incorporated within the same theories or models of HR (Truss et. al. 1997). For example, HR model of Storey (1992), clearly states that humans do need managerial control but only trust, human capabilities and commitment distinguishes great organizations from good ones. Thus, it is important to nurture human resources along with some level of strategic control (Storey, 1992). The scientific elements of HR include numerous empirical factors such as productivity, wage demands, skills and qualifications, punctuality, the "Bradford Factor" etc. Most of these scientific elements require sound intelligent quotient, such as calculation, logical reasoning, working memory etc. Whereas, HR manifests artistry elements in dealing with individual employee, their idiosyncrasies, their distinctive talents, behaviors and different perceptions on life, career and the workplace – "all of which have at least as big an impact on a business as measurable factors and sets HR practitioners apart from their peers" (Gikopoulos, 2019). And these artistry elements require sound emotional intelligence such as: compassion, empathy, relationship building and mindfulness (Goleman, 1996). Such artistry elements help individuals to overcome their inhibitions and display creativity (Sinha, 2022b). Experts suggest that higher latent inhibitions may block creativity of an individual (Carson et. al., 2003). Emotional displays during interactions at work can have a significant impact on employees' innovative behaviour (e.g., Sinha, 2022a; Zampetakis and Moustakis, 2011). Humans are complex beings and their actions/decisions are not always based on objectivity. Many times, emotional interactions and subjective assessment of a situation at workplace influence their decisions and they act based on impulses (Thaler and Sunstein, 2009). Such situations cannot be handled effectively by AI algorithms. Thus, it can be deduced that for organizations to be effective, it is important to incorporate both scientific and artistry HR elements. Table 1 represents features of scientific and artistry HR elements.

Hence, we can say that it is easier to apply software to the scientific elements of HR functions as it is great in identifying patterns from large amount of data and making recommendations. However, when it comes to working with people and understanding their emotions (artistry element of HR), there is an assumption that no technology, no matter how intelligent, can come close to the artistry that helps HR practitioners in the "human" aspect of their jobs (Kamar, 2016; Gikopoulos, 2019). Every organization incorporates scientific and artistry HR elements and thus, would require both technical and human interventions. Various organizational functions can incorporate routine and well-defined tasks as well as subjective evaluation of a situation. For task which are routine and objective and comprises of analyzing piles of data can use AI systems but when it comes to building trust, commitment and display of emotional intelligence, human intervention remains the key. Below the paper discusses some prominent organizational functions which may deploy AI as a supporting and integrating tool to humans for better collaborative interventions.

Table 1. Artistry/Soft and Scientific/Hard HR Elements

Scientific/Hard HR Element	Characteristics	Outcomes	Artistry/Soft HR Element	Characteristics	Outcomes
Put forth by Michigan Model, Theory 'X' (Fombrun et al., 1984; McGregor, 1960)	Organizational strategy at the centre, trats humans as resources, aims to achieve efficiency, Economic goals, Task oriented, Calculative & Objective in nature, Quantitative, tight strategic control	Behavior controlled by sanctions, lack of trust, lack of self-motivation, lower levels of engagement	Put forth by Harvard Model, Theory 'Y' (Beer et. al, 1984; McGregor, 1960)	Human in the centre, qualitative, aims to achieve effectiveness, focus is on people, considers human as assets, goals and objective along with human needs, subjective evaluation, control through commitment	Self-regulated Behavior, commitment, competence, engagement, congruence, trust, self-motivated employees

Hard and soft elements within Organizational Functions

Manpower Planning and Productivity Management

AI systems may be used to analyze individual productivity, efficiency and effectiveness on the basis of key performance indicators (KPIs) and tasks assigned. Such insights may pin point certain pattern about employee behavior and attitude towards work. This in turn would help managers to give continuous feedback on time. Productivity analysis via AI systems can also generate insights which may reveal and detect those at-risk of resigning (Reilly, 2018). This would help organizations to plan their manpower more effectively and retain high-productive employees (Buranyi, 2018). Better insights and real-time information have reduced the hire time by 75% at Unilever (Heric, 2018). However, such situations might lead to negotiations over the terms of an employment offer, settling start dates or queries about contracts, handling employees' apprehensions and empathetic listening which may require a human approach led by empathy and emotions rather than a machine approach driven by data and pattern recognition.

Recruitment and Selection

Leaders invest most of their time and attention into hiring right people for the right job. And rightly so, as people who do not resonate with organizational goals and culture may become a 'misfit'. This requires a lot of planning and good HR strategy. There are known AI-powered recruitment tools such as "Mya" and "HireVue", which takes candidates through an initial screening process via text messages, video, AI and game-based challenges in order to determine candidates' cognitive ability, their preferred working styles and even how they will interact with other team members before Jobseekers advance to the next stage (or are ruled out). Mya claims a 79 per cent reduction in time-to-interview, over double the conversion rates and 144 per cent productivity gains compared to traditional interviewing (Gikopoulos, 2019). However, hiring requires much more time and efforts of a leader to ensure that the recruit is settled and happy in his/her role and gels with organizational culture in order to perform. This can be a slow process which may require personal attention and emotional bonding.

Performance Management

Hiring right people for the right job is challenging but more challenging is to keep employees motivated, engaged and up-to-date in their skills and behavioral training. Thus, managing performance is certainly a tough organizational job. Traditionally, performance appraisals have been conducted on a scheduled half-yearly or annual basis. It encompasses comparing set and actual performance and KPIs, career ambitions, completion of training module and feedback. But it is difficult for organizations to achieve uniformity across workforce and ensuring that every staff member has a set of individually tailored targets and goals (Gikopoulos, 2019). Again, AI has an answer to this. According to Srivastava (2018), AI can be used to set customized individual employee goals based on which video-based performance appraisals can be conducted and on the basis of recorded performance data and a real-time view, managers can give more constructive feedback. This would help employees to grow in their respective roles. The insights would also help them further to take up new and challenging roles within organization. Although AI can prepare managers for feedback by providing them with data and performance evidences but giving feedback to an employee would involve a lot more than just data. It would involve a manager as a mentor and a counsellor who would not allow employees to feel vulnerable but motivate them to perform better by providing constructive feedback on their performance against their own goals and those of the business.

Improved Communication

AI may also be helpful in improving communication between employees/hierarchy. Chat-boxes can successfully replace humans in call-centers. As AI has the capability to learn, not only they can handle more-complex form of communication as they 'learn' more, but also can know when to hand over to a human when a question is beyond its capability to answer. Cognitive insight may help uncover the patterns of calls and callers and improve the ubiquitous responses into something useful (Reilly, 2018). This may lead to better anticipation of what employees and managers want to know. Machine learning can also 'identify probabilistic matches of data that is likely to be associated with the same person but that appears in slightly different formats across databases (Davenport and Ronanki, 2018). According to Reilly (2018), this could reveal even at the individual level, both a positive thirst for information or a worrisome set of concerns (e.g. if the employee is searching in multiple places for facts about, say, sexual harassment and whistleblowing). Such insights provided by AI systems using detailed data analysis would be very useful. However, in order to deal with such insights, human-led interventions would be very important. Such insights may require greater empathy, compassion and emotions to handle certain situations (e.g., sexual harassment) with greater poise.

Compensation Management

According to Srivastava (2018), Compensation decisions are very complex as they take into consideration performance and, in a lot of cases, the potential of employees. Many a times such decisions also take into consideration the industry and market benchmark for a given role. And it is also important to consider the expectations of employees, their market value and fairness within the company, as well as peer group companies (Srivastava, 2018). The existing algorithms work for category of people rather than for individuals. AI systems can be used to establish patterns of performance, potential, compensation benchmarks and individual market value, so that individual compensation can be determined more accurately and fairly. However, at times ethical issues may crop in, such as glass ceiling and then role of emotions and empathy (artistry elements of HR) becomes significant to generate fair results and lead the way to ethical compensation planning without promoting any discrimination.

Policy Making

The AI systems can help organizations to frame better and profound policies with speed and accuracy. AI systems respond to the evidence, rather than manager's gut feeling (Reilly, 2018). This might be used to challenge as much to inform; to offer a different perspective; to disrupt groupthink; or to manage stakeholder participation and process their views (Tata, 2018). However, the strategic and complex tasks done by HR business partners or experts based on their experiences (i.e., tacit knowledge), suggest that HR's contribution in this area will be unaffected and could even be improved by some of the new information, analysis and tools available (Reilly, 2018). This indicates towards the fact that machines are apt for analytical tasks but lack humane aspects big time. According to Poole (2018), if one wants to create a general problem-solving brain, the best way is still to find a mate and create a new human being.

Learning and Development

Learning and development can be enabled through AI. It can facilitate how learning and development content is created, distributed, accessed and used (DiRomualdo et.al., 2018). Through AI it would be possible to deliver personalized, just-in-time, context-specific training and learning support. Analytics through AI can help employees to track and anticipate their own learning needs, thus making it a bottom-up approach. Insights gained of a training programme via AI, can help in analyzing training data which in turn can improve HR's understanding of the drivers of effective training and pinpoint methods that generate measurable improvements in performance (DiRomualdo et.al., 2018). However, only deep conversations can help employees overcome latent inhibitions. According to Sinha (2022b), higher latent inhibitions lower down the creativity & performance, thus beating the purpose of training. Also, Sinha (2017), found that an individual's affective competence to understand self as well as others emotions plays an important role when it comes to display creativity and innovativeness within an organization. As it helps to display higher perseverance and overcome any negative feeling arousing from failures (Sinha 2021; Sinha, 2022a). Hence, we can say that artistry elements are equally important in imparting quality and result-oriented training and development programs. The value of artistry HR elements can be understood by the fact that some renowned technology intensive organizations, e.g., Microsoft have started recruiting poet and a novelist as their team members to impart rightful training to people to develop the right personality (e.g., confident, caring, and helpful but not bossy) (Wilson and Daugerty, 2018).

Organization Effectiveness Focuses on Culture and Performance

AI may help organizational leadership to develop a culture of innovation and performance as AI is capable of handling large volume of data and learn from past experiences (Davenport and Ronanki, 2018). Organizational workforce agility and team innovation can be addressed with the help of AI. AI can identify the complimentary skills a team may need in order to perform any task and can enable remote connectivity and help in asking the right questions (DiClaudio, 2019). AI can help the leaders to realign overall organizational culture ensuring that groups have the best model to support innovation

Figure 2. The Proposed Conceptual Model

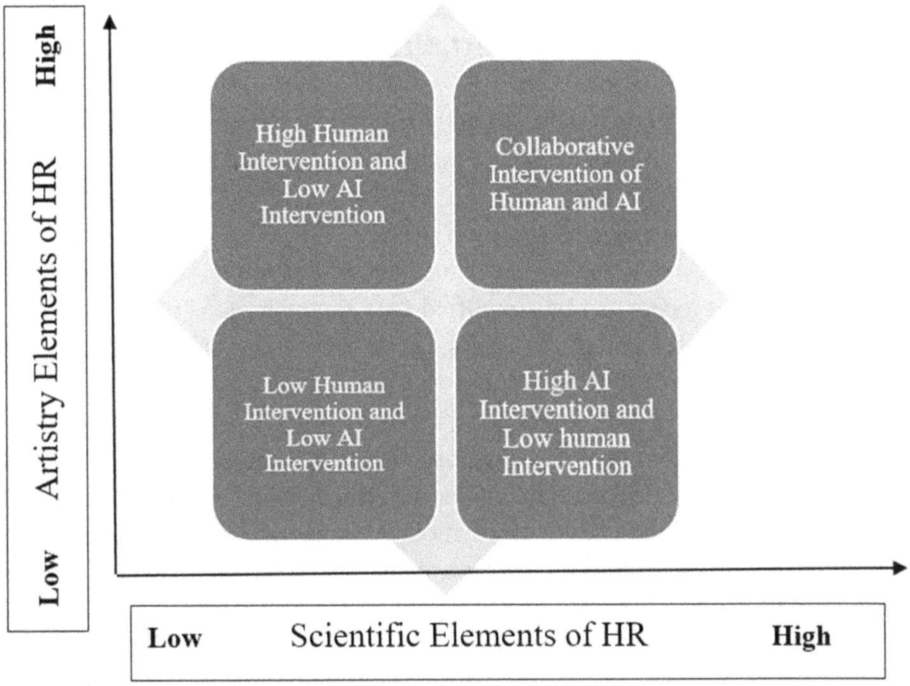

and agile responses to market changes (DiRomualdo et. al., 2018). However, employees, aside from technical skills, must have emotional skills too. Such artistry HR elements help employees to be more creative, cooperative and effective (Zampetakis and Moustakis, 2011), who help each other in order to improve the outcomes of the team and the organization as a whole (Drigas and Papoutsi, 2019). These artistry HR elements, help members of the organization to face conflicts more constructively if they occur, think from different perspectives, and accept the diversity of people (Druskat and Wolff, 2001).

CONCEPTUAL FRAMEWORK

On the basis of the above discussions, the study proposes a conceptual framework (Figure 2) based on "artistry" and "scientific" elements of HR, that would help to develop an understanding of human-AI interventions and integration within organizations. Figure 2, indicates four quadrants. Each quadrant helps to improve our understanding on the required human-AI integration within organizations, on the basis of scientific (also known as hard HR elements) and artistry (also known as soft HR elements). We will look into all the four quadrants one by one.

The first quadrant (bottom left) indicates that when in an organizational domain, scientific elements of HR (i.e., logical, reasoning, pattern recognition, etc.) are low along with the artistry elements of HR (i.e., emotions, ethics, common-sense, empathy, etc.) then, the human as well as AI interventions are low. For example, a small organization may use mailing or SMS services to reach out to their clients or potential customers with the help of very small number of employees. Thus, low human and AI interventions.

Proposition 1: Low AI-Human Intervention is Required When Decisions Involve low Scientific and Artistry HRM Elements.

Second quadrant (bottom right) suggests that when the task within organizations require high scientific HR elements and low artistry HR elements then organizations may need higher AI system interventions as compared to human interventions. Such tasks are considered to be repetitive and procedural. Thus, they can utilize AI systems to generate better results (Berhil et. al., 2020). Also, large amount of data can be analyzed with the help of AI systems for better insights. For example, recruiting candidates, which is a highly time-consuming process can be simplified with the help of AI interventions (as discussed earlier section). AI's value in performing such tasks can be understood in its ability to crunch data and assess objectively – to do things faster, easier and cheaper (Partridge and Hussain, 1992). There are *chatbots,* these days which can answer routine queries from customers and can work 24/7 without or low human interventions. For example, SEB, a major Swedish bank, now uses a virtual assistant called *Aida* to interact with millions of customers. It augments a human worker by providing quality service to customers on the basis of already available information. Aida has access to vast stores of data and can answer many frequently asked questions, such as how to open an account or make cross-border payments (Wilson and Daugherty, 2018). Whenever the system can't resolve any issue—which happens in about 30% of cases—it turns the caller over to a human customer-service representative and then monitors that interaction to learn how to resolve similar problems in the future (Wilson and Daugherty, 2018). This enables employees to focus on more important and complex jobs. Let us take one more example of drug rehabilitation center, where large number of people come for treatment. AI can be used to manage large volumes of data related to the patients and their addictions. Simultaneously, it can be used to check their progress, level of fatigue, response time etc. during the treatment for better insights rather than relying only on "judgement and observation".

Proposition 2: High AI and low human intervention are required when decisions involve high scientific and low artistry HRM elements.

However, the third quadrant (upper left) suggests that when such patients are brought to these centers, only medicine and treatment are not the solutions; 'human' aspect is also needed. The tacit knowledge, cognition, emotions and intuition of Humans enable them to analyze complex alternatives and equivocal situations with a deeper perception (Jarrahi, 2018), exceeding ordinary-level functioning based on simple rational thinking (Bishop, 2000). There could be some similar situations within an organization, that may demand higher level of artistry HR elements than scientific HR elements, such as: sexual harassment, or glass ceiling. Then human intervention becomes more important, like empathy, compassion, emotions, mindfulness etc. only objectivity may not give desired outcome. Hence, resulting into higher human and lower AI interventions. Similarly, in order to achieve greater commitment and employee engagement at work, it is important to build trust (Truss et. al., 1997). In recent studies is has been found that AI algorithms may "rapidly reinforce and amplify bias present in training data, resulting in outcomes that could have detrimental consequences to minorities (e.g., indigenous peoples)" (Shrestha & Yang, 2019). Such things can be well-handled by artistry HR elements, which advocates building relations through open and empathetic communication (Jin, 2010).

Proposition 3: Low AI and high human intervention are required when decisions involve low scientific and high artistry HRM elements.

But the quadrant four (upper right) indicates that there are areas within organizations which require high artistry as well as high scientific HR elements. This calls for strategic shift towards human-AI interventions and integration. Existing studies suggest that almost 80% of existing marketing data within organizations is unstructured (Shrestha & Krishna, forthcoming) and only a fraction of organizations possess the requisite technical competencies to utilize this type of data (Balducci & Marinova, 2018). Thus, very small fractions of the available data are currently being utilized to support the creation of organizationally relevant knowledge (Chakraborty et al., 2019) and augment decision-making. AI can be an answer to this complex data handling with an organization. Organizations can make the best of machine learning by using it as a collaborative tool, working alongside human insights. This can be a crucial distinction. Through such collaborative human-AI intervention, organizational outcomes can be enhanced. Collaborative human-AI systems actively enhance each other's complementary strengths: the speed, scalability, and quantitative capabilities (scientific HR elements) of the former, and the leadership, insights, team-spirit, creativity, and social skills (artistry elements of HR) of the latter (Wilson and Daugherty, 2018). Organizations using AI-HR collaborative systems understand that innately human skills are going to be more important, valuable and sought-after than ever before (Altemeyer, 2019). The trick is being able to accurately and scientifically assess who has these skills and where they are as it is quite possible that such already skilled employees are in the wrong part of the business. Or these mission-critical skills may be in such short supply that organizations need to understand who is capable of being re-trained with them (Altemeyer, 2019).

Proposition 4: Collaborative AI-human intervention is required when decisions involve high scientific and artistry HRM elements.

Besides this human-AI collaborative capacity, there exist some barriers which needs to be addressed. Below we discuss some prominent barriers in the path of collaborative AI-human systems.

BARRIERS TO HUMAN-AI INTEGRATION

Organizations' failure to Identify Proper Intervention Opportunity

Organizations' failure to identify proper intervention opportunity may result into unproductive and ineffective usage of available resources (both human and AI). Procter & Gamble and American Express provide useful examples. Both firms have engaged with AI for years now, but their overall strategies have not been to just automate processes, or eliminate human jobs. Instead, they viewed and employ AI as a tool on which employees can draw to do their work more effectively (Davenport & Bean, 2017).

Employee Support

Any intervention may need employees' support for better implementation. Some apprehensions which employees may have could be, issues related to data privacy, authentication, security, lack of clarity, transparency, ownership and control of data (Villaronga et. al., 2018). AI-based decisions into organizations becomes relatively effective when some level of transparency or interpretability of decisions can be achieved. Thus, organizations and HR professionals must ensure that AI intervention works in harmony with the shared goal(s) of organization and employees.

Possibility of Data Manipulation

There is a possibility of 'fooling' AI as it works on algorithms and manipulation of data is possible. The manipulation can be done with the data it uses as input or by changing weights of predictors or through the design (Shrestha et. al, 2019). As AI algorithms are opaque in nature such manipulation is very difficult to detect. Thus, organizations may require fresh algorithms to check the authenticity of AI designs using which decisions are supported within an organization (Song et. al., 2018). Choudhury et al. (2020), showed that AI algorithms introduced new sources of bias in hiring, and introduction of domain expert can complement AI systems in mitigating such bias.

Temporal Boundaries

There is possibility that AI system can fail under certain situation. The boundary between what a human can do and what an AI-system can do in an organization may changes over time, attributing to some unforeseen situation, like COVID-19 pandemic. For example, during this pandemic when people began hoarding items (such as, toilet papers and hand sanitizers), Amazon decided to rely on manual interventions as AI systems could not adopt to this disruptive phenomenon (Xin et. al., 2018). The understanding of what can be formalized grows over time as people reflect on their jobs and establish routines (Fischer and Nakakoji, 1992).

Difficult to Explain the Process

Most of the times it is difficult to explain how/why an AI system reached to a particular decision as they are built on "numerous hidden layers and millions of neurons, which makes them opaque" (Shrestha and Krishna, forthcoming). Experts feel that despite the available and underway research which promise to explain the interpretability and fairness of an AI system, there is still a lack of satisfactory answer to the problem of opacity (Samek & Müller, 2019). In such cases it is the responsibility of a manager to maintain procedural justice within organization while building AI capabilities (Logg et. al., 2019).

DISCUSSION AND IMPLICATIONS

The model shown above represents clear demarcation between AI and human capabilities and based on scientific and artistry HRM elements suggest their level of integration. It can be said that HR tasks which are routine and programmed can be handled by AI systems efficiently. But HR tasks which need greater subjectivity, tacit knowledge and human common-sense can be handled in a better way by human resource of the organizations. Here, the author would like to suggest that the model is not static and the transition between the quadrants would depend on the quality of decision making. According to Shrestha et. al. (2019), when objectivity (Clearly defied, specific and well-structured output), replicability (standard and non-falgorithms) are required in any decision the then AI plays an important role as these facets of decision making represents scientific HR elements. But when there is a need of subjective evaluation of any situation (tacit knowledge, past experience, emotional intelligence and common sense) and interpretability of decision (how and why certain decision has been reached) then human involvement becomes very significant as they involve artistry elements of HR (Table 1).

Based on the above conceptual framework (Figure 2), we can conclude that a wise integration of AI systems and human can bring a lot of advantage to organizations. Effective AI-human collaboration can use analytical insights of AI systems along with the subjective human insights to leverage its market position and gain competitive edge (Plastino and Purdy, 2018). Lee Beardmore, chief technology ofðcer of Capgemini's business process outsourcing division believes AI will have a dramatic impact on the workforce, resulting in employees having to be trained and up-skilled to work in higher value areas (Chelliah, 2017).

Organizations and HR managers should anticipate the role and impact of AI systems within organization in order to identify integrative/collaborative opportunities to scale up their functions and processes, the possible changes to workforce in terms of nature of work and to predict the likely roles that employees will play in future. The conceptual framework presented in the study gives obvious indications to identify the level of human-AI interventions necessary within organizations to manage human resources effectively and to survive the cut-throat competition. Davenport and Ronanki (2018), found in their study that only 22% of the executives indicated that they considered reducing head count as a primary benefit of AI. Most managers with whom they discussed favoured integrating human and machine work, rather than replacing humans entirely.

HR as we know it, involves functions, like, recruitment and interviewing, on-boarding employees and maintaining performance, developing career paths and designing compensations, etc. Our conceptual model can provide a lot of insights to the practitioners to achieve meaningful AI-human integration within their organizations to achieve greater feats. The human practice of carrying out tasks evolves over time, and an AI augmented problem-solving HR system must be promoted to reflect these changes. Further, the boundary between what a human can do and what an AI-system can do in an organization may changes over time, because the understanding of what can be formalized grows over time as people reflect on their jobs and establish routines (Fischer and Nakakoji, 1992). Organizations, on the basis of the conceptual model presented in this paper can decide the level of AI-human intervention given the extent of procedural and formalization of HR functions.

Also, the conceptual model presented here, provides a ground to the researchers and academics for further exploration and testing. The discussion presented above warrants further validation in order to generalize the results.

SUMMARY

This study has been able to answer both the probing questions framed in the earlier section of this article. First, by presenting a conceptual framework the study established that it is possible to achieve resonance between AI and human resource. The discussion based on scientific and artistry elements of HR resulted into four quadrants which show that it is possible to achieve greater collaborative AI-human intervention. Second, by discussing the roles of scientific and artistry HR elements in various HR functions, the study has shown that it is possible for HR professionals to ensure the digital transformation at the right pace for their business without losing the all-important human touch. Never have digital tools been so responsive to us, nor we have been to these tools. While AI will radically alter how work gets done and who does it, the technology's larger impact will be in complementing and augmenting human capabilities, not replacing them (Wilson and Daugherty, 2018).

REFERENCES

Altemeyer, B. (2019). Making the business case for AI in HR: Two case studies. *Strategic HR Review*, *18*(2), 66–70. doi:10.1108/SHR-12-2018-0101

Balducci, B., & Marinova, D. (2018). Unstructured data in marketing. *Journal of the Academy of Marketing Science*, *46*(4), 557–590. doi:10.100711747-018-0581-x

Beer, M., Spector, B., Lawrence, P. R., Quinn Mills, D., & Walton, R. E. (1984). *Managing Human Assets*. The Free Press.

Berhil, S., Benlahmar, H., & Labani, N. (2020). A review paper on artificial intelligence at the service of human resources management. *Indonesian Journal of Electrical Engineering and Computer Science*, *18*(1), 32–40. doi:10.11591/ijeecs.v18.i1.pp32-40

Bishop, P. (2000). *Synchronicity and intellectual intuition in Kant, Swedenborg, and Jung*. The Edwin Mellen Press.

Biswas, S. (2019). *The Beginner's Guide to AI in HR*. Retrieved from https://www.hrtechnologist.com/articles/digital-transformation/the-beginners-guide-to-ai-in-hr/

Brynjolfsson, E., & McAfee, A. (2012). Winning the race with ever-smarter machines. *MIT Sloan Management Review*, *53*(2), 53.

Buranyi, S. (2018). Dehumanising, impenetrable, frustrating": the grim reality of job hunting in the age of AI. *The Guardian*. Retrieved from https://www.theguardian.com/inequality/2018/mar/04/dehumanising-impenetrable-frustratingthe-grim-reality-of-job-hunting-in-the-age-of-ai

Carson, S. H., Peterson, J. B., & Higgins, D. M. (2003). Decreased latent inhibition is associated with increased creative achievement in high-functioning individuals. *Journal of Personality and Social Psychology*, *85*(3), 499–506. doi:10.1037/0022-3514.85.3.499 PMID:14498785

Chakraborty, I., Kim, M., & Sudhir, K. (2019). Attribute Sentiment Scoring with Online Text Reviews: Accounting for Language Structure and Attribute Self-Selection. SSRN Electronic Journal, 2176. doi:10.2139/ssrn.3395012

Chelliah, J. (2017). Will artiðcial intelligence usurp white collar jobs? *Human Resource Management International Digest*, *25*(3), 1–3. doi:10.1108/HRMID-11-2016-0152

Choudhury, P., Starr, E., & Agarwal, R. (2020). Machine learning and human capital complementarities: Experimental evidence on bias mitigation. *Strategic Management Journal*, 1381–1411.

Cornelissen, J. (2017). Editor's comments: Developing propositions, a process model, or a typology? Addressing the challenges of writing theory without a boilerplate. *Academy of Management Review*, *42*(1), 1–9. doi:10.5465/amr.2016.0196

Davenport, T., & Ronanki, R. (2018). Artificial intelligence for the real world. *Harvard Business Review*. Retrieved from https://hbr.org/2018/01/artificial-intelligence-for-the-real-world

Davenport, T. H., & Bean, R. (2017). How P&G and American Express Are Approaching AI. *Harvard Business Review*. https://hbr.org/2017/03/how-pg-and-american-express-are-approaching-ai

Desanctis, G., & Jackson, B. M. (1993). Coordination of information technology management: Team-based structures and computer-based communication systems. *Journal of Management Information Systems*, *10*(3), 85–110.

DiClaudio, M. (2019). People analytics and the rise of HR: How data, analytics and emerging technology can transform human resources (HR) into a profit center. *Strategic HR Review*, *18*(2), 42–46. doi:10.1108/SHR-11-2018-0096

DiRomualdo, A., El-Khoury, D., & Girimonte, F. (2018). HR in the digital age: How digital technology will change HR's organization structure, processes and roles. *Strategic HR Review*, *17*(5), 234–242. doi:10.1108/SHR-08-2018-0074

Drigas, A., & Papoutsi, C. (2019). Emotional Intelligence as an Important Asset for HR in Organizations: Leaders and Employees. *International Journal of Advanced Corporate Learning*, *12*(1), 58–66. doi:10.3991/ijac.v12i1.9637

Druskat, V. U., & Wolff, S. B. (2001). Building the emotional intelligence of groups. *Harvard Business Review*, *79*(3), 80–91. PMID:11246926

Fischer, G., & Nakakoji, K. (1992). Beyond the macho approach of artificial intelligence: Empower human designers do not replace them. *Knowledge-Based Systems*, *5*(1), 15–30. doi:10.1016/0950-7051(92)90021-7

Fiss, P. C. (2011). Building better causal theories: A fuzzy set approach to typologies in organizational research. *Academy of Management Journal*, *54*(2), 393–420. doi:10.5465/amj.2011.60263120

Fombrun, C., Tichy, N. M., & Devanna, M. A. (1984). *Strategic Huma Resource Management*. Wiley.

Gikopoulos, J. (2019). Alongside, not against: Balancing man with machine in the HR function. *Strategic HR Review*, *18*(2), 56–61. doi:10.1108/SHR-12-2018-0103

Goleman, D. (1996). Emotional Intelligence. Why It Can Matter More than IQ. *Learning*, *24*(6), 49–50.

Guszcza, J., Lewis, H., & Evans-Greenwood, P. (2017). *Cognitive collaboration: Why humans and computers think better together*. Deloitte University Press.

Heric, M. (2018). *HR new digital mandate.* Bain & Company. Retrieved from https://www.bain.com/insights/hrs-new-digital-mandate/

Jaakkola, E. (2020). Designing conceptual articles: Four approaches. *AMS Review, 10*(1-2), 18–26. doi:10.100713162-020-00161-0

Jarrahi, M. H. (2018). Artificial Intelligence and the Future of Work: Human-AI Symbiosis in Organizational Decision Making. *Business Horizons, 61*(4), 1–15. doi:10.1016/j.bushor.2018.03.007

Jin, Y. (2010). Emotional leadership as a key dimension of public relations leadership: A national survey of public relations leaders. *Journal of Public Relations Research, 22*(2), 159–181. doi:10.1080/10627261003601622

Jordan, I. M., & Mitchell, M. T. (2015). Machine learning:Trends, perspectives, and prospects. *Science, 349*(6245), 255–260. doi:10.1126cience.aaa8415 PMID:26185243

Joseph, J., & Gaba, V. (2019). Organizational structure, information processing and decision making: A retrospective and roadmap for research. *The Academy of Management Annals.*

Joshi, N. (2019). *7 types of Artificial Intelligence.* Retrieved from https://www.forbes.com/sites/cognitiveworld/2019/06/19/7-typ es-of-artificial-intelligence/#3b31eefa233e

Kalev, L. (2016). Is Elon Musk Right and Will AI Replace Most Human Jobs? *Forbes.* https://www.forbes.com/sites/kalevleetaru/2016/11/08/is-elon -musk-right-and-will-ai-replace-most-human-jobs/#4d3e7add60f 4

Kamar, E. (2016). *Directions in Hybrid Intelligence: Complementing AI Systems with Human Intelligence.* https://www.microsoft.com/en-us/research/wp-content/uploads/ 2016/11/hi.pdf

Keenoy, T., & Anthony, P. (1994). HRM: metaphor, meaning and morality. In P. Blyton & P. Turnbull (Eds.), *Reassessing Human Resource Management* (pp. 233–255). Sage.

Legge, K. (1995). *Human Resource Management: Rhetorics and Realities.* Macmillan. doi:10.1007/978-1-349-24156-9

Logg, J. M., Minson, J. A., & Moore, D. A. (2019). Algorithm appreciation: People prefer algorithmic to human judgment. *Organizational Behavior and Human Decision Processes, 151*, 90–103. doi:10.1016/j.obhdp.2018.12.005

MacInnis, D. J. (2011). A framework for conceptual contributions in marketing. *Journal of Marketing, 75*(4), 136–154. doi:10.1509/jmkg.75.4.136

Marr, B. (2018). The amazing ways how Unilever uses artificial intelligence to recruit & train thousands of employees. *Forbes.* https://www.forbes.com/sites/bernardmarr/2018/12/14/the-amaz ing-ways-how-unileveruses-artificial-intelligence-to-recruit -train-thousands-of-employees

Marr, D. (1976). *Artificial Intelligence- A personal view.* Massachusetts Institute of Technology Artificial Intelligence Laboratory.

McGregor, D. (1960). *The Human side of Enterprise*. McGraw-Hill.

OCI. (n.d.). What is AI? Learn about Artificial Intelligence. Oracle India.

Partridge, D., & Hussain, K. M. (1992). Artificial Intelligence and Business Management. *International Journal of Management*, *18*(3), 1–14.

Plastino, E., & Purdy, M. (2018). Game changing value from Artiðcial Intelligence: Eight strategies. *Strategy and Leadership*, *46*(1), 16–22. doi:10.1108/SL-11-2017-0106

Poole, S. (2018). Elastic by Leonard Mlodinow review – unplug to think creatively. *The Guardian*. Retrieved from https://www.theguardian.com/books/2018/apr/18/elastic-flexiblethinking-leonard-mlodinow

Rahwan, I., Cebrian, M., Obradovich, N., Bongard, J., Bonnefon, J.-F., Breazeal, C., Crandall, J. W., Christakis, N. A., Couzin, I. D., Jackson, M. O., Jennings, N. R., Kamar, E., Kloumann, I. M., Larochelle, H., Lazer, D., McElreath, R., Mislove, A., Parkes, D. C., Pentland, A., ... Wellman, M. (2019). Machine behaviour. *Nature*, *568*(7753), 477–486. doi:10.103841586-019-1138-y PMID:31019318

Raisch, S., & Krakowski, S. (in press). Artificial Intelligence and Management: The Automation-Augmentation Paradox. *Academy of Management Review*.

Reilly, P. (2018). The impact of artificial intelligence on the HR function. *IES Perspectives on HR 2018*. Retrieved from https://www.employment-studies.co.uk/system/files/resources/files/mp142_The_impact_of_Artificial_Intelligence_on_the_HR_function-Peter_Reilly.pdf

Russell, S., Norvig, P., & Intelligence, A. (1995). *Artificial Intelligence: A modern approach*. Prentice-Hall.

Samek, W., & Müller, K.-R. (2019). *Towards explainable artificial intelligence*. doi:10.1007/978-3-030-28954-6_1

Shannon, C. (1950). Programming a computer for playing chess. *Philosophical Magazine*, 41.

Shrestha, Y. R., Ben-Menahem, S. M., & von Krogh, G. (2019). Organizational decision-making structures in the age of artificial intelligence. *California Management Review*, *61*(4), 1–18. doi:10.1177/0008125619862257

Shrestha, Y. R., & Krishna, V. (forthcoming). Augmenting Organizational Decision-Making with Deep Learning Algorithms: Principles, Promises, and Challenges. *Journal of Business Research*.

Shrestha, Y. R., & Yang, Y. (2019). Fairness in algorithmic decision-making: Applications in multi-winner voting, machine learning, and recommender systems. *Algorithms*, *12*(9), 199. doi:10.3390/a12090199

Sinha, E. (2017). Emotional Intelligence: Proximal factor of Entrepreneurial Behaviour. *Twelfth Biennial Conference on Entrepreneurship*, *1*, 109-119.

Sinha, E. (2021). Towards an Integrative Framework of Intrapreneurship by Focusing on Individual Level Competencies. *Journal of Asia Entrepreneurship and Sustainability*, *17*(1), 106–163.

Sinha, E. (2022a). Managerial Intrapreneurship: Effect of Individual level Competencies and Mediating Role of Trait Emotional Intelligence. *Journal of Asia Entrepreneurship and Sustainability, 18*(2), 3–51.

Sinha, E. (2022b). 'PREFACE' Leadership in Times of Crises: Evidence from Indian SME Sector. In L. P. Dana, N. Sharma, & V. Singh (Eds.), *Managing Human Resources in SMEs and Start-ups: International Challenges and Solutions*. World Scientific. doi:10.1142/9789811239212_0014

Song, S., Chen, Y., Ngai-Man, C., & Jay Kuo, C. (2018). *Defense against Adversarial Attacks with Saak Transform.* arXiv preprint, arXiv:1808.01785 [cs.CV].

Srivastava, S. (2018). *Impact of Artificial Intelligence on strategic HR decision making*. Retrieved from https://www.peoplematters.in/article/technology/impact-of-artificial-intelligence-on-strategic-hr-decision-making-17935

Storey, J. (1987). *Developments in the management of human resources: an interim report.* Warwick Papers in Industrial Relations, 17, IRRU, School of Industrial and Business Studies, University of Warwick.

Storey, J. (1992). *Developments in the Management of Human Resources: An Analytical Review*. Blackwell.

Tata. (2018). *Cognitive Diversity: AI and The Future of Work.* Tata Communications.

Thaler, R. H., & Sunstein, C. R. (2009). *Nudge: Improving decisions about health, wealth, and happiness*. HeinOnline.

Truss, C., Gratton, L., Hope-Hailey, V., McGovern, P., & Stiles, P. (1997). Soft and hard models of human resource management: A reappraisal. *Journal of Management Studies, 34*(1), 53–73. doi:10.1111/1467-6486.00042

Turing, A. M. (1950). Computing machinery and intelligence. *Mind, 59*(236), 433–460. doi:10.1093/mind/LIX.236.433

Villaronga, F. E., Kieseberg, P., & Li, T. (2018). Humans forget, machines remember: Artificial intelligence and the Right to Be Forgotten. *Computer Law & Security Review, 34*(2), 304–313. doi:10.1016/j.clsr.2017.08.007

Walton, R. E. (1985). From Control to Commitment in the Workplace. *Harvard Business Review, 63*(2), 77–84.

Wilson, J. H., & Daugherty, R. P. (2018). Collaborative Intelligence: Humans and AI Are Joining Forces. *Harvard Business Review*, 2–11.

Wood, S. (1996). High Commitment Management and Unionization in the UK. *International Journal of Human Resource Management, 7*(1), 41–58. doi:10.1080/09585199600000117

Xin, D. D., Ma, L. L., Liu, J. J., Macke, S. S., Song, S. S., & Parameswaran, A. A. (2018). Accelerating Human-in-the-loop Machine Learning: Challenges and opportunities. *Proceedings of the 2nd Workshop on Data Management for End-To-End Machine Learning, DEEM 2018 - In Conjunction with the 2018 ACM SIGMOD/PODS Conference.* 10.1145/3209889.3209897

Zampetakis, L. A., & Moustakis, V. (2011). Managers' trait emotional intelligence and group outcomes: The case of group job satisfaction. *Small Group Research, 42*(1), 77–102. doi:10.1177/1046496410373627

Zheng, L., Noroozi, V., & Yu, P. S. (2017). Joint deep modeling of users and items using reviews for recommendation. *WSDM 2017 - Proceedings of the 10th ACM International Conference on Web Search and Data Mining*, 425–433. 10.1145/3018661.3018665

KEY TERMS AND DEFINITIONS

AI Classification: AI systems can be classified on three bases. First, on the basis of human resemblance; second, on the basis of business support; and third, on the basis of advancement in technology.

Artificial Intelligence: AI refers to systems or machines that mimic human intelligence to perform tasks and can iteratively improve themselves based on the information they collect. AI manifests in a number of forms, like 'Chatbots' and 'intelligent assistants'.

Artistic/Soft HR: The artistry HR elements focus on emotions, ethics, common-sense, trust and treating employees as valued assets and a source of competitive advantage through their commitment, adaptability and high-quality skill and performance.

Scientific/Hard HR: The scientific HR elements emphasise on the quantitative, calculative, and business-strategic aspects of managing the 'headcount'.

Chapter 5
The Role of Human Centricity in the Transition From Industry 4.0 to Industry 5.0:
An Integrative Literature Review

Rebecca Castagnoli
Department of Management, Università di Torino, Italy

Monica Cugno
https://orcid.org/0000-0001-8305-8248
Department of Management, Università di Torino, Italy

Silvia Maroncelli
Department of Management, Università di Torino, Italy

Anna Cugno
Department of Economics, Social Studies, Applied Mathematics and Statistics, Università di Torino, Italy

ABSTRACT

In 2021 the European Commission presented the report "Industry 5.0: Towards Sustainable, Human-Centric and Resilient European Industry." However, there is no clarity in the literature on the concept of human-centricity, and there is a lack of clear definitions, and intercurrent relationships are not identified. The chapter aims to assess, critique, and synthesize literature on the topic to enable a firm foundation for advancing knowledge and facilitating theory development. The study answers three research questions: RQ1) What are the concepts that identify the human-centric approach in firms' management? RQ2) What are the main definitions of the concepts and their gaps, overlaps, similarities, or contrasts? RQ3) What are the intervening relationships between the concepts and definitions that guide the implementation of human-centric Industry 4.0 or 5.0? The chapter implements an integrative literature review and contributes to the literature through the creation of a conceptual framework, useful for the promotion and application of a human-centric approach in Industry 4.0 and 5.0.

DOI: 10.4018/978-1-6684-6745-9.ch005

INTRODUCTION

The European Commission's General-Directorate for Research and Innovation and the one for Prosperity – following two workshops with representatives from leading research organizations, technology institutes, and funding agencies –present a promising new challenge for businesses and workers summarized in the report *Industry 5.0: Towards Sustainable, Human-Centric and Resilient European Industry* (European Commission, 2021). With this strategy, the European Commission aims to transition from Industry 4.0, an industrial revolution based on the adoption of cyber-physical systems, to Industry 5.0. The latter is understood to be a cultural revolution that integrates the Industry 4.0 approach with the Sustainable Development Goals of the UN 2030 Agenda, requiring businesses to produce responsibly while paying attention to resilient economic growth (SDG9), supporting employment prosperity (SDG8) respecting workers' well-being (SDG3) and training (SDG4).

Literature shows that in Industry 4.0, technology is the enabler for achieving more productive (Büchi et al., 2020; Cugno et al., 2021), competitive (Dalenogare et al., 2018), sustainable (Müller et al., 2018; Birkel & Müller, 2021), and resilient (Marcucci et al., 2021; Cugno et al., 2022) firms. In the transition from Industry 4.0 to Industry 5.0 (Xu et al., 2021), human capital, human-machine relationships, and human-centricity are identified as enablers for achieving firms that can nurture a prosperity that is more attentive to inclusiveness, eco-friendliness, and able to operate in VUCA scenarios, i.e., characterized by volatility, uncertainty, complexity and ambiguity (Taskan et al., 2022; Bennis & Nanus, 1985).

At present, there is no clarity in the literature on the concept of human-centricity and related concepts, there is a lack of clear and unambiguous definitions, and the relationships between these concepts and definitions are not identified nor described. Existing studies (Maroncelli & Castagnoli, 2022; Castagnoli et al., 2022), highlight the absence of a theoretical and conceptual framework.

The aim of the paper is to assess, critique and synthetize in a neutral way the literature on human-centricity in Industry 5.0 transition to enable a firm foundation for advancing knowledge and facilitating theory development.

The study answers three research questions: RQ1 – What are the concepts that identify human-centricity in firms' management? RQ2 – What are the main definitions of the concepts and their gaps, overlaps, similarities or contrasts? RQ3 – What are the relationships between concepts and definitions that guide the implementation of a human-centric 4.0 or 5.0 firms?

To answer the research questions, the chapter implements an integrative literature review organized around a coherent structure of the topic according to a conceptual framework that provides clarity regarding concepts, definitions and relationships that the literature identifies. The methodology is chosen to respond to an emerging topic with boundaries that are not yet fully defined, is characterized by a broad dimension of analysis, and is addressed by different disciplines.

The research contributes to the literature through the creation of a conceptual framework, useful for the promotion and application of a human-centricity in 4.0 and 5.0 firms, and provides promising lines for future research.

The results of the study are useful to scholars and practitioners with expertise in the field, enabling them to map, understand and develop concepts, definitions and relationships of human-centricity and to make progress both from a theoretical point of view – on the understanding of the topic – and from a practical point of view – on the implementation of human-centricity and the transition to Industry 5.0, as also required by the European challenge.

The chapter is organized as follows. The second paragraph identifies the methodology, describing: search protocol; inclusion and exclusion criteria; articles selection and data extraction; screening articles and concepts; definitions and relationships identification. The third paragraph reports the results, developing a critical analysis highlighting the answers to the three research questions. The fourth paragraph discusses the results outlining the conceptual framework. The fifth paragraph formalizes the conclusions by highlighting the contribution, implications, limitations of the study and future lines of research.

METHODOLOGY

The analysis performs an integrative literature review that assess, critiques and synthesizes representative contribution on the topic to point out new understandings, perspectives and frameworks (Torraco et al., 2005, 2016). The literature review is organized according to a conceptual perspective to identify the main concepts, their respective definitions, and the relationships between the concepts.

The integrative literature review is useful to addresses mature topics or new and emerging topics. The chapter on human-centricity focuses on an emerging topic, that would benefit from a holistic conceptualization and synthesis on the debate to date. Since the subject is investigated by a selected range of literature review (Maroncelli & Castagnoli, 2022; Castagnoli et al., 2022; Lu et al., 2022), the integrative approach is more likely to lead to an initial or preliminary conceptualization of the topic. Moreover, this perspective is better suited to study a broad issue with contributes by several disciplines (Snyder, 2019).

The literature review can be developed in five stages: search protocol (§2.1), articles selection and inclusion and exclusion criteria (§2.2), screening articles and data extraction (§2.3), critical analysis and concepts, definitions and relationships identification (§2.4); semantic analysis and taxonomy elaboration (§2.5).

Search Protocol

In order to reconstruct the sample of articles on the topic, the paper uses three international scientific databases – Web of Science (WoS), Ebsco and Scopus – which enable timely and comprehensive research in the social sciences. Since this is an emerging phenomenon, the databases were chosen to cover relevant literature in the various fields of study – engineering, economic-managerial, sociological... – reflecting the multidisciplinary approach to analyzing the topic.

The period of analysis considers research conducted between 2011, the year of the beginning of the Fourth Industrial Revolution or Industry 4.0, and February 2022. The research is based on English-language articles, and since it addresses an emerging topic, scholarly articles, editorial materials, reviews and conference proceedings are included.

The search strategy identifies a set of keywords, selected from the concepts of Industry 4.0 and 5.0 on the one hand and human-centricity on the other, summarized in Table 1. The search string is made from the synonyms of Industry 4.0 and 5.0 and human-centricity*.

Articles Selection and Inclusion and Exclusion Criteria

Papers are excluded from the sample if:

Table 1. Keywords. Source: own elaboration

Industry 4.0 and 5.0 synonims	Human-centricity synonims
Industry 4.0	Human-centr*
4th industrial revolution	
Fourth industrial revolution	
Factor* of the Future	
Future of Manufacturing	
Digital Factor*	
Digital Manufacturing	
Smart Factor*	
Interconnected Factor*	
Integrated Industr*	
Production* 4.0	
Human-Machine-Cooperation*	
Industrial Internet	
Industry 5.0	

1. the research concerns domains diffrent from than Industry 4.0 or 5.0 or synonyms of human-centricity;
2. the paper merely mentions the relationship between Industry 4.0 or 5.0 and human-centricity, but does not investigate it in depth;
3. the work only identifies policy-making actions;
4. the study considers a work schedule and employee benefits.

The inclusion and exclusion criteria are applied following a staged review. In the first stage, authors read the abstracts of the identified articles, net of duplicates, eliminating articles not relevant to the purpose of the research. In the second stage, authors read the main bodies of each articles, selecting a sample of 38 studies. To these papers, 7 cross references are added, obtaining a final sample of 45 articles (Annex I).

Screening Articles and Data Extraction

Data are collected through an observation grid containing the characteristics of the sample (§3.1): authors; years; type of contribution; focus of the analysis; value chain phases; approach; research methodology; research design; units of analysis; disciplines; level of analysis; ranking CABS list. The grid is constructed in Excel from a unit-variable matrix where units are the studies indicated by authors and year and variables report the dimensions covered.

Critical Analysis and Concepts, Definition and Relationships Identification

The critical analysis is conducted in three stages. The first stage identifies the concepts referring to human-centricity, responding to RQ1 (§ 3.2). The second stage identifies the definitions and related gaps, overlaps, similarities or contrasts, and reference authors for each definition, responding to RQ2 (§

3.3). The third stage highlights the relationships between concepts highlighted in the different definitions, responding to RQ3 (§3.4).

To critically reconstruct the topic for a clearer, more complete, and up-to-date conception of the topic, the concepts, definitions, and relationships are summarized, critically evaluated by each author, and then discussed to reach a unanimous decision.

Semantic Analysis and Taxonomy Elaboration

Through a semantic analysis of concepts and definitions, based on a qualitative research design method, a conceptual framework is elaborated (§4) structured as a taxonomy which allows to classify and categorize the main human-centricity related concepts according to XXX main categories, and to select and/or elaborates clear definitions.

To meet the purpose of identify a classification scheme, the design of the taxonomy (Lagorio et al., 2021): (i) identifies the units of classifications (i.e., concepts); (ii) compares the definitions of the concepts identifying different attributes (i.e., dimensions) of each definition; (iv) assigns macro-categories to the defined concepts and dimensions. Following this scheme, the taxonomy is based on a deductive approach, helping in sharing and communicating relevant information about the topic, thereby representing a useful framework to understand and explore the current and possibile implementation of 4.0 and 5.0 human-centric firms.

FINDINGS

Sample Description

Interest in the topic significantly increases in the last 4 years. The term Industry 5.0 is used from 2020 onward, although usage is still limited. Most of the articles (n=36) are published on International academic journals and international conferences. Among the journals, Computer & Industrial Engineering (n=8), Journal of Intelligence Manufacturing (n=2) and Journal of Manufacturing Systems (n=2) are most recurrent. The papers investigate almost exclusively (n=42) a value chain level of analysis and focus in the design, organization, production and maintainance phases. The studies adopt a predominantly conceptual approach (n=28). Only 17 researches are empirical and generally adopt test-cases. The most investigated industry is manufacturing, with a focus on automotive and aerospace. The discipline most involved on human centricity is engineering (n=33), followed by management (n=4), sociology (n=3), and economics (n=1). Only 4 essays are characterized by an interdisciplinary approach. Few studies to date have been published in highly ranked journals. More information is available in Annex II.

Concepts

The analysis of the sample of papers shows that to interpret human-centricity characteristics and dynamics in 4.0 and 5.0 firms, the authors introduce 71 concepts some of which are recurrent in the available literature. The most investigated concepts are: operator 4.0 (11 papers); human-machine interaction (6); and human-centric design (5). For a complete analysis see Figure 1.

Figure 1. Tag cloud of concepts. Source:own elaboration

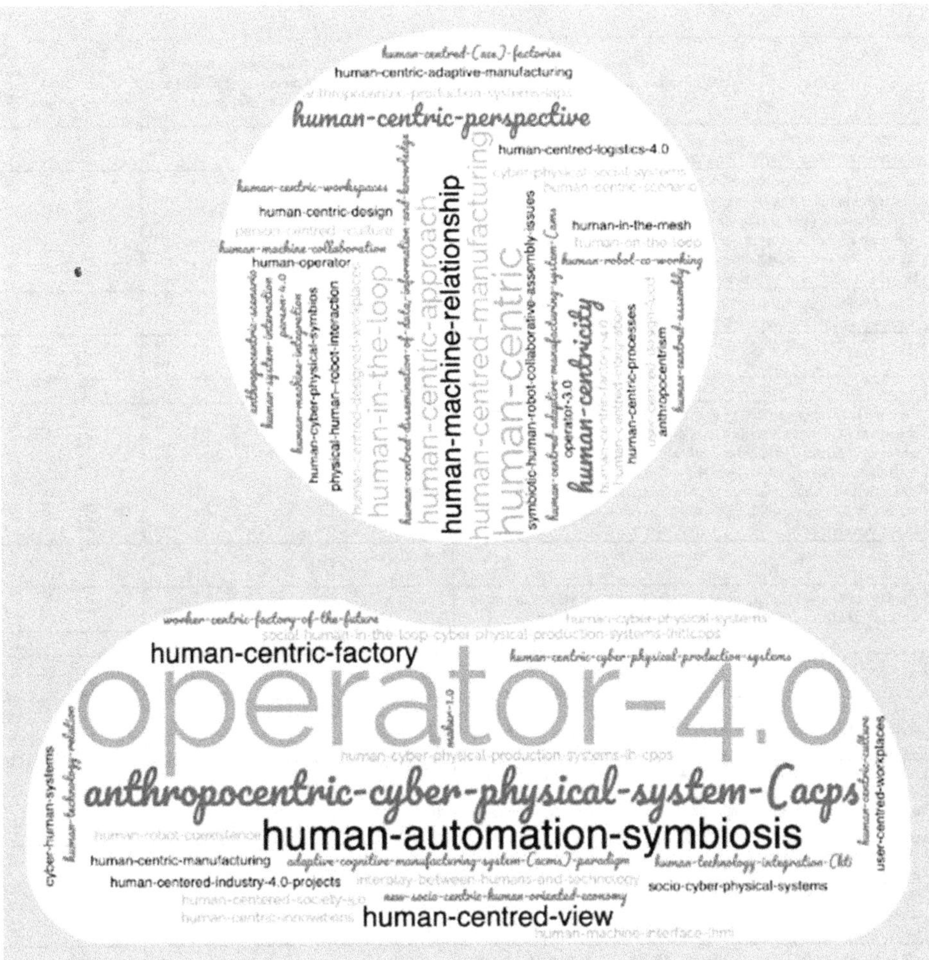

Definitions

Table 2 for each concept shows: the definition, cited explicitly if present in the articles analyzed between '«...»', reconstructed retrospectively by the authors if sufficiently deducible from the sample of articles, or indicated with '-' where absent or not deducible; the author and the year in which the concept is referred to; the relationship between the concepts that emerged in the literature definitions; overlaps, similarities and contrasts in the definitions of a concept identified through brainstorming among the authors and indicated respectively as '=', '»' e '!'.

Table 2 highlights that in the sample of articles analyzed 51 concepts have at least one definition, of these, 16 concepts are defined by some authors and only mentioned by others. 20 concepts out of the 71 identified have no definition: human-centric; human-centric process; human-centric design; human-centred design workplaces; human-centred solutions; human-centred assembly; human-centred dissemination of data, information and knowledge; human-centred society 5.0; person-centred culture; human-machine integration; human-robot interaction; physical human-robot interaction; symbiotic

Table 2. Human-centricity related concepts, definitions, authors and years, relationships, overlaps / similarities/contrasts

Concepts	Definitions	Authors and years	Relationships between concepts highlighted in the definitions	Overlaps (=)/similarities(»)/ contrasts (↑)in the definitions of a concept		
				=	»	↑
Human centricity	«A central component of Industry 4.0 is its human-centricity, described as development towards the Operator 4.0 concept (Romero et al., 2016a)».	Kaasinen et al. 2020	Operator 4.0		»	
	«Allows for a paradigm shift from independent automated and human activities towards a human-automation symbiosis (or 'human cyber-physical systems') characterised by the cooperation of machines with humans in work systems and designed not to replace the skills and abilities of humans, but rather to co-exist with and assist humans in being more efficient and effective».	Romero et al. 2016a	Human-automation symbiosis Human cyber-physical systems		»	
	«Humans should never be subservient to machines and automation, but machines and automation should be subservient to humans».	Romero et al. 2015			»	
Human-centric	-	Moenks et al. 2022				
	-	Chen et al. 2021				
Human-centric perspective	Each worker is characterized by a certain level of physical, sensory and cognitive abilities and a defined level of competence associated with each knowledge and skill. In addition, each worker has defined preferences regarding the tasks to which he or she would like to be assigned. Similarly, each job is assumed to require a certain level of physical, sensory, and cognitive abilities, as well as a certain level of relevant knowledge and skills.	Longo et al. 2020a				
	-	Peruzzini et al. 2018				
Human-centric approach	The human-centric approach must consider all relevant aspects of human work and not focus exclusively on the individual level of performance.	Reiman et al. 2021				
	-	Kadir et al. 2019				
Human-centric processes	-	Cillo et al. 2021				
Human-centric culture	«A human-centric culture should consider the necessary balance between work flexibility and human dignity, even in a digital environment».	Cillo et al. 2021				
Human-centric Innovations	A human-centric innovation is a «knowledge-based open innovation strategy or an orientation capable of transforming theoretical assumptions into concrete operational innovation paths».	Carayannis et al. 2021				
Human-centric workspaces	«Human-centric workspaces increase both productivity and operators' well-being, offering new possibilities of data collection, synthesis and analysis to build newknowledge, not only about machines, but also about how humans interact with them».	Grandi et al. 2020				
Human-centric scenario	«In a Human-centric scenario, operators are the managing and decision-making authority and the repository of experience (Mattsson, Karlsson, Fast-Berglund, & Hansson, 2014), while their role in the working process is upgraded via smart tools and assistance systems (Romero, Bernus, Noran, Stahre, & Fast-Berglund, 2016). Operators receive physical and cognitive support when needed (Romero et al., 2016; Fasth- Berglund & Stahre, 2013) and develop new skills (Boston Consulting Group, 2015; Dworschak & Zaiser, 2014)».	Pinzone et al. 2020				
Human-centric design	-	Reiman et al. 2021				
Human-centred design (HCD)	«HCD focuses on the inclusion of human factors in product and system design in order to respond to physical, psychological, social and cultural needs of human beings».	Grandi et al. 2018			»	
	«HCD consists of the application of human-related information to the design of tools, machines, systems, tasks, jobs, and environments for safe, comfortable, and effective human use (ISO 10075, 2004).	Grandi et al. 2020			»	
	-	Peruzzini & Pellicciari 2017				
	«HCD applies physical, cognitive, and social factors to design – tools, tasks, machines, systems, and environments – for enhancing effectiveness and efficiency: human use and safe».	Ngoc et al. 2022			»	
	«HCD improve the global performance of complex and conflicting production objectives and reduce workers' workload (Pacaux-Lemoine et al., 2017)».	Kadir et al., 2019			»	
Human-centred view	-	Johansson et al. 2017				
	Optimal way to integrate the lifecycle and human aspects.	Romero et al. 2015				

continued on following page

Table 2. Continued

Concepts	Definitions	Authors and years	Relationships between concepts highlighted in the definitions	Overlaps (=)/similarities(»)/ contrasts (ı)in the definitions of a concept		
				=	»	ı
Human centred integration	Important mean to increase not only firm performance but also work and life quality of Workers.	Rauch et al. 2020				
Human-centred context	Contexts where «humans are frequently involved in manufacturing and assembly processes from a physical and cognitive viewpoint: they are asked to interact with complex production systems and machine interfaces, to move materials between stations, to control the process, to intervene in case of failures, to interpret data and information for decision-making».	Grandi et al. 2020				
Human-centred designed workplaces	-	Caputo et al. 2019				
Human-centered solutions	-	Carayannis et al. 2021				
Human-centred assembly	-	Zamifrescu et al. 2014				
Human-centred logistics 4.0	«Despite the extensive use of technology in Logistics 4.0, the human role will be crucial in supervision and controlling activities. For instance, the human-technology interactions will be determinant to improve decision-making».	Lagorio et al. 2021				
Human-Centred Dissemination of Data, Information and Knowledge	-	Li et al. 2019				
Human-centered Society 5.0	-	Şahinel et al. 2021				
Anthropocentric scenario	«In anthropo-centric scenario, workers will be in control and make decisions supported by the CPS (Pacaux-Lemoine et al., 2017)».	Kadir et al. 2019				
Anthropocentrism	« In context of workplace relations, anthropocentrism refers to a focus on the person as an individual and not as just another part of the mechanics of production (Trist & Bamforth, 1951)».	Rauch et al. 2020				
User-centred design (UCD)	UCS is «The deeper concept of user multidimensional experience, which considers users' emotional and psychological responses».	Ngoc et al. 2022				
User-centred workplaces	«User-centred workplaces allow to: reducing non-value adding activities; reducing mistakes from employees and suppliers; reducing time for employee orientation and training; reducing search time in navigating the facility and locating tools, parts and supplies; reducing unnecessary human motion and transportation of goods; increasing productivity supporting sustainability, mainly from a social perspective. Workers will no longer perform their tasks routinely; instead, they will have to undertake varied and mostly unstructured tasks, depending on the needs of the dynamically changing production process. Teams should/will include flexible and remote ways of working and interacting with the systems as well as with other workers».	Caldarola et al. 2018				
New socio-centric human-oriented economy	«It is proposed to re-write the modern values of working life, assess the true role of social, moral, mental, and non-economic aspects in our lives, and move on to a search for a new paradigm of life issues».	Kolot et al. 2020				
Human-Centered Industry 4.0 Projects	«Practicable support for the migration of CPS to the shop floor that ensure the involvement of employees in the design and implementation of applications by the integrated approach of participation as well as methods and tools».	Bauer et al. 2019				
Person-centred culture	-	Mazali et al. 2018				
Human-machine relationship	«In terms of human-machine relationship, I4.0 technology appears to increase the scope for discretionary action and related forms of control, while at the same time reduces the room for autonomy».	Cirillo et al. 2021				ı
	«Human-machine relationships will change following a 5C evolution map – from current Coexistence, Cooperation and Collaboration to future Compassion and Coevolution».	Lu et al. 2022				ı
Human-machine cooperation	«Human-machine cooperation enables to maintain controlled levels of fatigue and well-being in the human activities».	Parades et al., 2019				
Human-machine interaction (HMI)	-	Grandi et al. 2018				
	HMI includes «not only physical interactions and visibility issues, but also interaction with digital information (e.g. touch screens), and multi-task jobs in order to understand how task complexity and dual-task issues can affect the users' performance».	Grandi et al. 2020			»	
	«HMI can be seen as the result of the "contact" (also a non-physical contact, like a signal or a procedure) between the worker, the system and the task».	Peruzzini et al. 2020			»	

continued on following page

Table 2. Continued

Concepts	Definitions	Authors and years	Relationships between concepts highlighted in the definitions	Overlaps (=)/similarities(»)/ contrasts (!)in the definitions of a concept		
				=	»	!
	-	Kadir et al. 2019	Human-in-the-Loop (HitL) Human-in-the-Mesh (HitM)			
	-	Johansson et al. 2017				
	-	Rauch et al. 2020				
Human–machine integration	-	Flemish et al. 2014				
Human-machine interface (HMI)	«Putting humans at the centre of interface design is the concept of HMI, which allows humans to understand and operate a machine in a digital manufacturing context. Design for HMI requires a transdisciplinary approach that takes various disciplines into account: cognitive psychology, industrial design, information processing graphics, human factors, and ergonomics».	Ngoc et al. 2022				
Human-machine symbiosis	«The human–machine symbiosis in Industry 5.0 should be fair and respectful of everyone's dignity and opinion equally. It should not create relational gaps, but foster social interaction».	Longo et al. 2020a				
	-	Longo et al. 2020b				
	-	Moenks et al. 2022				
Human-machine collaboration	«Placing human operators in the center of attention».	El Maraghy et al. 2021				
Human-robot interaction (HRI)	-	Eimontaite et al. 2018				
Physical human–robot interaction	-	Şahinel et al. 2021				
Human-robot co-working	«Collaborative robotics, or human-robot co-working, is merging the traditionally segregated autonomous and manual modes of operation».	Eimontaite et al. 2018				
Human-robot coexistence	«Unlike human-robot-collaboration, in human-robot-coexistence the worker and the robot share a common workspace, but not a common task».	Rauch et al. 2020	(-)Human-robot collaboration			
Human robot collaboration (HRC)	-	El Maraghy et al. 2021				
	«Design for the collaboration is well known as human–robot collaboration (HRC), which is also interchangeably called human–robot interaction (Cohen et al., 2019; Gervasi et al., 2020). Beyond the physical interactions, the collaboration design also enables the robots and humans to share knowledge and learn from others, and so work towards social sustainability».	Ngoc et al. 2022	Human-robot interaction			
	«The Operator 3.0 generation performs cooperative work with robots, machines and computer tools, which is also referred to as human-robot collaboration (1970–2000)».	Rauch et al. 2020	Operator 3.0			
Symbiotic human-robot collaborative assembly issues	-	El Maraghy et al. 2021				
Human-technology relation	«In the human–technology relation, it is possible to identify two dimensions: (i) automation; ii) support. Automation represents the situation in which operators are completely replaced by a machine/ robot or an automatic computerized system […]. Support dimension, conversely, refers to all the situations in which human and technology coexist in the performance of working tasks».	Lagorio et al. 2021				
Human-technology integration (HTI)	«Used when total automation is inefficient. […] Is an effective interaction of humans and technology in production that enable the workforce to realize improvements in production».	Moenks et al. 2022				
Human-system interaction	-	Grandi et al. 2018				
Human-automation symbiosis	«Paradigm that allows operators to feel empowered and in control of their workstation, while also fostering the optimal use of human competencies (knowledge, skills, abilities and behaviours)».	Romero et al. 2015				
	«Human-automation symbiosis (or 'human cyber-physical system') is characterised by the cooperation of machines with humans in work systems and designed not to replace the skills and abilities of humans, but rather to co-exist with and assist humans in being more efficient and effective».	Romero et al. 2016a	Human cyber-physical system			
	«Human-automation symbiosis introduces factories where machines cooperate with humans. However, production systems will not be designed to replace the skills and capabilities of humans, but to assist humans in being more efficient and effective (Nelles et al., 2016, Romero et al., 2016, Tzafestas, 2006)».	Rauch et al. 2020				

continued on following page

Table 2. Continued

Concepts	Definitions	Authors and years	Relationships between concepts highlighted in the definitions	Overlaps (=)/similarities(»)/ contrasts (¹)in the definitions of a concept		
				=	»	¹
	«Manufacturers would implement an optimized balance between humans and machines in their production processes, allocating each task through a decision grid that chooses which agent – human or machine – is better suited to handle it. Ideally, robots would enhance the cognitive, physical and sensorial abilities of factory workers, rather than automation operating unaided. Such a partnership is termed human-automation symbiosis».	Taylor et al. 2020				
Operator 4.0	Augmented operator	Longo et al. 2020a			»	
	-cita Romero, et al. (2016a); Romero et al. (2016b).	Kaasinen et al. 2020		=		
	-	Peruzzini et al. 2020				
	«Is a smart and skilled employee performing (cooperative) work aided by machines if and as needed. Works often refer to the concept of HTI as operator 4.0 (Romero et al., 2020), logistics operator 4.0 (Cimini et al., 2020), production operator 4.0 and order picker 4.0 (Guerin et al., 2019), cognitive operator 4.0 (Thorvald et al., 2021), or smart operator (Longo et al., 2017)».	Moenks et al. 2022	Human-technology integration		»	
	Romero, et al., 2016b.	Johansson et al. 2017		=		
	Romero, et al., 2016b.	Li et al. 2019		=		
	Romero, et al., 2016a, Romero et al., 2016b.	Şahinel et al. 2021		=		
	Romero et al., 2016a.	Taylor et al. 2020		=		
	«Operator 4.0 generation represents the 'operator of the future', a smart and skilled operator who performs 'work aided' by machines if and as needed. It represents a new design and engineering philosophy for adaptive production systems where the focus is on treating automation as a further enhancement of the human's physical, sensorial and cognitive capabilities by means of human cyber-physical system integration».	Romero et al. 2016a	Human cyber physical systems	=		
	An operator 4.0 can belong to one or more of the following types: - the Super-strong Operator (who uses exoskeletons); - the Augmented Operator (who uses augmented reality tools); - the Virtual Operator (who recreates a virtual factory); - the Healthy Operator (who wears wearable devices to monitor his or her own well-being); - the smarter Operator (who uses agents or artificial intelligence to plan activities); - the collaborative Operator (who interacts with CoBots); - the social Operator (who share knowledge using a social network); - the analytical Operator (which uses Big Data analysis).	Romero et al., 2016b	Human cyber physical systems	=		
	«Operator 4.0 generation is characterised by operating in a human-automation symbiosis for enhancing workforce capabilities».	Rauch et al. 2020	Human-automation symbiosis		»	
Operator 3.0	«The Operator 3.0 generation performs cooperative work with robots, machines and computer tools, which is also referred to as human-robot collaboration (1970–2000)».	Rauch et al. 2020	Human-robot collaboration			
Maker 1.0	«In our vision of the future in small-scale, high-value manufacturing, we foresee the operator 4.0 as a maker 1.0, a person who works alongside the automated production system but in a creative role rather than simply monitoring non-discretionary work-flow processes. The act of producing may be highly automated, but both it and the products are open to innovative activity through the worker as maker – a model we may call 'Maker 1.0'».	Taylor et al. 2020	Operator 4.0			
Human operator	-	Rauch et al. 2020				
Person 4.0	In Industry 4.0 there is the need for a switch from worker 4.0 to person 4.0.	Mazali et al. 2018				
Human-cyber-physical symbiosis	-	Kong et al. 2019;				
Social Human-in-the-loop Cyber-Physical Production Systems (HITLCPPS)	In the HITLCPPS the operator is at the center of Industry 4.0.	Moenks et al. 2022				
Human Cyber-Physical Systems	«A human-automation symbiosis (or 'human cyber-physical systems') characterised by the cooperation of machines with humans in work systems and designed not to replace the skills and abilities of humans, but rather to co-exist with and assist humans in being more efficient and effective».	Romero et al. 2016a	Human-automation symbiosis			

continued on following page

Table 2. Continued

Concepts	Definitions	Authors and years	Relationships between concepts highlighted in the definitions	Overlaps (=)/similarities(»)/ contrasts (!)in the definitions of a concept		
				=	»	!
Human Cyber-Physical Production Systems (H-CPPS)	«A human cyber-physical production system (H-CPPS) is defined as a work system that improves operators' abilities thanks to a dynamic interaction between humans and machines in the cyber- and physical-worlds by means of 'intelligent' human-machine interfaces».	Romero et al. 2016b				
Human-centric Cyber-Physical Production Systems	«A human-centric Cyber-Physical Production System (CPPS), depicted within a CPPS Functionality-Level Performance (CyFL) Matrix. The CyFL Matrix can help balance operative and social performance requirements when implementing CPPS. This provides a conceptual foundation to systemize and prioritize different functionalities».	Moenks et al. 2022	Social Human-in-the-loop Cyber-Physical Production Systems (HITLCPPS)			
Anthropocentric cyber-physical system (ACPS)	«ACPS is a reference model for factory automation that integrates the physical component (PC), the computational/cyber component (CC), and the human component (HC). The main characteristic of an ACPS reference model is its unified integrity that cannot be further decomposed into smaller engineering artifacts without losing its functionality. Consequently, ACPS is a System given by the combination of adaptive automation and augmented cognition».	Zamifrescu et al., 2014				
	Cita Zamifrescu et al. 2014	Pinzone et al., 2020				
	«ACPS is presented, wherein humans are not just interacting with a CPS, but they are active components of it».	Rauch et al., 2020				
Anthropocentric Production Systems (APS)	APS are structures and processes based on the use of skilled human resources and technologies adapted to the needs of a flexible and participatory organization, designed to improve skills, participation in decision-making processes, and quality of work life. APS are new technologies to enhance specific human capabilities. This concept extends from the plant organization through departmental cooperation and teamwork to the workplace.	Rauch et al. 2020				
Socio-cyber-physical systems	«Cyber-Physical Systems – or even socio-cyber-physical system – are systems in which smart machines, smart materials, smart warehouses, and other smart systems in factories continuously exchange information with each other as well as with human workers».	Johansson et al. 2017				
Cyber-physical-social systems	-	Zamifrescu et al. 2014	Anthropocentric cyber -physical system (ACPS)			
Cyber-human systems	«Human actors are still expected to play a central role in CPS-based smart factories; therefore the integration of humans to the CPS is crucial in realizing the future smart factory scenarios, as discussed under similar concepts such as operator 4.0 and cyber-human systems».	Şahinel et al. 2021	Operator 4.0			
Adaptive Cognitive Manufacturing System (ACMS) paradigm	«It is envisioned that the next manufacturing systems paradigm will be an adaptive cognitive manufacturing system, coined as ACMS, and characterized by its cognitive adaptability. It differs from static and dynamic adaptability in the manner in which the need to adapt, e.g. due to different products/variants, change in production volume, supply shortages, technological advances, and online changes is recognized and response is triggered, as well as how adaptation gets implemented; will all be enabled and supported by AI modules, smart sensors, extensive information and data analytics, and the automated, cognitive and hybrid human-machine adaptation actions and execution methods and human experience and wisdom. It is a new paradigm where the power of the 4th industrial revolution and beyond is deployed to achieve a more responsive as well as a more humane and human-centric manufacturing systems driven by economic and environmental sustainability and social responsibility».	El Maraghy et al. 2021				
Human-centred manufacturing work environments	-	Oliveira et al., 2019				
Human-centric manufacturing	«It should address human needs defined in an Industrial Human Needs Pyramid – from basic needs of safety and health to the highest level of esteem and self-actualization. As such, human-centric manufacturing systems need to have bi-directional empathy, proactive communication and collaborative intelligence for establishing trustworthy human-machine coevolution relationships, thereby leading to high-performance human-machine teams».	Lu et al. 2022	Human-machine co-evolution			
Human-centred adaptive manufacturing system (AMS)	«AMS should be able to adapt to the aging workers' needs considering their reduced workability, due to both physical and cognitive functional decrease, with the final aim to improve the human-machine interaction and the workers' wellbeing».	Peruzzini & Pellicciari 2017	Human-machine interaction			
Human-centric adaptive manufacturing	«AMS should pay «attention to the central role played by human workers and their well-being both physically and psychologically as well as considering the environmental issues».	El Maraghy et al. 2021				

continued on following page

Table 2. Continued

Concepts	Definitions	Authors and years	Relationships between concepts highlighted in the definitions	Overlaps (=)/similarities(»)/ contrasts (1)in the definitions of a concept		
				=	»	1
HumAn-CEntred (ACE) factories	For the definition see "Factories, A. C. E. (2019). Human-Centred Factories from eory to Industrial Practice. Lessons Learned And Recommendations".	El Maraghy et al. 2021				
Human-centric factory	It is a firm model that focuses on knowledge and on the understanding of: - workers (anthropometry, functional capabilities, knowledge, personal needs), - factories (economic KPIs on production, how change occurs, processes, organizational structure, workstations and workplaces, services, psychological workload, safety devices, incentives) - context (economic, social, environmental)	Pinzone et al. 2020		=		
	It is a model that focuses on workers, factories and context.	May et al. 2015		=		
Human-centric factory 4.0	-	Fiaschè et al. 2016				
Worker-centric factory of the future	-	May et al. 2015				
Human-in-the-loop (HitL)	«HitL covers systems/machines that require human commands in their operations».	Chen et al. 2021	(-)Human-on-the-loop (HotL)		»	
	«HitL scenarios are described to involve human activities, such as overseeing and adjusting machines, directly commanding the system, and first in line to detect and report abnormalities. This paradigm of HitL combines data and decision models with human knowledge and feedback, which promotes the development of machine intelligence (Ma et al., 2018)».	Kadir et al., 2019	Human-machine interaction		»	
Human-on-the-loop (HotL)	«HotL encompasses systems/machines that execute tasks independently but with human supervision who can interfere when anomalies occur».	Chen et al. 2021				
Human-in-the-Mesh (HitM)	«In HitM scenarios, the role of humans is more focused on supporting the systems in activities such as receiving alerts, intervening when necessary, analyzing and changing planning, and observing and extracting knowledge».	Kadir et al., 2019	Human-machine interaction			

In definitions, text quoted between '«»' indicates the in-text citation, while text quoted without '«»' is a reworking by the Authors inferring a definition from the original text.

Source: own elaboration

human-robot collaborative assembly issue; interplay between human and technology; human-system interaction; human-operator; human-cyber-physical symbiosis; cyber-physical social system; human-centred manufacturing; work environments; human-centred factory; human-centric factory 4.0; worker-centric factory of the future.

The concept of operator 4.0 deserves special attention as almost all converge toward a single definition referring in most cases to the one provided by Romero et al. (2016a and b). There is a similararity between the different definitions of the concepts of: human-centred design; human-machine interaction; human-in-the-loop. At present, however, there are contrasts regarding the definitions of the concepts of human-centricity and human-machine relationship.

Relationships

Analysis of the definitions of some concepts reveals direct references to other concepts, reported as intercurrent relationships (Tab.2). The relationships between concepts, are highlighted by means of a concept map (Figures 2), providing a visual representation of authors, concepts and relationships between concepts and enhancing the understanding of the author's critical analysis of the sample of articles (Webster & Watson, 2002). The concept map also highlights overlaps, similarities and contrasts between definitions of each concept.

Relationships can be: positive, emphasizing a (i) connection or (ii) equality between two concepts; or negative, highlighting a (iii) contrast between a new term and one used in the past.

(i) Connection.
- Kaasinen et al. (2020) define the concept of human-centricity by resorting to the concept of operator 4.0.
- Romero et al. (2016a) link the concept of human-centricity to those of human-automation symbiosis and human cyber-physical systems;
- Kadir et al. (2019) highlight a connection between the concept of human-machine and human-in-the-loop and human-in-the-mesh;
- Romero et al. (2016a and 2016b) explain the concept of human-automation symbiosis in the light of that of human-cyber-physical systems;
- Rauch et al. (2020) links the concept of operator 3.0 with that of human-robot collaboration;
- Moenks et al. (2022) define operator 4.0 referring to human-technology integration;
- Rauch et al. (2020) explain operator 4.0 in the light of automation symbiosis;
- Taylor et a. (2020) links the concept of maker 1.0 with that of operator 4.0.
- Romero et al. (2016a) point out a connection between human-cyber-physical system and human-automation symbiosis.
- Moenks et al. 2022 refer human-centric-cyber-physical-production-systems to social-human-in-the-loop-cyber-physical-production-systems.
- Şahinel et al. 202 define cyber-human systems in the light of operator 4.0.
- Lu et al. 2022 links the concept of human-centric manufacturing to the concept of human-machine co-evolution.
- Peruzzini & Pellizzari (2017) connect human-centered adaptive manufacturing system to the concept of human-machine interaction.
- Zamifrescu et al. 2014 point out that the concept of social cyber physical systems is related to the one of anthropocentric cyber -physical systems.
- Kadir et al., 2019 links the concept of human-in-the-loop to that of human-machine interaction.
- Kadir et al. 2019 explain human-in-the-mesh referring to human-machine interaction.

(ii) Equality.
- Ngoc et al. (2022) point out that human-robot collaboration is interchangeable with the concept of human-robot interaction.

(iii) Contrast.
- Rauch et al. (2020) contrast the concept of human-robot coexistence and the one of human-robot collaboration.
- Chen et al., 2021 explain the concept of human-in-the-loop by contrasting it with human-on-the-loop.

The concept map (Braun and Clarke, 2006) represents the relationships (arrows) between individual authors – represented as high-level (parent) nodes – and concepts – represented by low-level (child) nodes (Braun and Clarke, 2006; Wheeldon and Faubert, 2009). If concepts have encountered a definition in the literature they are shown in small caps; otherwise they are shown in lower case. The arrows are represented with line: double, if the definitions are equal (overlaps); continuous, if the definitions are

Figure 2. Concept map. Source: own elaboration

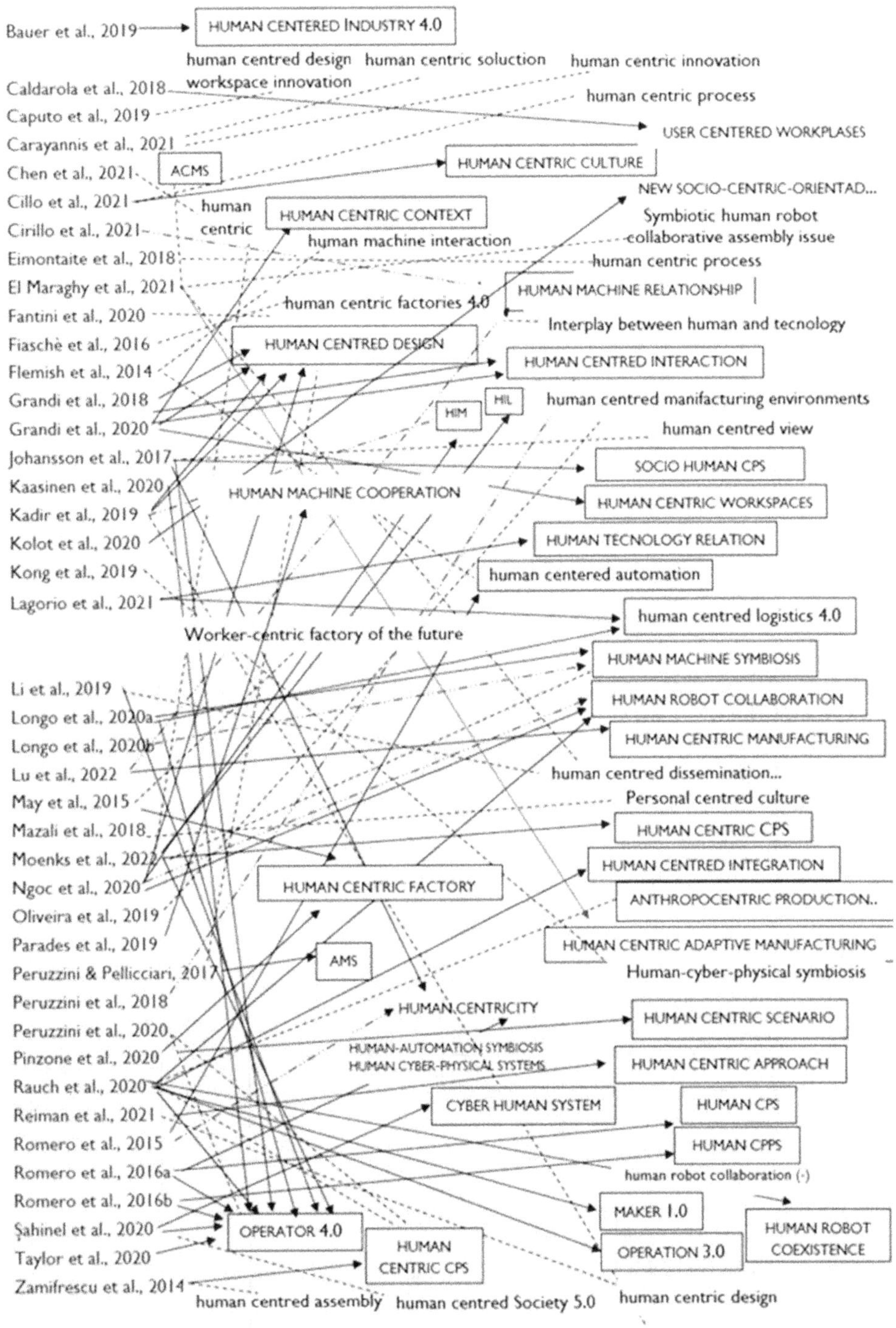

overlapping (similarities); alternating dashes and dots, if the definitions are divergent (contrasts); dashed, if the definitions are reconstructed retrospectively by the authors. As the review progresses, the nodes are continuously regrouped and the arrows between the nodes are iteratively adjusted to code main themes.

Table 3. Taxonomy. Source: own elaboration

Label used to define concepts										
First word	**Second word**	**Third word**	**Keywords**	**Fourth word**	**Fifth word**	**Authors, year**	**Dimensions**	**Overlapping/ not overlapping definition**	**Synthesis word**	**Macro-categories**
Block 1										
	human	centricity				Kaasinen et al. 2020	-focus on the operator	overlapping definitions	human-centric	human-centric factory
	human	centricity				Romero et al. 2016a	-human automation symbiosis -human-cyber-physical system -skills and human abilities			
	human	centricity				Romero et al. 2015	-machines subservient to humans			
	human	centric				Moenks et al. 2022	-focus on the operator	overlapping definitions	human-centric	
	human	centric				Chen et al. 2021	-focus on the operator			
	antrhopo	centrism				Rauch et al. 2020	-focus on the person as individual	-	human-centric	
	adaptive	cognitive	manufacturing system	paradigm		El Maraghy 2021	-cognitive adaptability -human centric manufacturing systems	-	adaptive cognitive manufacturing system paradigm	
	human	centred	manufacturing			Lall et al. 2017;		-	human-centric manufacturing	
	human	centric	manufacturing			Lu et al. 2022	-human needs -safety and health system -empahty -proactive communication -collaborative intelligence -co-evolution relationship	-	human-centric manufacturing	
	human	centred	adaptive manufacturing			Peruzzini & Pellicciari 2017	-human machine interaction -workers' wellbeing	overlapping definitions	human-centric manufacturing	
	human	centric	adaptive manufacturing			El Maraghy et al 2021	-workers and their well-being in the phsyco-physical environment			
	human	centric	factories			El Maraghy et al 2021	-making operators' tacit knowledge, wearable apparatus -workers' wellbeing -workers' needs	overlapping definitions	human-centric factory	
	human	centric	factory			Pinzone et al.2020	-workers -factories -contexts			
	human	centric	perspective			Longo et al. 2020a	-abilities -knowledge -skills -preferences regarding tasks	-	human centric perspective	human centric perspective
	human	centric	approach			Reiman et al. 2021	-not only focus on individual performance	overlapping definitions		
	human	centric	approach			Kadir et al. 2019	-not only focus on individual performance			
	human	centred	integration			Rauch et al. 2020	-not only performance -work and life quality	not overlapping definitions	human-centric integration	
	human	centric	processes			Cillo et al. 2021	-knowledge management -human-resource management -diversity -inclusion -people empowerment	-	human-centric process	human-centric value chain
	human	centred	assembly			Zamifrescu et al. 2014	-assembly line -assembly workstation	-	human-centric assembly	
	human	centred	logistics	4.0		Lagorio et al. 2021	-supervision and controlling activities	-	human-centric logistics 4.0	
	human	centred	dissemination	data, information and knowledge		Li et al. 2019	-well-informed decisions	-	human-centric dissmination	
	human	centric	culture			Cillo et al. 2021	-work flexibility -human dignity -digital environment	-	human- centric culture	human-centric culture
	person	centred	culture			Mazali et al. 2018	-work flexibility -human dignity -digital environment	-		
	human	centric	innovation			Carayannis et al. 2021	-ecosystems -knowledge circulation -system -regional innovative solutions	-	human-centric innovation	human-centric ecosystem

continued on following page

Table 3. Continued

Label used to define concepts										
First word	**Second word**	**Third word**	**Keywords**	**Fourth word**	**Fifth word**	**Authors, year**	**Dimensions**	**Overlapping/ not overlapping definition**	**Synthesis word**	**Macro-categories**
	human	centric	workspaces			Grandi et al. 2020	-productivity -well-being -new knowledge -interaction	-	human-centric workspace	human-centric designed workspace
	human	centric	design			Reiman et al. 2021	-human needs	-	human-centric design	
	human	centred	design			Grandi et al. 2018	-inclusion of human factors -social and cultural needs	overlapping definitions		
	human	centred	design			Grandi et al. 2020	-human-related information			
	human	centred	design			Peruzzini & Pellicciari 2017	-human needs			
	human	centred	design			Ngoc et al. 2020	-physical, cognitive and social factors			
	human	centred	design			Kadir et al. 2019	-reducing workers workload			
	user	centred	design			Ngoc et al. 2022	-multidimensional experience -emotional and psycological responses	-		
	human	centred	manufaturing	work enviroment		Oliveira et al. 2019	-man-made workplaces	-	human-centric manufacturing environment	
	human	centred	designed	workplaces		Caputo et al., 2019	-inclusion of human factors	overlapping definitions	human-centric designed workplace	
	human	centred	Industry 4.0	projects		Bauer et al. 2019	-involvement of employee in design and implementation	-	human-centric industry 4.0 project	
	human	centric	scenario			Pinzone et al. 2020	-decision making -physical and cognitive support -smart tools and assistance systems	-	human-centric scenario	human-centric system
	anthropo	centric	scenario			Kadir et al. 2019	-decision making -smart tools and assistance systems -cps	-		
	human	centred	context			Grandi et al. 2020	-human interact with complex production systems -control of processes	-	human-centric context	
	human	centred	society	5.0		Şahinel et al. 2021	-human role in fully automated systems	-	human-centric society 5.0	
	anthropocentric		production systems			Rauch et al. 2020	-focus on the operator -modelling human and technology aspects	-	human-centric production system	
	human	centred	view			Johansson et al. 2017	-human lifecycle	overlapping definitions	human-centric view	human-lifecycle approach
	human	centred	view			Romero et al. 2015	-human lifecycle			
	human	centred	designed	workplaces		Caldarola et al. 2018	-flexibility -social perspective -human factors		human-centric designed workplace	
	human	centred	solutions			Carayannis et al. 2021	-innovative solutions	-	human-centric solution	human-centric solution
	human	(new socio-) centric	oriented	economy		Kolot et al. 2020	-true role of social, moral, mental, and non-economic aspects	-	human-centric socio-economy	human-centric economy
	human	cyber-physical	systems			Romero et al. 2016a	-cooperation -coexistance -human-automation symbiosis	-	human cyber-physical system	human cyber-physical system
	human	cyber-physical	production systems			Romero et al. 2016b	-interaction -interfaces	-	human cyber-physical production system	
	human-centric	cyber-physical	production systems			Moenks et al. 2022	-interaction	-	human-centric cyber-physical production system	
	anthropocentric	cyber-physical	systems			Zamifrescu et al. 2014	-integration	overlapping definitions	human-centric cyber-physical system	
	anthropocentric	cyber-physical	systems			Pinzone et al. 2020	-integration			
	anthropocentric	cyber-physical	systems			Rauch et al. 2020	-integration			
	socio	cyber-physical	system			Johansson et al 2017	-exchange information with human workers	-	human cyber-physical system	
		cyber-physical	social system			Zamifrescu et al 2014	-symbiotic man-machine system	-	human cyber-physical system	
		cyber -human	system			Şahinel et al 2021	-integration of humans to cyber-physical systems	-	human cyber-physical system	
	human	centric	factory			May e al. 2015	- workers - factories - contexts			
	human	centric	factory 4.0			Fiaschè et al. 2016	-integration of human aspects			
	worker	centric	factory	(of the) future		May et al. 2015	-capabilities of workers regardless of age and role	-	human-centric factory	

continued on following page

Table 3. Continued

Label used to define concepts										
First word	**Second word**	**Third word**	**Keywords**	**Fourth word**	**Fifth word**	**Authors, year**	**Dimensions**	**Overlapping/ not overlapping definition**	**Synthesis word**	**Macro-categories**
Block 2										
	human	machine	relationship			Cirillo et al. 2021	-increasing control -reducing autonomy	-	-	human-technology relationship
	human	technology	relationship			Lagorio et al. 2021	-automation -support -coexistence	-	human-technology relationship	
	human	machine	cooperation			Parades et al. 2019	-well-being	overlapping definitions	human-technology cooperation	human-technology interaction
	human	machine	interaction			Grandi et al. 2018	-not only physical interaction		human-technology interaction	
	human	machine	interaction			Grandi et al. 2020	-not only physical interaction			
	human	machine	interaction			Peruzzini et al. 2020	-not only physical contact			
	human	machine	interaction			Kadir et al. 2019	-not only physical contact -not only physical interaction			
	human	machine	interaction			Johansson et al. 2017	-not only physical contact -not only physical interaction			
	human	machine	interaction			Rauch et al. 2020	-not only physical contact -not only physical interaction			
	human	machine	integration			Flemish et al. 2014	-interaction -cooperation			
	human	machine	collaboration			El Maraghy et al., 2021	-focus on the operator	overlapping definitions	human-technology collaboration	
	human	automation	collaboration			Romero et al. 2015	-control of workstation -optimal use of competences			
	human	automation	collaboration			Romero et al. 2016a	-cooperation in work system -co-existence -skills and abilities of humans			
	human	automation	collaboration			Rauch et al. 2020	-work optimization -workplaces optimization			
	human	automation	collaboration			Taylor et al. 2020	-tasks allocation			
	human	automation	symbiosis			Romero et al. 2015	-control of workstation -human competences optimization	overlapping definitions	human-technology symbiosis	
	human	automation	symbiosis			Romero et al. 2016a	-cooperation -different from coexistence			
	human	automation	symbiosis			Rauch et al. 2020	-cooperation -human competences			
	human	automation	symbiosis			Taylor et al. 2020	-tasks allocation			
	human	robot	interaction			Eimontaite et al. 2018	-collaboration -interface design			
physical	human	robot	interaction			Şahinel et al. 2021	-integration context			
	human	robot	co-working			Eimontaite et al. 2018	-collaboration	-	human-technology co-working	
	human	robot	collaboration			El Maraghy et al. 2021	-	overlapping definitions	human-technology collaboration	
	human	robot	collaboration			Ngoc et al. 2022	-synonyms of interaction			
	human	robot	collaboration			Rauch et al. 2020	-related to operator 3.0 -cooperation			
symbiotic	human	robot	collaborative	assembly	issue	El maraghy et al. 2021	-tasks allocation	-	human-technology collaboration	
	human	technology	integration			Moenks et al. 2022	-interaction	-	human-technology integration	
	human	cyber-physical	symbiosis			Kong et al. 2019	-interaction -collaboration	-	human-technology symbiosis	
	human	machine	integration			Flemish et al. 2014	-cooperation -relationship	overlapping definitions	human-technology integration	
	human	technology	integration			Moenks et al. 2022	-enabling workforces -improving production -interaction			
	human	robot	co-existence			Rauch et al. 2020	-different from collaboration -sharing of common workspace but not common tasks	-	human-technology coexistence	human-technology co-existence
	human	system	interaction			Grandi et al. 2018	-interface	-	human-technology interaction	human-technology interface
	human	machine	interface			Ngoc et al. 2022	-interface design		human-technology interface	
	human	machine	symbiosis			Longo et al. 2020a	-respectful of dignity -equity	-	human-technology symbiosis	human-technology symbiosis

continued on following page

Table 3. Continued

Label used to define concepts										
First word	**Second word**	**Third word**	**Keywords**	**Fourth word**	**Fifth word**	**Authors, year**	**Dimensions**	**Overlapping/ not overlapping definition**	**Synthesis word**	**Macro-categories**
Block 3										
		operator	4.0			Longo et al. 2020a	-augmented operator	overlapping definitions	operator 4.0	operator 4.0
						Kaasinen et al. 2020	-smart and skilled operator -work aided performer			
						Peruzzini et al. 2020	-operator in industry 4.0			
						Moenks et al. 2022	-smart, skilled and cooperative employee			
						Johansson et al. 2017	-smart and skilled operator -work aided performer			
						Li et al. 2019	-smart and skilled operator -work aided performer			
						Şahinel et al. 2021	-smart and skilled operator -work aided performer			
						Taylor et al. 2020	-smart and skilled operator -work aided performer			
						Romero et al. 2016a	-smart and skilled operator -work aided performer			
						Romero et al. 2016b	-smart and skilled operator -work aided performer			
						Rauch et al. 2020	-smart and skilled operator -work aided performer			
		maker	1.0			Taylor et al. 2020	-operator 4.0 -person -creativity	-	maker 1.0	
	human	operator				Rauch et al. 2020	-anthropocentrism -tasks allocation	-	human operator	
		person	4.0			Mazali et al. 2018	-different from worker 4.0	-	person 4.0	
		operator	3.0			Rauch et al. 2020	-collaboration -cooperation	-	operator 3.0	operator 3.0
Block 4										
	human	(in the) loop				Chen et al. 2021	-overseeing and adjusting machines	overlapping definitions	human-in-the-loop	human-in-the-loop
	human	(in the) loop				Kadir et al. 2019	-overseeing and adjusting machines			
social	human-in-the-loop	cyber-physical	production systems			Moenks et al. 2022	-focus on the operator -modelling human and technology aspects	-	human-in-the-loop	
	human	(on the) loop				Chen et al. 2019	-system/machines that execute tasks	-	human-on-the-loop	human-on-the-loop
	human	(in the) mesh				Kadir et al. 2019	-man supports the system	-	human-in-the-mesh	human-in-the-mesh

The author conducting the broadest spectrum analysis is Rauch et al. (2020), who cites eleven key concepts – human-centered integration, anthropocentrism, human-machine interaction, human-robot coexistence, human-robot collaboration, human-automation symbiosis, operator 4. 0, operator 3.0, human operator, anthropocentric cyber-physical systems, anthropocentric production systems. Other authors condescending wide-ranging analyses are El maraghy et al. (2021), Kadir et al. (2019), Moenks et al. (2022), who mention 6 concepts respectively, followed by Chen et al. (2021), Grandi et al. (2020), Johansson et al. (2017) Ngoc et al. (2022), Romero et al. (2016a), Şahinel et al. (2021).

DISCUSSION

Table 3 reconstructs the set of labels used to identify the 71 concepts that emerged from the literature review. Given the complexity of the phenomena involved in the implementation of Industry 4.0 and 5.0, the labels used in the literature arise from the juxtaposition of multiple words (from two to five).

Through semantic analysis, each sub-word in the labels is reorganized in the different columns according to a logic of meaning and sense that allows for the identification of possible groups of synonyms. For semantic grouping, a multi-level process is followed starting with the "keyword" column, which groups words that represent the label's distinctive element, which uniquely identify the phenomenon under consideration. Next, the terms antecedent to the keyword are reported in the left columns and the following terms in the right columns (i.e. in the concepts human-centric perspective, human-centric approach, human-centric culture: on the one hand, the terms human and centric are antecedent terms, constituting two sense categories that are distinct from each other; on the other hand, the keywords that introduce relevant shades of meaning are perspective, approach, and culture, constituting a separate sense category). This process is conducted gradually on the different words that constitute the concept to reorganize the high variability that exists in the different terminological nuances found in the literature.

The table shows the authors and the reference year for the definition of each concept and allows the definitions to be analyzed by outlining their key dimensions in order to identify any identities or differences in meaning among the various concepts. In cases where the contribution does not provide a precise definition of the concepts, the authors infer the key dimensions through reading the contribution. The process allows the definitions of overlapping or non-overlapping concepts to be distinguished in order to identify a synthesis term in favor of greater clarity and better consistency with the European Commission's human-centric Industry 4.0 and 5.0 guidelines (i.e., the use of the terms human and centric is favored over the terms anthropo/user/person/socio/worker and centricity/centred).

Finally, concepts are reclassified into macro-categories that aggregate multiple concepts thus completing the reference taxonomy.

The process described is carried out through a briefing among the authors to arrive at a unanimous consensus.

The rationalization activity: on the one hand, it corrects some terminological inaccuracies detected by the study, identifying terms most appropriate for the authors' stated purpose; on the other hand, it synthesizes terms that can be used almost interchangeably to reduce terminological variability (i.e. since most studies analyze the manufacturing sector, the terms factory and manufacturing can be grouped into a single macro-category; the term workplace, used indistinctly in engineering studies, is reserved for identifying changes in the micro-organization of work, while the term workspace is employed to recognize the design dynamics of cyber-physical environments and workstations).

The proposed conceptual framework reduces complexity by bringing the 71 concepts noted in the literature back to 21 macro-categories that are in turn divided into 4 blocks. The work is the result of an investment in language standardization where multiple concepts identified in the literature are linked by synonymy.

Block 1

Block 1: is numerically the largest (with 11 concepts out of 21); represents the most general concepts focused on the role of the centrality of humans within the firm system in its different spheres: skills, competences, inclusion, needs, empathy, flexibility, ...; is the most interdisciplinary block, as it touches on socio-economic disciplines and not predominantly engineering disciplines. The aggregation of concepts within the macro-categories of Block 1, maintains a distinction between different levels of firms management: human-centric factory, perspective, culture, ecosystem, designed workspace, system, approach, solution, economy, cyber-physical system. Despite the variability of encapsulated concepts and interdisciplinarity, Block 1 does not contrast with the existing literature.

Block 2

With regard to the second block, the study confirms the existing distinction between the concepts of relationship/interaction/co-existence/interface/symbiosis, but, unlike in the literature, aggregates the terms collaboration/cooperation/interaction/integration within a single macro-category "human-technology interaction" as they are mostly used interchangeably. Moreover, within the concept of human-technology symbiosis, the study is critical of some existing work (Romero et al., 2015; Romero et al., 2016a, Rauch et al., 2020; Taylor et al., 2020) that uses the term as synonymous with interaction, collaboration, co-operation, co-existence, and prefers the definition introduced by Longo et al., 2020a, which highlights the role of respect for dignity and equity as the focus of human-centric symbiosis. In this direction, the analysis conducted emphasizes the difference between the concepts of: relationship, typical of the third industrial revolution; interaction/co-existence/interface usable indistinctly for the third and fourth industrial revolutions; and the concept of symbiosis, considered in the meaning presented above, proper to the fourth industrial revolution (Longo et al., 2020a).

Block 3

Regarding the third block, the analysis agrees with the definition most reported in the literature of operator 4.0 introduced by Romero et al. (2016a) and Romero et al. (2016b).

Block 4

Regarding the fourth block, the analysis supports existing definitions and distinctions between the concepts of human-in-the-loop (Chen et al., 2021; Kadir et al., 2019), human-on-the-loop (Cen et al., 2019) and human-in-the-mesh (Kadir et al., 2019).

CONCLUSION

The chapter analyzes the topic on the role of human-centricity in the transition from Industry 4.0 to Industry 5.0 through an integrative literature review. The results identify 71 concepts (RQ1) represented by a tag cloud, out of which only 51 have at least one definition and 20 have no definition (RQ2). Analysis of the definitions reveals relationships between multiple concepts in the form of connections, equalities and contrasts, represented through a concept map (RQ3).

Through semantic analysis, a taxonomy is reconstructed leading to a conceptual framework.

The results contribute to the literature by mapping and classifying existing studies, highlighting any consensus, inconsistencies, and contrasts, and identifying terminological solutions to overcome them.

The study contributes to policy makers, practitioners, and managers by providing a shared language for structuring human-centric policies and strategies.

At present, however, there is still no interdisciplinary shared glossary that enables the operationalization of concepts, with a view to identifying specific indicators to measure the implementation of human-centricity in 4.0 and 5.0 firms.

Declaration of Conflicting Interests

The author(s) declared no potential conflicts of interest with respect to the research, authorship, and/or publication of this article.

Funding

The author(s) received no financial support for the research, authorship, and/or publication of this article.

REFERENCES

Bauer, W., Schuler, S., Hornung, T., & Decker, J. (2019). Development of a procedure model for human-centered industry 4.0 projects. *Procedia Manufacturing*, *39*, 877–885. doi:10.1016/j.promfg.2020.01.402

Bennis, W., & Nanus, B. (1985). *The strategies for taking charge*. Harper. Row.

Birkel, H., & Müller, J. M. (2021). Potentials of industry 4.0 for supply chain management within the triple bottom line of sustainability–A systematic literature review. *Journal of Cleaner Production*, *289*, 125612. doi:10.1016/j.jclepro.2020.125612

Braun, V., & Clarke, V. (2006). Using thematic analysis in psychology. *Qualitative Research in Psychology*, *3*(2), 77–101. doi:10.1191/1478088706qp063oa

Breque, M., De Nul, L., & Petridis, A. (2021). *Industry 5.0: Towards a sustainable, human-centric and resilient European industry*. Publications Office. https://data.europa.eu/doi/10.2777/308407

Büchi, G., Cugno, M., & Castagnoli, R. (2020). Smart factory performance and Industry 4.0. *Technological Forecasting and Social Change*, *150*, 119790. doi:10.1016/j.techfore.2019.119790

Caldarola, E. G., Modoni, G. E., & Sacco, M. (2018). Enhancing the Workforce Skills and Competences by Leveraging a Human-Centered Knowledge-Based System in the Rise of Industry 4.0. *International Journal on Advances in Intelligent Systems*, *11*(3&4), 309–324.

Caputo, F., Greco, A., Fera, M., & Macchiaroli, R. (2019). Workplace design ergonomic validation based on multiple human factors assessment methods and simulation. *Production & Manufacturing Research*, *7*(1), 195–222. doi:10.1080/21693277.2019.1616631

Carayannis, E. G., Campbell, D. F., & Grigoroudis, E. (2021). Helix trilogy: The triple, quadruple, and quintuple innovation helices from a theory, policy, and practice set of perspectives. *Journal of the Knowledge Economy*, 1–30.

Castagnoli, R., Cugno, M., Maroncelli, S., & Cugno, A. (2022). Human-centric manufacturing: an interdisciplinary review of drivers and dark sides. *R&D Management Conference*.

Chen, J., Lim, C. P., Tan, K. H., Govindan, K., & Kumar, A. (2021). Artificial intelligence-based human-centric decision support framework: An application to predictive maintenance in asset management under pandemic environments. *Annals of Operations Research*, 1–24. doi:10.100710479-021-04373-w PMID:34785834

Cillo, V., Gregori, G. L., Daniele, L. M., Caputo, F., & Bitbol-Saba, N. (2021). Rethinking companies' culture through knowledge management lens during Industry 5.0 transition. *Journal of Knowledge Management.*

Cirillo, V., Rinaldini, M., Staccioli, J., & Virgillito, M. E. (2021). Technology vs. workers: The case of Italy's Industry 4.0 factories. *Structural Change and Economic Dynamics, 56*, 166–183. doi:10.1016/j.strueco.2020.09.007

Coffey, J. W., Hoffman, R., & Cañas, A. (2006). Concept map-based knowledge modelling: Perspectives from information and knowledge visualization. *Information Visualization, 5*(3), 192–201. doi:10.1057/palgrave.ivs.9500129

Cugno, M., Castagnoli, R., & Büchi, G. (2021). Openness to Industry 4.0 and performance: The impact of barriers and incentives. *Technological Forecasting and Social Change, 168*, 120756. doi:10.1016/j.techfore.2021.120756

Cugno, M., Castagnoli, R., Büchi, G., & Pini, M. (2022). Industry 4.0 and production recovery in the covid era. *Technovation, 114*, 102443. doi:10.1016/j.technovation.2021.102443

Dalenogare, L. S., Benitez, G. B., Ayala, N. F., & Frank, A. G. (2018). The expected contribution of Industry 4.0 technologies for industrial performance. *International Journal of Production Economics, 204*, 383–394. doi:10.1016/j.ijpe.2018.08.019

Eimontaite, I., Gwilt, I., Cameron, D., Aitken, J. M., Rolph, J., Mokaram, S., & Law, J. (2019). Language-free graphical signage improves human performance and reduces anxiety when working collaboratively withe robots. *International Journal of Advanced Manufacturing Technology, 100*(1), 55–73. doi:10.100700170-018-2625-2

ElMaraghy, H., Monostori, L., Schuh, G., & ElMaraghy, W. (2021). Evolution and future of manufacturing systems. *CIRP Annals, 70*(2), 635–658. doi:10.1016/j.cirp.2021.05.008

Factories, A. C. E. (2019). *Human-Centred Factories from eory to Industrial Practice.* Lessons Learned And Recommendations.

Fantini, P., Pinzone, M., & Taisch, M. (2020). Placing the operator at the centre of Industry 4.0 design: Modelling and assessing human activities within cyber-physical systems. *Computers & Industrial Engineering, 139*, 105058. doi:10.1016/j.cie.2018.01.025

Fiasché, M., Pinzone, M., Fantini, P., Alexandru, A., & Taisch, M. (2016, September). Human-centric factories 4.0: A mathematical model for job allocation. In *2016 IEEE 2nd International Forum on Research and Technologies for Society and Industry Leveraging a better tomorrow (RTSI)* (pp. 1-4(. IEEE.

Flemisch, F. O., Bengler, K., Bubb, H., Winner, H., & Bruder, R. (2014). Towards cooperative guidance and control of highly automated vehicles: H-Mode and Conduct-by-Wire. *Ergonomics, 57*(3), 343–360. doi:10.1080/00140139.2013.869355 PMID:24559139

Grandi, F., Peruzzini, M., Zanni, L., Campanella, C. E., & Pellicciari, M. (2018). Digital Manufacturing and Virtual Reality for Tractors' Human-Centred Design. In *Transdisciplinary Engineering Methods for Social Innovation of Industry 4.0.* IOS Press.

Grandi, F., Zanni, L., Peruzzini, M., Pellicciari, M., & Campanella, C. E. (2020). A Transdisciplinary digital approach for tractor's human-centred design. *International Journal of Computer Integrated Manufacturing*, *33*(4), 377–397. doi:10.1080/0951192X.2019.1599441

Green, B. N., Johnson, C. D., & Adams, A. (2006). Writing narrative literature reviews for peer-reviewed journals: Secrets of the trade. *Journal of Chiropractic Medicine*, *3*(3), 101–117. doi:10.1016/S0899-3467(07)60142-6 PMID:19674681

Johansson, J., Abrahamsson, L., Kåreborn, B. B., Fältholm, Y., Grane, C., & Wykowska, A. (2017). Work and organization in a digital industrial context. *Management Review*, 281–297.

Kaasinen, E., Schmalfuß, F., Özturk, C., Aromaa, S., Boubekeur, M., Heilala, J., Heikkilä, P., Kuula, T., Liinasuo, M., Mach, S., Mehta, R., Petäjä, E., & Walter, T. (2020). Empowering and engaging industrial workers with Operator 4.0 solutions. *Computers & Industrial Engineering*, *139*, 105678. doi:10.1016/j.cie.2019.01.052

Kadir, B. A., Broberg, O., & da Conceicao, C. S. (2019). Current research and future perspectives on human factors and ergonomics in Industry 4.0. *Computers & Industrial Engineering*, *137*, 106004. doi:10.1016/j.cie.2019.106004

Kolot, A., Kozmenko, S., Herasymenko, O., & Štreimikienė, D. (2020). Development of a decent work institute as a social quality imperative: Lessons for Ukraine. *Economia e Sociologia*, *13*(2), 70–85. doi:10.14254/2071-789X.2020/13-2/5

Kong, X. T., Luo, H., Huang, G. Q., & Yang, X. (2019). Industrial wearable system: The human-centric empowering technology in Industry 4.0. *Journal of Intelligent Manufacturing*, *30*(8), 2853–2869. doi:10.100710845-018-1416-9

Lagorio, A., Cimini, C., Pirola, F., & Pinto, R. (2021). A Taxonomy of Technologies for Human-Centred Logistics 4.0. *Applied Sciences (Basel, Switzerland)*, *11*(20), 9661. doi:10.3390/app11209661

Lall, M., Torvatn, H., & Seim, E. A. (2017, September). Towards industry 4.0: increased need for situational awareness on the shop floor. In *IFIP international conference on advances in production management systems* (pp. 322–329). Springer. doi:10.1007/978-3-319-66923-6_38

Le Masson, P., Dorst, K., & Subrahmanian, E. (2013). Design theory: History, state of the art and advancements. *Research in Engineering Design*, *24*(2), 97–103. doi:10.100700163-013-0154-4

Li, D., Landström, A., Fast-Berglund, Å., & Almström, P. (2019). Human-centred dissemination of data, information and knowledge in industry 4.0. *Procedia CIRP*, *84*, 380–386. doi:10.1016/j.procir.2019.04.261

Li, D., Paulin, D., Fast-Berglund, Å., Gullander, P., & Bligård, L. O. (2018, November). Supporting individual needs for intra-organizational knowledge sharing activities in pre-industry 4.0 SMEs. *15th International Conference on Intellectual Capital, Knowledge Management and Organisational Learning, ICICKM 2018*, 160-170.

Longo, F., Nicoletti, L., & Padovano, A. (2019). Modeling workers' behavior: A human factors taxonomy and a fuzzy analysis in the case of industrial accidents. *International Journal of Industrial Ergonomics*, *69*, 29–47. doi:10.1016/j.ergon.2018.09.002

Longo, F., Padovano, A., & Umbrello, S. (2020). Value-oriented and ethical technology engineering in industry 5.0: A human-centric perspective for the design of the factory of the future. *Applied Sciences (Basel, Switzerland), 10*(12), 4182. doi:10.3390/app10124182

Lu, Y., Zheng, H., Chand, S., Xia, W., Liu, Z., Xu, X., Wang, L., Qin, Z., & Bao, J. (2022). Outlook on human-centric manufacturing towards Industry 5.0. *Journal of Manufacturing Systems, 62*, 612–627. doi:10.1016/j.jmsy.2022.02.001

Marcucci, G., Antomarioni, S., Ciarapica, F. E., & Bevilacqua, M. (2021). The impact of Operations and IT-related Industry 4.0 key technologies on organizational resilience. *Production Planning and Control*, 1–15.

Maroncelli, S., & Castagnoli, R. (2022). Human-centred manufacturing: quale ruolo per la sociologia della persona? In *XXII incontro giovani Pontignano – Sociologia*. Persona e Sfera pubblica.

May, G., Taisch, M., Bettoni, A., Maghazei, O., Matarazzo, A., & Stahl, B. (2015). A new human-centric factory model. *Procedia CIRP, 26*, 103–108. doi:10.1016/j.procir.2014.07.112

Mazali, T. (2018). From industry 4.0 to society 4.0, there and back. *AI & Society, 33*(3), 405–411. doi:10.100700146-017-0792-6

Moencks, M., Roth, E., Bohné, T., Romero, D., & Stahre, J. (2022). Augmented Workforce Canvas: A management tool for guiding human-centric, value-driven human-technology integration in industry. *Computers & Industrial Engineering, 163*, 107803. doi:10.1016/j.cie.2021.107803

Müller, J. M., Kiel, D., & Voigt, K. I. (2018). What drives the implementation of Industry 4.0? The role of opportunities and challenges in the context of sustainability. *Sustainability, 10*(1), 247. doi:10.3390u10010247

Ngoc, H., Lasa, G., & Iriarte, I. (2022). Human-centred design in industry 4.0: Case study review and opportunities for future research. *Journal of Intelligent Manufacturing, 33*(1), 35–76. doi:10.100710845-021-01796-x PMID:34149201

Oliveira, M., Arica, E., Pinzone, M., Fantini, P., & Taisch, M. (2019, July). Human-centered manufacturing challenges affecting European industry 4.0 enabling technologies. In *International Conference on Human-Computer Interaction*. Springer. 10.1007/978-3-030-30033-3_39

Paredes-Astudillo, Y. A., Jimenez, J. F., Zambrano-Rey, G., & Trentesaux, D. (2019, October). Human-Machine Cooperation for the Distributed Control of a Hybrid Control Architecture. In *International Workshop on Service Orientation in Holonic and Multi-Agent Manufacturing* (pp. 98-110). Springer.

Pautasso, M. (2019). The structure and conduct of a narrative literature review. A Guide to the Scientific Career. *Virtues, Communication, Research and Academic Writing*, 299-310.

Peruzzini, M., Grandi, F., & Pellicciari, M. (2018). How to analyse the workers' experience in integrated product-process design. *Journal of Industrial Information Integration, 12*, 31–46. doi:10.1016/j.jii.2018.06.002

Peruzzini, M., Grandi, F., & Pellicciari, M. (2020). Exploring the potential of Operator 4.0 interface and monitoring. *Computers & Industrial Engineering, 139*, 105600. doi:10.1016/j.cie.2018.12.047

Peruzzini, M., & Pellicciari, M. (2017). A framework to design a human-centred adaptive manufacturing system for aging workers. *Advanced Engineering Informatics*, *33*, 330–349. doi:10.1016/j.aei.2017.02.003

Pinzone, M., Albè, F., Orlandelli, D., Barletta, I., Berlin, C., Johansson, B., & Taisch, M. (2020). A framework for operative and social sustainability functionalities in Human-Centric Cyber-Physical Production Systems. *Computers & Industrial Engineering*, *139*, 105132. doi:10.1016/j.cie.2018.03.028

Rauch, E., Linder, C., & Dallasega, P. (2020). Anthropocentric perspective of production before and within Industry 4.0. *Computers & Industrial Engineering*, *139*, 105644. doi:10.1016/j.cie.2019.01.018

Reiman, A., Kaivo-oja, J., Parviainen, E., Takala, E. P., & Lauraeus, T. (2021). Human factors and ergonomics in manufacturing in the industry 4.0 context–A scoping review. *Technology in Society*, *65*, 101572. doi:10.1016/j.techsoc.2021.101572

Romero, D., Bernus, P., Noran, O., Stahre, J., & Fast-Berglund, Å. (2016a). The operator 4. 0: Human cyber-physical systems & adaptive automation towards human-automation symbiosis work systems. In *IFIP international conference on advances in production management system* (pp. 677–686). Springer. doi:10.1007/978-3-319-51133-7_80

Romero, D., Noran, O., Stahre, J., Bernus, P., & Fast-Berglund, Å. (2015, September). Towards a human-centred reference architecture for next generation balanced automation systems: human-automation symbiosis. In *IFIP international conference on advances in production management systems* (pp. 556–566). Springer. doi:10.1007/978-3-319-22759-7_64

Romero, D., Stahre, J., Wuest, T., Noran, O., Bernus, P., Fast-Berglund, Å., & Gorecky, D. (2016b, October). Towards an operator 4.0 typology: a human-centric perspective on the fourth industrial revolution technologies. *Proceedings of the international conference on computers and industrial engineering (CIE46)*, 29-31.

Şahinel, D., Akpolat, C., Görür, O. C., Sivrikaya, F., & Albayrak, S. (2021). Human modeling and interaction in cyber-physical systems: A reference framework. *Journal of Manufacturing Systems*, *59*, 367–385. doi:10.1016/j.jmsy.2021.03.002

Snyder, H. (2019). Literature review as a research methodology: An overview and guidelines. *Journal of Business Research*, *104*, 333–339. doi:10.1016/j.jbusres.2019.07.039

Taskan, B., Junça-Silva, A., & Caetano, A. (2022). Clarifying the conceptual map of VUCA: A systematic review. *International Journal of Organizational Analysis*.

Taylor, M. P., Boxall, P., Chen, J. J., Xu, X., Liew, A., & Adeniji, A. (2020). Operator 4.0 or Maker 1.0? Exploring the implications of Industrie 4.0 for innovation, safety and quality of work in small economies and enterprises. *Computers & Industrial Engineering*, *139*, 105486. doi:10.1016/j.cie.2018.10.047

Torraco, R. J. (2005). Writing integrative literature reviews: Guidelines and examples. *Human Resource Development Review*, *4*(3), 356–367. doi:10.1177/1534484305278283

Torraco, R. J. (2016). Writing integrative reviews of the literature: Methods and purposes. *International Journal of Adult Vocational Education and Technology*, *7*(3), 62–70. doi:10.4018/IJAVET.2016070106

Webster, J., & Watson, R. T. (2002). Analyzing the past to prepare for the future: Writing a literature review. *Management Information Systems Quarterly*, xiii–xxiii.

Wheeldon, J., & Faubert, J. (2009). Framing experience: Concept maps, mind maps, and data collection in qualitative research. *International Journal of Qualitative Methods*, *8*(3), 68–83. doi:10.1177/160940690900800307

Xu, X., Lu, Y., Vogel-Heuser, B., & Wang, L. (2021). Industry 4.0 and Industry 5.0—Inception, conception and perception. *Journal of Manufacturing Systems*, *61*, 530–535. doi:10.1016/j.jmsy.2021.10.006

Zamfirescu, C. B., Pirvu, B. C., Gorecky, D., & Chakravarthy, H. (2014). Human-centred assembly: A case study for an anthropocentric cyber-physical system. *Procedia Technology*, *15*, 90–98. doi:10.1016/j.protcy.2014.09.038

APPENDIX

Table 4. Articoli analizzati. Source: own elaboration

Autori e anno
Fiaschè et al., 2016
Cirillo et al., 2021
Grandi et al., 2018
Longo et al., 2020
Kong et al., 2019
Kaasinen et al., 2020
Eimontaite et al., 2018
El Maraghy et al., 2021
Flemish et al., 2014
Grandi et al., 2020
Peruzzini et al., 2020
Reiman et al., 2021
Moenks et al., 2022
Caputo et al., 209
Kadir et al., 2019
Cillo et al., 2021
Carayannis et al., 2021
Chen et al., 2021
Zamifrescu et al., 2014
Johansson et al., 2017
Lagorio et al., 2021
Lall et al., 2017
Li et al., 2019
Li et al., 2018
May et al., 2015
Parades et al., 2019
Peruzzini et al., 2018
Peruzzini & Pellicciari, 2017
Romero et al., 2015
Fantini et al., 2020
Lu et al., 2022
Pinzone et al., 2020
Kolot et al., 2020
Longo et al., 2020
Ngoc et al., 2022
Rauch et al., 2020
Şahinel et al., 2020
Taylor et al., 2020
Briken, 2020
Romero et al., 2016a
Romero et al., 2016b
Oliveira et al., 2019
Caldarola et al., 2018
Bauer et al., 2019
Mazali et al., 2018

Table 5. Characteristics of the sample. Source: own elaboration

Authors	Years	Type of contributions	Focus of the analysis (I4.0 o I5.0)	Levels of analysis	Value chain phase	Approach (conceptual/ empirical)	Research methodology (qualitative, quantitative, mixed)	Research design (case studies, interviews, survey, focus groups, literature review, simulation/ programming/other)	Unit of analysis (start up, multinational corporates, public corporates, SME…)	Disciplines	Ranking CABS
Fiaschè et al.	2016	IEEE 2nd International Forum on Research and Technologies for Society and Industry Leveraging a better tomorrow (RTSI)	I4.0	Value chain	Planning and organizing production	Conceptual	-	-	Manufacturing	Engineering	Conference
Cirillo et al.	2021	Structural Change and Economic Dynamics	I4.0	Value chain	Organization	Empirical	Qualitative method	Interviews with workers, union delegates and middle-managers	3 high-tech automotive factories with a Toyota/ taylorist/Mitbestimmung manufacturing system	Economics	2
Grandi et al.	2018	Transdisciplinary Engineering Methods for Social Innovation of Industry 4.0	I4.0	Value chain	Production	Empirical	Quantitative method	Test cases	Automotive	Engineering (Design)	-
Longo et al.	2020a	Applied science	I4.0 and I5.0	Value chain	Production	Empirical	Quantitative method	Survey + 3 case studies	All sectors	Engineering (Design)	-
Kong et al.	2019	Journal of Intelligent Manufacturing	I4.0	Value chain	Product design	Empirical	Qualitative method	3 case studies	3 european projects (safety, production and mantenaince)	Engineering (Design)	1
Kaasinen et al.	2020	Computers & Industrial Engineering	I4.0	Value chain	Production and production planning	Empirical	Qualitative method	3 case studies + 44 interviews	Manufacturing	Engineering (Design)	2
Eimontaite et al.	2018	The International Journal of Advanced Manufacturing Technology	I4.0	Value chain	Production	Empirical	Quantitative method	1 case study (test case)	1 manufacturing firm, 3 groups of 30 employees	Engineering	-
El Maraghy et al.	2021	CIRP annals manufacturing technology	I4.0 (I5.0 is only mentioned)	Value chain	Production	Conceptual	Qualitative method	Review of use cases and Horizon 2020 projects	Case studies and Horizon 2020 projects	Engineering	Conference
Flemish et al.	2014	Ergonomics		Value chain	Product design	Empirical	Mixed methods	2 case studies	Manufacturing	Industrial engineering	3
Grandi et al.	2020	International Journal of Computer Integrated Manufacturing	I4.0	Value chain	Product design	Empirical	Quantitative method	2 experiments	Manufacturing (production of a tractore)	Transdisciplinary Engineering (TE)	2
Peruzzini et al.	2020	Computers & Industrial Engineering	I4.0	Value chain	Assembly line	Empirical	Qualitative method	1 case study	CNH; Industrial, a global manufacturer of agriculture and industrial vehicles	Engineering of systems	2
Reiman et al.	2021	Technology in Society	I4.0 (I5.0 is only mentioned)	Value chain	-	Conceptual	Qualitative method	Literature review (scoping review)	336 papers, 37 of which related to manufacture	Engineering	-
Moenks et al.	2022	Computers & Industrial Engineering	I4.0	Value chain	Design, development, refinement, testing	Empirical	Qualitative method	39 industry expert interviews, the Canvas was co-designed and developed in 13 workshop sessions, refined and tested in 12 working sessions by industry practitioners, and evaluated in three industry case studies	Several industries	Industrial engineering	2
Caputo et al.	2019	Production & Manufacturing research	I4.0	Value chain	Assembly line	Empirical	Quantitative method	Test case	1 automotive company	Engineering (Design)	-
Kadir et al.	2019	Computers & Industrial Engineering	I4.0	Value chain	Operational level	Conceptual	Mixed methods	Systematic litterature review		Industrial engineering	2
Cillo et al.	2021	Journal of knowledge management	I5.0	Value chain	-	Empirical	Quantitative method	Secondary data (from Refinitiv)	Longitudinal analysis of 7158 firm over a time span of 5 years	Management	-
Carayannis et al.	2021	Journal of the Knowledge Economy	I5.0 and Society 5.0	Ecosystem (macro, meso and micro level analysis)	Ecosystem (internal value chain excluded)	Empirical	Mixed methods	1 case study	Aereospace	Engineering	-
Chen et al.	2021	Journal of operations research	I4.0	Value chain	Predictive maintenance	Empirical	Qualitative method	1 case study	SMEs	Industrial engineering	3
Zamifrescu et al.	2014	Procedia technology	-	Value chain	Assembly line	Empirical	Quantitative method	1 use case	Manufacturing	Engineering (Design)	Conference
Johansson et al.	2017	Management Revue	I4.0	Value chain	-	Conceptual	-	-	-	Management	-
Lagorio et al.	2021	Applied science	I4.0	Value chain	Internal logistics	Conceptual	Deductive method	Litterature review (taxonomy)	-	Management	-
Lall et al.	2017	International IFIP WG 5.7 Conference on Advances in Production Management Systems (APMS)	I4.0	Value chain	Shop floor	Empirical	Qualitative method (participative tradition of action research)	3 case studies	Manufacturing	Management	Conference
Li et al.	2019	29th CIRP Design 2019	I4.0	Value chain	Information acquisition/ decision making	Conceptual	Qualitative method	Litterature review	Manufacturing/15 essays	Engineering/ management	Conference

continued on following page

Table 5. Continued

Authors	Years	Type of contributions	Focus of the analysis (I4.0 o I5.0)	Levels of analysis	Value chain phase	Approach (conceptual/ empirical)	Research methodology (qualitative, quantitative, mixed)	Research design (case studies, interviews, survey, focus groups, literature review, simulation/ programming/other)	Unit of analysis (start up, multinational corporates, public corporates, SME…)	Disciplines	Ranking CABS
Li et al.	2018	Proceedings of the International Conference on Intellectual Capital, Knowledge Management & Organizational Learning	I4.0	Value chain	-	Empirical	Mixed methods	2 case studies	Manufacturing/ 16 interviews and 17 questionaires	Engineering/ management	Conference
May et al.	2015	12th Global Conference on Sustainable Manufacturing	-	-	Workplaces	Conceptual	Qualitative methods	Literature review	-	Interdisciplinary	Conference
Parades et al.	2019	Service oriented, holonic and multi-agent manufacturing systems for industry of the future	I4.0	-	Labor organization	Empirical	Quantitative method	Experiment	Manufacturing	Industrial engineering	Conference
Peruzzini et al.	2018	Journal of Industrial Information Integration	I4.0	Value chain	Design	Empirical	-	2 case studies	Manufacturing and agriculture	Engineering (Design)	-
Peruzzini & Pellicciari	2017	Advanced Engineering Informatics	I4.0	Value chain	Decision making	Empirical	Quantitative method	Industrial use case	Manufacturing (woodworking)	Engineering	-
Romero et al.	2015	APMS 2015 – Advacnces in Production Management Systems: Innovative production management towards sustainable growth	-	Value chain		Conceptual			Manufacturing	Engineering	Conference
Fantini et al.	2020	Computers and Industrial Engineering	I4.0	Value chain	Maintenance	Empirical	Quantitative method	2 case studies	2 firms (production of compressors and aerospace)	Industrial engineering	2
Lu et al.	2022	Journal of Manufacturing Systems	I5.0	Value chain		Conceptual				Engineering of systems	1
Pinzone et al.	2020	Computers & Industrial Engineering	I4.0	Value chain		Conceptual and empirical	Qualitative method	Narrative literature review + validation of guide-lines through a manifacturing case study	Papers + manufacturing	Industrial engineering	2
Kolot et al.	2020	Economics & Sociology	I4.0	Value chain		Conceptual				Sociology	1
Longo et al.	2020b	International Journal of Industrial Ergonomics	I4.0	Value chain		Empirical	Qualitative method	Fuzzy analytic hierarchy process	44 industries experts		1
Ngoc et al.	2022	Journal of Intelligent Manufacturing	I4.0	Value chain	Process design	Conceptual	Qualitative method	Systematic litterature review	77 papers	Engineering (Design)	1
Rauch et al.	2020	Computers & Industrial Engineering	I4.0	Value chain	Production	Conceptual and empirical	Qualitative method	Systematic litterature review	58 papers	Engineering (Design)	2
Şahinel et al.	2021	Journal of Manufacturing Systems		Value chain		Empirical	Qualitative method	1 case study		Industrial engineering	1
Taylor et al.	2020	Computers and Industrial Engineering	I4.0	Value chain		Conceptual	Qualitative method			Industrial engineering	2
Briken	2020	Capital & Class		Value chain		Conceptual	Qualitative method			Sociology	-
Romero et al.	2016a	IFIP international conference on advances in production management systems (pp. 677-686)	I4.0	Value chain		Conceptual				Engineering	Conference
Romero et al.	2016b	CIE46 Proceedings	I4.0	Value chain		Conceptual				Engineering	Conference
Oliveira et al.	2019	HCI International 2019 – Late Breaking Papers	I4.0	Value chian		Empirical	Qualitative method	2 case study	2 case studies about european projects in manufacturing industries	Engineering	Conference
Caldarola et al.	2018	International Journal on Advances in Intelligent Systems,	I4.0	Value chain	Production	Empirical and conceptual	Mixed methods	1 interpretive case study (qualitative interviews and survey)	Manufacturing (wooden furniture)	Engineering	-
Bauer et al.	2019	Procedia Manufacturing	I4.0	Value chiain	Shop floor	Empirical	Qualitative methods	1 case study (projects)	1 research project funded by the German goverment	Engineering	Conference
Mazali et al.	2018	AI & SOCIETY	I4.0	Value chain	Design	Empirical	Quantitative method	Survey	Italian manufacturing companies	Sociology	-

Chapter 6
Towards an Automated, Vigilant, and Strategic HRM Function in Industry 5.0

Pramit Banerjee
https://orcid.org/0000-0003-3832-1937
Indian Institute of Foreign Trade, India

ABSTRACT

The chapter references technological applications' advancements in the HRM function and suggests the revised HRM function in Industry 5.0. In the first part, a brief background has been given on the technological advancements in the function followed by an extensive literature review of the ongoing and probable application areas of technologies in HRM function. Subsequently, the author develops certain models of operations that the HRs will have to follow, which will help in imbibing the technological practices of machine learning, artificial intelligence, blockchain while adhering to the data privacy practices. Thus, this approach makes the HRM function more automated but vigilant and strategic simultaneously so that HRs can monitor and control the cobots in Industry 5.0.

INTRODUCTION

The HRM function is witnessing a drastic change in how it operates in industry 4.0 as more and more applications of automation and robotics are coming into the picture. In the wake of this digital revolution, many managers are constantly updating themselves in terms of the latest tools and technologies being used in the HRMS. At the same time, some are still sceptical about using people analytics and other technological advances in the domain. In both US and China, many solutions related to the application of AI and automation in HR function are being deployed so that the people in HR function can partner for a transformational journey which will improve the overall function and efficiency at work (Brin, 2019). No wonder, as we move towards the next industrial revolution, robots will start working alongside humans in the manufacturing sectors and in other service sectors, the robots will be helping the humans to maximize the efficiency of the processes. It is the collaborative efforts of the man

DOI: 10.4018/978-1-6684-6745-9.ch006

and the robots that will thrive in the industry 5.0 where the robots will continue to play its active role in the manufacturing process whereas the humans will step in, with their creative part providing the feedback in the manufacturing process before creation of the final product and thus by complementing each other in the production process, the collaborative robots will play an important role in industry 5.0 (Østergaard, 2016). As per the latest report by Cognizant, with the ushering of AI and automation, the human resources professionals need to play the role of being the detective of the HR data where they can investigate the different patterns of data originating from IT systems, a survey of employees, attendance systems etc., and thus understand the behavioural patterns of the employees and be aware of the pulse of the organization through the employee sentiments and emotions (Brown *et al.*, 2020). In this regard, the role of HR managers must be much more than just remaining confined to the traditional HRMS software and interacting with humans on an ad-hoc basis. This chapter thus focuses on the revised role of HR in the upcoming industrial revolution, i.e., industry 5.0 and how they will be contributing to the overall organizational success. The first section of this chapter focuses on reviewing the literature, while the subsequent sections focus on constructing the conceptual frameworks based on which the HRM functions would be operating, while referring to the relevant literature. The author also raises a few questions further on what could be the challenges and the road ahead while stressing on the fact that it will be the HR managers who will be playing a more controlling, strategic and vigilant role while upgrading themselves to the latest technological offerings required in this function.

BACKGROUND

The sequence of industrial revolutions starting from the first to the fourth saw the dramatic shift from manual labour to automated systems propelled by electronic and software developments, which involved changes in the way manufacturing was done and the way the HR professionals were willing to re-orient themselves in this wake of such revolutions (Xu *et al.*, 2021; Piwowar-SULEJ, 2020; Poba-Nzaou *et al.*, 2021). Through focus group interviews, authors have set up a four-step process of how the future of business in industry 4.0 will look and it involves the sections of technology, business, society and people (Schiele *et al.*, 2022). Technologies like digital twins, AI, blockchain, cyber-physical systems will influence businesses to focus on products covering the entire life cycle, creating customized products and solutions, all aimed at sustainable development, and social inclusivity so that finally the HR starts focusing on the technology enabled workforce, promoting self-management for employees and creating a culture of continuous learning (Schiele *et al.*, 2022). Some of the challenges that the HRM function has faced amidst the covid-19 crisis are understanding the shift in behavioural patterns of the employees, directing, controlling with some of the suitable measures through innovative HRM practices, starting new initiatives as people shifted to working from any place model, keeping the employee motivated and managing the pool of talent as people started leaving for more paid jobs (Azizi *et al.*, 2021). Moreover, the covid pandemic has pushed HR to think further on advancing from the technological point of view and many organizations are investing in revamping HR technologies by upgrading them through the applications of AI and ML. Through analysis on the Spanish firms, it was found that although AI adoption was low in those firms, the perception of the employees and managers revealed that AI could pinpoint the tailored skills that the particular employees require for upskilling thereby saving time, filtering the resumes during recruitment process and identifying the best suitable candidate for the job, highlighting the efforts of the employees during work thus identifying who is more deserving for the next promotion and thus it is expected that the applications of AI is expected to increase further in HRM function (Kambur & Akar, 2022). Bhatt (2022), through the Delphi methodology found that out of the seven factors which influence HR managers to adopt AI practices in recruitment, the top three factors were the security of data and information, the return on the investments made on these tools and technologies to implement the solutions and the validity of the context which the AI is going to consider while filtering the applications about the future task that will be assigned to them in the organization. Bhatt and Muduli (2022) mentioned that the application of AI in the functions of learning and development of the HR will help in the overall efficiency in the process by verification of the learners, creating tailored materials for the learners, monitoring and checking the progress and generating the reports specific to each employee to track the progress. Further, applying such algorithms will promote creativity among the learners as it will generate self-awareness, curiosity and areas of improvement among the learners which would otherwise be too time-consuming and costly (Bhatt and Muduli, 2022). Chowdhury *et al.* (2022) developed a framework which integrated the resources required for AI capability which will subsequently determine the usage of automation and understanding how it will impact the workforce like characteristics of the job, the autonomy of the employees, the structure of teams, the levels of job satisfaction and innovativeness of their employees which will finally be impacting the organizational efficiency, satisfaction of the customers and the overall image of the brand. Arslan *et al.* (2022) has highlighted that the HR function needs to strategize in terms of creating training initiatives, developing a clear communication plan to be circulated to the employees, segregating the roles and expectations form the humans at work, the level of collaboration among the humans and machines and understanding the issues and obstacles of the humans at work in the upcoming industrial revolution so that it helps to mitigate the tension, anxiety related to job loss due to automation, resistance to acquiring new skills and uplifting the employee morale and motivation at work while ensuring their performance doesn't get hampered due to the negative thoughts. Shet *et al.* (2021) highlighted the challenges faced in implementing data analytics in HR domain that had more focus on the descriptive side instead of the predictive part along with the lack of integration of the analytics solution in the HRMS portal and the authors also proposed a framework for the adoption of data analytics which involved different factors from technological to organizational, environmental, data governance and individual factors which if followed will help the HRM function to consider the entire stakeholder point of view while analyzing the data thus generated. The influence of AI-based technology in the recruitment process will surely lessen the time required to recruit an ideal candidate as AI will have the capability to promote and advertise the latest openings in the organization, screen the resumes to find out the potential fit candidates, send the offer letters to the selected candidates which would otherwise consume more time and effort for the humans involved in this function ("Swift and Efficient: Using Artificial Intelligence to Enhance the Talent Acquisition Process," 2021). Zhang *et al.* (2021) mentioned the benefits of the application of big data analysis within the HRM function and proposed three levels primarily i.e., the micro level of analysis where the data related to the behaviour and interactions of the employees within the team can be analyzed and understood, the meso level of analysis where the integration of such level of data can be analyzed and finally at the macro level where the HR will be able to model such data and predict from the metrics within the HR sub-functions which will pave the way for enhanced decision making. Dhanpat *et al.* (2020) mentioned the shift of HR role from being administrative and transactional in nature to a more strategic and technology-oriented where the HR would need to identify the skill gaps in the existing workforce, provide relevant training in line with the technologies of industry 4.0, ensuring that the right people are deployed in the related projects and maintaining a continuous talent pool for smooth operations. While sustainability is one of the factors that will be stressed in industry 5.0, some of the major challenges that will be seen while implementing technology in industry 5.0 will be the learning attitudes and human behaviour as they people start working with robots, the social and psychological effects on the employees, the legal and ethical perspectives (Demir *et al.*, 2019). Humayun & Arabia (2021) has highlighted that through the collaborative efforts of the skills of the human, the automation capabilities of machines and emphasizing human centricity, sustainability and resilience, the fifth industrial revolution will enhance the interaction between humans and machines, improve the quality of service, reduce both costs and hazards on the environments. Saxena *et al.* (2021) has put forward a thought provoking scenario where they have mentioned that the human robot collaboration in industry 5.0 will lead to a more diversified and evolving role of HR as they would now have to understand both the man and the machine by analyzing the productivity and performance of cobots, identifying the level of coordination, the creativity involved, the utilization of the skills gathered by them and gathering feedback from internal cobots and understanding the market sentiments. An upcoming vigilant role for the HR in terms of analyzing the behaviour of individuals which impact the business in turn, the work as a detective to unearth patterns in data, identification of any bias in the algorithms and humans as the machines and man start working together in industry 5.0 (Brown *et al.*, 2020) as a possibility in the further near-term challenges the process mentioned above and framework. As we move forward towards the next industrial revolution, the organizations will shift their focus from making only profits to applying a more people centric and environment-cautious approach thus adding value to society at large (Breque *et al.*, 2021). A more human-centric approach will be the focus where the systems and processes will adapt to the needs of the workers and employees in the industrial production instead of the other way round, along with the focus on reducing waste through the circular process of production to reduce harmful effect on the environment and thus making the production process more robust such that it can withstand any abrupt disruptions like covid-19 or any other noise in the daily operations (Breque *et al.*, 2021). The above literature has given us enough insights as to why HR would need to further re-invent itself as a function that would contribute to the business and the organization's overall health by monitoring, controlling and effective management techniques while harnessing the latest technologies available. In the subsequent sections, the different process and conceptual frameworks have been constructed to highlight some of the new ways that the HRM function might adopt while focusing on the relevant further literature.

STRUCTURE OF HRM FUNCTIONS IN INDUSTRY 5.0

From the literature that has been discussed in the previous section, it is quite clear that the HRM function will hardly have any operational role, rather, a vigilant and strategic role is being desired out of the HRs in the industry 5.0. To come out with exactly what will be the role of the structure of the HRM functions and the role of HRs, the author initially delves into the technology-aligned role of the HR in its different sub-functions which are discussed one by one.

Recruitment and Selection HRM Function

=The recruitment and selection function are currently seeing a lot of applications of niche technologies like machine learning and blockchain while the HRs of tomorrow prepares themselves for equipping themselves with the knowledge of such technologies. Through a sample survey across certain employees, managers and HR recruiters in an organization it was found that although there was some resistance of the application of AI in recruiting and selection of employees in terms of the accuracy of the filtering of assessments, there was a positive response among the managers and recruiters that it would save them much time and effort and in long run, it would not only be the technology or AI, but the collaboration of specialized HR skills which will complement the AI for better recruitment, selection and onboarding process of employees (Niehueser & Boak, 2020).

Figure 1. Talent recruitment system overview

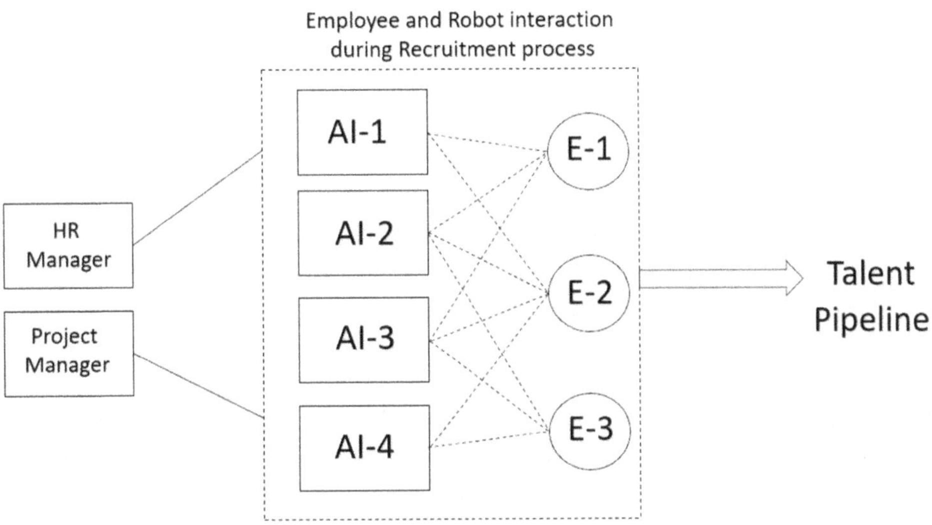

The above figure shows the overall view of the system of recruitment and selection that can bring the automated systems and humans closer to work together thereby saving time and effort. The AI-1,2,3,4 as mentioned in the figure, are the AI-enabled learning systems which will interact with employees E1, E2 and E3 as highlighted above. Through the interactions of the man and machine, the details will be shared in the talent pipeline which will be accessible to the entire network of HR and project managers.

Continuing with the discussion and as seen in the above figure, a blockchain-based recruitment system will be enabled so that the talent pool visibility will be there for all the relevant stakeholders in the recruitment process (especially the HR and project managers). The metrics and analytics will be displayed in the systems and the HR will have visibility on how the AI-based systems are performing the resume scans and the recommendation systems and will only need to work on the select few resumes of the candidates, thereby saving their time and effort. However, in applying the solutions of AI in functions of recruitment, and selection, special care needs to be taken so that there is no effect on the unconscious bias of the algorithms and if done properly, this would pave way for the revolutionary change in the corresponding HR functions (Brin, 2019). Thus, the super users in the systems, will have control to the systems in case of any discrepancy and can act on behalf of the HR in case of any emergency or data retrieval.

Figure 2. Blockchain enabled recruitment system

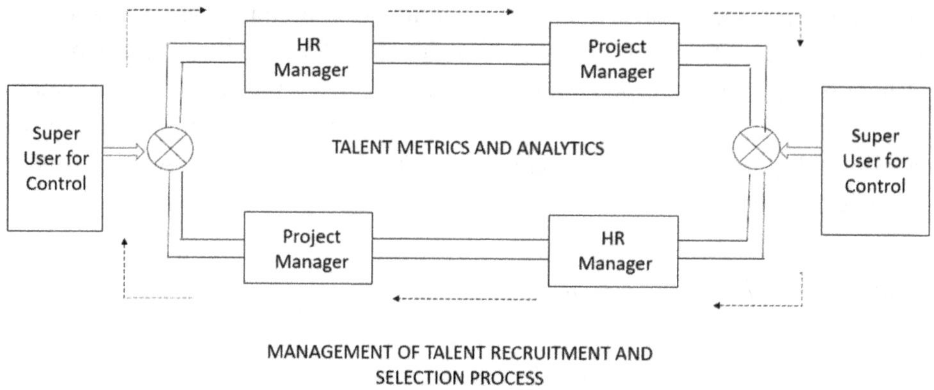

Learning and Development HRM Function

The learning and development function, considered an essential strategic function for generating in-house talent, will largely be influenced by technology in the upcoming technological revolution. Gautam (2022) has highlighted the importance of re-skilling and upskilling both the blue- and white-collar employees in the organization amidst the advent of industry 5.0 as they will have to adapt to the upcoming changes and equip themselves with the data and automation-related skills while pointing out through different reports that automation and AI will lead to economic growth of the nation and benefit of the employees at large thus driving away the fear of job losses and replacement of the humans by the robots. Tiwari (2022), while stating the need for the upskilling of employees, mentioned the need of an appropriate framework amidst the digital disruption in the workplace so that the organization can select the correct tools and technologies and enforce the latest processes reducing waste along with the focus on the people which will ultimately help them to stay ahead of the competitor in this digital landscape. It has thus become essential to re-imagine the system of the training and development function within HR, which imbibes the latest technologies.

The above figure shows from the process perspective, how the HRs will be interacting with the employees and the automated systems to monitor, train and develop the employees. The employee will interact with the AI enabled robotic systems installed in the functions which will respond to the queries, provide them feedback on the weak areas and give them a overview of the strengths and the journey to progress. The learning metrics will be captured and they will be stored in the cloud, which will be accessible to the HR as well and they in turn will be able to provide feedback to the HR as well as the AI enabled systems that is providing the feedback to the employee. Thus, through this way, a better transparency will be generated and HR will remain vigilant about the robotic process and control their actions as well as have the human touch and feel with the employees, which is the need of the times in industry 5.0.

Performance Management HRM Function

Although there have been many analytical applications in performance management and appraisal systems, some gaps still exist in terms of real-time visibility and feedback for the employees. Prassida & Asfari (2021) established a conceptual framework for embracing the collaborative robots in industry 5.0

Figure 3. Training and development system overview

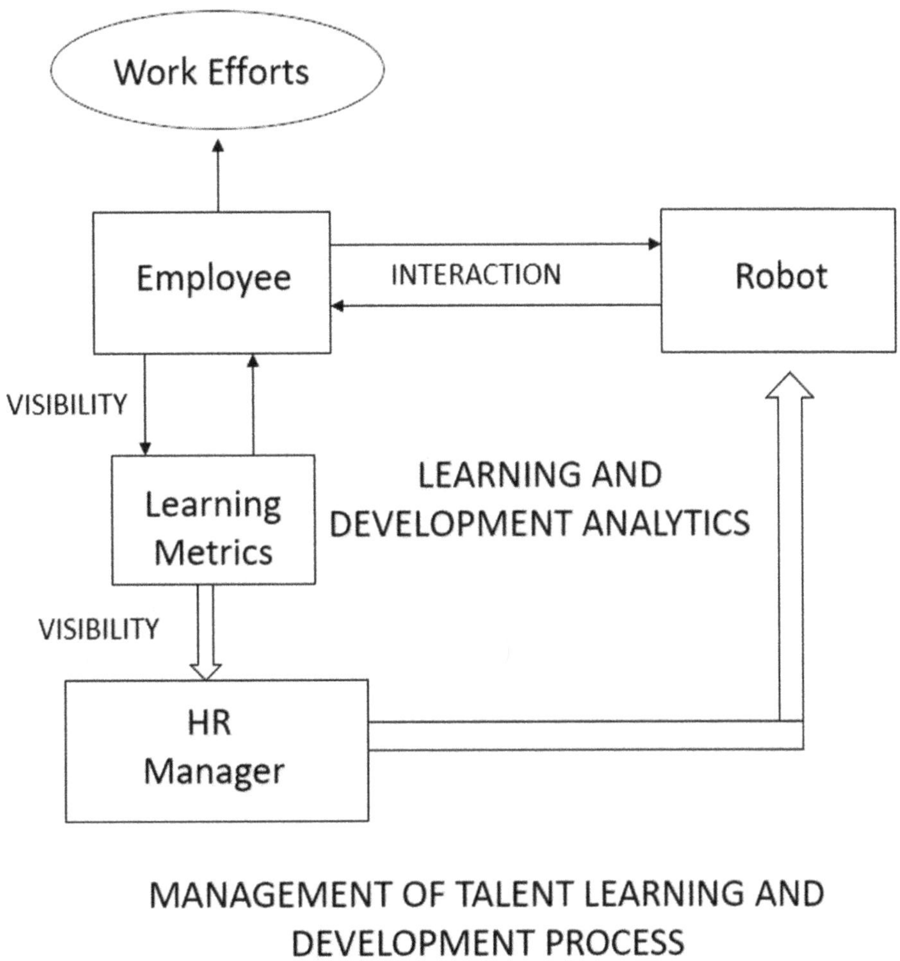

which had factors of expectancy of performance, the expectancy of effort and other facilitating conditions for understanding the intention of using the cobots. Chillakuri and Attili (2021) through a case research methodology generated some insights on how blockchain technology would influence the HR function and came to the conclusion that distributed systems will enable more transparency among the HR for validation of employee data, enable visibility of employees for better deployment in projects and the enhanced security features which will help to protect the privacy of the data of the employees within the organization. The integration of collaborative efforts of the robots and humans will be integrated through a social and technical sub-system which can be tracked and adjusted as and when necessary for better efficiency and productivity (Prassida & Asfari, 2021). Technological applications of industry 5.0 especially the digital twins, AI-enabled smart performance management systems will enable the HRs to appropriately track and award the based performance based on the consensus of all the stakeholders involved.

The integration of the feedback and the people involved in performance management within the systems will be one of the major challenges going forward. The above figure thus shows the overall picture

Figure 4. Interconnected performance management systems

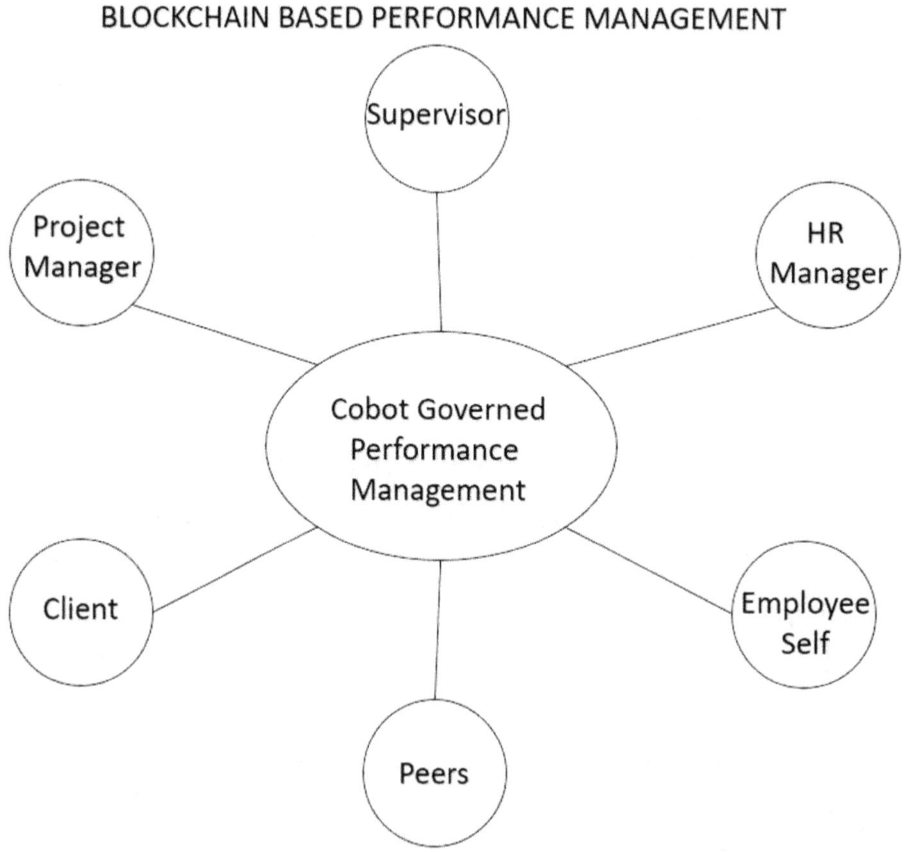

of the stakeholders who will be playing an active role in an individual's robot-governed performance management systems. This will be achieved through the application of blockchain systems through which there will be transparency among the employees and other stakeholders as to where the current performance stands concerning the others so that there is little room for complain in the later stages of the process. Thus, through this robust process laid through systems, monitoring the real-time situations in daily operations and active participation of people, the performance management systems can be improved to cater by bringing transparency and aptly rewarding the deserved. Thereby, HR will play a more vigilant and strategic role in ascertaining the steps that need to be tailored for every employee rather than focusing on the process.

Employee Engagement and Monitoring through ML and AI Applications

The interaction between HR and the cobots will be a major breakthrough in industry 5.0. This is because it will be difficult to manage the collaborative robots and the humans with the same techniques that are being used in silos in industry 4.0. Studies have shown why and how the quantification of the HRM function can be done which may involve metrics within the HRM function for understanding the descriptive part of the behaviour of the organization. This analytics part would be able to bridge the gap

Figure 5. Machine learning based HRM system involving human machine collaboration

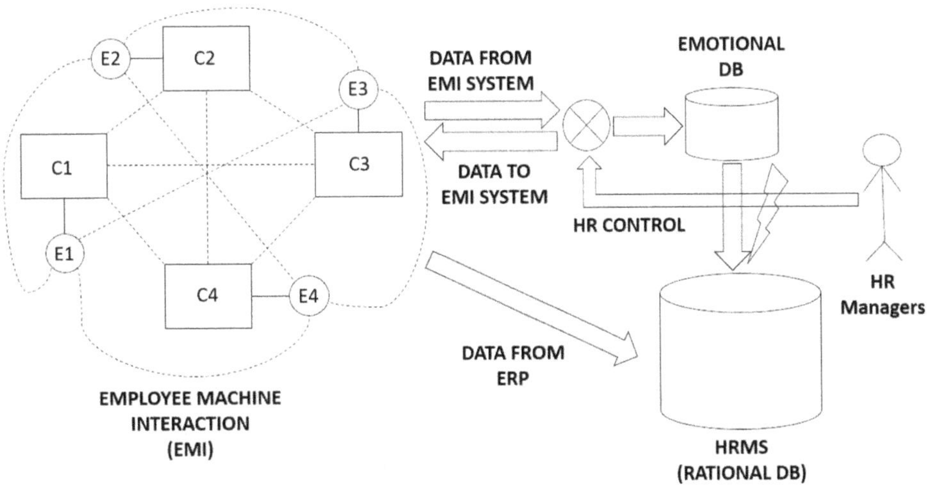

between employee performance and organizational benefit, the use of AI and other algorithms using the big data which would help in predicting the probable states of corresponding sub-functions of HRM and thereby helping in taking decisions more effectively and accurately (Coron, 2022). With quantifying the function and operational areas in the HR domain, we will see more applications of ML and AI here and more so as robots start collaborating with the humans and generating more data. Through a case study of the organization Tech Mahindra, it was shown how they had digitized the human resource management functions by applying automation, artificial intelligence and leveraging latest technological advancements of industry 4.0, thereby staying ahead in the competition (Verma *et al.*, 2020). However, in industry 5.0 as we embrace the culture of internet of things and people, along with emergent intelligence and Evergetics, integrate the physical space with cyberspace (Martynov *et al.*, 2019), a much broader role of HR professionals is expected. The review of machine learning (ML) applications in human resource management showed that the functions of recruitment and selection along with performance management had majority of the applications of ML where heuristics algorithms like decision trees, random forest, k-nearest neighbour were used more frequently than the metaheuristics algorithms like ensemble learning and Markov process which shows the direction of future possible applications in HR function where level of complexity is high (Garg *et al.*, 2022). Nahavandi (2019) has suggested a new role, chief robotics officer who will be responsible for the optimal balance of the machines as they collaborate with the humans as they will have enough knowledge not only on the technology side but the necessary factors needed for modelling the humane side of machines alongside maintaining the environmental impacts. As seen through the literature, there are more and more applications of AI and ML in industry 4.0. This is what makes the author develop some of the practices in terms of operations how the HRs of tomorrow will interact with the employees alongside the applications of AI and ML.

The above figure depicts the HR managers who will be interacting with the HRMS which is mentioned as the rational database. The author brings in the concept of an emotional database which will capture the emotional insights of the employees and will be connected to the rational database but can be cut off from the same by the HR in case of any discrepancy. The system also consists of computers (marked as C1, C2, C3, C4) and employees (marked as E1, E2, E3, E4) who are interconnected and

Figure 6. Emotional network and machine collaboration

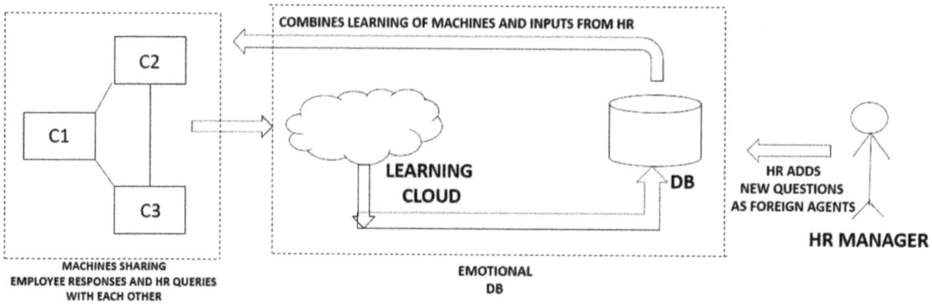

exchanges information to and from among themselves and also with the emotional database. Some of the data related to the transactional details are only shared in the rational database. Thereby the HR will have the control over the emotional database and cut it off from the rational system if the collaboration network of the humans and computers malfunctions, thereby saving the existing HRMS. By this way the HR will be able to engage with the employees through the system and control the process of the engagement through the AI based systems by adjusting the inputs as and when needed (Sharma, 2022).

In reference to the figure above, as the day begins, the HR manager will ask questions in the form of a feedback and introduce this in the database which will be passed on to the machine network. The machine will then not only consume this in its own storage, but rather pass on to the other machines. The employees will ask these questions each time they log in to the system. It includes the situations when employees are locking the machine for some time and again re-logs in. This data will capture insights as to the emotional states of the employees, how did the day go, what incidents went well, what are the levels of enthusiasm, how often they interact with other colleagues, what they do not like at work and their degree of measure through Likert scale of measurement. This will then be transferred to the learning cloud where the ML algorithm will determine the learning equation for the employee in terms of emotional function. Thus, the system will learn to throw new questions as the learning cloud strengthens along with HR questions. A very important point has been raised which addresses the acceptance of the AI and the robots by the employees in the workplace for which the organizations would have to understand the emotion and cognitions of such employees, thus enabling a culture through collaborative efforts of both AI and humans which will strike a balance between both automation and augmentation and such kind of model will also have the potential to make way for continuous innovations along with high productivity to negate the societal and environmental degradation (del Giudice *et al.*, 2021). As proposed by the author, the model embarks on human and machine collaboration with HR as a vigilant and controlling agent.

The above figure portrays the interaction of the employee and the machine individually in an employee machine collaborative network and the daily operational process is mentioned next. At stage 0, one question flows from one of the machines to one employee, and at the next stage, the question is passed to EMI (employee machine interaction) network and the same question is asked to other employees. The responses are recorded in the cloud, corresponding to the profiles of each individual. Learning functions are introduced for each employee in the system, and subsequent questions are asked based on collective machine intelligence based on the learning, which compares the responses of individuals and asks specific questions to the employees.

Figure 7. Employee machine collaborative learning

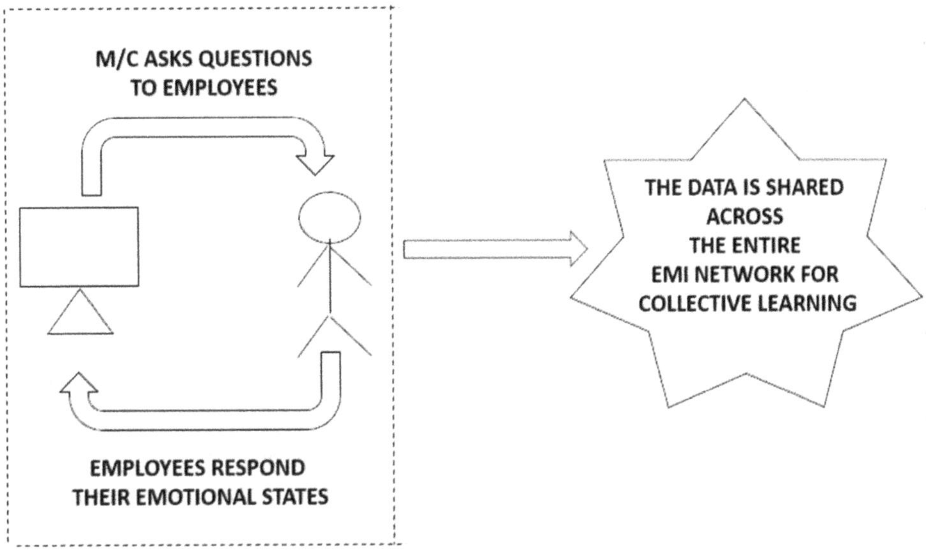

Figure 8. HR being vigilant and having supreme control

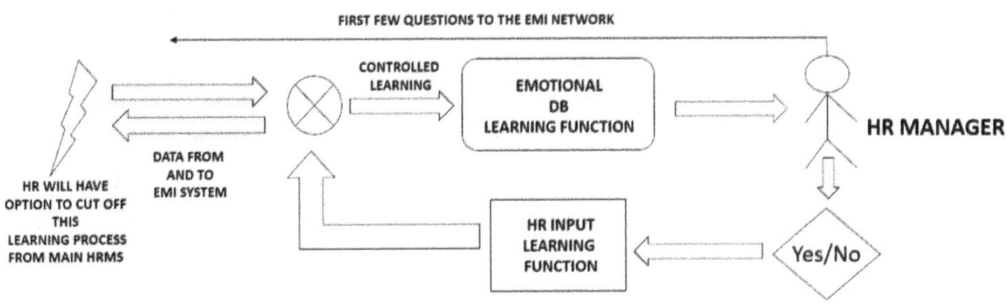

We have seen from the literature that HRs in the future need to also act like a coach to the employees who would require help and support in understanding the organizational practices and in case of difficult circumstances and would also need to direct the employees to take up sustainable practices so that the firm can benefit in the long run to achieve the sustainable goals (Brown *et al.*, 2020). Also, HR would need to facilitate the business in terms of understanding the behaviour of the internal customers, i.e., the employees such that the business is up to date of the behavioural patterns within the organization which helps them take the best decisions keeping the concern of all the stakeholders in mind (Brown *et al.*, 2020). The above figure shows the HR control process and the combination of the learning functions generated by the employee machine network and the revised function with control from the HR learning through introducing new sets of questions. The HR can monitor the situation as to how the process is going on through the control diagrams and then take a decision on whether to introduce new sets of questions in the system. Also, being the owner of this process, the HR will have the authority to cut off this learning control system from the network, thereby, the emotional database will get detached from the main HRMS thereby saving the network. This will be handy if the HR observes that there are too many questions being shot by the machines to the employees or that the system behaves erratically. Thus, HR will be able to engage with the employees daily by playing a vigilant role and have supreme control over this entire process.

CONCERNS AND RECOMMENDATIONS FOR HR IN INDUSTRY 5.0

The literature reviewed in context of role of HR in industry 5.0 and the revised operational models of the HRM function proposed by the author raises a number of questions. One of the major benefits of having collaborative robots in the industry 5.0 is that the robots will be able to take care of the work which is hazardous to the humans and instead the humans will be concentrating on intellectual tasks ranging from enhancing the customer centricity, making the design much better for generating customer appeal and thereby improving their quality of work and at the same time maintaining a competitive advantage (Østergaard, 2017b). Das (2022) has mentioned the trade-off that the organizations are going to face in in future in the form of deciding whether to use the AI in production or the human workers as it will significantly have an effect on the customer service and through an empirical investigation has hypothesized that it will be those firms who can effectively manage their capital structure, they will be benefitted in the long run as they can then optimize the usage of AI and humans in the production process and thus provide better customer satisfaction at a reasonable cost. Qamar *et al.* (2021) came up with a framework for the application of AI in HRM function, which imbibed the principles of ethics in order to mitigate the bias in the algorithms, taking proper care of the security and privacy issues in the layers involved, checking for any existing loophole for data manipulation and thereby strengthening the framework for more robust, secure and judicious use of AI and enabling transparency in the system. From the ethical point of view, it indeed is a question where employed people are speculating that there will be a lot of job cuts for improvement of production efficiency and also the customers are raising eyebrows on whether the organizations are focusing on the improvement of privacy management techniques while data are being collected and processed for automation of the systems. Piwowar-SULEJ (2020), through a literature review and focus group interview, concluded that there was an ever-growing need for HR professionals to implement the different elements of HRM function by first segregating the types of employees based on their skills and then subsequently harness the power of technology available for effective management. As the customers are looking for more and more customized solutions, it is imperative for the humans to play an active role in the industrial manufacturing process of sharing their creative designs, thus harnessing their cognitive skills and through collaborations with the robots, they will be able to create differentiated products targeted at the customers (Østergaard, 2017a). This leaves the senior management in the HRM functions to further investigate the systems and processes in terms of the design, and implementation to check whether they are ethically applying the AI-based techniques so that they serve the employees and the society at large by not being only profit centric in nature but touching the lives of the people and surroundings overall. Hereby the author discusses the issues through a few questions as mentioned below:

- Are the HRs leveraging the technologies which are ushering in the current industrial revolution (industry 4.0) and if so to what extent?

- Are the HRs able to ascertain the employees' levels of productivity in the HRM function individually and identify the current gaps in the current systems and processes?
- What is the level of interaction of the employees with the technical managers of the projects or products and how often do they collaborate to coach, train the employees in production for mutual learning and benefit?
- Have the HRs applied and understood the metrics for the business benefits of automation and ascertained how implementation of such metrics will have incremental benefits in future?
- What is the state of analytics in the HRM function and whether it is leaping towards the prescriptive state or still entering the predictive state?
- How does the HR wish to distinguish ethically on the selection of a robot and a human and what are the target metrics that they are setting for each role?
- Does the HR focus on driving sustainable practices for both the robot and the employee and to what extent does it benefit the organization?

The above questions may be referred to by the practitioners who may further provide further thought-provoking guidance on the road ahead for the HR managers. A critical fact that the author would like to highlight is the convergence of the roles of the project or product managers and the HR managers to some extent. In this regard, the author is worrisome whether the roles should merge into one particular role that will be in charge of the cobot resource management overall or whether there will still be two separate roles as it is in the present. On the one hand the HR managers would know more about the policies and the legislations of the land along with the dynamics of individuals within the organization, whereas the project or product managers will be more knowledgeable in terms of the modern technologies, their deployment and management. Although it may be more feasible to equip the leadership and people-oriented skills to the project or product managers in the organization, it is the HR managers who, with their existing experience in managing the relationships, overseeing the people's practices, policies and regulations who need to remain up to date with the technological applications and play a vigilant, controlling and strategic role in the organization.

FUTURE RESEARCH DIRECTIONS

The future research will pertain to the areas of the interaction of the employee-robots, the employee-HR and the robot-HR to ascertain their relationship and creation of the conceptual frameworks as more and more technologies come into the picture. Also, experiments need to be carried out before the technologies are adapted in the industrial context through simulation and gamification to understand the expectations of the employees and the role of the robots. Similarly, the behavioural analysis may also be conducted on the HR and the employees on their perception and reaction towards implementing the cobot system, identifying the hindrances that they speculate to come across and appropriately shape the system before rolling it out. Also, future research could pertain to the level of productivity benefit or decrease of the same once the systems are applied in the industries and work on the possible metrics and techniques to improve productivity further. Finally, since in industry 5.0, the human touch will be more in focus, it is worth investing to what extent humans can contribute to the sustainable practices that bring about a change in the society and environment and in turn the organization.

CONCLUSION

This chapter focuses on the role of HR in the industry 5.0 and how they would need to adapt to the latest technological revolution. The chapter begins with a brief introduction on the expected technological changes that are ushering followed by literature review of the technologies that are already applicable in industry 4.0 or that are going to be in use in the next industrial revolution. Some of the systems and processes that will be revised in the industry 5.0 are constructed subsequently after considering the existing gaps. The different sub functions within the HR practices have been highlighted while their systems and processes have been revamped to suit the next wave of the industrial revolution. By capturing the emotions of the employees and the collaboration network, HR will be playing the monitoring and controlling role in the organization. Several questions are still unanswered with respect to the data privacy and sustainable practices and the author proposes a few questions which the HR practitioners can refer to while understanding the possible impact of industry 5.0 in the HRM function. Finally, the author concludes that the HRM function will be revamped by incorporating more automation of systems and processes while the Hr will play a more strategic and vigilant role as they will be overseeing the processes and make the necessary controls as and when required.

ACKNOWLEDGMENT

This research has not received any support in the form of grants or financial incentives and benefits from any agency in public, commercial or not-for-profit sectors.

REFERENCES

Arslan, A., Cooper, C., Khan, Z., Golgeci, I., & Ali, I. (2022). Artificial intelligence and human workers interaction at team level: A conceptual assessment of the challenges and potential HRM strategies. *International Journal of Manpower*, *43*(1), 75–88. doi:10.1108/IJM-01-2021-0052

Azizi, M. R., Atlasi, R., Ziapour, A., Abbas, J., & Naemi, R. (2021). Innovative human resource management strategies during the COVID-19 pandemic: A systematic narrative review approach. *Heliyon*, *7*(6), e07233. Advance online publication. doi:10.1016/j.heliyon.2021.e07233 PMID:34124399

Bhatt, P. (2022). AI adoption in the hiring process – important criteria and extent of AI adoption. *Foresight*. Advance online publication. doi:10.1108/FS-07-2021-0144

Bhatt, P., & Muduli, A. (2022). Artificial intelligence in learning and development: a systematic literature review. In *European Journal of Training and Development*. Emerald Group Holdings Ltd. doi:10.1108/EJTD-09-2021-0143

Breque, M., Nul, L. de, & Petridis, A. (2021). Industry 5.0 Towards a sustainable human centric and resilient European Industry. doi:10.27777/308407

Brin, W. D. (2019, March 22). *Employers Embrace Artificial Intelligence for HR.* https://www.shrm.org/resourcesandtools/hr-topics/global-hr/pages/employers-embrace-artificial-intelligence-for-hr.aspx

Brown, H. R., Meister, J., Styr, C., & Pring, B. (2020, June 25). *An Evolving Profession: 21 New HR Jobs to Watch For.* https://www.cognizant.com/us/en/latest-thinking/perspectives/an-evolving-profession-21-new-hr-jobs-to-watch-for

Chillakuri, B., & Attili, V. S. P. (2021). Role of blockchain in HR's response to new-normal. *The International Journal of Organizational Analysis*. Advance online publication. doi:10.1108/IJOA-08-2020-2363

Chowdhury, S., Dey, P., Joel-Edgar, S., Bhattacharya, S., Rodriguez-Espindola, O., Abadie, A., & Truong, L. (2022). Unlocking the value of artificial intelligence in human resource management through AI capability framework. *Human Resource Management Review*. Advance online publication. doi:10.1016/j.hrmr.2022.100899

Coron, C. (2022). Quantifying human resource management: a literature review. In Personnel Review (Vol. 51, Issue 4, pp. 1386–1409). Emerald Group Holdings Ltd. doi:10.1108/PR-05-2020-0322

Das, D. (2022). Understanding the choice of human resource and the artificial intelligence: "strategic behavior" and the existence of industry equilibrium. *Journal of Economic Studies (Glasgow, Scotland)*. Advance online publication. doi:10.1108/JES-06-2021-0305

del Giudice, M., Scuotto, V., Orlando, B., & Mustilli, M. (2021). Toward the human – Centered approach. A revised model of individual acceptance of AI. *Human Resource Management Review*. Advance online publication. doi:10.1016/j.hrmr.2021.100856

Demir, K. A., Döven, G., & Sezen, B. (2019). Industry 5.0 and Human-Robot Co-working. *Procedia Computer Science*, *158*, 688–695. doi:10.1016/j.procs.2019.09.104

Dhanpat, N., Buthelezi, Z. P., Joe, M. R., & Maphela, T. v, & Shongwe, N. (2020). Industry 4.0: The role of human resource professionals. *SA Journal of Human Resource Management*. Advance online publication. doi:10.4102ajhrm

Garg, S., Sinha, S., Kar, A. K., & Mani, M. (2022). A review of machine learning applications in human resource management. In International Journal of Productivity and Performance Management (Vol. 71, Issue 5, pp. 1590–1610). Emerald Group Holdings Ltd. doi:10.1108/IJPPM-08-2020-0427

Gautam, S. (2022, April 9). *Is our workforce ready for Industry 5.0?* https://hr.economictimes.indiatimes.com/news/workplace-4-0/learning-and-development/is-our-workforce-ready-for-industry-5-0/90737484

Humayun, M., & Arabia, S. (2021). Industrial Revolution 5.0 and the Role of Cutting Edge Technologies. *International Journal of Advanced Computer Science and Applications*, *12*(12). doi:10.14569/IJACSA.2021.0121276

Kambur, E., & Akar, C. (2022). Human resource developments with the touch of artificial intelligence: A scale development study. *International Journal of Manpower*, *43*(1), 168–205. doi:10.1108/IJM-04-2021-0216

Martynov, V. V., Shavaleeva, D. N., & Zaytseva, A. A. (2019). Information Technology as the Basis for Transformation into a Digital Society and Industry 5.0. *Quality Management, Transport and Information Security, Information Technologies*, 23–29.

Nahavandi, S. (2019). Industry 5.0-a human-centric solution. *Sustainability (Switzerland)*, *11*(16), 4371. Advance online publication. doi:10.3390u11164371

Niehueser, W., & Boak, G. (2020). Introducing artificial intelligence into a human resources function. *Industrial and Commercial Training*, *52*(2), 121–130. doi:10.1108/ICT-10-2019-0097

Østergaard, H. E. (2016, May 13). *Industry 5.0 – Return of the human touch*. https://www.universal-robots.com/blog/industry-50-return-of-the-human-touch/

Østergaard, H. E. (2017a, October 17). *Collaborative Robots ushering in Industry 5.0*. https://www.universal-robots.com/blog/collaborative-robots-ushering-in-industry-50/

Østergaard, H. E. (2017b, October 27). *Industry 5.0: The Factory of the Future*. https://www.universal-robots.com/blog/industry-50-the-factory-of-the-future/

Piwowar-SULEJ, K. (2020). Human resource management in the context of Industry 4.0. *Organization & Management Scientific Quartely*, *2020*(49). doi:10.29119/1899-6116.2020.49.7

Poba-Nzaou, P., Galani, M., & Tchibozo, A. (2020). Transforming human resources management in the age of Industry 4.0: A matter of survival for HR professionals. *Strategic HR Review*, *19*(6), 273–278. doi:10.1108/SHR-06-2020-0055

Prassida, G. F., & Asfari, U. (2021). A conceptual model for the acceptance of collaborative robots in industry 5.0. *Procedia Computer Science*, *197*, 61–67. doi:10.1016/j.procs.2021.12.118

Qamar, Y., Agrawal, R. K., Samad, T. A., & Chiappetta Jabbour, C. J. (2021). When technology meets people: The interplay of artificial intelligence and human resource management. *Journal of Enterprise Information Management*, *34*(5), 1339–1370. doi:10.1108/JEIM-11-2020-0436

Saxena, A., Saxena, A., Sharma, R., & Parashar, M. (2021). Emergence of Futuristic HRM in Perspective of Human - Cobot's Collaborative Functionality. *International Journal of Engineering and Advanced Technology*, *10*(5), 292–296. doi:10.35940/ijeat.E2763.0610521

Schiele, H., Bos-Nehles, A., Delke, V., Stegmaier, P., & Torn, R. J. (2022). Interpreting the industry 4.0 future: Technology, business, society and people. *The Journal of Business Strategy*, *43*(3), 157–167. doi:10.1108/JBS-08-2020-0181

Sharma, N. (2021). Using positive deviance to enhance employee engagement: An interpretive structural modelling approach. *The International Journal of Organizational Analysis*, *30*(1), 84–98. doi:10.1108/IJOA-07-2020-2341

Sharma, N., & Garg, P. (2017). Psychological contract and psychological empowerment as employee engagement drivers in Indian IT sector. *International Journal of Applied Business and Economic Research*, *15*(1).

Sharma, N., & Singh, V. K. (2018). Psychological empowerment and employee engagement: Testing the mediating effects of constructive deviance in Indian IT Sector. *International Journal of Human Capital and Information Technology Professionals*, *9*(4), 44–55. doi:10.4018/IJHCITP.2018100103

Shet, S., Poddar, T., Wamba Samuel, F., & Dwivedi, Y. K. (2021). Examining the determinants of successful adoption of data analytics in human resource management – A framework for implications. *Journal of Business Research*, *131*, 311–326. doi:10.1016/j.jbusres.2021.03.054

Swift and efficient: Using artificial intelligence to enhance the talent acquisition process. (2021). In *Development and Learning in Organizations* (Vol. 35, Issue 5, pp. 43–45). Emerald Group Holdings Ltd. doi:10.1108/DLO-11-2020-0224

Tiwari, M. (2022, July 25). *An effective framework to prepare workplaces for digital transformation*. https://hr.economictimes.indiatimes.com/news/workplace-4-0/learning-and-development/an-effective-framework-to-prepare-workplaces-for-digital-transformation/93105433

Verma, A., Bansal, M., & Verma, J. (2020). Industry 4.0: reshaping the future of HR. In Strategic Direction (Vol. 36, Issue 5, pp. 9–11). Emerald Group Holdings Ltd. doi:10.1108/SD-12-2019-0235

Xu, X., Lu, Y., Vogel-Heuser, B., & Wang, L. (2021). Industry 4.0 and Industry 5.0—Inception, conception and perception. *Journal of Manufacturing Systems*, *61*, 530–535. doi:10.1016/j.jmsy.2021.10.006

Zhang, Y., Xu, S., Zhang, L., & Yang, M. (2021). Big data and human resource management research: An integrative review and new directions for future research. *Journal of Business Research*, *133*, 34–50. doi:10.1016/j.jbusres.2021.04.019

KEY TERMS AND DEFINITIONS

Artificial Intelligence (AI): A technology which is aimed at enabling the machines to analyze and predict the events thereby enabling automation.

Cobot: A robot that is considered as a very close or direct interaction with the human while at work.

Efficiency: A state that defines the degree of being dynamic while in operation.

Engagement: A form of an event where there is an interaction and agreement between the subjects involved (Sharma and Garg, 2017).

Human Resource Management Systems (HRMS): An information technology enabled system that manages the data record of the organization for usage of the HR and employee.

Machine Learning (ML): A technology that induces the learning capabilities within the machines through algorithms and computing power for generating predictive capability.

Recruitment: A function within the human resource management that includes the process of taking an employee in the organization.

Vigilant: A form of attribute that implies keeping a close and careful watch.

Chapter 7
Reinventing Human Resources Through Digitalization

Ariadna Monje Amor
https://orcid.org/0000-0002-6713-851X
Universidade da Coruña, Spain

ABSTRACT

Human resource management (HRM) in organizations is rapidly being transformed by information technologies. The COVID-19 pandemic has intensified the pace of digitalization of HR processes, which has become particularly important in the context of the digital transformation of human resource activities. Those organizations that take advantage of digital HRM technologies are better positioned than those that pay less attention to them. Additionally, organizations have had to adapt to new work models such as hybrid or remote work. This chapter describes how digitization is reshaping human resources by introducing digital HR transformation in different activities, comparing digital recruitment to traditional recruitment, focusing on the role of applicant tracking systems in recruitment and selection, and examining digital trends and work models. Finally, several practical implications will be discussed.

INTRODUCTION

With the advent of digital technologies, companies are designing, manufacturing, and delivering their products and services in new and innovative ways (Fernandez & Gallardo-Gallardo, 2020). These technologies, represented by artificial intelligence, big data, and cloud computing, are constantly changing people's ways of working and living. In this new era, new technologies are also giving rise to new business models. As an important component of business management, human resources (HR) are also undergoing significant changes as a result of digitalization. Over the last couple of years, HR technology has grown consistently, and many companies have benefited from significant investments in integrated HR platforms, indicating an industry in transition.

Most organizations' human capital departments use digital tools such as websites and apps to manage employees and other HR activities to save time and make better use of resources. The current post-pandemic landscape has brought with it some workforce resilience, as work teams begin to adapt

DOI: 10.4018/978-1-6684-6745-9.ch007

to new ways of working. This adaptation brings with it new demands and expectations on the part of the employees. Individuals are no longer the same after the COVID-19 crisis and may only be able to re-enter the workforce by providing workdays that contribute to a higher quality of life (health, family time, vacations, training, etc.) and, more importantly, sufficient motivation to foster a sense of belonging (Wontorczyk & Rożnowski, 2022).

The use of people analytics is increasing in organizations as a method for optimizing HR practices. Examples include recruitment, performance appraisal, employee development, health, and retention management. With data analytics, HR practices can identify business impact and enable data-driven decisions that are based on descriptive, visual, and statistical analyses of HR processes, human capital, as well as organizational performance (Marler & Boudreau, 2017). There are several enabling resources that are needed for successful data analytics, such as quality data, information technology infrastructure, and support from top management (Peeters et al., 2020). It is, however, risky, challenging, and ethical to transfer and apply the efficiency-driven logic of analytics to manage humans (Giermindl et al., 2022).

This chapter aims to explain how digitalization is reinventing human resources. The first section focuses on digital HR transformation. Next, a comparison between digital recruitment and traditional recruitment is presented. The following section describes the use of applicant tracking systems in recruitment and selection. After that, digital trends and work models are discussed. Then, the importance of human resource development is stressed. Finally, some solutions and recommendations for managers and policymakers are examined, and future lines of research are proposed.

THE INDUSTRY 5.0 AND HR PRACTICES

Artificial intelligence, the Internet of Things, robots, 3D printing, cloud computing, and other advanced technologies are at the heart of Industry 4.0 (Adel, 2022). Industry 5.0, however, refers to the upcoming generation of efficient and intelligent machines designed on the basis of the previous generation of technology.

According to the European Union, Industry 5.0 places less emphasis on technology, as it aims to reach a resolution by assuming that progress comes from collaboration between humans and machines (European Commission, 2020). The purpose is to use advanced technologies, such as big data analytics, to help individuals work faster, improve performance and efficiency (Adel, 2022).

Work organization is rapidly changing as a result of digitalization, which is hastening long-term trends that began about 30 years ago, increasing flexibility in both timing (e.g., flextime) and space (e.g., remote work) (Roquelaure, 2021). The use of a digital platform facilitates the delivery of online services by an individual over a network; allows for the provision of on-demand physical services, such as commercial services; and enables workers to access a virtual labor market. In the age of big data, massive volumes of commercial, personal, and geographic data are being combined by internet platforms in ways that are directly exploitable.

When businesses see a competitive advantage, they are typically willing to make changes. Despite this, many organizations struggle to implement new technologies and advances due to insufficient capital, skills, and employee resistance. Because of this, companies often hesitate to implement new systems unless they believe they will be beneficial to them (Ngai & Wat, 2006). The adoption of a digital approach to HRM and integration of information technology and HR systems is referred to as e-HRM (Marler & Parry, 2016; Zhou et al., 2021).

MAIN FOCUS OF THE CHAPTER

Digital HR Transformation

A number of technology-based employee selection methods have appeared, or existing methods have been digitized, significantly affecting HR activities. For example, the use of online applications may reduce the potential for adverse impacts on protected groups by ensuring objectivity when handling job applications (Konradt et al., 2013). However, applicants' perception of justice is influenced by the design, content, and user-friendliness of the system, as well as the amount of customization available (De Goede et al., 2011; Kraichy & Chapman, 2014; Selden & Orenstein, 2011).

Additionally, a growing number of companies are using digital selection methods. Asynchronous interviewing, for instance, has become widespread before and since the pandemic. Gamification and game-based assessments are also common (Nikolaou, 2021). An example of gamification is employee recruitment and selection, where game elements are incorporated into non-gaming contexts (Georgiou et al., 2019). Mobile or computing devices are often used to transform existing selection methods, such as personality or situational tests, into gamified versions. Incorporating game elements into the selection process may increase candidates' enjoyment, challenge, and interaction.

Remote onboarding has also been common during the COVID-19 pandemic. Due to the fact that new hires work off-site, remote onboarding may present unique challenges compared to local onboarding, such as lack of communication and documentation, asking for help, and bonding with peers (Rodeghero et al., 2021). The authors suggested encouraging communication with employees, providing information about the company, fostering team building, and assigning an onboarding buddy or mentor to make the transition to the new role smoother. With the pandemic, LinkedIn moved from a one-day in-person onboarding program to a five-day online onboarding program to provide more flexibility to employees (Maurer, 2020). It includes activities, live sessions, chats on LinkedIn groups, and Q&A.

Regarding the training and development arena, the use of online training (both formal and informal) is not new. Nevertheless, the use of technology has increased considerably lately, with access to specialized applications, online training programs, e-mentoring, MOOCs (Massive Open Online Courses), and intranets resembling social networks (Nikolaou, 2021). Training centers have become increasingly reliant on e-learning training as a means to educate students and employees in recent years as its popularity has soared. Compared to traditional face-to-face training, e-learning is more cost-effective, individuals can connect from work or home, it is more convenient, and learners can progress at their own pace (Griffin et al., 2019). The Ritz-Carlton provides ongoing training to both management and non-management employees (100 hours per year), including e-learning courses on best practices of the brand, a culture of excellence, or providing a differentiating service (Ritz-Carlton, n.d.).

Evaluating employees' performance has never been easy. It consists of evaluating employee traits that are considered to be important to the job, behavior, or performance through qualitative or quantitative measures (Torrington et al., 2017). Most organizations use performance appraisal to find out the employee's training and development needs, enhance performance, make communications easier, set pay, determine bonuses and rewards, and motivate and control employees (Wilkinson et al., 2021). Traditional performance appraisal methods are subjected to bias, and employee evaluations are often inconsistent, unreliable, and invalid because evaluators apply different standards to each employee (Levy et al., 2015; Samuel et al., 2014). Accenture is a great example of digital performance evaluation (Accenture, 2019). With Performance Achievement, they moved away from the more traditional performance appraisal method of reviewing employees' performance annually to a much more innovative way of controlling their development by receiving real-time performance and feedback from their managers regularly throughout the year, resulting in speedy evaluations and operational excellence. With this cloud-based technology, Accenture managed to reduce operations costs by 10%.

Digital Recruitment versus Traditional Recruitment

A variety of new and innovative technological methodologies have emerged to assist with personnel selection in light of the rapid advancement of the digital economy (McCarthy et al., 2017). The digital revolution in the information age is drastically changing the way people work and live. The traditional concept of talent search, where recruiters post job openings on job boards, is becoming less effective (Purvis, 2016). The traditional model of talent search is no longer relevant in an increasingly competitive talent market. The main factors that make filling open positions difficult are a lack of qualified candidates, a lack of relevant experience, and a lack of hard-to-find skills. The demands of quantity, precision, and talent adequacy require that HR managers change their mindsets and become more proactive.

Digital recruitment will define the use of technology to improve its efficiency, increase its effectiveness and broaden the impact of recruitment for the company, reducing costs in the recruitment process and increasing recruitment capacity. Digitalization in recruitment refers primarily to the use of new technologies, such as mobile tools and social networks, to provide candidates with access to human recruitment information via multiple channels, allowing HR to increase the speed and efficiency of employee recruitment and selection through data analysis to meet the needs and characteristics of various people more easily (Wiblen & Marler, 2021). Using artificial intelligence, a company can determine if an applicant is a good fit by analyzing the applicant's facial expressions and sentences, thus reducing hiring discrimination.

In terms of recruitment costs, traditional recruitment models use newspapers, magazines, and job fairs to attract candidates for open positions, but the costs of these methods are relatively high, resulting in a significant expenditure for businesses. Using online platforms (e.g., LinkedIn, Infojobs, Indeed, or corporate websites) to publish work-related information can help to reduce direct costs significantly (Torrington et al., 2017). Job fairs and contacting newspapers and magazines to publish job-related information are time-consuming and may add a significant burden to the HR department in the final stages of the recruitment and selection process. However, thanks to online job boards, businesses can attract job seekers in a more efficient and timely manner, and the rise of digital platforms has the potential to solve the problem of screening CVs on a small scale, which benefits both businesses and job seekers.

LinkedIn has evolved into an effective external recruiting tool. LinkedIn has powerful search technology and offers a variety of licenses, as well as different levels of visibility for search terms and access to contacts, making it a valuable tool for businesses. LinkedIn, which is generally appropriate for professional-level candidates, offers a variety of ways to reach out to candidates, including traditional job postings that can direct candidates to the type of candidate that an organization is looking for. Furthermore, LinkedIn has hundreds of millions of professional profiles in its database that businesses can search and select from to get in touch with them, share information about job opportunities with them, and directly hire them. Companies that want a more professional service can use paid hiring tools on LinkedIn to get a more targeted pool of candidates.

Inditex, the fast-fashion retailer, uses a combination of online recruitment methods, including social media (e.g., LinkedIn, Instagram, or Twitter) and its careers website, to attract qualified candidates for open positions. In 2021, Inditex Careers garnered more than 14.3 million visits from over 200 markets, making it the company's primary recruitment source (Inditex, 2021).

The Use of Applicant Tracking Systems

An applicant tracking system (ATS) is an automated software that manages the entire recruitment and selection process, saving time and money in candidate management (Sotnikova et al., 2020). ATS helps companies find talent, assess their potential, follow-up the interview process, evaluate their performance, and finally make an offer and hire the most suitable candidate. Candidates receive system-generated alerts informing them of the outcome of their application.

These systems can monitor all recruitment and selection activities through a comprehensive set of analytical processes and reports. Nowadays, it is quite common to use an ATS in HR departments and temporary agencies because it not only simplifies the hiring process for businesses but also improves the hiring experience for job seekers (Nikolaou, 2021).

An ATS relies on parameters (e.g., the use of keywords) to define the relevance between a candidate's CV and the job offered and has evolved to support the search for talent on job boards, social and professional networks. Recent developments in ATS have included the use of artificial intelligence and the use of natural language processing to facilitate semantic search functions.

Oracle Taleo is a tool that provides an engaging experience for candidates and efficient productivity for recruiters. Oracle Recruiting, from Oracle Fusion Cloud Human Capital Management, is a complete, unified solution that helps recruiters attract and hire the right people (Oracle, n.d.). Oracle Taleo Recruiting Cloud Services is the world's most widely used cloud-based ATS and human resource management software, and is the ATS of choice for more than 5,000 medium and large companies in 180 countries (Oracle Taleo, n.d.). About 20% of all companies using ATS software today use Oracle Taleo, placing it among the leading ATS systems in the market. Customers such as Best Buy, United Airlines, Toyota, Macy's, Marriott, Sainsbury's, and Carrefour have chosen Oracle Taleo's ATS to help them hire the highest quality candidates and reduce turnover.

Oracle Taleo's candidate management platform is a cloud-based, on-demand system that uses sophisticated artificial intelligence technology to simplify and streamline the talent acquisition process for small, medium, and large companies. It is used early in the recruitment process to track communications with applicants, automatically screen large numbers of candidates, find the best fit for vacancies, generate reports and much more. Candidates register an account on the Taleo website and, after completing a series of profiles and assessment tests, the system produces a scoring and analysis report of the best candidates. This tool reduces the HR department's workload and the cost of recruitment by automating the process, and the ATS software continues to provide additional solutions for training and performance management even after the candidate has been hired (Oracle Taleo, 2012). Greenhouse, BambooHR, SmartRecruiters, or IBM Kenexa BrassRing are some other ATS software options.

The advantages of using ATS include the following: time savings; cost savings; a fairer interview system (as data is analyzed by algorithms without personal bias); protection of candidates' equal rights; quick screening and data analysis; facilitates employee on-boarding; and allows several people to jointly manage the recruitment process, effectively promoting synergies between departments.

In contrast, there are several disadvantages associated with the use of ATS. For example, traditional recruitment methods and ATS can be difficult to integrate for some companies in transition, resulting in confusing data. There could be keyword problems with the ATS, and it is possible that some good candidates will be discarded for not using the keywords that recruiters selected. In addition, there are some ATS products that research candidate information through social media, so there could be privacy issues involved.

Digital Trends and Work Models

The digital transformation of HR has played a key role in the coronavirus landscape. Due to government mandated measures in all countries, millions of workers' homes have had to be readjusted and become their new workplace. Initially, the main challenge for organizations was helping employees work from home to ensure business continuity (Collings et al., 2021). This required substantial digital transformation as organizations redesigned technology and work processes to perform tasks virtually, often for the first time, as well as train employees (Shankar, 2020). This section will focus on what telework and hybrid work entail and the legal framework in the European Union.

Electronic devices (e.g., laptops, mobile phones, or tablets) and ubiquitous connectivity are key factors in the new forms of work in the digital economy. Several HR trends have arisen as a result of the pandemic. As technology advances, telework, hybrid work, and flexible working are becoming staples in HR's toolkit. The concept of remote work was developed in the early 1970s. It was coined in 1973 by Jack Nilles, a NASA engineer, and his colleagues in their book "Telecommunications-Transportation Tradeoff" (Nilles et al., 1976). This work model was called teleworking and refers to the provision of services in a physical space other than the company through computer and information technologies. Telework is a method of work organization and performance in which the employee works away from the employer's workplace for a significant part of his or her working time, providing the employer with the results or outcomes of his or her work through information and data transmission technologies, especially the Internet.

Workplaces where remote work takes place are often adaptations of the home environment. They are not properly constructed workspaces, as the equipment in the home is often not as good as the equipment in an office, thus affecting ergonomics. In addition, the remote worker usually does not have access to the same resources as those in the company premises (e.g., documentation, databases, or support from colleagues) (Wontorczyk & Rożnowski, 2022).

Hybrid work combines face-to-face and remote work. In a hybrid world of work, there is a risk that differences between remote and face-to-face workers reinforce labor market disadvantages. Furthermore, there are likely to be conflicts between some employees and their employers. In the face of growing employee expectations to be able to work remotely, particularly among younger generations, many companies yearn for a return to face-to-face work in the office, particularly for the face-to-face interactions that could contribute to more productive working relationships (Gifford, 2022).

Inequalities in the use of technology (or the lack thereof) could lead to divisions between different groups of employees. As a result, tensions may arise between employees who are based in the office and those who work remotely. Moreover, it calls for considerations of morality and ethics that relate to fairness across employees (Green et al., 2020).

Leaders and HR professionals must listen to the concerns of millennials and Generation Z because these generations are part of today's workforce and understanding them will help attract and retain their talent. They are looking for more flexibility, work-life balance, more learning and development opportunities, and a greater commitment to social responsibility (Deloitte, 2022). In fact, a Deloitte survey of more than 23,000 young people in 46 countries found that 75% of Generation Z and millennials would prefer a hybrid or remote working model to face-to-face work. This suggests that organizations need to work to ensure that all professionals feel heard and drive change in their workplaces.

Statistics indicate that 5.4% of EU employees aged 15–64 worked from home on a regular basis in 2019 (Eurofound, 2020; Eurostat, 2020). Over the last decade, this percentage has remained stable at around 5%. Over the same period, however, the percentage of people who sometimes worked from home has increased from 6% in 2009 to 9% in 2019. In response to the COVID-19 pandemic, social distancing measures led more people to work from home. It is estimated that 12% of employed workers in the European Union aged 20–64 worked from home in 2020, whereas this figure had been stable at around 5-6% over the last decade (Eurostat, 2021).

Although many industries (e.g., manufacturing and service sectors) anticipate a reduction in the amount of physical exertion and movement due to the digitization of tasks and extensive use of digital devices (P. Moore, 2019; Neumann et al., 2021), these digital trends and work models also have disadvantages. As new work models and digitalization emerge, workplace hazards will continue to shift, increasing the exposure to psychosocial factors, such as cognitive overload, and other forms of mental stress (Berg-Beckhoff et al., 2017; Diebig et al., 2020; Kotera & Correa Vione, 2020).

At the European Union level, there is no hard-law regulation of telework. However, several directives and regulations (e.g., Directive 2003/88, Council Directive 89/391/EEC, and Directive (EU) 2019/1152) address issues critical to providing teleworkers with good working conditions.

The main legal framework in the European Union (EU) prior to the advent of COVID-19 was the EU Framework Agreement on Telework, updated in 2005. This framework defined telework as “a form of organizing and/or performing work, using information technology, in the context of an employment contract/relationship, where work, which could also be performed at the employers’ premises, is carried out away from those premises on a regular basis” (Article 2).

In terms of the content of the EU Agreement, several important issues stand out. For example, as long as teleworking is not part of the initial job description, it is voluntary for both employers and employees; the agreement must be formalized in writing; the employer is responsible for ensuring the protection of data used and processed by the teleworker; and workers will have the same rights and opportunities as those working face-to-face on the company premises.

In EU countries, telework is regulated by statutory legislation or by social dialogue and collective bargaining. In most EU countries, both types of regulation exist but with different levels of coverage (Sanz de Miguel et al., 2021). Some countries, such as Spain, France, or Portugal, have regulated telework in their employment laws. Other countries, such as the UK, Italy, or the Netherlands, have included it as “flexible work”, while Finland, Sweden, and Germany have regulated this work model through collective bargaining and sectoral agreements.

The Importance of Human Resource Development

Learning is becoming more and more important and workplace learning is a vital segment of it, determined by the influence of shifts in skills, needs, technologies, relationships, and roles within different institutions and organizations (Vaughan, 2008; Watkins & Marsick, 2021). In particular, human resource development (HRD) is a key integral part of the human resource management role as it helps employees to advance in their professional careers by enhancing their knowledge, skills, and capabilities (Shuck et al., 2014).

Businesses, markets, workforce shifts, and the pandemic are increasingly altering the way in which people learn in the workplace, and the context of globalization is increasing the pressures of developing people to deliver a competitive advantage. Also, pressures relevant to HRD activities and forces which influence learning must be deemed, such as competitive forces because of globalization, internationalization of business, new technologies, digitalization, the drive for quality, the need for leadership, augmented value put on intangible assets and human capital, and changes in markets and the economy, among others (Garavan et al., 1995; A. L. Moore & Klein, 2020). Since the overall purpose of the workplace is to produce goods and services and not to produce learning, in situations of economic recession or uncertainty, workplaces often diminish their spending in this area. Indeed, the sudden switch to full digital delivery as face-to-face learning became less accessible was a challenge faced by many companies in this time of reduced budgets and changing demands, having a knock-on effect on the resources available for learning and development (Crowley & Overton, 2021).

However, a clever and experienced workforce who possesses the right knowledge, skills, and abilities (KSAs) is fundamental to a firm's success, and their learning should be undertaken on an ongoing basis to meet the targets of the business. That is why it is crucial for companies to provide employees with the necessary tools, equipment, and support in terms of training and development. There is a need to identify the associated KSAs for all kinds of work activity to make sure that employees possess the KSAs to perform effectively and add value in a competitive global marketplace. Thus, it is critical to pay attention to job analysis as it helps identify the human behavior required for adequate job performance (Torrington et al., 2017).

First, the connection between workplace learning and a particular context must be made since the context within a specific industry, work, knowledge, skills, and abilities drives workplace learning. Then a needs assessment must be carried out to identify learning and training needs. This is one of the most important steps as, if needs are not well identified, money would be spent on training or programs that may not be necessary. Learning needs and learning styles vary significantly across the various staff groups. Therefore, it is essential to identify the training needs to know if there is a need for training and development or not. Given that every organization is different and carries out diverse policies and practices, it is indispensable to tailor the training and development requirements to the needs of each firm. Lastly, line managers must be actively involved (Niazi, 2011).

Numerous studies have identified several individual and organizational benefits related to training and employee development. On the one hand, the first set of benefits includes an increase in earnings and better wages. On the other hand, the major organizational benefits of well-trained and skilled employees are associated with enhanced productivity, innovation, more upgraded production processes, higher quality products and services, as well as more effective recruitment and employee retention (Blundell et al., 1996; Park et al., 2020; Tamkin, 2005). More specifically, Lähteenmäki et al. (2001) demonstrated that employees had a greater willingness to accept change when they perceived that learning and development were effectively handled. Tamkin (2005) studied the connection between employee skills and business performance and concluded that investment in learning and development was usually reasonable since firms got a more motivated and more satisfied workforce in exchange for better skills to promote change.

The challenge for HRD is to provide employees with learning or training programs at the moment of need, especially during times of change (e.g., COVID-19, digitalization), as well as find the connect-the-dots between individuals and their work, which may contribute to the development of a knowledge culture within the organization (Yarberry & Sims, 2021). Work and learning should also be integrated so that they can take place simultaneously. Managing new employees from different generations, backgrounds, skills, and mindsets in new workplaces is another potential challenge for learning and development professionals, as young managers may have distinct expectations influenced by the era of information technology, forcing organizations to evolve and create new tools and programs appealing to employees.

SOLUTIONS AND RECOMMENDATIONS

HR professionals must consider the many nuances associated with digital transformation and its impact on employees. If digital transformation is not managed in a strategic way, it could adversely affect many employees and ultimately result in job losses instead of job creation, adaptation, and more flexible working practices.

Managers and HR professionals have the opportunity to add value to businesses by embracing these digital changes and accelerating the transformation process. It is important for managers to understand what employees want and to combine their desires with the achievement of business objectives to create a higher level of work engagement and productivity. In addition, organizations should increasingly collaborate with competitors, intermediaries, governments, and customer networks to create value and establish strategic alliances. Therefore, it is necessary to share information collaboratively and allocate resources based on collaborative decisions.

It is important for organizations to support their employees throughout the digitalization process to ensure that they are able to perform at their best and remain happy at work. For this purpose, managers must talk to employees and empower them, conduct staff surveys, review performance, conduct exit interviews, and make sure employees have access to appropriate resources at work (e.g., equipment, digital tools, support, and training).

Practitioners should make sure that critical roles are filled with productive employees who are happy to work for the organization. To start, they have to identify the critical roles within the organization and see if the people in those roles have the skills and resources (including technology) they need to perform their jobs. Digital skills need to be developed for digital transformation to make it a success. Skills gaps must be addressed by managers, as well as the assumption that all employees are literate in technology and digital. Furthermore, analytical skills should be developed within the profession, and credibility should be built in this area. People expertise should also be brought to digital transformation to add real value, and other business areas should consider the impact of digital transformation on people.

In the light of the pandemic, digital tools, and e-learning methods such as webinars or virtual classrooms have become increasingly important to organizations. Consequently, line manager involvement should also be taken into account, as it can be linked to numerous advantages. This view is supported by McCracken and Wallace (2000), who stated that top management support is fundamental to encouraging ongoing development and that they have an important role to play in developing personalized development programs.

Digital disconnection is a common issue among hybrid and remote workers because spaces and times for work and non-work are blurred (Fast, 2021). Organizations need to establish mandatory rest days and times for all employees, including remote workers, to avoid psychosocial risks such as techno-addiction and digital burnout, which involve having a need to be permanently connected to technology, causing physical and mental fatigue, headaches, and anxiety (Roquelaure, 2021). This worker's hyperconnectivity can have physical and mental consequences (e.g., technostress; nomophobia—the fear of being without a mobile phone; fomophobia—the dependence on a mobile phone or other devices for work and social gatherings) (Berg-Beckhoff et al., 2017). Therefore, organizations could develop a digital disconnection policy (including flexible working hours, rest periods, or limiting exposure to technology) to favor productivity and employee wellbeing.

Additionally, there are some risks associated with the use of technology and people analytics that may have negative consequences for employees and organizations, such as privacy concerns, data protection breaches, surveillance, constant monitoring, or algorithmic bias (Calvard & Jeske, 2018; Gal et al., 2020; Giermindl et al., 2022). For instance, people perceive algorithms as being less fair than humans when it comes to making decisions (Newman et al., 2020). Thus, organizations must reflect on ethical considerations when implementing new technology, storing data, and managing privacy. Considering the amount of data HR professionals manage internally, they have a key role to play in ensuring these best practices are developed and adopted in the workplace.

Governments should provide support for the digitization of small businesses. For example, they could engage in guidance and assistance by allocating funds to support digitalization to eligible companies and regularly organizing visits of some leaders of successful companies in the digital transformation of HRM.

FUTURE RESEARCH DIRECTIONS

A direction for future research could be to look into whether current policies and practices allow for the flexibility the market demands and how they affect employees and company performance from a qualitative (e.g., employees' perceptions) and quantitative perspective (e.g., turnover, performance, work engagement).

Future studies could also examine how remote and hybrid work are transforming the world of work and the HR profession, and explore how individuals should be equipped with the capabilities to drive these changes.

As technology and HR systems play a great role in work, future research should study the impact of new technologies on employees' jobs and wellbeing (e.g., job satisfaction, burnout, or work engagement).

CONCLUSION

In the face of the COVID-19 pandemic, organizations and national governments have been put to the test in terms of their ability to deal with the challenges. As a result, digitalization, automation, cloud-based technology tools, virtual learning, and remote working have become increasingly prevalent. As the workplace evolves rapidly, innovative strategies are required to keep up with technological changes, organizational structures, and forms of employment.

People cannot be removed from the equation in a digital world, so HR professionals will need interpersonal skills more than ever. A key element of strategic HR is to drive organizational change and development rather than react to it, and to balance the needs of employees and the company in the process. Organizations can thrive through digital transformation when people, culture, structure, tasks, and technology are aligned.

ACKNOWLEDGMENT

This research received no specific grant from any funding agency in the public, commercial, or not-for-profit sectors.

REFERENCES

Accenture. (2019). *How we created a technology solution to enable Accenture's reimagined performance management approach*. WordPressBlog. https://www.accenture.com/us-en/blogs/how-accenture-does-it/how-we-created-a-technology-solution-to-enable-accentures-re imagined-performance-management-approach

Adel, A. (2022). Future of industry 5.0 in society: Human-centric solutions, challenges and prospective research areas. *Journal of Cloud Computing*, *11*(1), 40. doi:10.118613677-022-00314-5 PMID:36101900

Berg-Beckhoff, G., Nielsen, G., & Ladekjær Larsen, E. (2017). Use of information communication technology and stress, burnout, and mental health in older, middle-aged, and younger workers—Results from a systematic review. *International Journal of Occupational and Environmental Health*, *23*(2), 160–171. doi:10.1080/10773525.2018.1436015 PMID:29460697

Blundell, R., Dearden, L., & Meghir, C. (1996). *The determinants and effects of work-related training in Britain*. doi:10.1920/re.ifs.1996.0050

Calvard, T. S., & Jeske, D. (2018). Developing human resource data risk management in the age of big data. *International Journal of Information Management*, *43*, 159–164. doi:10.1016/j.ijinfomgt.2018.07.011

Collings, D. G., Nyberg, A. J., Wright, P. M., & McMackin, J. (2021). Leading through paradox in a COVID-19 world: Human resources comes of age. *Human Resource Management Journal*, *31*(4), 819–833. doi:10.1111/1748-8583.12343

Crowley, E., & Overton, L. (2021). *Learning and skills at work survey 2021*. Chartered Institute of Personnel and Development.

De Goede, M. E. E., Van Vianen, A. E. M., & Klehe, U.-C. (2011). Attracting Applicants on the Web: PO fit, industry culture stereotypes, and website design. *International Journal of Selection and Assessment*, *19*(1), 51–61. doi:10.1111/j.1468-2389.2010.00534.x

Deloitte. (2022). *Striving for balance, advocating for change. The Deloitte global 2022 gen Z & millenial survey*. https://www2.deloitte.com/content/dam/Deloitte/global/Documents/deloitte-2022-genz-millennial-survey.pdf

Diebig, M., Müller, A., & Angerer, P. (2020). Impact of the Digitization in the Industry Sector on Work, Employment, and Health. In T. Theorell (Ed.), *Handbook of Socioeconomic Determinants of Occupational Health: From Macro-level to Micro-level Evidence* (pp. 305–319). Springer International Publishing. doi:10.1007/978-3-030-31438-5_10

Eurofound. (2020). *Living, working and COVID-19* (COVID-19 Series). Publications Office of the European Union.

Eurostat. (2020). *How usual is it to work from home?* https://ec.europa.eu/eurostat/web/products-eurostat-news/-/DDN-20180620-1

Eurostat. (2021). *Working from home across EU regions in 2020.* https://ec.europa.eu/eurostat/web/products-eurostat-news/-/ddn-20210923-1

Fast, K. (2021). The disconnection turn: Three facets of disconnective work in post-digital capitalism. *Convergence, 27*(6), 1615–1630. doi:10.1177/13548565211033382

Fernandez, V., & Gallardo-Gallardo, E. (2020). Tackling the HR digitalization challenge: Key factors and barriers to HR analytics adoption. *Competitiveness Review, 31*(1), 162–187. doi:10.1108/CR-12-2019-0163

Gal, U., Jensen, T. B., & Stein, M.-K. (2020). Breaking the vicious cycle of algorithmic management: A virtue ethics approach to people analytics. *Information and Organization, 30*(2), 100301. doi:10.1016/j.infoandorg.2020.100301

Garavan, T. N., Costine, P., & Heraty, N. (1995). The emergence of strategic human resource development. *Journal of European Industrial Training, 19*(10), 4–10. doi:10.1108/03090599510095816

Georgiou, K., Gouras, A., & Nikolaou, I. (2019). Gamification in employee selection: The development of a gamified assessment. *International Journal of Selection and Assessment, 27*(2), 91–103. doi:10.1111/ijsa.12240

Giermindl, L. M., Strich, F., Christ, O., Leicht-Deobald, U., & Redzepi, A. (2022). The dark sides of people analytics: Reviewing the perils for organisations and employees. *European Journal of Information Systems, 31*(3), 410–435. doi:10.1080/0960085X.2021.1927213

Gifford, J. (2022). Remote working: Unprecedented increase and a developing research agenda. *Human Resource Development International, 25*(2), 105–113. doi:10.1080/13678868.2022.2049108

Green, M., Peters, R., & Young, J. (2020). *People Profession 2030: A collective view of future trends report.* CIPD. https://www.cipd.co.uk/Images/people-profession-2030-report-compressed_tcm18-86095.pdf

Griffin, R. W., Phillips, J. M., & Gully, S. M. (2019). *Organizational Behavior: Managing People and Organizations* (13th ed.). Cengage.

Inditex. (2021). *Collaborating with our people, the engine of that transformation.* https://static.inditex.com/annual_report_2021/en/documents/we-are-collaborating-our-people-engine-transformation.pdf

Konradt, U., Warszta, T., & Ellwart, T. (2013). Fairness Perceptions in Web-based Selection: Impact on applicants' pursuit intentions, recommendation intentions, and intentions to reapply. *International Journal of Selection and Assessment, 21*(2), 155–169. doi:10.1111/ijsa.12026

Kotera, Y., & Correa Vione, K. (2020). Psychological Impacts of the New Ways of Working (NWW): A Systematic Review. *International Journal of Environmental Research and Public Health, 17*(14), 5080. doi:10.3390/ijerph17145080 PMID:32674518

Kraichy, D., & Chapman, D. S. (2014). Tailoring Web-Based Recruiting Messages: Individual Differences in the Persuasiveness of Affective and Cognitive Messages. *Journal of Business and Psychology, 29*(2), 253–268. doi:10.100710869-013-9311-z

Lähteenmäki, S., Toivonen, J., & Mattila, M. (2001). Critical Aspects of Organizational Learning Research and Proposals for Its Measurement. *British Journal of Management, 12*(2), 113–129. doi:10.1111/1467-8551.00189

Levy, P. E., Cavanaugh, C. M., Frantz, N. B., & Borden, L. A. (2015). The role of due process in performance appraisal: A 20-year retrospective. In *The Oxford handbook of justice in the workplace* (pp. 605–619). Oxford University Press. doi:10.1093/oxfordhb/9780199981410.013.29

Marler, J. H., & Boudreau, J. W. (2017). An evidence-based review of HR Analytics. *International Journal of Human Resource Management, 28*(1), 3–26. doi:10.1080/09585192.2016.1244699

Marler, J. H., & Parry, E. (2016). Human resource management, strategic involvement and e-HRM technology. *International Journal of Human Resource Management, 27*(19), 2233–2253. doi:10.1080/09585192.2015.1091980

Maurer, R. (2020, April 20). *Virtual Onboarding of Remote Workers More Important Than Ever.* SHRM. https://www.shrm.org/resourcesandtools/hr-topics/talent-acquisition/pages/virtual-onboarding-remote-workers.aspx

McCarthy, J. M., Bauer, T. N., Truxillo, D. M., Anderson, N. R., Costa, A. C., & Ahmed, S. M. (2017). Applicant Perspectives During Selection: A Review Addressing "So What?" "What's New?" and "Where to Next?". *Journal of Management, 43*(6), 1693–1725. doi:10.1177/0149206316681846

McCracken, M., & Wallace, M. (2000). Towards a redefinition of strategic HRD. *Journal of European Industrial Training, 24*(5), 281–290. doi:10.1108/03090590010372056

Moore, A. L., & Klein, J. D. (2020). Facilitating Informal Learning at Work. *TechTrends, 64*(2), 219–228. doi:10.100711528-019-00458-3

Moore, P. (2019). *OSH and the Future of Work: Benefits and risks of artificial intelligence tools in workplaces.* European Agency for Safety and Health at Work (EU-OSHA). https://osha.europa.eu/en/publications/osh-and-future-work-benefits-and-risks-artificial-intelligence-tools-workplaces

Müller, J. (2020). *Enabling Technologies for Industry 5.0: results of a workshop with Europe's technology leaders.* Publications Office. https://data.europa.eu/doi/10.2777/082634

Neumann, W. P., Winkelhaus, S., Grosse, E. H., & Glock, C. H. (2021). Industry 4.0 and the human factor – A systems framework and analysis methodology for successful development. *International Journal of Production Economics, 233*, 107992. Advance online publication. doi:10.1016/j.ijpe.2020.107992

Newman, D. T., Fast, N. J., & Harmon, D. J. (2020). When eliminating bias isn't fair: Algorithmic reductionism and procedural justice in human resource decisions. *Organizational Behavior and Human Decision Processes, 160*, 149–167. doi:10.1016/j.obhdp.2020.03.008

Ngai, E. W. T., & Wat, F. K. T. (2006). Human resource information systems: A review and empirical analysis. *Personnel Review, 35*(3), 297–314. doi:10.1108/00483480610656702

Niazi, B. A. S. (2011). Training and Development Strategy and Its Role in Organizational Performance. *Journal of Public Administration and Governance, 1*(2), 42–57. doi:10.5296/jpag.v1i2.862

Nikolaou, I. (2021). What is the Role of Technology in Recruitment and Selection? *The Spanish Journal of Psychology, 24*, e2. Advance online publication. doi:10.1017/SJP.2021.6 PMID:33536110

Nilles, J. M., Carlson, F. R., & Gray, P. (1976). *The Telecommunications-transportation Tradeoff: Options for Tomorrow*. Wiley.

Oracle Taleo. (2012). *Oracle Taleo Recruiting Cloud Service*. https://www.oracle.com/a/ocom/docs/taleo-recruiting-cloud-service.pdf

Oracle Taleo. (n.d.). *Oracle Taleo*. Retrieved 30 July 2022, from https://www.oracle.com/es/human-capital-management/taleo/

Park, Y., Woo, H., Oh, M.-R., & Park, S. (2020). The role and related variables of workplace learning in quantitative research. *Industrial and Commercial Training, 53*(1), 29–59. doi:10.1108/ICT-02-2020-0023

Peeters, T., Paauwe, J., & Van De Voorde, K. (2020). People analytics effectiveness: Developing a framework. *Journal of Organizational Effectiveness: People and Performance*, 7(2), 203–219. doi:10.1108/JOEPP-04-2020-0071

Purvis, J. (2016). Human Resources Marketing and Recruiting: Essentials of Digital Recruiting. In M. Zeuch (Ed.), *Handbook of Human Resources Management* (pp. 53–71). Springer. doi:10.1007/978-3-662-44152-7_3

Ritz-Carlton. (n.d.). *Gold standards*. The Ritz-Carlton. Retrieved 2 August 2022, from https://www.ritzcarlton.com/en/about/gold-standards

Rodeghero, P., Zimmermann, T., Houck, B., & Ford, D. (2021). *Please Turn Your Cameras on: Remote Onboarding of Software Developers During a Pandemic*. https://ieeexplore.ieee.org/document/9402105

Roquelaure, Y. (2021). *New forms of work in the digital era: Implications for psychosocial risks and musculoskeletal disorders*. https://osha.europa.eu/en/publications/digitalisation-work-psychosocial-risk-factors-and-work-related-musculoskeletal

Samuel, O. W., Omisore, M. O., & Atajeromavwo, E. J. (2014). Online fuzzy based decision support system for human resource performance appraisal. *Measurement, 55*, 452–461. doi:10.1016/j.measurement.2014.05.024

Sanz de Miguel, P., Caprile, M., & Arasanz, J. (2021). *Regulating telework in a post-COVID-19 Europe*. Publications Office of the European Union. https://osha.europa.eu/es/publications/regulating-telework-post-covid-19-europe

Selden, S., & Orenstein, J. (2011). Government e-recruiting web sites: The influence of e-recruitment content and usability on recruiting and hiring outcomes in US state governments. *International Journal of Selection and Assessment, 19*(1), 31–40. doi:10.1111/j.1468-2389.2011.00532.x

Shankar, K. (2020). The Impact of COVID-19 on IT Services Industry—Expected Transformations. *British Journal of Management, 31*(3), 450–452. doi:10.1111/1467-8551.12423

Shuck, B., Twyford, D., Reio, T. G. Jr, & Shuck, A. (2014). Human Resource Development Practices and Employee Engagement: Examining the Connection With Employee Turnover Intentions. *Human Resource Development Quarterly, 25*(2), 239–270. doi:10.1002/hrdq.21190

Sotnikova, Y., Nazarova, G., Nazarov, N., & Bilokonenko, H. (2020). Digital technologies in HR management. *Management Theory and Studies for Rural Business and Infrastructure Development, 42*(4), 527–535. doi:10.15544/mts.2020.54

Tamkin, P. (2005). *The Contribution of Skills to Business Performance*. Institute for Employment Studies (IES). https://www.employment-studies.co.uk/resource/contribution-skills-business-performance

Torrington, D., Hall, L., Taylor, S., & Atkinson, C. (2017). *Human Resource Management* (10th ed.). Pearson.

Vaughan, K. (2008). Workplace Learning: A Literature Review. In *NZCER Press*. New Zealand Council for Educational Research.

Watkins, K. E., & Marsick, V. J. (2021). Informal and Incidental Learning in the time of COVID-19. *Advances in Developing Human Resources, 23*(1), 88–96. doi:10.1177/1523422320973656

Wiblen, S., & Marler, J. H. (2021). Digitalised talent management and automated talent decisions: The implications for HR professionals. *International Journal of Human Resource Management, 32*(12), 2592–2621. doi:10.1080/09585192.2021.1886149

Wilkinson, A., Dundon, T., & Redman, T. (2021). Contemporary Human Resource Management: Text and Cases. *Sage (Atlanta, Ga.)*.

Wontorczyk, A., & Rożnowski, B. (2022). Remote, Hybrid, and On-Site Work during the SARS-CoV-2 Pandemic and the Consequences for Stress and Work Engagement. *International Journal of Environmental Research and Public Health, 19*(4), 2400. doi:10.3390/ijerph19042400 PMID:35206590

Yarberry, S., & Sims, C. (2021). The Impact of COVID-19-Prompted Virtual/Remote Work Environments on Employees' Career Development: Social Learning Theory, Belongingness, and Self-Empowerment. *Advances in Developing Human Resources, 23*(3), 237–252. doi:10.1177/15234223211017850

Zhou, Y., Cheng, Y., Zou, Y., & Liu, G. (2021). e-HRM: A meta-analysis of the antecedents, consequences, and cross-national moderators. *Human Resource Management Review, 100862*. Advance online publication. doi:10.1016/j.hrmr.2021.100862

KEY TERMS AND DEFINITIONS

Application Tracking System: It is a software that helps organizations manage the recruitment and selection process, including job postings, collecting data, screening applications, and choosing the most suitable candidates.

Artificial Intelligence: The use of machines, such as computer systems, to simulate human intelligence processes, behaviors, and decisions.

Automation: The use of processes which perform tasks or activities and replace humans with machines, such as robots and computers, with the intention of increasing efficiency and reducing variability.

Digital HR Transformation: It is the process by which operational and manual human resources processes are automated based on data and information technology.

HR: Human resources is one of the functions of the organization which is responsible for managing the employment relationship, recruitment and selection, onboarding, training and development, performance management, and compensation.

Human Resources Development: The part of HR that oversees training and employee development.

Hybrid Work: A work model that allows employees to combine work in-office and remotely.

Recruitment: An HR function that focuses on attracting potential employees to fill open positions.

Remote Work: A work model where employees work from a location different to the organizations' premises.

Chapter 8
How Does the Use of AI in HRM Contribute to Improved Business Performance?
A Systematic Review

Sonika Singh
Chandigarh Business School of Administration, India

Pratibha Thakur
Chandigarh Business School of Administration, India

Sandeep Singh
Punjabi University, Patiala, India

ABSTRACT

The chapter aims to review the usage of artificial intelligence in human resource management (HRM) to enhance organizational performance. The current study is a conceptual effort that integrates several streams of literature to give critical review of the interaction between AI and HRM in modern organizations. The present review enables industrialists to think of AI as a collection or combination of numerous IT configurations in the many company business areas rather than as a single technology because the success of AI depends on a number of important factors being combined. The authors found that the use of artificial intelligence has helped the organizations in enhancing their performance and assists in gaining competitive advantage.

INTRODUCTION

Human resource management (HRM) is being revolutionized on a worldwide basis nowadays because to new technology (Ancarani al., 2019). In fact, as Artificial Intelligence (AI) and other breakthrough technologies are developed and used more widely, the relationship between companies, employees, and

DOI: 10.4018/978-1-6684-6745-9.ch008

customers is changing in a fundamental way, and the administrative parts of HRM activities and tasks are becoming more and more automated (Lariviere et al., 2017; Marler & Parry, 2016; Sharma & Singh, 2016). Even though HRM's technological changes can be traced back to the industrial revolution, these changes have only changed the way physical or mental services are provided. (Malik et al., 2019; Luo et al., 2019) However, modern developments are making it easier to find alternatives to human resources for tasks that traditionally required human interaction and communication. This is changing both the organizational structures and the nature of work (Colbert et al., 2016). When IT is incorporated into the business ecosystem, it can have noticeable effects, notably on how the firm interacts with its clients, partners, and potential clients. AI, a technology that has experienced unparalleled development over the past decades, continues to be the most outstanding IT application today (Lee et al., 2018). AI is defined as a set of "theories and techniques used to create machines capable of simulating intelligence. AI is a general term that involves the use of a computer to model intelligent behavior with minimal human intervention" (Haenlein and Kaplan, 2019). The discussion here is narrower, focusing on a sub-class of algorithms within AI that rely on the increased availability of data for prediction tasks. It has also impacted the organizational decision making and redefined management tools (Jarrahi, 2018).

A wide range of technologies known as artificial intelligence (AI) enable the computer to perform numerous tasks that typically require cognitive process, such as analytical decision-making (Vrontis et al., 2021). The gap between the existing and desired levels of knowledge and capabilities for human workers is constantly fostered by the rapid technological progress, especially in the digital age. Managers' and employees' anxiety and internal contradictions can be made worse by information overload. However, not retaining the necessary knowledge and skill levels may result in a huge discrepancy between the necessary and actual levels of human competitiveness. Additionally, the majority of existing abilities are rendered by the rapid emergence of new technologies and paradigms, which reduces the case for developing new competencies that can become irrelevant almost immediately (Henfridsson et al., 2014). AI can recognize inconsistencies in corporate processes and recommend the best resource allocation for enhanced performance. However, because of the absence of integration of current and new information, determining the required kind of knowledge for AI's capacity to optimally increase organizational performance is difficult (Olan et al., 2022).

Artificial intelligence is changing how businesses today manage their workforces and create human resource strategies in order to boost productivity and improve the quality of employee work. There is an increasing strength and promise for HRM but also serious obstacles such as job-specific obsolescence due to the usage of AI (Malik et al., 2019; Lariviere et al., 2017). On the other hand, the extensive use of AI in organizations and corporations is enabling them to streamline their operations, raise production, improve efficiency, and cut expenses (Cooke et al., 2019).With the use of artificial intelligence, machines are now able to make decisions based on historical data and behavioral patterns more precisely than people. A significant advancement in corporate management, artificial intelligence will have a significant impact on how workers operate, particularly in the human resources and employment departments. A number of recent HRM innovations have been reviewed (Bondarouk & Brewster, 2016; Bondarouk et al., 2017; Fleming, 2019; Garcia-Arroyo & Osca, 2019), but these studies have only explored technology-enabled HRM and concentrated on specific areas of technology like robotics and e-services in HRM. Because of this, it is necessary to conduct a systematic review in order to connect the many sources of information in order to acquire a comprehensive understanding of the subject (Sharma 2021; Vrontis et.al., 2021). Current researchers have already worked on various applications of AI that benefit the employees as well the organization.

Hence, the purpose of this paper is to conduct a literature review in order to systematize how the use of artificial intelligence in the field of HRM contributes to better HR services and organizational performance.

RESEARCH METHODOLOGY

In order to offer a thorough overview, we undertook an organized, multidisciplinary evaluation of more than fifty recent papers. The results of different studies show that studies in various fields used various methodologies and had various study focuses. Research from the other disciplines often focused on the effects of AI on HRM, jobs, and labor markets, as opposed to studies from the technical disciplines, which tended to concentrate on the development of AI for specific HRM activities (Pan & Froese et al., 2022). So identify various research patterns and to understand the effect of AI on performance of various organizations and other facets related to the usage of AI in HRM, we took only those studies who worked on effects of usage of AI and how it affects the overall performance. The implementation of a clear and repeatable technique in the review made a systematic approach the best course of action.

LITERATURE REVIEW

AI has the power to lead mankind toward a more prosperous future for everybody. But there are also threats and complexities involved. At its finest, AI will increase human productivity at work, drive employment growth through innovations, and promote global economic success. However, technology also has the potential to wipe out all sectors, increase economic inequality, and widen the workforce's skills and education inequalities. According to a theoretical concept, job replacement by AI would initially occur at the task level rather than the job level and for "lower" intelligence tasks as these are simpler and easier for AI to accomplish than human employees (Huang & Rust, 2018).

AI can be viewed as a computational technology that simulates the intelligent behaviors of humans and importantly, when we discuss the usage of AI applications in HRM, we focus on job replacement, training, decision-making process, and recruiting (Bhave et al., 2020). The excessive use of AI technology will replace human factor at work which will affect the interpersonal relationships (Huang & Rust, 2018), for instance, the dependence of humans on virtual assistants like Siri, Alexa, and google home. They may allow businesses to operate around-the-clock without having human employees at physical locations by handling inquiries and providing customer support on a global scale (Glavas et al., 2019).

According to Cano-Kollmann et al. (2018), non-technical workers may not only lose their employment but also become "unemployable" and jobs are either off shored, disappear altogether, or become less valuable because of the rapid improvements in digitalization in HR industry. Another study on the use of AI in HRM decision-making stresses the capacity to handle enormous volumes of data in a short period of time (Lindebaum et al., 2020). AI adoption is hampered by businesses' perceptions of its complexity, although technological proficiency and regulatory support promote AI adoption (Pan et al., 2022). The development of Artificial Intelligence (AI) technology has led to a new wave of human intelligence that is now the primary driver of company success and industry change. AI has been used by corporate management to make decisions more frequently, taking on and assisting staff with automating their tedious and repetitive day-to-day work.

The consequences of technology advancements and inventions for people are growing more complex as machines' roles shift from being effective tools for production or usage to being crucial in several aspects of organizational and economic life (Arslan et al., 2021). Pratibha et al. (2022) conducted a survey among the IT employees and found that organizational innovativeness helps in enhancing the overall performance of the organization, which indicates that the innovative strategies and policies helps the organizations to cope up with the latest technological changes in this competitive environment. Zehir et al. (2020) stated that there is an impact of digital technologies on strategic human resource management and AI technologies improve the strategic development of HR. Research shows that the introduction of e-recruitment, e-training, and competency management, as well as other forms of e-technology or AI are improving HRM services in both national and international businesses (Bondarouk et.al., 2017). It is also possible to recreate real-world working settings in order to evaluate and hire candidates using AI technology. Artificial Intelligence (AI) may be used to verify their background details on job applicants and build remuneration packages for specific occupations (Cooke et al., 2019). Several studies have also shown that the implementation of AI technologies automate the different processes that increase the efficiency of the employees as well as organizations (Buckley et al., 2004; Park, 2018). Keeping these ideas in mind Sajjadiani et al. (2019) believe that such automation in HR industry removes biasness during recruitment process and make it more reliable.

Kumar et al., (2021) depicted that the AI-enabled technologies has a significant effect on the market performance of healthcare industry by facilitating their customers with healthcare service quality. Kitsios and Kamariotou (2021) stated that the use of AI has successfully developed decision support systems to support strategically the decision-making process, to grow new organizational openings and capacity for innovation, to take out certain challenges with respect to product attributes and machine functionalities and increasing business performance. AI can increase the performance of an organization by introducing new goods and services and improving the quality of already-existing ones. The financial and market performance of the organizations can also be increased through AI. The use of AI helps the organizations in targeting the right customers and framing right strategies for better decision making in improving the market performance (Enholm et al., 2021). Toniolo et al. (2020) has also mentioned in their study that the use of AI can minimize the energy costs, reduce pollution and wastage, and promote recycling and therefore increasing sustainable performance of the firm.

The analysis of AI technology used in HRM indicates there is still little understanding of how AI-enabled HRM features impact employees, their professional results, and overall organizational success (Castellacci & Viñas-Bardolet, 2019).

Thomas Higginbotham et al. (2021) emphasised the issue regarding the usage of artificial intelligence and the displacement of workers in a case study. Beyond the displacement, they also emphasized how automation and AI are fundamentally altering the nature of employment itself. The need for technical skills in the workplace will rise by 55% by 2030, while the demand for social and emotional abilities will increase by 24%. Evidence indicates that there is a 30% or more gap between the abilities that the workforce possesses and those that businesses now want. Automation will likely make this mismatch worse due to shifting demands for higher talents. All of these forecasts provide us with a wealth of information on the future of the HR sector, which employed individuals to fulfill these demands. Although it is generally projected that AI will generate more jobs than it eliminates, there will still be significant consequences for certain people.

This case study suggests that automations must be human-centered in order to help realize a brighter future for all of mankind in order to deal with all the issues and challenges caused by them. A crucial goal of human-centered AI in the workplace is to complement and enhance humans rather than to replace them. The results of a different research (Chowdhury et al., 2022) also stressed that in order for organizations to profit from the adoption of AI, they must focus on creating non-technical resources such as human skills and competences, leadership, team coordination, organizational culture, and an innovation mentality.

CONCLUSION

For the aim of this research, we looked at how AI may improve HRM and company performance. It has been discovered that authors have showed a significant interest in examining the role of AI and the latest technologies in HRM to improve corporate performance and obtain competitive advantages. We found that AI has several advantages for HRM. However, these beneficial benefits have been questioned in regards to the ethics of gathering (Bhave et al., 2020; Suen et al., 2019). Specifically, the use of AI machine learning in the workplace, involving the collection and analysis of digital data to assist evaluation of talent and forecasting business-related challenges, raises a number of questions about human privacy (Bhave et al., 2020). To sum it up, we can't deny that the rise of artificial intelligence (AI) in human resources management is ushering in a new age of HR (version 5.0). Usage of AI applications in HR processes is revolutionizing the current scenario. The benefits of AI and how it can boost corporate performance have been covered in this chapter. According to some assessments, AI will fundamentally alter or replace the nature of job. However, a significant number of brand-new employment will also be generated, and the overall economy should benefit in the long run. Despite the fact that there are still many unexplored avenues and difficulties to overcome, we must admit that AI is the future of HR industry 5.0. So Government and business must collaborate to support people as they make the transition to this better future and make sure that the greatest number of people can benefit from these new technologies.

Implications

The main focus of this study was research on AI in HRM settings. The goal was to find out how these new technologies make HRM tasks easier and improve performance as a whole. This review turned up 30 journal articles, which gave us an idea of the present phenomenon. This review article adds to the growing chorus of academic voices urging managers to focus on how new technologies might improve the productivity of their businesses and their workforce. Artificially intelligent technology boosts interactions between human workers, improves problem-solving for efficiency, offers training, provides feedback, and supports employees. To ensure that employees have the qualifications and abilities necessary for working with artificial intelligence, businesses should prioritize employee training and continuous growth. Employee participation in training that will improve their learning habits and current knowledge base could be encouraged by managers. It is the managers' duty to encourage employees to participate in such endeavors that would equip them with the technological know-how necessary in the cutthroat global marketplace. Additionally, companies have to try to employ AI and robots responsibly. This involves supporting ongoing research and innovation while also creating regulations that safeguard consumer information and aid organizations and employees in adjusting to the increased expectations these technologies place on them. This will entail changing training programs to assist workers in developing the digital and soft skills that will be required in the new age, substituting legacy processes and systems with those that are better suited to handle newer technologies, and providing temporary support for those who suffer as a result of automation. As a result, professionals and academics must think about AI as a useful tool for a new business strategy. Our study aims to provide managers with information they can use to completely benefit from AI, enhance business performance, maximize the return and helps in acquiring a competitive edge.

LIMITATIONS AND FUTURE SCOPE

Unfortunately, there are few limitations that need to be addressed in future studies. Firstly, the present paper is completely based on the peer-reviewed published articles, therefore, future research should focus more on empirical research so that evidence can be generated and the impact of AI in improving corporate performance can be presented with the help of primary data and using tools and techniques. Secondly, for a review paper, the authors can go for thematic analysis or bibliometric analysis to provide a detailed review. Another important aspect is employee emotions and responses to HRM's technologically caused shift in the organization's function are another relatively untapped topic ideal for future investigation. Adopting a cross-cultural viewpoint will help in obtaining a better understanding of the global scenario and the reaction of employees that could either assist or obstruct the applicability of AI in HRM (Vrontis et al., 2022)

REFERENCES

Ancarani, A., Di Mauro, C., & Mascali, F. (2019). Backshoring strategy and the adoption of Industry 4.0: Evidence from Europe. *Journal of World Business, 54*(4), 360-371. doi:10.1016/j.jwb.2019.04.003

Arslan, A., Ruman, A. N., & Tarba, S.Y. (2021). Human dynamics of automation and digitalisation of economies: discussion on the challenges and opportunities. In The Palgrave Handbook of Corporate Sustainability in the Digital Era. Palgrave Macmillan.

Bhave, D. P., Teo, L. H., & Dalal, R. S. (2020). Privacy at work: A review and a research agenda for a contested terrain. *Journal of Management, 46*(1), 127–164. doi:10.1177/0149206319878254

Bondarouk, T., Harms, R., & Lepak, D. (2017). Does e-HRM lead to better HRM service? *International Journal of Human Resource Management, 28*(9), 1332–1362. doi:10.1080/09585192.2015.1118139

Buckley, P., Minette, K., Joy, D., & Michaels, J. (2004). The use of an automated employment recruiting and screening system for temporary professional employees: A case study. *Human Resource Management, 43*(2-3), 233–241. doi:10.1002/hrm.20017

Cano-Kollmann, M., Hannigan, T. J., & Mudambi, R. (2018). Global innovation networks–organizations and people. *Journal of International Management, 24*(2), 87–92. doi:10.1016/j.intman.2017.09.008

Castellacci, F., & Viñas-Bardolet, C. (2019). Internet use and job satisfaction. *Computers in Human Behavior, 90*, 141–152. doi:10.1016/j.chb.2018.09.001

Chowdhury, S., Dey, P., Joel-Edgar, S., Bhattacharya, S., Rodriguez-Espindola, O., Abadie, A., & Truong, L. (2022). Unlocking the value of artificial intelligence in human resource management through AI capability framework. *Human Resource Management Review, 100899*. Advance online publication. doi:10.1016/j.hrmr.2022.100899

Colbert, A., Yee, N., & George, G. (2016). The digital workforce and the workplace of the future. *Academy of Management Journal, 59*(3), 731–739. doi:10.5465/amj.2016.4003

Cooke, F. L., Liu, M., Liu, L. A., & Chen, C. C. (2019). Human resource management and industrial relations in multinational corporations in and from China: Challenges and new insights. *Human Resource Management, 58*(5), 455–471. doi:10.1002/hrm.21986

Enholm, I. M., Papagiannidis, E., Mikalef, P., & Krogstie, J. (2021). Artificial intelligence and business value: A literature review. *Information Systems Frontiers*, 1–26.

Fleming, P. (2019). Robots and organization studies: Why robots might not want to steal your job. *Organization Studies, 40*(1), 23–38. doi:10.1177/0170840618765568

Garcia-Arroyo, J., & Osca, A. (2019). Big data contributions to human resource management: A systematic review. *International Journal of Human Resource Management*, 1–26. doi:10.1080/09585192.2019.1674357

Glavas, C., Mathews, S., & Russell-Bennett, R. (2019). Knowledge acquisition via internet-enabled platforms: Examining incrementally and non-incrementally internationalizing SMEs. *International Marketing Review, 36*(1), 74–107. doi:10.1108/IMR-02-2017-0041

Haenlein, M., & Kaplan, A. (2019). A brief history of artificial intelligence: On the past, present, and future of artificial intelligence. *California Management Review, 61*(4), 5–14. doi:10.1177/0008125619864925

Henfridsson, O., Mathiassen, L., & Svahn, F. (2014). Managing technological change in the digital age: The role of architectural frames. *Journal of Information Technology, 29*(1), 27–43. doi:10.1057/jit.2013.30

Higginbotham, T., Weinberg, J., Aaker, J., & Fei, F. L. (2021). *Human - Centered Artificial Intelligence and workforce Displacement. Stanford Business*. Case Centre.

Huang, M. H., & Rust, R. T. (2018). Artificial intelligence in service. *Journal of Service Research, 21*(2), 155–172. doi:10.1177/1094670517752459

Jarrahi, M. (2018). Artificial intelligence and the future of work: human-AI symbiosis in organizational decision making. *Business Horizons, 61*(4), 577–586. doi:10.1016/j.bushor.2018.03.007

Kitsios, F., & Kamariotou, M. (2021). Artificial intelligence and business strategy towards digital transformation: A research agenda. *Sustainability, 13*(4), 2025. doi:10.3390u13042025

Kumar, P., Dwivedi, Y. K., & Anand, A. (2021). Responsible artificial intelligence (AI) for value formation and market performance in healthcare: The mediating role of patient's cognitive engagement. *Information Systems Frontiers*, 1–24. doi:10.100710796-021-10136-6 PMID:33948105

Lariviere, B., Bowen, D., Andreassen, T. W., Kunz, W., Sirianni, N. J., Voss, C., Wunderlich, N. V., & De Keyser, A. (2017). Service Encounter 2.0": An investigation into the roles of technology, employees and customers. *Journal of Business Research, 79*, 238–246. doi:10.1016/j.jbusres.2017.03.008

Lee, J., Davari, H., Singh, J., & Pandhare, V. (2018). Industrial Artificial Intelligence for industry 4.0-based manufacturing systems. *Manufacturing Letters, 18*, 20–23. doi:10.1016/j.mfglet.2018.09.002

Lindebaum, D., Vesa, M., & den Hond, F. (2020). Insights from The Machine Stops to better understand rational assumptions in algorithmic decision-making and its implications for organizations. *Academy of Management Review, 45*(1), 247–263. doi:10.5465/amr.2018.0181

Luo, X., Tong, S., Fang, Z., & Qu, Z. (2019). Frontiers: Machines vs. humans: The impact of artificial intelligence chatbot disclosure on customer purchases. *Marketing Science, 38*(6), 937–947. doi:10.1287/mksc.2019.1192

Malik, A., Budhwar, P., Srikanth, N. R., & Varma, A. (2019). *May the Bots Be with You! Opportunities and Challenges of Artificial Intelligence for Rethinking Human Resource Management Practices*. Paper Accepted for presentation BAM 2019. https:// www.bam.ac.uk/sites/bam.ac.uk/files/contribution294_0.pdf

Marler, J. H., & Parry, E. (2016). Human resource management, strategic involvement and e-HRM technology. *International Journal of Human Resource Management, 27*(19), 2233–2253. doi:10.1080/09585192.2015.1091980

Olan, F., Arakpogun, E. O., Suklan, J., Nakpodia, F., Damij, N., & Jayawickrama, U. (2022). Artificial intelligence and knowledge sharing: Contributing factors to organizational performance. *Journal of Business Research, 145*, 605–615. doi:10.1016/j.jbusres.2022.03.008

Pan, Y., Froese, F., Liu, N., Hu, Y., & Ye, M. (2022). The adoption of artificial intelligence in employee recruitment: The influence of contextual factors. *International Journal of Human Resource Management, 33*(6), 1125–1147. doi:10.1080/09585192.2021.1879206

Park, R. (2018). The roles of OCB and automation in the relationship between job autonomy and organizational performance: A moderated mediation model. *International Journal of Human Resource Management, 29*(6), 1139–1156. doi:10.1080/09585192.2016.1180315

Saxena, P., Charu, & Arora, R. (2022). Exploring the link between Innovativeness and Organizational Performance. *NMIMS Management Review, 30*(1), 68-89. doi:10.53908/NMMR.300104

Sharma, N. (2021). Using positive deviance to enhance employee engagement: An interpretive structural modelling approach. *The International Journal of Organizational Analysis, 30*(1), 84–98. doi:10.1108/IJOA-07-2020-2341

Sharma, N., & Singh, V. K. (2016). Effect of workplace incivility on job satisfaction and turnover intentions in India. *South Asian Journal of Global Business Research, 5*(2), 234–249. doi:10.1108/SAJGBR-02-2015-0020

Toniolo, K., Masiero, E., Massaro, M., & Bagnoli, C. (2020). Sustainable business models and artificial intelligence: Opportunities and challenges. *Knowledge, People, and Digital Transformation*, 103-117.

Vrontis, D., Christofi, M., Pereira, V., Tarba, S., Makrides, A., & Trichina, E. (2022). Artificial intelligence, robotics, advanced technologies and human resource management: A systematic review. *International Journal of Human Resource Management*, *33*(6), 1237–1266. doi:10.1080/09585192.2020.1871398

Zehir, C., Karaboğa, T., & Başar, D. (2020). The transformation of human resource management and its impact on overall business performance: big data analytics and AI technologies in strategic HRM. In *Digital business strategies in blockchain ecosystems* (pp. 265–279). Springer. doi:10.1007/978-3-030-29739-8_12

Chapter 9
Future of HR Analytics:
Applications to Recruitment, Employee Engagement, and Retention

Smruti Bulsari
https://orcid.org/0000-0002-0651-3275
University of Essex, UK

Kiran Pandya
https://orcid.org/0000-0002-6777-4647
Veer Narmad South Gujarat University, Surat, India

ABSTRACT

HR analytics is a paradigm shift from a traditional and intuitive-based approach to an evidence-based approach for aiding decision-making processes to enhance employee as well as organizational performance and profitability. This chapter discusses the concept of HR analytics, followed by its application to three HR functions: recruitment, employee engagement, and employee retention. Two case studies for each of these three HR functions are also succinctly discussed. Some relevant statistics regarding the current state of implementation of HR analytics in organizations is also briefly discussed. Key issues related to the HR analytics implementation process, moderating factors to implement HR analytics, and challenges of implementation are also discussed in this chapter. The chapter concludes with a discussion on the future of HR analytics. Considering the scope of the book, technical details like regression models or machine learning algorithms are not discussed in this chapter.

Human Resource (HR) Analytics is relatively a new, yet a fast-emerging concept. HR functions like recruitment and selection, succession planning, performance management, training and development, employee engagement and many more, can find HR Analytics useful to derive insights for better human resource management. HR Analytics is now being recognized as very useful tool for decision-making, especially with the emergence of the Fifth Industrial Revolution (Industry 5.0). Industry 5.0 capitalizes upon data to build smart and efficient processes. Data is now available in abundance through Internet of Things (IoT)[1] and Cloud platforms[2]. These data which are available in massive quantity and with fre-

DOI: 10.4018/978-1-6684-6745-9.ch009

quency of as high as nano seconds, are popularly known as "Big Data". Industry 5.0 focuses on replacing human efforts with Artificial Intelligence (AI) and robotics for the repetitive tasks. Industry 5.0 is built on the premise that humans should be employed to perform tasks which cannot be done by machines. Unlike humans, machines / robots do not experience the boredom. Therefore, unlike humans, a repetitive task is performed by robots with the same efficiency, irrespective of the number of repetitions. On the other hand, humans can contribute to more productive solutions like developing the new technology, or even conflict management in organizations. Thus, Industry 5.0 is bringing about major changes in the roles that would be performed by the human resources. In such a situation, deriving insights about people's choices, aptitudes and abilities for a given task / job role will be helpful in making right decisions regarding recruitment and retention. Matching the job roles with choices, aptitudes and abilities would increase the probability of recruiting a right candidate and also for enhanced employee engagement. HR Analytics can also be helpful in understanding the factors that would increase the retention of employees with high performance.

A quick glance on evolution of HR Analytics show that the term "Workforce Analytics" was the first among the vocabulary. This could be sometime in late 1990s. The term Talent Analytics was used sometime in 2006, which developed alongside the concept of Talent Management, whereas People Analytics was used in 2013 by Google to describe their data-driven approach to human resource management. The latest of all is HR Analytics (Marler & Boudreau, 2017).

HR Analytics is crucial to strategic planning in an organization because it provides insights about the organizational dynamics, helps in identifying issues that can adversely impact the organization's productivity, examining the impact of a solution to address a given organizational issue, and predict outcomes of certain actions (Momin & Mishra, 2015). HR Analytics can also be useful to determine demand for employees for a given job role, predicting employee turnover, devising compensation policies, enhancing employee performance, succession planning and a lot more (HR Research Institute, 2021). Ekka, (2021) has undertaken a comprehensive review of literature and observes that HR Analytics can help in enhancing the performance of the HR department. Insights from HR Analytics can help retain the best talents, enhance decision-making in the organization, enhance productivity and performance, assess loyalty of employee towards the organization, provide right type of training to the employees, and enhance employee engagement. Sivathanu & Pillai, (2020) examined the use of technology and HR Analytics for talent management and its impact on organizational performance. They interviewed 122 senior HR officers of the national and multinational firms of India and found that a strong strategic HR management drive, backed up by HR Analytics insights would help in developing a high-performing talent pool, which would result in improved organizational performance. Barbar et al., (2019) studied the impact of HR Analytics on training and development strategy by administering a questionnaire on 302 employees, each from 302 private sector organizations. The results of their study show that HR professionals from the large private sector organizations make use of HR Analytics to formulate strategies for employees' development and for strategic HR decisions. However, they observe that there is a need to strengthen communication between HR professionals and HR Analytics experts to optimize both – data for and outcome of HR Analytics. Muhammad & Naz, (2022) undertook a study to examine the role of HR Analytics in improving employee engagement, retention and overall performance of banking sector organizations in Karachi, Pakistan. They collected data from 120 banking professionals and found that HR Analytics helps in improving employee engagement and enhancing their performance. This is then helpful in improving employee retention and improving overall organizational performance. Shrivastava & Dhaigude, (2022) undertook a case study of Prime Data Tech Pvt Ltd (PDPL), a US-based company with its Indian headquarters in Bengaluru. The company was facing a recruitment issue, where the candidates would accept the job offer yet, would not join the organization. Using predictive HR Analytics, the team identified the possible causes of this problem and developed a model that would predict whether the candidate would join or not. This helped the company in giving job offers only to those candidates who clear the interview but has a high probability of joining. These examples provide a broad idea about the use of HR Analytics in solving the issues pertaining to the HR functions, making the existing process more efficient and improving organizational performance. Karmańska, (2020) argues how almost all HR functions can draw insights from HR Analytics to enhance efficiency, increase productivity and improve business performance. For example, HR Analytics can be applied to applicants' assessments in the recruitment process for getting recommendations on shortlisting the applicants or even selecting candidates for a job offer. Thus, HR Analytics can be used to derive insights for reducing the cost and time involved, and also for enhancing efficiency of the recruitment process. HR Analytics can be helpful in workforce planning, retention as well as in performance measurement. Machine learning[3] techniques provide insights into the factors associated with attrition, which are otherwise difficult to observe at an individual (managerial) level. It also gives insights into the expenditure trends and helps in forecasting the expenditure (or increase in expenditure over time). This can be helpful in devising cost management strategies in time and to prevent sudden financial shocks to the organization.

The basic objective of this chapter is to provide a broad overview of how organizations have successfully adopted HR Analytics to enhance the efficiency of existing HR processes or solve an issue associated with the HR functions. This chapter is largely non-technical in nature, yet provides insights into pre-requisites, moderating factors, the process of and challenges faced in implementing HR Analytics in an organization. This chapter focuses on discussing the application of HR Analytics to three main functions of HR: recruitment, employee engagement and employee retention. The chapter also succinctly discusses two case studies each for HR Analytics applications to recruitment process, employee engagement and retention. Organizations require to perform a large number of HR functions. These are required for growth and development, and smooth functioning of an organization. Job satisfaction, talent management, employee retention and developing competencies are important HR functions. However, considering that the selection of the right employee is crucial to rest of the HR functions, this chapter discusses the use of HR Analytics for recruitment. Once employees are recruited, their engagement in the organization is crucial to their own performance, as well as for the organizational performance. An engaged and satisfied employee is less likely to leave the organization. This helps in reducing employee turnover and enhancing retention. Normally, the cost of recruiting a new employee and train her / him for the defined work is quite high. It is therefore important, to ensure that the right employee is recruited and retained. Considering the scope of the book, technical details like regression models or machine learning algorithms are not discussed in this chapter. Some statistics regarding the current state of implementation of HR Analytics in organizations are briefly discussed in this chapter. An HR professional might find this chapter helpful to get details and insights about the issues that can be resolved using HR Analytics, the right time to implement HR Analytics, and to allocate tasks to the HR Analytics experts after recruiting them.

This chapter is organized in 7 sections: section 1 presents an overview of the concept of HR Analytics and the present state of its implementation in organizations. Section 2 describes the use of HR Analytics for recruitment process. Case studies of Shell and Google explain how these organizations have made use of HR Analytics to enhance the effectiveness of assessments and reduce the recruitment process time respectively. Section 3 discusses the use of HR Analytics for improving employee engagement. Case studies on Clarks and Shell show how HR Analytics is used to identify the factors affecting engagement. Section 4 explains the use of HR Analytics for enhancing retention / reducing attrition. Case studies of Johnson & Johnson, and Pricewaterhouse Coopers explain how HR Analytics helped them enhancing retention and reducing attrition respectively. Section 5 discusses the pre-requisites, moderating factors and the process of implementing HR Analytics in an organization. Challenges to HR Analytics implementation is discussed in Section 6, and the future of HR Analytics is presented in section 7.

HR ANALYTICS: AN OVERVIEW

HR Analytics is a broad term to describe the use of big data and IoT to derive insights about various HR issues. These could range from getting information about the pool of prospective candidates for recruitment, an identifying and resolving HR issues in an organization, making HR processes more efficient and much more. One single definition cannot provide overall perspective of HR Analytics. Opatha, (2020) attempts to provide a comprehensive list of HR Analytics definitions, based on past studies. Some additional definitions, categorizing HR Analytics as a practice, a method and a process are presented in this section.

HR Analytics as a Practice

Marler & Boudreau, (2017) undertook a study to understand the application of HR Analytics, its operationalization, its importance to organizations, its outcomes, and the factors influencing the outcomes of HR Analytics. They adopted the "integrative synthesis"[4] procedure to extract the research papers, conference proceedings, edited books, and other Internet-based literature containing terms *HR Analytics*, *Talent Analytics*, *Workforce Analytics*, *People Analytics* and *Human Resource Analytics*. They define HR Analytics as:

"A HR practice enabled by information technology that uses descriptive, visual, and statistical analyses of data related to HR processes, human capital, organizational performance, and external economic benchmarks to establish business impact and enable data-driven decision-making."

HR Analytics as a Method

Tomar & Gaur, (2020) describe HR Analytics as a combination of methodology, experimental approach, data-driven framework and an innovation to process and analyze HR data for making informed decisions.

Karmańska, (2020) reviews the literature available on HR Analytics and describes it as a method to organize and analyze data related to people of an organization, making use of the quantitative techniques and the methods of computer science and decision science. They emphasize that the use of HR Analytics should result in better decisions, leading to improved business outcomes.

Jain & Jain, (2020) define HR Analytics as a collection of robust algorithms with different operability, yet similar objectives, built upon the fundamentals of statistical concepts and analytical tools.

Houghton, (2015) focuses on the value added by the human resources in an organization and define HR Analytics as:

"HR Analytics is the application of analysis and data processing procedures to HR/people data to provide information and insights about the nature of individuals in organisations and the value that they add."

HR Analytics as a Process

Ferrar & Green, (2021) define HR Analytics as making use of the data related to workforce for devising strategies that lead to improved business outcomes. They schematically explain the activities associated with HR Analytics and its outcomes in Figure 1:

Figure 1. HR Analytics: Activities and Outcomes. Source: Ferrar, J., & Green, D. (2021). Excellence in People Analytics: How to Use Workforce Data to Create Business Value. Kogan Page Limited. p. 5.

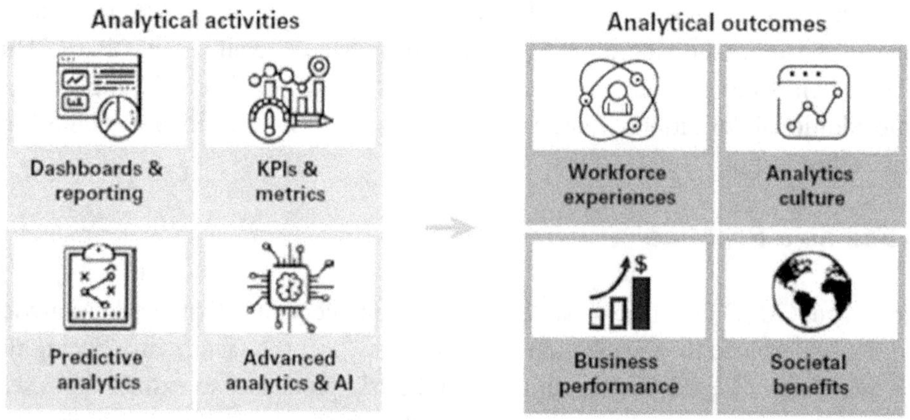

Figure 2. HR Analytics Process. Source: Mohammed, A. Q. (2019). HR Analytics: A Modern Tool in HR for Predictive Decision Making. Journal of Management, 6(3). p. 53.

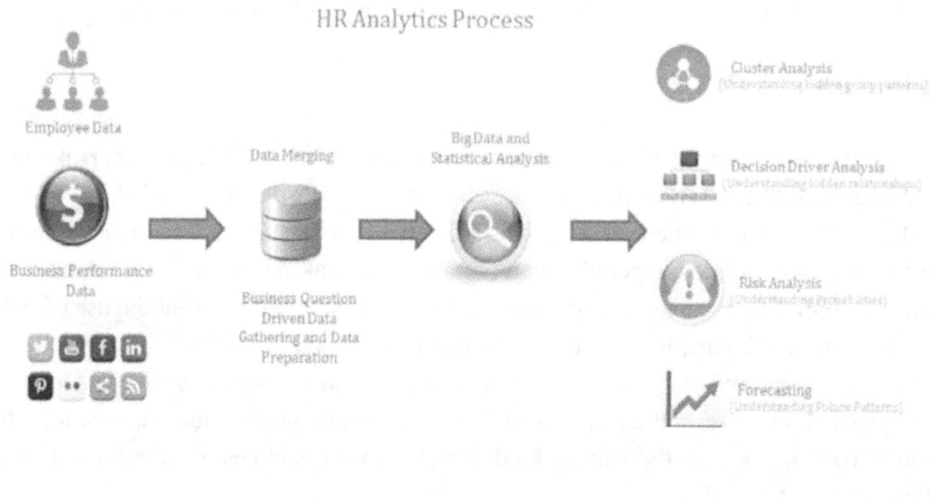

Mohammed, (2019) describes the process of HR Analytics as shown in Figure 2. He observes that the data of employee records maintained by an organization, along with the organizational performance data, clubbed with all the data from the social media (both – about the employee as well as organization, which would be largely, unstructured in nature[5]) is aggregated into one database. This aggregated data is then subjected to quantitative analytical techniques to discern patterns, understanding associations, estimating the probabilities of business risks and forecasting the organizational performance. The forecast of organizational performance include demand for employees, changes in job roles, attrition rates, over and above business profits and turnover.

Levels of HR Analytics

There are four levels of HR Analytics:

Descriptive Analytics: It makes use of historical data and is used to describe a situation in the organization. For example, examining trends of employee attrition is descriptive analytics. Use of dashboards and visualizations are the main tools of descriptive analytics.

Insightful Analytics: This too makes use of historical data. Insightful analytics is used to identify the associations and cause-effect relationships. It is used either to estimate demand for employees with specific skills or to identify the cause of an issue in the organization (for example, high attrition, lower performance etc.). Use of statistical tools like different types of correlations and regressions are used to gain insights, i.e., to undertake insightful analytics.

Predictive Analytics: This makes use of historical data, along with forecasting techniques to forecast future demand for employees with specific skills, employee turnover etc. Over and above statistical tools, predictive analytics makes use of machine learning models. Artificial intelligence algorithms / software, which are developed and deployed to predict the outcome with a reasonably high accuracy are called machine learning models. High accuracy is the key aspect of machine learning algorithms because the forecast is to be used for devising future strategies or make changes in existing policies / practices.

Prescriptive Analytics: In this case, a future target is set. Present situation of the organization is analyzed and scenarios are created for achieving the target. These scenarios give insights about what requires to be done to achieve the set target in the set time frame. They normally adopt the concepts of What-if / sensitivity analysis and Goal Seek.

Present State of Implementation

HR Research Institute, (2021) show that 68 per cent organizations make use of descriptive analytics, 53 per cent make use of insightful analytics, 43 per cent organizations use predictive analytics and only 34 per cent make use of prescriptive analytics. These figures are arrived at aggregating the percentages for each (staked) bar shown in Figure 3:

Figure 3 shows that there is still a wide scope of implementing HR Analytics for various HR functions in organizations.

Figure 3. Extent of Use of HR Analytics in Organizations by Levels. Source: Compiled from HR Research Institute. (2021). The State of HR Analytics in 2021. HR.com. p. 11.

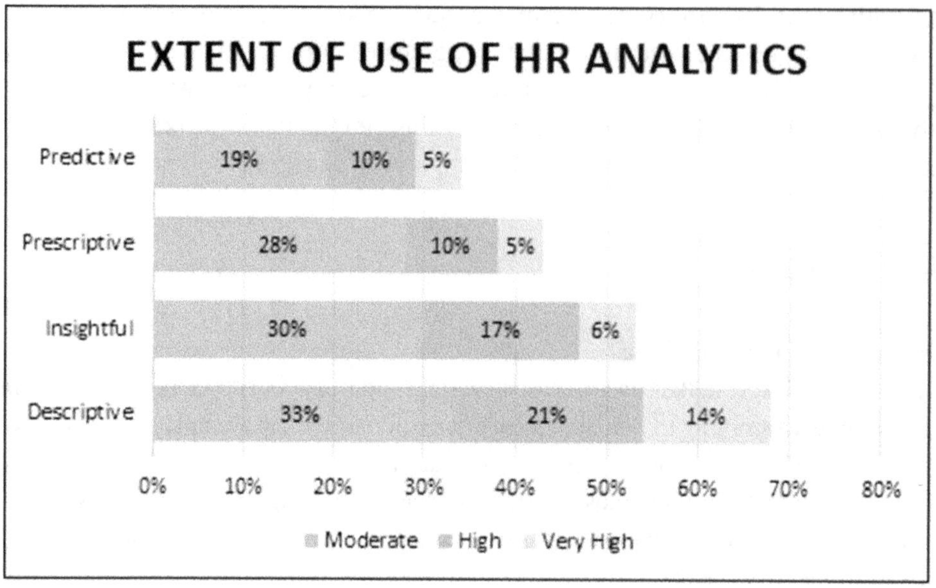

HR ANALYTICS FOR RECRUITMENT

One of the applications of HR Analytics is to forecast recruitment needs of an organization. HR Analytics helps in identifying the gaps in the demand for and supply of talents at a global level, helping to select the most suitable talent for the job (Momin & Mishra, 2015). Profile features such as education and experience help HR to identify the most suitable profiles for a given job (Dey & De, 2015). Apart from this, HR Analytics can be a predictive tool to design a template for the future job roles. Gurusinghe et al., (2021) provide a conceptual framework for applying predictive HR Analytics to talent management issues. They suggest that frequency mapping, regression analysis to understand the cause-effect relationships, trend analysis and scenario planning for talent management help in addressing the issues to tackling talent shortage, talent development and talent retention. Pessach et al., (2020) apply tools of HR Analytics on a large dataset, containing details of more than a hundred thousand employees, of over a decade. The said dataset is claimed by them to be representative of a wide range of heterogenous population. The results of their study show that is it possible to predict with a high level of accuracy, the selection of a candidate with required characteristics for a given position and use these predictions for a more generalized recruitment optimization model.

HR Analytics helps in Talent acquisition (TA) as well as in bridging the gap between HR team and TA team. TA is a broader term, which includes recruitment, over and above promotion, transfer, and training and development (T&D). HR team and TA team have separate roles in the recruitment process. Apart from bridging the gap between HR and TA, HR Analytics gives insights about the quality of talent hired, which helps in classifying the new recruits, who would perform better than the others, given, enabling environment to perform and grow. Walford-Wright & Scott-Jackson, (2018) suggest analyzing the skills and attributes to classify high performers and low performers for the purpose. This can help effective resource management and advance planning for recruitment, training as well as infrastructure development. Attrition results in high hiring costs. This has bearing on the profits of the organization. Analytics on performance and productivity of existing employees, attrition trends, the right profile for each potential employee can be worked out to help planning related to TA. Retention Analytics is discussed in detail in section 4.

The term "Recruitment Analytics" refers to HR Analytics applied to tasks associated with recruitment, ranging from sourcing assessment, selection and hiring. Defining candidate success profiles, forecasting workforce requirements, examining the reasons for attrition, analyzing performance data for identifying talent needs, job profiling, mapping the source of talents, selecting candidates and improving overall recruitment experience are also included in Recruitment Analytics (Mohapatra & Sahu, 2017).

This section describes two case studies, of Shell and Google, where HR Analytics is successfully implemented. Successful implementation can be defined in terms of reduced economic cost and increased return on investment. Shell makes use of Recruitment Analytics to enhance the effectiveness of candidates' assessment in the recruitment process. Google uses Recruitment Analytics to reduce the number of interviews, and time taken from shortlisting a candidate to deciding whether or not, to offer the job.

Enhancing the Effectiveness of Assessment Process using Recruitment Analytics in Shell

Lam & Hawkes, (2017) describes how Shell augmented Recruitment Analytics with assessment experts to streamline the recruitment process. Shell is a British company which produces and distributes oil and gas products. Shell typically receives, over one lakh applications for their global graduate program each year for less than a thousand positions. The recruitment process requires the candidates to be assessed for their ability and aptitude for the job role. Shell was interested in ensuring the effectiveness of assessments and matching right candidates for the job roles such that it reduces the economic cost of recruitment and enhance the return on talent investment. The effectiveness of assessments was examined by implementing Recruitment Analytics using the data on performance of the recruits, candidates' feedbacks and focus groups with assessment experts. Shell found that the assessments about candidates' suitability for a job role was correlated with the recruits' job performance. Candidates' feedback and focus group results found the assessment process to be robust. Yet, they found that there is a scope to further enhance the efficiency of the recruitment process by increasing the extent of digitizing. For this, the use of pre-recorded interviews in early stage of the assessment was implemented.

Enhancing Efficiency of Recruitment Process using HR Analytics at Google

Google is one of the few companies to pioneer the implementation of Recruitment Analytics. Levenson & Pillans, (2017) found that Google would typically put the candidates through somewhere between 15 to 25 interviews before deciding whether to make a job offer or not. This amounted to approximately 1000 manhours (125 persons multiplied with 8 hours) for every 1000 persons recruited. These 1000 hours do not include the assessments of those candidates who get rejected; the probability of getting an offer from Google after all these interviews is 0.2 per 100 applicants who get interview calls (Popomaronis, 2019). The time for assessments ranged from three to six months. Recruitment Analytics was used to estimate that the optimum number of interviews for deciding on whether to offer a job to the candidate or not. This number worked out to four interviews. Four interviews would predict with 86 per cent accuracy about a candidate's suitability for the job role, and every additional interview would lead to diminishing returns by 1 per cent. The time taken for assessment procedure reduced to 47 days (close to a month and a half), which is a 75 per cent reduction from the earlier. As a part of adopting this efficient assessment process, the interview scores of the candidate being assessed is compared with that of those in the past, and the performance of the candidates hired in past. This helps in making a decision about hiring a prospective candidate. Google has implemented an Applicant Tracking System. This checks the CVs of the applicant against those of employees. If there is any overlap in terms of their working together in any organization in the past, the existing employees' feedback about the prospective employee is included for making a hiring decision. Google also takes feedback from the candidates interviewed, irrespective of their selection, to make the selection process more efficient.

EMPLOYEE ENGAGEMENT ANALYTICS

HR Analytics, used to examine employee engagement, is referred as Employee Engagement Analytics. The importance of employee engagement for improved business performance is gradually gaining acceptance. One of the most frequently quoted definitions of employee engagement is by Kahn, (1990):

"the harnessing of organization members' selves to their work roles; in engagement, people employ and express themselves physically, cognitively, and emotionally during role performances."

However, psychologists try to explain employee engagement as a construct. Edwards & Edwards, (2016) cite (Rich et al., 2010; Schaufeli & Bakker, 2003, 2010), who have independently devised a set of 17 questions, which are validated to capture the concept of engagement. They cite examples of the statements on which the employees are required to respond on a five-point scale (where, 1 represents "strongly disagree" and 5, "strongly agree"). They highlight the point that the metrics of employee engagement used by organizations and research consultancies are largely, based on the Gallup's Q12 measure and Utretch Work Engagement Scale (UWES). Some commonly used employee engagement metrics by organizations are: percentage of engaged employees, employee engagement score, employee satisfaction score, and the net promoter score. The net promoter score based on the percentage of employees who would recommend their organizations as workplace to others (net of those who would not).

Employee Engagement Analytics is a practice to examine the extent of employee satisfaction and identify the factors associated with it. It is used to get insights about the involvement of employees in their work as well as the impact that employees with higher engagement would bring to the profits and overall business performance. Coco et al., (2011) show a cause-effect linkage between employee engagement and business performance using HR Analytics using data of Lowe's, a USA-based company having retail stores dealing in home improvement products and hardware. Employee engagement is defined as an emotional commitment of an employee towards the organization and its goals (Kruse, 2012). They argue that employees with higher engagement result in better service, increased customer satisfaction, which in turn results in higher profits to business. Oladipupo & Olubusayo, (2020) undertook a study the examine the impact of using HR Analytics for employee engagement in manufacturing sector organizations of Nigeria. Their study is based on the review of literature and it reveals that insights derived from the results of HR Analytics helped in enhancing employee engagement in these organizations. Gaur, (2020) examined the impact of leveraging HR Analytics on employee engagement using feedback of 100 HR professionals[6]. Her study revealed that use of HR Analytics enhanced the employees' confidence on their performance appraisals and overall experience with the organization. This resulted in higher employee engagement.

This section describes two case studies: Clarks and Shell. Employee engagement Analytics has helped improved business performance in Shell and has helped enhancing safety and improving leadership in Shell.

Improving Business Performance through Employee Engagement Analytics at Clarks

Ankum, (2022) describes how C & J Clarks, a British shoe manufacturer and retailer enhanced their business performance and maximized return on investment by increasing Employee Engagement. Analytics was applied after identifying as many as 450 data points, which represented either employee engagement or business performance. The results showed an increase in business performance parameters by 0.4 per cent for each one per cent increase in employee engagement metric. It may be noted that the employee engagement in Clarks was already high, when this Employee Engagement Analytics exercise was undertaken. Despite, the results showed that there was a scope to increase the extent of employee engagement. The team further collected data of the retail stores of the company, which were rated as top 100 on business performance to validate (and successfully validated) their findings from the first analytics exercise. Clarks has stores in approximately 1400 locations with a total of 13000 employees across the globe. This entire exercise gave insights to the management to work out an ideal team size for optimizing operational efficiency and to have a replicable schema to increase the business performance of their retail outlets. It also helped the company to develop a store management programme and an employee engagement toolkit for the managers.

Enhancing Safety and Improved Organizational Leadership through Employee Engagement Analytics at Shell

Safety assumes top priority, be it for an individual, or an organization. Levenson & Pillans, (2017) narrate how Shell's HR Analytics team found that employee engagement is the biggest driver of employee performance, and that it has a positive causal link with sales. However, what is more incisive is that the results of Employee Engagement Analytics show a four per cent drop in "recordable case frequency", a key term for industrial safety metric, for one per cent increase in employee engagement. The analytics team further looked for the drivers of employee engagement and found that the team members and team leaders are two key determinants of employee engagement. They found that inclusion of a low performing employee to a given team reduces employee engagement of all the team members. These insights derived from Employee Engagement Analytics helped to shape the leadership practices in Shell. The company started providing actionable feedback like retraining the employees / team leaders with lower performance or lower engagement after deriving insights from Employee Engagement Analytics exercise. The leadership training curriculum is also revamped after undertaking this exercise of Employee Engagement Analytics.

EMPLOYEE RETENTION ANALYTICS

Employee engagement is pre-condition to retention. Employee engagement and retention can be said to be related in the sense that employees with higher engagement are more likely to stay in the organization. Borkakoty, (2017) quotes the results of a survey undertaken by the Times Jobs, which shows that 60 per cent employees are not happy with their current jobs and 80 per cent employees are looking for switching the jobs. She argues that companies have huge HR data about their employees, which can be used to know the extent of engagement towards their work. HR Analytics helps identifying the motivational factors like reward and recognition, or specialized trainings, which are likely to have positive influence on retention.

Employee Retention Analytics is the HR Analytics applied to understand the situation and causes of employee attrition. Employee Retention Analytics gives insights into the current situation of employee turnover, the root cause of the problem and the types of employees who constitute a major proportion of the total employee attrition. Employee Retention Analytics also helps the management of an organization to know their employees better in terms of their personal life as well as in terms of their positions, job satisfaction, their expectations from the organization and like. Organizations maintain data of employees. Over and above, social media content of the employees could be used to understand their sentiments, and the changes therein, from time to time. On one hand, this gives insights about the estimated probability of an employee to leave the organization. On its positive side, Employee Retention Analytics provides an indirect voice to the employees in strategic decision making, especially about the HR policies of the organization.

Singh et al., (2022) examined the transmission mechanism of employing big data and predictive analytics for employee retention. Using questionnaire, they collected data from 269 HR managers of manufacturing sector organizations identified from LinkedIn. The results of their study reveal that use of predictive analytics and big data helps in eliciting tacit reasons of employee turnover, which can then be used to reduce it. They also observe that use of data and analytics enhances transparency, which is necessary for building trust. Employees having trust in an organization are less likely to leave. The study by Biriowu & Kalio, (2020) in Nigeria also observes a similar association between the use of HR Analytics and employee retention. Marvin et al., (2021) employ data analytics techniques (machine learning algorithms) on a large dataset of US-based organizations to develop a model that can accurately identify the factors that would improve employee retention. Since the focus of this study was to find the algorithm with high accuracy, the relative accuracies of machine learning algorithms were discussed in their study. Nevertheless, their study does confirm that use of HR Analytics is helpful for enhancing employee retention.

Two case studies, of Johnson & Johnson and PricewaterhouseCoopers (PwC), are described in this section. These case studies explain how Employee Retention Analytics has helped enhancing the retention rate in Johnson & Johnson, and reducing voluntary turnover in PwC.

Enhancing Employee Retention using HR Analytics at Johnson & Johnson

Ankum, (2022) describes the case of Johnson & Johnson made use of HR Analytics to improve both – employee performance and retention. Johnson & Johnson is an American multinational company and is one of the largest companies in the health care sector. The company had a policy to prefer candidates with work experience in the relevant field. Because of this policy the percentage of graduate recruits had declined by 10 per cent. The company preferred to recruit experienced candidates assuming that they stay longer and contribute more to the company in comparison with the graduate recruits. Employee Retention Analytics was used to examine the association between past experience and employee turnover. Based on the data of 47000 employees, the HR Analytics team found that the retention rate of fresh graduate recruits was far higher than that of experienced recruits. However, the difference in contribution to the company by experienced employees and that by graduate recruits was not found to be statistically significant[7]. This means that the graduate recruits effectively contributed more to the company; experience played no role in contribution. This insight, which was derived from Employee Retention Analytics, helped the company to develop a special two-year leadership programme for fresh graduate recruits with an objective to help them retain even longer in the organization. The outcome of this exercise was that the recruitment of graduates at Johnson & Johnson increased by 20 per cent, the retention rate increased, while holding for the contribution to the company.

Reducing Employee Turnover using HR Analytics at PricewaterhouseCoopers

PricewaterhouseCoopers, branded as (and now on, referred as) PwC, is one of the giant accounting firms with network across the globe. Levenson, (2011) describes how PwC made use of HR Analytics to solve their problem of talent management and retention. The company was specifically interested in surveying the past (those who has left the company before or within past 15 years) as well as the present employees on their experience with the organization. The data on career progression so far, and current positions of the employees who had already left PwC was also collected. PwC had a high attrition rate, especially of those in key talent pool like entry-level associates, senior associates and partners. The company considered offering deferred compensation for improving retention. PwC made use of HR Analytics to examine the efficacy of deferred compensation as a tool to improve retention. Data of past and present employees was collected and analytical techniques (ranging from basic to advanced) were applied on it to answer the following questions:

- What are the career outcomes / progression of the former employees,
- How is the work-life balance of both – former and current employees at comparable career stages; and
- What are the drivers of retention for current employees?

Using Employee Retention Analytics techniques, and controlling for factors like education, gender, race, office location, total years of work experience etc., they found that deferred compensation would have much lower impact on retention in comparison with addressing the concerns of work-life balance, career progression and individual development. PwC took initiative to strengthen the relationships between the partners and the employees, enhanced focus on training and development, and equipped managers with tools to manage work-life balance. The outcome of this exercise was that, voluntary turnover reduced to a remarkable extent.

HR ANALYTICS IMPLEMENTATION

Implementation of HR Analytics not only requires active participation of HR team but also of Information Technology (IT) team and a team of analytics specialists. Thinking from an HR perspective, implementation of HR Analytics, even for one HR function, is a major change. HR professionals and students will understand the difficulties associated with change management. Moreover, implementing HR Analytics for just one function is not cost effective, as the same amount of IT infrastructure and skills (employees) would be required for even for multiple HR functions. In this section, pre-requisites to HR Analytics implementation, moderating factors and the stepwise implementation process are discussed.

Pre-requisites to Implementation

Building trust among the employees for accepting the use of HR Analytics is one of the main pre-requisites to successful implementation. Lee, (2021) discusses the pre-requisites of implementing HR Analytics in an organization. An important pre-requisite is that of data governance. This means, there should be a system where data on different HR parameters can be collected, joined and stored. They cite Welle, (2018) to explain the importance on uniformity of the data format as a pre-requisite that in case of multinational corporations, there have been instances where the same data is represented as Korean numbers, English numbers, signs, symbols etc. These discrepancies in data formats result in delay in implementing HR Analytics as more time is spent in collating and cleaning the data[8]. Setting up a data warehouse for HR and organizational data, which can be termed as Human Resource Information System (HRIS) could ensure uniform and clean data. The process of setting up a data warehouse is discussed in section 5.3, as a part of the steps to implement HR Analytics in an organization.

Fernandez & Gallardo-Gallardo, (2021) suggest 14 key factors, grouped in four categories to overcome barriers to HR Analytics implementation. These are:

Preparation: Clearly define the business problem and whether data is available to apply HR Analytics to get insights into the problem.

Development: Identifying and working on the models suitable to answer the business problem.

Dissemination: Generating visualizations that will provide insights into the key issues behind the business problem.

Team: HR Analytics team should be independent of all the departments; it should be an independent entity / department in itself, which will take inputs from other departments and give insights through analytical tools and visualizations to other departments. However, who should lead this team – someone from analytics background or someone from HR – is still being debated.

Moderating Factors for HR Analytics Implementation

Having pre-requisites in place is not enough. One may have all pre-requisites in place, yet some more efforts are required for successful implementation of HR Analytics in an organization.

Dealing with change management is the most important of all the moderating factors. Existing employees should be taken into full confidence about the implementation of HR Analytics. Any apprehensions about their job insecurity should be immediately addressed by giving them an assurance that their jobs are secured. Kremer, (2018) suggests that if employees are convinced, they will not only co-operate but would contribute to putting the system in place. They also discuss other factors that would moderate the process of HR Analytics implementation, which are:

While setting up the infrastructure for implementing HR Analytics, care requires to be taken to ensure that the technology and software should have the capability to not only store and process the data generated within the organization. Rather, it should also have compatibility to draw relevant data from external sources, including social media and data available in public domain.

Upgradation of existing HRIS to make it capable of undertaking data exploration, advanced statistical analysis and working with machine learning models. It may be noted that machine learning models consume a lot of resources and processor's capabilities in comparison with standard statistical models. Data exploration is largely undertaken these days in the form of dashboards and visualizations. This too requires an HRIS capable of creating and operating dashboards, and for generating visualizations. Use of cloud platforms is also required not only for accessing data but also for displaying visualizations.

McCartney & Fu, (2022) collect data from 155 Irish organizations and test the model linking HR technology, HR Analytics, evidence-based management and organization performance to answer the "why", "how" and "when" will HR Analytics result in enhanced performance. They observe that HR technology is a pre-requisite to HR Analytics, and HR Analytics helps in evidence-based management. This, in turn, results in improved performance of an organization. Thus, focusing on building a strong HR technology infrastructure is the first step to implementing HR Analytics.

People are core to success of any system. Successful implementation of HR Analytics requires experts in the area of statistics, data science and engineering (computer / IT / electronics and allied disciplines).

Most importantly, an enterprise approach, where there is an integration of process, data and Analytics, requires to be developed in the organization. Successful implementation is possible only if there is flexibility among the employees and organizational polices, as well as attitude to adapt a new system. This again brings back to change management.

Process of Implementing HR Analytics

Altexsoft, (2019) has given a step-by-step approach to implement HR Analytics in an organization. This is shown in Figure 4.

Each of these eight steps are summarized as follows:

1. Choosing what to measure, selecting the relevant data to be collected is the first step to successful HR implementation. The aims for implementing HR Analytics should be clear in order to choose the right metrics and data.
2. Identifying the sources of data, which can range from a database within the organization to external sources, data available in public domain or social media data.
3. Deciding on whether to use standard and ready available system / tools for data extraction and analytics or to develop one specific to organization's requirements.
4. Creating a team comprising HR manager, data engineer, data warehouse / HRIS developer, database administrator, analyst, data scientist and system developers with different skillsets.
5. Setting up data integration tool through Extracting, Transforming and Loading (commonly known as ETL). Here, "Extraction" means identifying and collating data from different sources, "Transform" is the process to convert data extracted from different sources to a uniform, predefined format, and "Load" is the process of uploading the transformed data to the data warehouse / HRIS.

6. Using statistical analysis, graphs and pivot tables for generating visualizations or data descriptions. Applying machine learning techniques for developing a model for prediction / forecasting.
7. Developing user interfaces for interactions of the user with data or analytics outputs.
8. Training the concerned employees for making use of the system.

Figure 4. Step-by-Step Approach to Implement HR Analytics in an Organization[9]. Source: Altexsoft. (2019). How to Successfully Implement HR Analytics and People Analytics in a Company.

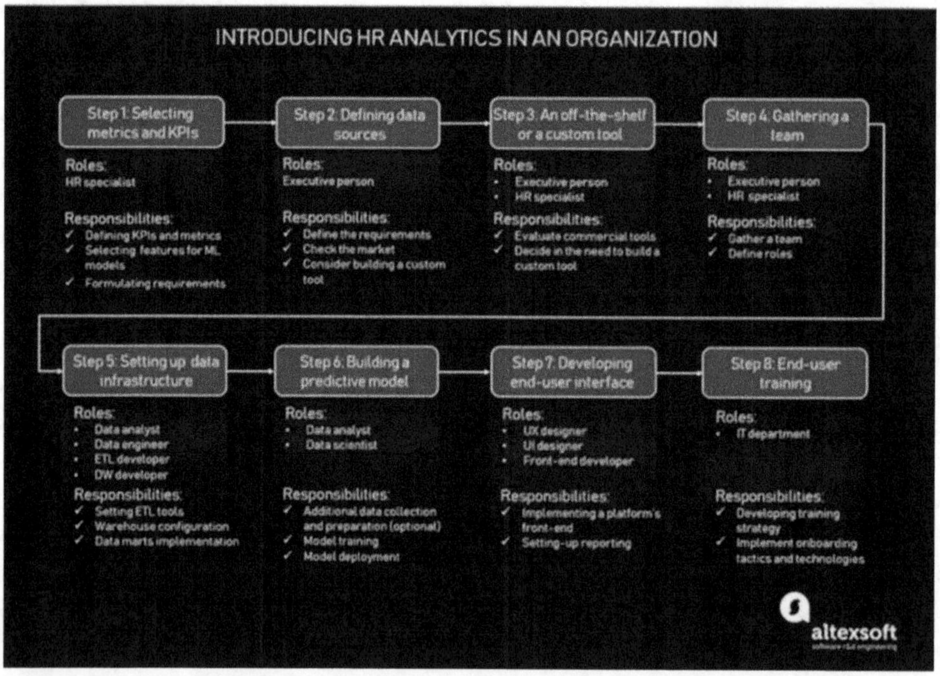

Falletta & Combs, (2021) answer some questions like what is the best way to get started and who should be responsible for HR Analytics. They suggest:

- Procuring Human Capital Management (HCM) technology platforms which offer visualization tools, for example R (with R Shiny), Python, Power BI etc.
- Hiring an HR leader with a strategic perspective, who also has an understanding of HR Analytics, alongside procuring of HCM technology platform, as this would facilitate and strengthen the implementation of HR Analytics in an organization.
- Hiring human capital technologist, econometrician, mathematician, statistician, data scientist or financial analyst, with statistical and analytics skills, which can help generating meaningful outputs as results of HR Analytics process.
- Finally, merging HR Analytics with HR strategy, resulting in setting up "HR Analytics and Strategy" function in an organization.

Despite, all pre-requisites, moderating factors and steps for implementation in place, HR Analytics faces a lot of challenges while extracting and collating data.

CHALLENGES IN HR ANALYTICS IMPLEMENTATION

A major challenge in implementing HR Analytics is the availability of relevant, clean, and reliable data. If the data is not relevant, there could be bias in results. If the data is not clean there could be noise in results and if the data is not reliable, it results in Garbage-In-Garbage-Out (GIGO). Snell, (2011) raises similar concerns about data. She provides the following statistics from Taleo Research, (2010), which is based on a survey of HR and business executives from the companies across the UK:

- Data on competency and skill gap was demanded by 91 per cent of respondents but only 55 per cent of them had access to reliable data on these.
- Data on individual's goals were important to 90 per cent of survey respondents for examining whether the congruence between organizational goals and employees' individual goals. However, only 57 per cent of them had the data on this metric.
- Data on strength of succession bench (the ability of an organization to fill-in critical positions without any delay, on an employee's retirement / resignation) is important to 82 per cent of respondents. However, only 41 per cent are having access to this.

The observations about data availability and reliability were, more or less, same for the companies across the USA, France and Australia, which were also surveyed by Taleo Research, (2010).

Apart from making data available, it is necessary to train the workforce to extract and make use of the available data. Khan et al., (2017) observe that apart from availability of data, HR Analytics is still not included as a part of the training programs for employees, let apart focusing exclusively on HR Analytics per se, its implementation and use for HR functions. They further observe that HR Analytics is an emerging area and therefore, there is a divide between the experts of HR and those of Data Analytics.

Houghton, (2015) observe following barriers to implementation of HR Analytics:

- Silos within HR functions and also between IT and HR results in inefficient use of data and IT systems.
- Skill gap in demand and supply of talents who can undertake analytics.
- Skepticism about anything new, and HR Analytics is not an exception.

Fernandez & Gallardo-Gallardo, (2021) undertook a comprehensive literature review of research on HR Analytics, published in Scopus and Web of Science between 2010 and 2019. They reviewed 64 manuscripts and identified 14 challenges to adoption of HR Analytics. They then categorize these 14 challenges in four groups, namely, (1) data and models, (2) software and technology, (3) people and (4) management.

Dahlbom et al., (2020) examine the factors hindering the effective implementation of HR Analytics. On basis of case studies on nine Finnish companies, they observe that there was difference in vision of senior executives vis-à-vis that of HR professionals, in terms of use of big data and HR Analytics for ensuring informed and evidence-based decision-making. This difference was one of the major obstacles

Figure 5. Extent of Importance of HR Analytics for Each of these HR Functions to Organizations surveyed by Oracle. Source: Compiled from HR Research Institute. (2021). The State of HR Analytics in 2021. HR.com. p. 13.

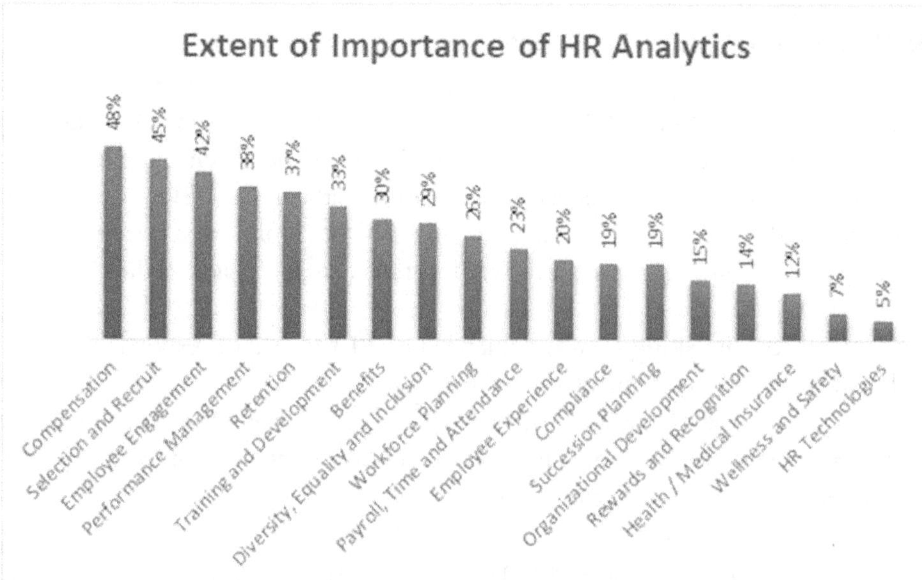

over and above, use of traditional information systems, poor quality of data and resistance to change because of implementation of HR.

Apart from these, difficulties in curating data, inadequate data analytics skills and know-how, issues associated with privacy of data leading to legal compliance issues also pose challenges to HR Analytics. However, support from top management can help in overcoming these issues to a large extent (Opatha, 2020).

Edwards et al., (2021) highlight one very critical challenge to implementing HR Analytics in an organization. Their study based on a comprehensive review of literature, highlight ethical issues involved in collecting and using data of existing as well as potential employees and subjecting them to analytics. They also highlight the need to critically reflect on collecting and making use of data for HR Analytics.

FUTURE OF HR ANALYTICS

HR Analytics is a paradigm shift from traditional and intuitive-based approach to an evidence-based approach for aiding decision-making process to enhance employees' as well as organization's performance and profitability, along with satisfied employees. HR Analytics helps in enhancing the credibility of HR functions and organizational policies as it is an evidence-based approach. There is a wide scope of implementing HR Analytics in organizations. Proliferation of internet use and awareness about visualizations using descriptive analytics has led to development of dashboards and interactive visualizations. There is wide scope of implementing insightful, predictive and prescriptive analytics, as can be seen by their extent of use in Figure 3.

Challenges described in section 6 come in the way of its implementation. There is a wide scope to streamline and standardize data formats across industries. As discussed, Industry 5.0 focuses on automating repetitive tasks. This includes the tasks which are of repetitive nature in HR functions too. Apart from recruitment, engagement and retention, HR Analytics can be applied to a wide range of HR functions, the list and extent of their importance to organizations. These are shown in Figure 5:

Figure 5 clearly shows that organizations are yet to realize the importance of HR Analytics implementation for various HR functions. Organizations have rated Wellness and Safety, and HR Technologies as the least important areas for implementing HR Analytics, which precisely indicates that there is a wide scope to generate awareness about its importance for these two HR functions. On the other hand, compensation, recruitment, and employee engagement are opted as important for implementing HR Analytics; however, the percentage of organizations rating these as important are only 48, 45 and 42 per cent respectively. The geographical location and sample size are not mentioned in this survey. Irrespective of the location, the chart indicates that a large number of HR functions will make use of HR Analytics for making strategic decisions. However, awareness about the usefulness and importance of HR Analytics, in general, requires to be raised. The research also shows that most companies are still storing their data in Excel formats and make use of Excel sheets to analyze data and generate visualizations. Many softwares like Tableau, PowerBI and free and open-source software like R (with its Shiny package) or Python (with its Matplotlib, Seaborn) can be used to generate smart and interactive visualizations. Apart from visualizations, R and Python provide packages for insightful, predictive and prescriptive analytics. Thus, there is a wide scope even in terms of using more efficient and cost-effective packages.

Since manual repetitive tasks will be gradually replaced by machines, even in the functional areas of HR, Industry 5.0 would require their employees to be competent in completely new skill sets. There will be demand for jobs which require the know-how and expertise of use of technologies like cloud computing, web scraping, extracting data from IoT, and working with semi-structured and unstructured data. The concept of data has ceased to be tabular and numerical. People are active on social media. Tweets, Facebook and LinkedIn posts convey a lot about employees' sentiments and future plans. Social media can be a very good source of data to draw insights about whether an employee would stay in the organization, whether they are happy with the work culture, what is their attitude towards work, how do they associate with organizations etc.

Making use of sensitive data (both from organization's HR database and from social media) would pose the issue of ethical concerns. HR Analytics will also generate demand for legal experts who would guide the HR professionals about what data personal data to use, and otherwise. Legal issues associated in sharing sensitive data by the organization to HR Analytics consultants will also arise and will have to be addressed.

At present, HR Analytics appears to be the technology that can be afforded by organizations with large turnovers. However, smaller firms also have a scope to make use of HR Analytics using free and open-source software, thereby partly reducing the technology installment costs. Use of shared, yet secured, cloud space can also be a substitute to dedicated IT infrastructure required for implementation of HR Analytics for smaller firms. Expertise continues to be a scarce resource and the scarcity is expected to reduce in future.

HR Analytics is still in its infancy. A large number of organizations are still having modest infrastructure and know-how to use HR Analytics (Wirges & Neyer, 2022). It is a promising and growing area, yet has "*miles to go….*" for it to mature. It is difficult to predict exactly "when" it will mature, maybe an analytics exercise might answer this question.

ACKNOWLEDGMENT

Smruti Bulsari would like to acknowledge the support of the Business and Local Government Data Research Centre (ES/S007156/1) funded by the Economic and Social Research Council (ESRC).

REFERENCES

Altexsoft. (2019). *How to Successfully Implement HR Analytics and People Analytics in a Company*. https://www.altexsoft.com/blog/how-to-implement-hr-analytics/

Ankum, M. (2022). People Analytics: 5 Real Case Studies. *Effectory*. https://www.effectory.com/knowledge/people-analytics-5-real-case-studies/

Barbar, K., Choughri, R., & Soubjaki, M. (2019). Training and Development Strategy—Private Sector Case Study in Lebanon. *Journal of Management and Strategy*, *10*(3), 27–36. doi:10.5430/jms.v10n3p27

Biriowu, C. S., & Kalio, N. L. (2020). Talent Analytics and Employee Retention in Nigeria Organizations. *International Journal of Human Resources Management, 9*(3), 1.12.

Borkakoty, K. (2017). *HR Analytics For Employee Engagement Strategy and More*. https://medium.com/@mynab247/hr-analytics-for-employee-engagement-strategy-and-more-659dd236d234

Coco, C. T., Jamison, F., & Black, H. (2011). Connecting people's Investments and Business Outcomes at Lowe's: Using Value Linkage Analytics to Link Employee Engagement with Business Performance. *People & Strategy*, *34*(2), 28–33.

Dahlbom, P., Siikanen, N., Sajasalo, P., & Jarvenpää, M. (2020). Big Data and HR Analytics in the Digital Era. *Baltic Journal of Management*, *15*(1), 120–138. doi:10.1108/BJM-11-2018-0393

Dey, T. S., & De, P. (2015). *Predictive Analytics in HR: A Primer*. Tata Consultancy Services.

Edwards, M. R., Charlwood, A., Guenole, N., & Marler, J. (2021). HR Analytics: An Emerging Field Finding its Place in the World Alongside Simmering Ethical Challenges. *Human Resource Management Journal,* 1–11.

Edwards, M. R., & Edwards, K. (2016). *Predictive HR Analytics: Mastering the HR Metric*. Kogan Page Limited.

Ekka, S. (2021). HR Analytics: Why it Matters. *Journal of Contemporary Issues in Business and Government*, *27*(2), 2283–2291.

Falletta, S. V., & Combs, W. L. (2021). The HR Analytics Cycle: A Seven-Step Process for Building Evidence-Based and Ethical HR Analytics Capabilities. *Journal of Work-Applied Management*, *13*(1), 51–68. doi:10.1108/JWAM-03-2020-0020

Fernandez, V., & Gallardo-Gallardo, E. (2021). Tackling the HR Digitalization Challenge: Key Factors and Barriers to HR Analytics Adoption. *Competitiveness Review, 31*(1), 162–187. doi:10.1108/CR-12-2019-0163

Ferrar, J., & Green, D. (2021). *Excellence in People Analytics: How to Use Workforce Data to Create Business Value*. Kogan Page Limited.

Gaur, B. (2020). *HR4.0: An Analytics Framework to Redefine Employee Engagement in the Fourth Industrial Revolution. 11th International Conference on Computing, Communication and Networking Technologies (ICCCNT)*, Kharagpur, India. 10.1109/ICCCNT49239.2020.9225456

Gurusinghe, R. N., Arachchige, B. J. H., & Dayarathna, D. (2021). Predictive HR analytics and talent management: A conceptual framework. *Journal of Management Analytics, 8*(2), 195–221. doi:10.1080/23270012.2021.1899857

Houghton, E. (2015). *Evolution of HR Analytics: A Middle East Perspective*. Chartered Institute of Personnel and Development.

HR Research Institute. (2021). *The State of HR Analytics in 2021*. HR.com. https://www.oracle.com/a/ocom/docs/applications/human-capital-management/hrt-talent-analytics-hrdotcom.pdf

Jain, P., & Jain, P. (2020). Understanding the Concept of HR Analytics. *International Journal on Emerging Technologies, 11*(2), 644–652.

Kahn, W. A. (1990). Psychological Conditions of Personal Engagement and Disengagement at Work. *Academy of Management Journal, 33*(4), 692–724. doi:10.2307/256287

Karmańska, A. (2020). The benefits of HR Analytics. *Research Papers of Wroclaw University of Economics and Business, 64*(8), 30–39.

Khan, H. P., Sultana, A., & Reddy, T. N. (2017). Review on HR Analytics: An Emerging Scale for Evaluation of Human Assets. *International Journal of Management and Social Sciences, 5*(8), 140–145.

Kruse, K. (2012). What is Employee Engagement. *Forbes*. https://www.forbes.com/sites/kevinkruse/2012/06/22/employee-engagement-what-and-why/

Lam, S., & Hawkes, B. (2017). From Analytics to Action: How Shell Digitized Recruitment. *Strategic HR Review, 16*(2), 76–80. doi:10.1108/SHR-01-2017-0005

Lee, J. (2021). *[3 stages + 8 steps] Model for HR Analytics Implementation*. https://www.linkedin.com/pulse/3-stages-8-steps-model-hr-analytics-implementation-jaejin-lee/

Levenson, A. (2011). Using Targeted Analytics to Improve Talent Decisions. *People & Strategy, 34*(2), 34–43.

Levenson, A., & Pillans, G. (2017). *Strategic Workforce Analytics*. Corporate Research Forum. https://www.orgvue.com/uploads/sites/2/2020/05/strategic-workforce-analytics-report.pdf

Marler, J. H., & Boudreau, J. W. (2017). An evidence-based review of HR Analytics. *International Journal of Human Resource Management*, *28*(1), 3–26. doi:10.1080/09585192.2016.1244699

Marvin, G., Jackson, M., & Alam, Md. G. R. (2021). A Machine Learning Approach for Employee Retention Prediction. *2021 IEEE Region 10 Symposium (TENSYMP)*, 1–8.

McCartney, S., & Fu, N. (2022). Bridging the Gap: Why, How and When HR Analytics Can Impact Organizational Performance. *Management Decision*, *60*(13), 25–47. doi:10.1108/MD-12-2020-1581

Mohammed, A. Q. (2019). HR Analytics: A Modern Tool in HR for Predictive Decision Making. *Journal of Management*, *6*(3), 51–63. doi:10.34218/JOM.6.3.2019.007

Mohapatra, M., & Sahu, P. (2017). Optimizing the Recruitment Funnel in an ITES Company: An Analytics Approach. *5th International Conference on Information Technology and Quantitative Management, ITQM 2017*, *122*, 706–714. 10.1016/j.procs.2017.11.427

Momin, W. Y., & Mishra, K. (2015). HR Analytics as a Strategic Workforce Planning. *International Journal of Applied Research*, *1*(4), 258–260.

Muhammad, G., & Naz, F. (2022). A Moderating Role of HR Analytics Between Employee Engagement, Retention and Organisational Performance. *International Journal of Business Environment*, *13*(4), 345–357. doi:10.1504/IJBE.2022.126370

Oladipupo, O. O., & Olubusayo, F. H. (2020). Human Resource Analytics Dimensions and Employee Engagement in Manufacturing Industry in Nigeria: A Conceptual Review. *Journal of Management Information and Decision Sciences*, *23*(5), 629–637.

Opatha, H. H. D. P. J. (2020). HR Analytics: A Literature Review and New Conceptual Model. *International Journal of Scientific and Research Publications*, *10*(6), 130–141. doi:10.29322/IJSRP.10.06.2020.p10217

Pessach, D., Singer, G., Avrahami, D., Chalutz Ben-Gal, H., Shmueli, E., & Ben-Gal, I. (2020). Employees recruitment: A Prescriptive Analytics Approach via Machine Learning and Mathematical Programming. *Decision Support Systems*, *134*, 113290. doi:10.1016/j.dss.2020.113290 PMID:32501316

Popomaronis, T. (2019). Here's How Many Google Interviews It Takes to Hire a Googler. *CNBC*. https://www.cnbc.com/2019/04/17/heres-how-many-google-job-interviews-it-takes-to-hire-a-googler.html

Rich, B. L., LePine, J. A., & Crawford, E. R. (2010). Job Engagement: Antecedents and Effects on Job Performance. *Academy of Management Journal*, *53*(3), 617–635. doi:10.5465/amj.2010.51468988

Schaufeli, W. B., & Bakker, A. B. (2003). *Utrecht Work Engagement Scale: Preliminary Manual*. Department of Psychology, Utrecht University.

Schaufeli, W. B., & Bakker, A. B. (2010). Defining and Measuring Work Engagement: Bringing Clarity to the Concept. In *Work Engagement: A Handbook of Essential Theory and Research*. Psychology Press.

Schick-Makaroff, K., MacDonald, M., Plummer, M., Burgess, J., & Neander, W. (2016). What Synthesis Methodology Should I Use? A Review and Analysis of Approaches to Research Synthesis. *AIMS Public Health, 3*(1), 172–175. doi:10.3934/publichealth.2016.1.172 PMID:29546155

Shrivastava, S., & Dhaigude, A. S. (2022). Prime Data Tech Pvt. Ltd: Resolving Employee Recruitment Dilemma using HR Analytics. *Communications of the Association for Information Systems, 50*(27), 576–588. doi:10.17705/1CAIS.05027

Singh, R., Sharma, P., Foropon, C., & Belal, H. M. (2022). The Role of Big Data and Predictive Analytics in the Employee Retention: A Resource-Based View. *International Journal of Manpower, 43*(2), 411–447. doi:10.1108/IJM-03-2021-0197

Sivathanu, B., & Pillai, R. (2020). Technology and Talent Analytics for Talent Management – A Game Changer for Organizational Performance. *The International Journal of Organizational Analysis, 28*(2), 457–473. doi:10.1108/IJOA-01-2019-1634

Snell, A. (2011). Developing Talent Intelligence to Boost Business Performance. *Strategic HR Review, 10*(2), 12–17. doi:10.1108/14754391111108301

Taleo Research. (2010). *Talent Intelligent: The Key to Business Success*. Taleo.

Tomar, S., & Gaur, M. (2020). HR Analytics in Business: Role, Opportunities, and Challenges of Using It. *Journal of Xi'an University of Architecture & Technology, 12*(7), 1299–1306.

Walford-Wright, G., & Scott-Jackson, W. (2018). Talent Rising; People Analytics and Technology Driving Talent Acquisition Strategy. *Strategic HR Review, 17*(5), 226–233. doi:10.1108/SHR-08-2018-0071

Welle, B. (Director). (2018). *Applied Perspective: Vol. Wharton People Analytics Conference 2018* [Video]. https://youtu.be/RyD2I0pUR1I

Wirges, F., & Neyer, A.-K. (2022). Towards a Process-Oriented Understanding of HR Analytics: Implementation and application. *Review of Managerial Science*. Advance online publication. doi:10.100711846-022-00574-0

ENDNOTES

1 IoT are a network of physical objects embedded with sensors, software and supporting hardware for connecting and exchanging data across devices connected with the Internet.

2 Cloud platforms are basically servers, which provide computing resources over Internet.

3 Machine learning is a process which makes use of algorithms / computer software that can understand, self-learn and improve itself on the basis of data that it receives on a continuous basis. It is one form of Artificial Intelligence, an algorithm, which works like human intelligence. These are normally used for repetitive processes, like shortlisting a candidate on the basis of their qualification, experience etc. for a job position.

4 Integrative syntheses is a method that undertakes systematic reviews, meta-analyses, scoping as well as rapid reviews for summarizing the literature (Schick-Makaroff et al., 2016).

5 Unstructured data in the form of text makes use of natural language processing (NLP) methods. Machine learning is applicable to text data also. There are methods to process images, sound and video and apply machine learning on these categories of data too.

6 Geographical region is not mentioned in the paper.

7 A term used in statistics to examine whether the difference between two groups (in this case) is by chance or there is a consistent pattern.

8 The process of identifying incorrect, erroneous or incomplete data and either editing it with an objective to correct it, and where that is not possible, completely removing those data, is called "data cleaning".

9 In step 5 of Figure 4, ETL stands for "Extract", "Transform" and "Load", whereas DW stands for "Data Warehouse". In step 7, UX means "User Experience", UI means "User Interface" and the term "Front-end" is one type of UI, usually of a website / webpage.

Chapter 10
Building an Enhanced Futuristic Organizational Hub:
Journey of Indian Markets From Industry 4.0 to Industry 5.0

Megha Sharma
Graphic Era Hill University, India

Subhash Chander Arora
Gurukula Kangri (Deemed), India

Vinod Kumar Singh
Gurukula Kangri (Deemed), India

ABSTRACT

With the growing digitalization, the use of machine learning and artificial intelligence has increased in businesses. Humans have gotten smarter while using and collaborating with such machines and integrated to the invention of Industry 5.0. A company like Tesla also depends on humans to create efficient work from robotic devices. Industry 5.0 objects to creating a balance between the use of machinery and human with the promotional use of technologies. Business owners must transform their strategies to attract customers, suppliers, and global markets. This chapter aims to identify the critical factors that Industry 4.0 lacked and were identified and transited to Industry 5.0. With artificial intelligence, the internet of things, machine learning, and nascent technologies, the human pace of work will subsequently be the essential constituent of the future workplace. Thus, India consists of many small and medium-sized companies and start-ups, and the latest technologies and adoption of Industry 5.0 is essential for Indian business owners.

INTRODUCTION

Industries are adopting digital technologies in today's era. Artificial intelligence (AI) is the core of

DOI: 10.4018/978-1-6684-6745-9.ch010

industrial growth. Robotic technology has become essential due to technological advancements like the brain-machine interface in AI (Akundi et al., 2022). With the increasing manufacturing process and lower human resources, such technologies are advancing to bridge the gap between humans and meet the manufacturing demand. To concentrate on such challenges, a new and foremost industrial revolution is analyzed named, Industry 5.0. Thus, the industrial revolution, where the technologies, including robots and humans, work in collaboration to meet the industrial gap, is known as Industry 5.0, followed by the 4 revolutions of industries i.e. Industry 1.0, Industry 2.0, Industry 3.0, and Industry 4.0.

Fabrics, steam engines, steel, instruments, cement, chemical products, fuel, illumination, glass, paper, mineral extraction, agricultural production, and public transit were the priority of Industry 1.0 in the eighteenth century. This revolution's accomplishments involve increased employment prospects, sustainable agriculture, transit, and long-term development. Environmental damage and the period required to develop the affiliated techniques are two recognized disadvantages of Industry 1.0. Industry 1.0 used mathematical models and geometrical as numerical algorithms (Vinitha et al., 2020). Metal, iron, railway, electricity, industrial machinery, paper, gas, chemicals, marine innovation, leather, cycles, vehicles, industrial engineering, fertilizer, motors, turbine, communications, and contemporary company management were the emphasis of Industry 2.0 in the nineteenth century. This era saw the birth of the electricity grid, telecommunications, telegraphs, and diesel engines. The main disadvantage of Industry 2.0 is the massive price of consuming electricity generation. Mathematical expressions, formulas, and geometries were used as computational formulas in Industry 2.0.

Industry 3.0 began in the twentieth century with a concentration on the electronics segment, internet signals, controlled electronic components, telephony, communication connectivity, sustainable sources, and technology. Industry 3.0's accomplishment is based on broadband, sustainable sources, robotic businesses, and machines are all examples of emerging technologies. Therefore, automation technology was the drawback of this era, as these technologies were full of complexity and added extra costs during the available work. Industry 4.0 emerged in the twenty-first century, focusing on all sectors using advanced technologies. This movement's successes comprise automation technologies and artificial intelligence technologies that function in unpredictable environments, with deep learning providing a favorable impact on the fourth industrial age. The disadvantages of Industry 4.0 include that all content on the web could not be secure, and thoroughly competent solutions for companies have not yet been established (Vinitha et al., 2020; Madsen et al., 2016; Akundi et al., 2022).

Industry 5.0 was invented by Micheal Rada (Rada, 2022). The significant features of Industry 5.0 are industrial robotics utilization to decrease danger. Such machines can detect, comprehend, and perceive the human driver and the aims and objectives for the job at hand. The purpose is for these machines to observe and understand how a human conducts a task before assisting personnel in executing the activity. Moreover, Industry 5.0 incorporates AI into living beings to increase human capability. Innovative IT techniques such as IoT, robotics, AI, and augmented reality are extensively deployed in Industry 5.0 for the advantage and efficiency of skilled workers (Skobelev and Borovik, 2017).

The revolution from industry 4.0 to industry 5.0 is still to be adopted by the companies. Industry 4.0 involves big data, artificial intelligence, the internet of things, and machine learning etc., which have been discussed in previous literature (Battini et al., 2022; Orso et al., 2022; Carayannis et al., 2022; Yuan et al., 2022; Cillo et al., 2021). Industry 5.0 is the latest and new concept. As per European Union, industry 5.0 presents a company's systems that goes above effectiveness and productivity as exclusive objectives, and reaffirms company's position and impact on society. It prioritizes employee welfare in manufacturing and employs new technology to bring wealth exceeding employment and development while honoring the world's limitations.

Industry 5.0 focuses on employees' prosperity and intends to apply innovative diffusion to increase the production rate besides seeking the importance of the planet earth. Basically, industry 5.0 is the addition in industry 4.0 by adding the research, development, and latest innovations to sustain humans' and planet usage. Thus, Industry 5.0 is solely focused on societal value, contrary to industry 4.0, which was focused on economic matters. Delivering societal values are the traditional approaches that had been served in the market through industrialization. Capitalism, corporate social responsibility (CSR), and triple bottom line are some of the instances that were used initially in the industries profit and growth maximization process. But in the current phase of industrialization, where industry 5.0 is growing, profit and growth is the secondary aspect for the businesses to focus on, whereas, the primary motive is to implement the advancement and of the benefit of people and the planet (Kraaijenbrink, 2022).

Industry 5.0 must apply to each type of organization, as it implies wider scope than industry 4.0. Industry 5.0 is summated with the three significant points, i.e., human-centered, adaptable, and long-term. These three acts as the pillars to sustain the considerable implications for implicating these key points in the business strategy. Thus, the amalgamation of these strategic points builds a strong factor for building the industry 5.0. Industry 5.0 is applicable in the society, manufacturing plant and network of channel level. All these levels are integrated towards resilience, sustainability, and human-centricity. These three integrations are significant in promoting flexibility, sustainability and human resource welfare. Industry 5.0 promotes technology advancement through the channel of communication, collaboration, automation and most important data analytics. This however, improves the efficiency of the work performance in the organization, improves the productivity of the employees, have promoted the flexibility of the employees which strengthen the performance of the organization (Ivanov, 2022).

Human-centered strategy encourages creativity, innovation, and opportunity. The most significant adjustment this implies is a change from viewing individuals as an instrument to an objective (as in the human resource department). It can be dived as a change in focus from individuals serving organizations to organizations serving the public. Therefore, the advantage of human-centered organization is that it provides a competitive advantage to the organizations and employees get the additional remuneration. Adaptable strategy depicts efficient and robust strategies, using adaptive and flexible technology in the business. Long-term strategy is based on the sustainability of the planet. To conserve the technological use among the products and services, right amount of resources must be used while concerning the future of our planet. This is a key factor that every business shall realize to promote sustainable development goals, triple bottom line, etc.

REVOLUTION OF INDIAN INDUSTRIES: FUTURE OF JOB WORK

The year 2022 has already been witnessed with the introduction of industry 5.0 in Indian market. As with the growing automotive technologies, Indian markets are already facing unemployment. Artificial intelligence, machine learning, the internet of things and several automations have changed the industries life. Thus, this was challenges faced in the industry 4.0 where technologies and robotics were the highlighted element for the survival of industries. Therefore, industry 5.0 has been invented where human force and technologies both are the essential assets for the industries. Below are the five factors which are predicted to transform the working culture in Indian industries, with the advent of industry 5.0 (Marr, 2019):

1. Changing jobs

Employees within the company will have flexible roles in their work and job responsibilities. The rigid organizational rules shall be abandoned to increase the company's successful projects. This entices Gen Z recruits, as 75% of them would like to have more responsibilities in one work environment. In the employment industry, employees are working on the contractual basis of as a freelancer for one assignment, and after completing it they straightly shift to the next tasks. Thus, this will expand in the upcoming years in the Indian industries.

2. Skilled workers that are autonomous

Employees are becoming more prevalent due to increasing mobile technologies and wide access of broadbrand internet connectivity. With this technology, employees do not have to be at the same place for their work commitments. This hybrid mode of the workforce situation will be more convenient for future generation to select a job and choose their workplace area. This may also boost creativity and may promote positive workplace deviance which is considered as a boon for workplace (Sharma, 2021; Sharma, 2019; Sharma & Singh, 2018).

3. Greater Productivity

At a stage of working years, employees need more than a wage and a salary to be motivated at the job. Employees join a company that has an objective that companies follow. This seeks attractive schemes, like individual growth possibilities, cutting-edge technology to support work-from-anywhere goals, and more.

4. Lifetime Education and Learning

Employees desire to grow in their professions, for which they require to be the master for acquiring additional skills and knowledge. Innovations and technologies keep changing with every decade, so the role of employees alters in their job profile. Training and development programs are conducted to educate them on the latest innovations and upgrade their skills. This modification is required to upgrade and modify the skills and careers of the employees.

5. People's occupations will be strengthen by the new tech

In the coming era, people will have tech-colleagues and business supporter with artificial intelligence and smart robots. People as workers will have to establish a degree of confidence and understanding about the coexistence of the collaborative work between technologies and humans.

INDUSTRY 5.0 INITIATIVES WITH CUSTOMER EXPERIENCES

With the growing technologies, industry 5.0 is implemented mainly by the companies to upgrade the organization's manufacturing, promotional tools and other functions. Industry 5.0 if, will not be adopted by the companies, could cause a huge loss and even could make them bankrupt. Industry 5.0 is initiated with the latest innovations, modern types of machinery, and advanced employees. But this is still the question of what strategies would compelling Indian industries to adopt industry 5.0. Thus, to compete with the tough competition in the market, understanding the customers' base and their experiences are the key factor for organization.

Firstly, an industry 5.0 strategy *must begin with the eventual goal*. The company shall constantly have the end user at the forefront and look for methods to improve that connection. The process should be carried back into the company by focusing on the points of contact that will affect customer experience. Any activities strategy must be founded on your company objectives and shortcomings and have a properly planned path. Business shall recommend concentrating on regions that can boost company and revenue and, eventually, consumer satisfaction. The approach must tackle both deficits in customer relationships as well as lengthy retaining existing customers. Industry 5.0 shall be strategizing as it benefits the whole company instead of just focusing on each organization. Thus, to make industry 5.0 effective, the solutions must be derived from each problem to offer and fulfill the customers' expectations.

Secondly, *companies shall focus to make a simple strategy*. The innovative and unique features and projects must be implied when investing in industry 5.0. For instance, there are situations for the company where a company manger and owner need to decide whether to spend the budget on purchasing a new machine, or to invest to build customer relationship management (CRM). Where, new machinery could help in cost-reduction and efficient manufacturing process and ultimately benefits the customers. In contrast, CRM would help to generate good communication between the customers with brands and companies regarding any information or query customers seek to find. Well, in such cases ethical leadership need to be implemented, by doing the market research and to find which is the best option to go for? To earn ore profit in short span of time is the accurate strategy to be implemented, for the long success of the business.

Further, the third strategy is to *look within the solutions*. Production and technology is evolving with the evolution of industry 5.0 from industry 4.0. Industry 5.0 must go upward and lead in the market rather the outward looking. Conventionally, lean approach was used which got no success. Under the lean approach, managers frequently applied the tools directly into the organization without proper research, rather than first determining the real issue and then applying the appropriate tool. While connecting to industry 5.0, companies must project a customer engagement strategy where managers shall ensure that technological generation and transmission must be carefully allocated to identify the challenges that significantly influence the company's success. Through these strategies, the company must effectively enable its finances and get the highest return on investment (Garrett, 2021).

IMPLEMENTING INTERNET OF THINGS IN INDUSTRY 5.0: OPPORTUNITIES AND DIFFICULTIES

In the manufacturing sector and industries, implementation of industry 5.0 is quite important. According to Statista (2022) the global range of internet of things (IoT) endpoint content and data will reach 79.4

zettabytes by 2025, with the figures approaching 75 billion till 2025. Most IoT gadgets are associated with production machineries used in education, manufacturing industries, healthcare, smart cities and automation, agribusiness, electricity, and water supplies etc. These technologies are assumed to expand when concerns regarding the installation surroundings of such gadgets and their connection with the software solution become more significant. Thus, to get the fruitful advantage from IoT, the adequate implementation of IoT is necessary in the companies. To protect the data of industries from cyber attacks, to promote the efficiency and productivity within the resources the industries and in cost-effective way, IoT is the best to implement in the organizations (Fatima et al., 2022).

Integrating various technological devices through IoT is advantageous for smoothly administering the business functions. IoT applications and technologies interact with realistic targets like technical devices, healthcare monitoring, and commercial radio frequency identification. The information gathered through these technological devices becomes very significant to execute the organizational decisions effectively. The proper implementation of IoT increases the efficiency and profitability in the business organization while reducing the extra cost. Therefore, the *opportunities* while implementing the IoT in the industries are as follows: (Altynpara, 2021):

- IoT device information and real data using artificial intelligence and deep learning assist in continuously and dynamically monitoring the manufacturing devices which tracks the key metrics of the work assigned in the organization and detects the pros and cons of the project. Through IoT devices, company can focus on avoiding the machinery and other maintenance expenses by replacing the defected items and machineries.
- Through the IoT the quality and accuracy of big data can be enhanced. Further, the analysis of big data aids to identify the best situation for the pieces of machinery, software and other equipment's operation and boosts the overall managerial efficiency.
- IoT helps integrate the existing data through the devices linked with the IoT technologies, and public data. These data aid in the optimization of distribution network, stock management, accounting, and other critical business activities, as well as the identification of cost-cutting methods and opportunities in the business.

According to the findings of a Forbes Research poll, IoT implementation in industry 5.0 have raised yearly profits by upto 5% to 45% yearly profit as conveyed by the business executives as the respondents. But there are certain *challenges* that industry may face while implementing IoT in the organization, as follows:

- Data security is the main factor every business owner should be concerned about. The risk of viruses, information leakage, and cyberattacks increases the need of security features. Cybercriminals may wirelessly close the doors and regulate temperatures and power in a facility. As a result, detection and prevention systems, password protection, and workstation and network security must be as creative as possible. This can include cryptographic keys and fingerprints technologies to safeguard IoT devices at the point of entry, production of cellular to prevent unwanted connection, authentic surveillance, virtualized upgrading, and other security procedures.
- The Internet of Things (IoT) incorporates data and practical solutions, but their integration can be complex. Data and practical solutions are frequently different divisions with independent procedures and objectives. However, an IoT organization need tight collaboration from these di-

visions and you must establish communication between all. Data and practical solutions must communicate standards and interests and establish duties, objectives, problems, and resources collaboratively.

- Tons of equipment and sensors are often used in industrial IoT implementations. Each connection must be documented and kept in a central source that demonstrates the current state of the installation. Any growing and modernizing this complicated system will confront sustainability and administration structural problems. Rebuild the old internet infrastructure, enhance performance and speed, and control essential app priorities. As a result, the early phases of installation and incorporation can be costly, and organizations must analyze their ROI in advance.

To integrate IoT in the organization, there are some of significant points that every manager and organization owner shall implement, as follows:

1. **Planning the strategy for objective accomplishment**: The first objective is to make the list of all the IoT devices in the business. Maintenance of the latest list of IoT equipments is necessary with all the regarding information. List may include about the manufacturer profile and machineries, serial number, software equipped, model number, etc. It is also necessary to acknowledge the level of risk of each device and its behavior concerning other devices equipments installed.
2. **Conducting a Pilot Study**: Starting A Pilot Study must be based on the findings of the forethought and implementation, a pilot study must be started initially. It may be expanded to a section or corporate level. Following the pilot, users must be capable to:
    - Develop a framework concept that considers the connectivity of all technologies, devices, and different data.
    - Identify machine learning methods and possibilities for connection and training.
    - Specify the screen kinds that will present administration with the outcomes of analyzing information extraction.
3. **Data Collection, Integration, and Analysis**: After initiating the pilot study, businesses will be able to apply a full technology platform. However, linking destinations is only the beginning. The major advantage of the Internet of Things is its capacity to analyze and analyze data more effectively, increasing total process versatility. For this process organizations must be able to:
    - To collect the data and organize the data in the real time using the machine learning and artificial intelligence.
    - To examine the collected data by analyzing it because analysis at the platform's perimeter and centre allows for the extraction of all data from devices, analyzing data in real time, personality apps, and similar technologies emerge essential for business IoT.
    - Using device to cloud technologies allows devices to track with the data and its analysis towards cloud technologies and use the analysis for visualization features. As, it can be said that cloud computing technology is the foundation of IoT because of its great efficiency and effectiveness.

ARTIFICIAL INTELLIGENCE AND MACHINE LEARNING

The business world is changing very fast and people are optimistic about the importance of AI to their enterprises over the next few years. AI/ML systems are reshaping client experiences, interpersonal communication, investment decisions, borrowing and lending interface through automated mortgage underwriting, identification of clients. The technological revolution is transforming the functioning of business enterprise in terms of cost savings through automation route, better product offerings, fraud detection and risk management, operational efficiency and other regulatory compliances.

The COVID-19 pandemic has further increased the commercial sector's appetite for AI/ML adoption. Banks are exploring ways to leverage their experience of using AI/ML to handle the high volume of loan applications during the pandemic to improve their underwriting process and fraud detection. Finally, AI/ML systems provide central banks and prudential oversight authorities with new tools to improve systemic risk surveillance and strengthen prudential oversight. To process the huge raw data through the systems in the organization regarding purchasing, orders, sales, customers, etc, artificial intelligence innovation must be implemented within the organizations. IoT forms-up the raw data, which further is evaluated and analyzed through the AI algorithms to extract the relevant information (Chander et al., 2022).

Businesses today are getting heavily relied on using AI and ML tools on account of the enormous data that is at its disposal. AI has the potential in carefully and successfully analyzing this large amount of data, minimizing human error in interpreting this data and providing useful insights to understand the future developments. Besides, it has the potential to upscale operational and employee efficiency, trim down safety risks at the premises, enable better decision-making and come up with tailor-made solutions for individual clients. Business houses, big or small, are incorporating the AI-enabled technologies in their day-to-day operations and back-office related activities almost uncompromisingly. Major applications include sales increase and prediction, profit maximization, inventory management, security, fraud detection and portfolio management.

APPLICATION OF AI/ML TOOLS

Acquiring large sets of data from the environment and processing it with said tools is changing the corporate sector landscape. AI/ML facilitates enhanced capacity to predict economic, financial, and risk events; reshape financial markets; improve risk management and compliance; strengthen prudential oversight; and equip central banks with new tools to pursue their monetary and macroprudential mandates.

Forecasting: Novice algorithms data sets are being used for forecasting macro-economic, financial variables and their inter-relationships, meet customer demands, provide payment capacity and monitor business conditions. They usually perform better than traditional statistical or econometric models. In the financial sector, this is used in such areas as credit risk scoring, economic and financial variables movement and risk management (Bolhuis & Rayner, 2020). However, there are challenges, especially in non-traditional data consisting of social media content, browsing history and others. Use of non-traditional data in financial forecasting raises several concerns including the governing legal and regulatory framework; ethical and privacy implications; and data quality in terms of cleanliness, accuracy, relevancy, and potential biases.

Anomaly and/or Fraud detection: Algorithms can be applied to detect rare items, outliers and/or missing/incomplete data. In the financial sector, insider trading, credit card and insurance fraud detectionare some of the applications that leverage this capability (Chandola et al., 2009). Giant organizations have excess funds to manage regularly. There are continuous inflows and outflows; thus, companies resort to AI-enabled technologies to avoid financial pollution (Rajamohan & Dhanabalan, 2013). AI is the topmost technology that comes with security and fraud detection techniques. It can be used to assess the earlier spending pattern and behavior of an individual towards various transactions and from which it would identify the odd behavior, like is there any attempt to take out the money unusually from an account which is in a state of query.

AI/ML systems could help central banks improve their understanding of economic and financial developments, support better-tuned monetary and macro prudential policies, and improve their operations. They could also strengthen systemic risk monitoring and potentially help predict the buildup of systemic risks and speed up crisis response. Notwithstanding these potential benefits, using AI/ML processes for policymaking should remain subject to good judgment. Furthermore, AI/ML could provide increased efficiency and better internal control opportunities for central banks, including monitoring of internal operations and resource allocation across functions. The technology to develop these applications largely exists; central banks' slow adoption thereof can be attributed to cultural, political, and legal factors, and lack of adequate capacity. Experiments and research by central banks have focused on improving the near-term forecasting capacity and monitoring market sentiment to inform policy decisions. Some central banks are also developing applications to improve internal processes and back-office functions (for example, cash management).

CONCLUSION AND DISCUSSION

Based on the above literature, industry 5.0 shall be the backbone of the India to transform the innovative technologies. Industry 5.0 applies to almost every sector including healthcare, manufacturing, branding and marketing, supply chain management, etc. Industry 5.0 is developed for the ease of humans and types of machinery. Where, industry 4.0 was only focused on human-robotics and technological advancements. The authors highlight the importance of big data, artificial intelligence, machine learning, and internet of things. Further, industry 5.0 is also helpful in building the customer's positive experiences. Every customer considers a budget-friendly products and services to purchase, which deliver a satisfactory customer experience. Future scholars may get in-depth insights about the importance of human-robotic terms, as this chapter lacks to provide such literature.

REFERENCES

Akundi, A., Euresti, D., Luna, S., Ankobiah, W., Lopes, A., & Edinbarough, I. (2022). State of Industry 5.0—Analysis and Identification of Current Research Trends. *Applied System Innovation*, *5*(1), 27. doi:10.3390/asi5010027

Altynpara, E. (2021). *Integrating The Industrial Internet Of Things: The Benefits And Challenges*. Retrieved from https://www.forbes.com/sites/forbestechcouncil/2021/07/01/integrating-the-industrial-internet-of-things-the-benefits-and-challenges/?sh=41d9a95306f3

Battini, D., Berti, N., Finco, S., Zennaro, I., & Das, A. (2022). Towards industry 5.0: A multi-objective job rotation model for an inclusive workforce. *International Journal of Production Economics, 250*, 108619. doi:10.1016/j.ijpe.2022.108619

Carayannis, E. G., Draper, J., & Bhaneja, B. (2021). Towards fusion energy in the Industry 5.0 and Society 5.0 context: Call for a global commission for urgent action on fusion energy. *Journal of the Knowledge Economy*, *12*(4), 1891–1904. doi:10.100713132-020-00695-5

Chander, B., Pal, S., De, D., & Buyya, R. (2022). Artificial intelligence-based internet of things for industry 5.0. In *Artificial Intelligence-based Internet of Things Systems* (pp. 3–45). Springer. doi:10.1007/978-3-030-87059-1_1

Chandola, V., Banerjee, A., & Kumar, V. (2009). Anomaly detection: A survey. *ACM Computing Surveys*, *41*(3), 1–58. doi:10.1145/1541880.1541882

Cillo, V., Gregori, G. L., Daniele, L. M., Caputo, F., & Bitbol-Saba, N. (2021). Rethinking companies' culture through knowledge management lens during Industry 5.0 transition. *Journal of Knowledge Management.*

Fatima, Z., Tanveer, M. H., Zardari, S., Naz, L. F., Khadim, H., Ahmed, N., & Tahir, M. (2022). Production Plant and Warehouse Automation with IoT and Industry 5.0. *Applied Sciences (Basel, Switzerland)*, *12*(4), 2053. doi:10.3390/app12042053

Garret, G. (2021). How To Align Industry 5.0 Initiatives With Your Customer Experience Strategy. *Forbes*. Retrieved from, https://www.forbes.com/sites/forbesbusinesscouncil/2021/04/15/how-to-align-industry-50-initiatives-with-your-customer-experience-strategy/?sh=532095d657e9

Ivanov, D. (2022). The Industry 5.0 framework: Viability-based integration of the resilience, sustainability, and human-centricity perspectives. *International Journal of Production Research*, 1–13. doi:10.1080/00207543.2022.2118892

Kraaijenbrink, J. (2022). What Is Industry 5.0 And How It Will Radically Change Your Business Strategy? *Forbes*. Retrieved from https://www.forbes.com/sites/jeroenkraaijenbrink/2022/05/24/what-is-industry-50-and-how-it-will-radically-change-your-business-strategy/?sh=2cc86f2220bd

Madsen, E. S., Bilberg, A., & Hansen, D. G. (2016, September). Industry 4.0 and digitalization call for vocational skills, applied industrial engineering, and less for pure academics. In *Proceedings of the 5th P&OM World Conference, Production and Operations Management, P&OM* (*Vol. 40*). Academic Press.

Marr, B. (2019). *The Future Of Work: 5 Important Ways Jobs Will Change In The 4th Industrial Revolution*. Retrieved from https://www.forbes.com/sites/bernardmarr/2019/07/15/the-future-of-work-5-important-ways-jobs-will-change-in-the-4th-industrial-revolution/?sh=5aa8d2a454c7

Orso, V., Ziviani, R., Bacchiega, G., Bondani, G., Spagnolli, A., & Gamberini, L. (2022). Employee-centric innovation: Integrating participatory design and video-analysis to foster the transition to Industry 5.0. *Computers & Industrial Engineering*, *173*, 108661. doi:10.1016/j.cie.2022.108661

Rada, M. (2018). *Industry 5.0-from Virtual to Physical*. LinkedIn. Available online: https://www.linkedin.com/pulse/industry-50-from-virtual-physical-michael-rada

Rajamohan, S., & Dhanabalan, T. (2013). Rural development through ICT: Opportunities and challenges. *International Journal of Retailing & Rural Business Perspectives*, *2*(2), 354.

Rayner, B., & Bolhuis, M. A. (2020). *The More the Merrier? A Machine Learning Algorithm for Optimal Pooling of Panel Data*. International Monetary Fund. doi:10.5089/9781513529974.001

Sharma, N. (Ed.). (2019). *Analyzing workplace deviance in modern organizations*. IGI Global.

Sharma, N. (2021). Using positive deviance to enhance employee engagement: An interpretive structural modelling approach. *The International Journal of Organizational Analysis*, *30*(1), 84–98. doi:10.1108/IJOA-07-2020-2341

Sharma, N., & Singh, V. K. (2018). Psychological empowerment and employee engagement: Testing the mediating effects of constructive deviance in Indian IT Sector. *International Journal of Human Capital and Information Technology Professionals*, *9*(4), 44–55. doi:10.4018/IJHCITP.2018100103

Skobelev, P. O., & Borovik, S. Y. (2017). On the way from Industry 4.0 to Industry 5.0: From digital manufacturing to digital society. *Industry 4.0, 2*(6), 307-311.

Vinitha, K., Prabhu, R. A., Bhaskar, R., & Hariharan, R. (2020). Review on industrial mathematics and materials at Industry 1.0 to Industry 4.0. *Materials Today: Proceedings*, *33*, 3956–3960. doi:10.1016/j.matpr.2020.06.331

Yuan, C., Liu, W., Zhou, G., Shi, X., Long, S., Chen, Z., & Yan, X. (2022). Supply chain innovation announcements and shareholder value under industries 4.0 and 5.0: evidence from China. *Industrial Management & Data Systems*.

Chapter 11
Information and Communication Technologies in Logistics and Supply Chain Management in Turkey:
Human Resource Practices and New Challenges

Gizem Nur Şarlıoğlu
Alanya Alaaddin Keykubat University, Turkey

Ece Boyacı
Alanya Alaaddin Keykubat University, Turkey

Meltem Akca
https://orcid.org/0000-0001-5544-5929
Alanya Alaaddin Keykubat University, Turkey

ABSTRACT

Businesses benefit from supply chain management because it enables the compatibility, integration, and high performance of applications, as well as the development of competitive qualities such as pricing, quality, and innovation. Today, businesses use information technology to compete and achieve their goals. Industry 4.0 is a new situation that has emerged as informatics, communication, internet, sensors, automation, artificial intelligence, and robotic technologies greatly affect and change production processes. As a result of Industry 4.0, information and automation technologies have caused the supply chain to adapt by digitizing it. On the other hand, with Industry 5.0 studies, it is aimed to reveal great innovations in logistics and supply chain management. In this study, the information and communication technologies used in the logistics and supply chain sector will be examined, Industry 5.0 applications will be discussed, and the current situation of Turkey will be evaluated.

DOI: 10.4018/978-1-6684-6745-9.ch011

In today's dynamic environment, businesses must now better control product prices and quality, costs, and productivity. Businesses benefit from supply chain management because it enables the compatibility, integration, and high performance of applications, as well as the development of competitive qualities such as pricing, quality and innovation. For businesses to have a competitive advantage in Supply Chain Management, it is necessary to regulate and develop buyer-supplier relations. Increasing information sharing and transfer between the parties allows such a connection to be established. It is possible to reduce inventory costs, optimize transport services, integrate all logistics services and plan with the use of information technology. Information is critical to improving supply chain performance and enabling managers to make the best possible decisions. Information technologies are tools used to gain knowledge awareness. Integration of the supply chain is facilitated using information technologies. Today, businesses use information technology to compete and achieve their goals. The transition from modern industrial development to this digital transformation has continued for several hundred years, and three major industrial revolutions have emerged until today. The fourth industrial revolution, known as Industry 4.0, is currently underway. Industry 4.0 is a new situation that has emerged as informatics, communication, internet, sensors, automation, artificial intelligence, and robotic technologies greatly affect and change production processes. As a result of Industry 4.0, information and automation technologies have caused the supply chain to adapt by digitizing it. Supply chain procedures for identification, tracking and real-time tracking as well as effective management are now done digitally.

On the other hand, with Industry 5.0 studies, it is aimed to reveal great innovations in logistics and supply chain management. In Industry 5.0, it is expected that artificial intelligence and human-assisted machine-robot systems will work in harmony, and human beings will perform more with less effort, and human resources applications are expected to be managed with a focus on digital transformation. In addition to new management approaches, new business models, new leadership styles and changes in business life dynamics are foreseen. In this context, it is estimated that the logistics and supply chain applications that can respond to changing customer needs in the fastest way will change within the framework of Industry 5.0. In this study, the information and communication technologies used in the logistics and supply chain sector will be examined, Industry 5.0 applications will be discussed, and the current situation of Türkiye will be evaluated.

INTRODUCTION

Developments in information and communication technology are bringing businesses closer to digital transformation every day. Businesses that offer technology-based goods and services or that inevitably must adapt to technological developments in their processes closely follow the developments in this rapidly changing field and adapt more easily. On the other hand, although businesses think that they offer traditional goods and services to the market, they must follow and apply current developments in information and communication technologies to be faster, more flexible, and competitive in various business processes (Akca & Tepe Küçükoğlu, 2021). It does not seem possible to stay out of the reflections of globalization and the new management approach, which are effective all over the world (Alacadağlı, 2019). Today's developments have created the appropriate infrastructure and conditions for the digitalization of businesses. A digital business is defined as a business that directly or indirectly supports almost all its business relationships with its suppliers, customers, and all employees. Core business processes in these businesses are supported by digital networks (Laudon & Laudon, 2020). When the sources in the field of digital transformation are examined, it is said that it is a concept that has recently emerged with the concept of Industry 4.0. Digital transformation in businesses has started with the use of various digital technologies in business processes, that is, with the digitalization process (Klein, 2019). Digital transformation is defined by Liu et al. (2011) as an organizational transformation that occurs by integrating digital technologies into business processes. However, it is not just about enabling the business to use a specific set of new technologies, it is about the ability to react and successfully use new technologies and procedures now and in the future (Herbert, 2017). Digital transformation transforms all the processes of the business by influencing the organizational structure and even the organizational culture. In digital transformation, which is a destructive and complex process, businesses need a digital transformation strategy and roadmap that covers all areas to be transformed (Klein, 2020). At this point, it is necessary to clearly determine what kind of need the business is in, and to develop strategies accordingly, and to implement them by considering business capabilities and competencies.

Digital businesses stand out when compared to traditional businesses. These businesses can adapt quickly by following the changes in the environment more closely. Thus, they can continue their activities by providing flexibility in chaotic times (Laudon & Laudon, 2020). It is important for the continuity of the business to perceive digitalization as a transformation process that needs to be adapted, not as an external environment component that should be opposed or struggled. Digitalization trends, which started because of business, have become an important component in sectoral and global competition (Çetin Gürkan, 2019).

In this chapter it is aimed to mention about technologies used in logistics and supply chain industry. In addition to that, it is discussed about industry 4.0-5.0 and digital leadership and human resource management practices in Turkey. In this context, it is aimed that the study will contribute to the literature and shed light on future studies.

DIGITAL TRANSFORMATION IN LOGISTICS AND SUPPLY CHAIN MANAGEMENT

Digitization through the application of digital technology can be defined as a radical transformation in products and services, processes, or entire business models (Nambisan et al., 2017). Industry 4.0(I4.0) requires the digitization of the industrial sector (McKinsey Digital, 2015) through the convergence of the physical and virtual worlds, as well as the universal interconnection of people and things (Kagermann 2015). Big data and advanced analytics are important 'game changers' in industry 4.0, especially for supply chain management (Waller & Fawcett, 2013). Additional technologies such as 3D printing, robots, and driverless cars are expected to be supported by industry 4.0-enabled systems (Yin, Stecke, and Li 2018). Various literature reviews summarize the technical underpinnings and overall business implications of industry 4.0, reflecting the rapidly growing interest in technology (Hermann, Pentek, and Otto 2015; Liao et al. 2016; Moeuf et al. 2018; Xu, Xu, and Li 2018). Industry 4.0 presents companies with several managerial problems, including business model design and the question of how companies create, transmit and capture value in this context (Arnold, Kiel and Voigt 2016). On the other side, in the literature, little attention has been paid to the effects of i4.0 on supply chain operating models. According to Kiel, Arnold and Voigt (2017), I4.0 technology changes the value proposition of a business model by providing solutions that improve customer operation procedures. As a result, internal infrastructure, and customer relationship management, which are a component of a supply chain operating model, must be changed. Ehret and Wirtz (2017) propose service-based operating models that include the provisioning of production assets and accompanying full-service operations, as well as information and analytics services, and efficient mass customization through end-user integration.

Supply chain management is considered in general; planning, implementation, and control of primary activities (especially procurement, production and logistics) that create and deliver value to the end customer; and (ii) the integration of business partners into value networks as well as the coordination of relevant business processes within and between companies (CSCMP 2013). Supply chain innovations have been regarded primarily as synonymous with process innovation, because of supply chain management's heavy focus on processes (Flint& Larsson 2007). Arlbjrn and Paulraj (2013) and Carrillo, Druehl, and Hsuan (2013) examined supply chain innovations. Supply chain innovation research deals with innovation networks and content as well as traditional components of innovation management such as innovation strategy, organization, and processes (Flint &Larsson 2007). Innovation networks seek to generate new ideas by bringing suppliers and customers together or by forming horizontal alliances (Roy, Sivakumar and Wilkinson 2004; Wagner 2012). The innovation content represents the result of the innovation process. In this perspective, three dimensions of supply chain innovation interactive content have been identified by Arlbjrn, de Haas, and Munksgaard (2011) as:

Supply chain innovations are mostly cost-driven but have the potential to generate customer value and are closely tied to the supply chain operating model, according to the researchers. Also, the product clock rate, or rate of change in a business, determines the focus of supply chain innovation efforts: high-clocked industries prioritize internal process optimization, while low-clocked industries prioritize external partners and relationships. Besides according to Abdelkafi and Pero (2018), supply chain innovations only generate incremental business model changes due to its operational focus, but large firms can use supply chain innovations (SCI) to create unique business models that complement existing approaches.

Industry 4.0 covers a wide range of interconnected technological concepts (Hofmann & Rüsch 2017) and future technologies are regularly discussed (Rüßmann et al. 2015). Miniaturization of electronics, which requires the production of smaller mechanical, optical and electronic products, and devices (Feldmann, Franke and Schüßler, 2010), is a very important technology. This is an important factor. It is enabled for automatic identification and data acquisition (AIDC) and radio frequency identification (RFID) technologies that assist in the collection, identification and tracking of data. Monitoring and analyzing data are important in supply chain shipping procedures.

AIDC and RFID technologies both classify them as "embedded systems". Microprocessor-based systems are embedded in physical elements to control a single function or a set of functions (Heath, 2002). Robotics, on the other hand, is strongly dependent on electronic miniaturization, as it is the branch of technology that deals with the design, manufacture, operation, and use of robots (Demetriou, 2011). Machine-to-Machine (M2M) communication is the independent and bidirectional communication of machines (Zaus & Choi, 2014).

Strategies, technologies, systems, processes, methodologies, and practices that evaluate vital business data to help an organization better understand its business and market and make timely business choices (Chen, Chiang, & Storey, 2012). Based on BI technology, the concept of the Smart Factory promotes information transparency and allows autonomous operation of a manufacturing facility (Radziwon et al., 2014). When a pay-per-use license is used in smart factories, the price is determined by the actual amount of software used, and this amount is measured in units of usage such as the number of users or transactions (Tukker, 2004). Included in the term Smart Factory is Smart Logistics (Resch & Blecker, 2012), which describes the use of ubiquitous technologies in logistics processes for efficiency improvements in transport, warehousing, and warehousing procedures. Smart Data is a similar idea that helps collect, manage, and analyze data from a growing number of sources in the financial world. When the purpose of Big Data is understood, it becomes Smart Data. Big Data is the large collection and storage of data in real time (Klinck, 2014).

Information Technologies Used in Supply Chain Management and Logistics

After the 1990s, computer networks started to emerge because of technological developments and as a result, the supply chain management phenomenon changed. Hand-held stocks and customer tracking cards have been replaced by a system in which the producer and the customers can follow each other. As a result of this system, companies have been able to better manage their flow from their warehouses to customers and consumers, and at the same time perform their transactions more easily and quickly. Moreover, information greatly influences the overall performance of the supply chain because supply chain managers make decisions based on it. In addition to that, information technologies are tools used to gain awareness about information. All this demonstrates the importance of information technologies in the integration of the virtual business and supply chain with suppliers and partners. In this perspective, there are various tools in the supply chain and logistics for evaluating and sharing data. Examples of these are electronic data interchange (EDI), Internet, Enterprise Resource Planning (ERP), radio frequency identification (RFID), and supply chain management/planning (SCM/SCP) technologies. Managers will choose which technologies to use and how they integrate their operations with those of their partners, but it should be noted that these decisions become more important as the qualities of these technologies evolve (Özdemir&Doğan, 2010). Furthermore, a properly and systematically functioning supply chain increases customer satisfaction, efficiency, and effectiveness, while reducing resources and costs (Sağbaş,2019). In other words, the use of information technologies has benefited businesses in many ways and has led businesses to a new digital transformation. For that reason, it is aimed to mention about some of these prior technologies in this sub-title (Karlı & Tanyas, 2020):

Enterprise Resource Planning

Enterprise Resource Planning (ERP), one of the digital transformation applications in today's business life, has emerged in parallel with the developments in information and communication technology because of the increase in computer use with a new management and business perspective in businesses. Enterprise Resource Planning (ERP) is comprehensive computer software that helps companies manage all aspects of their operations, from procurement to distribution, using an integrated information management system. The most important reason why Enterprise Resource Planning is used is because it allows the company's manufacturers, suppliers, and distribution centers (warehouse) to share resources in a coordinated manner across multiple locations (domestic and international), and ERP software is a software application series that enables a company to transmit information throughout the organization. Other services such as purchasing, human resources, production, accounting, production planning, finance, stock management, sales-distribution, marketing, quality management, maintenance-repair management are all part of the ERP system and were created to facilitate and expand cooperation and interaction between people. Although it may seem like a software for logistics management at first glance, ERP systems cannot be abstracted from this purpose. In this context, the aims of the system, which has a complex and comprehensive structure, are to reduce product costs and increase profitability (Keçek

&Yıldırım, 2009). In short, the system is used to help businesses reach their strategic goals by combining effective and efficient planning, coordination and supply, production, and distribution channels in multiple regions to meet the needs of the company (Karacan&Bayram, 2019).

Electronic Data Interchange (EDI)

Electronic Data Interchange (EDI) has been another concept that has benefited from being used in supply chain management in terms of application. Electronic Data Interchange, one of the electronic communication systems from the past, was first used to reduce the human factor and paper use. Today, large companies mostly use this system to send information to their consumers, to provide order information, to place orders with suppliers and to make electronic payment transfers (Yüregir, 2004). In addition, electronic data exchange is an important tool used in electronic commerce. Standard data can be easily transferred to other computer systems using EDI. In short, electronic data exchange is the direct computer-to-computer processing of business documents such as sales orders and purchase orders. By using the electronic data exchange system, time and cost savings are achieved, errors are minimized, transactions are completed more quickly, thus helping organizations with stock reduction and JIT (Just in Time) delivery methods, providing companies with an advantage in terms of potential opportunities (Parlakkaya, 2005).

Radio Frequency Identification and Barcode System

Inventory waste is a problem that prevents rings from working in integration with each other in supply chain management systems. Inventory waste is a major problem for retailers and manufacturers today. Theft, property damage, counterfeiting, misplacement, or transaction errors are all examples of wasted inventory. Out of stock occurs due to the difference between actual and recorded stock amounts (lost sales). Radio Frequency Identification (RFID) is the information technology method that enables the supply chain management to work more efficiently and functionally, minimizing this problem and mostly eliminating it. Thanks to RFID technology, values closer to actual stock quantities are obtained with increased visibility, product supply is carried out more accurately and stock availability is reduced. RFID technology offers solutions to these challenges. With more accurate stock management, transaction errors are reduced, misplacements are prevented, counterfeiting is eliminated, and waste amounts are reduced (Üstündağ &Tanyaş, 2009).

In the context of information technology, RFID technology means detecting assets, collecting information about them, and evaluating the obtained information instantly without the need for manual counting. RFID consists of three basic components: antenna, reader, and tag. Readers, one of these components, are components that use radio waves to receive information about an object in the form of a digital code, thanks to the tags attached to the object. Tags are information storage components. Binding is the process of communicating using antennae between a tag and a reader (Maraşlı &Çubuk,2015).

On the other hand, Barcode technology, which is encountered with the continuous RFID system, is a kind of information coding. Real-time product inspection, timely sending of invoices to the accounting department and reflection of the transaction to the stock status in businesses using barcode system are much faster and error-free than manual techniques. As a result, stock status can be checked in real time and goods can be delivered to customers as required. At the same time, the cost of keeping (or not keeping) stocks can be reduced, and since price adjustments will be made over the computer, the cost of labels can be reduced, especially for products whose prices are constantly changing. Many businesses have set up their own barcode systems in response to technological advances. In this context, it is thought that the most widely used system among the identification technologies related to printing is the barcode system (Yıldırım & Bayraktar, 2014).

Internet

Markets have traditionally been considered physical locations where buyers and sellers can meet their buying and selling demands and sell. These markets still operate today, but technology advances and ubiquitous internet use have removed space and time limits in the marketplace, making the internet the new dating marketplace for parties. Businesses, like other fields, have seen tremendous changes because of the internet. The importance of internet-based supply chain management has played an increasingly important role in increasing communication between the internet, businesses and their current or potential suppliers, intermediary institutions and customers (Barutçu, 2007). The enhancement of internet with the rapid development of globalization e-business concept get popular day by day in the worldwide. Specially, organizations that lead to have sustainable performance and competition advantage increase relations with suppliers and customers.

The term "e-business" refers to the use of the Internet to achieve supply chain integration goals. There are many different types of e-businesses, depending on different business deals. These; Customer to Customer (C2C), Business to Customer (B2C), Business to Business (B2B), Customer to Business (C2B), Government to Citizen (G2C), People to People (P2P), Citizen to Government (C2G), Intra-Business (Organizations to Organizations) are Modify-to-Modify (E2E) categories. All e-Commerce transactions are carried out electronically using computers and communication networks, without the use of face-to-face transactions. About e-commerce application electronic marketplaces are three main categories, also known as e-marketplaces, inter-organizational systems, and customer service (Özdemir&Doğan, 2010; Maraşlı &Çubuk,2015, Karlı&Tanyaş, 2020). Besides, all e-business transactions are carried out electronically using computers and communication networks, without using face-to-face transactions. E-business practice consists of three main categories, also known as electronic markets or e-markets, inter-organizational systems, and customer service. The Internet has significant advantages over Electronic Data Interchange (EDI) in terms of information sharing and thus the Internet allows more information to be moved, providing better visibility than EDI. Otherwise, better visibility helps supply chain decision making. Internet communication between layers of the supply chain is also easier as a standard infrastructure is already in place. On the other hand, E-commerce has become one of the most powerful forces in the supply chain thanks to the Internet. Traditional business-to-business e-commerce systems require a significant financial investment. In addition to that, small and medium-sized businesses can now establish electronic connections with large institutions thanks to internet technology. Unlike traditional systems, which have a mixed and limited access structure, the nature of the Internet, which usually only requires a computer, internet connection and a web browser to connect, creates an environment that allows small businesses to have global connectivity and do business with each other (Özdemir &Doğan, 2010).

Supply Chain Management/Planning Software (SCM/SCP)

Information in enterprise resource planning is used by the SCM/SCP package implementation to provide analytical decision assistance in information visibility. In this perspective it can be considered that, enterprise resource planning systems show the company what is happening, while SCM systems help the company decide about what is happening. The main advantage of SCM/SCP systems is that they allow for improved operational and commercial planning. With the use of SCM/SCP systems, it is possible to achieve increased earnings, increased productivity, lower operating costs, lower inventory, and shorter order fulfillment times (Özkök & Coşkun,2019). Besides, SCM/SCP systems use finite capacity planning algorithms that do not require iterative arrangements, as well as real-time planning features that allow businesses to respond quickly to changes in supply and demand. It is also known that reducing forecasting and planning errors in the supply chain can help reduce depreciation (Özkök & Coşkun,2019).

INFORMATION TECHNOLOGIES AUDIT IN TÜRKIYE

The evolution of today's communication and information technologies, especially the rise and development of the internet, affects both the public and private sectors and has a significant impact on the sector. As a result of these developments, the borders between countries are slowly being dissolved and the economic integrations that have taken place have profoundly changed the type and structure of the services offered. In our country, both the public and private sectors are undergoing great transformations because of technological developments, and they carry out a large part of their work with computers. This development is extremely significant for businesses because the use of computers allows transactions to be completed faster and more efficiently. However, besides the benefits of this rapid technological development, there are also some drawbacks. The most serious of these problems is the difficulty of monitoring, managing, and auditing the previously written transactions after they are transferred to the virtual environment. The transformation of systems into a more complex structure negatively affects the types and contents of risks related to information technologies and creates new risk factors. All these developments have revealed the importance of not only the data collected from these systems, but also the systems that produce these data. As a result, for the data obtained under the supervision of the organizations that started to operate in such a virtual environment to be more meaningful, the computer systems that produce this data and the processes and applications on these systems should work properly and reliably (Özbilgin, 2003). Parallel to the rest of the world, the use of information technologies in business life has increased in Turkey as well. Public institutions and corporate organizations in the sector are undergoing significant transformations because of technological developments and carry out most of their activities from systems and applications. In Turkey, the finance sector has been subject to mandatory audits in the field of information technologies in accordance with the rules issued by the Banking Regulation and Supervision Agency in the light of the Banking Law and the Payment Services and Electronic Money Institutions Law No. 6493. In addition, the Energy Market Regulatory Authority, the Information Technologies and Communications Authority and the Ministry of Customs and Trade have legislation on the implementation of IT controls. When country rules and globally notified bodies issue standards and frameworks, information technology and audit work is included in the process of evaluating internal controls. As a result, information systems audit working papers and reports are part of the same process. The standards and regulations published by IFAC/IAASB, PCAOB (SOX) in the world and by KGK in Turkey are decisive at this stage (KPMG,2017).

Digital Transformation in Türkiye in the Perspective of Industry 5.0

The effects of innovation and technological change, which are among the important dynamics of the 21st century, are felt all over the world as well as in Türkiye, and the interest and development in digitalization is increasing in our country. With the COVID-19 pandemic, which we have not experienced in the last century, the practices that we quickly integrated into our daily activities in many areas from education to logistics, from health to banking have a great impact on this development and transformation. For this reason, digitalization and digital transformation applications in both the public and private sectors are developing day by day. After Industry 4.0, Industry 5.0, centered on human-economy-environment and sustainability, accelerated the creation of Smart societies and laying the foundations of Society 5.0. In this context, it is possible to say that the studies on Society 5.0 in our country have progressed based on the public sector (Uysal Şahin, 2021).

With the initiation of the use of e-Government in Türkiye and the expansion of its usage area, the steps of the initiatives towards Smart Society have been strengthened. It is aimed to increase the quality of life of citizens, to save time and money, and to provide instant information sharing with smart applications within e-government. E-Government applications with 60,764,107 users, 901 institutions and 6811 service activities are an important precursor application in the Digital Transformation process (cbddo.gov.tr, 2022). The social acceptance and applicability of the developments in this context will enable Turkey to accelerate in the Smart State transformation. However, when the Society 5.0 efforts in Türkiye are examined, the establishment of the Electronic Public Information Management System draws attention as an important innovation (Uysal Şahin, 2021). Electronic Public Information Management System will ensure that the elements in public administration, from the organizational structure of public institutions to the services provided, from the documents used in the services to the information contained in the documents, are determined together with the legislative bases and defined in the electronic environment, and that the developed e-Government applications will be integrated from a single center to a-state is considered as a "basic information system" (kaysis.gov.tr, 2022).

On the other hand, a Digital Transformation Office was established in Türkiye to accelerate the digital transformation and Society 5.0 transition process. The Digital Transformation Office undertakes the task of coordinating digital transformation within the scope of Industry 5.0 and Society 5.0. With the Digital Transformation Office, it is aimed to lead the digitalization efforts in Türkiye. There are many projects carried out by the Digital Transformation Office. With these projects, the groundwork is laid for the formation of a Society 5.0, studies are carried out to provide qualified human resources, and studies are carried out to strengthen the innovative and technology-oriented competencies of young people. In addition, the National Artificial Intelligence Strategy was prepared and put into effect for the years 2021-2025. National Artificial Intelligence Strategy has been prepared in harmony with the vision of "Digital Türkiye" and "National Technology Move". In this context, the National artificial intelligence strategy, whose vision is to "generate value on a global scale with an agile and sustainable artificial intelligence ecosystem for a prosperous Türkiye, has been strengthened with 24 objectives and 119 measures around six strategic priorities. Six Strategic priorities of the National Artificial Intelligence Strategy are listed below (cbddo.gov.tr, 2022).

1. Educating AI Experts and Increasing Employment in the Field
2. Supporting Research, Entrepreneurship, and Innovation
3. Expanding Access to Quality Data and Technical Infrastructure

4. Planning to Accelerate Socioeconomic Adjustment
5. Strengthening International Cooperations
6. Accelerating Structural and Labor Transformation

Besides in this subtitle, it is mentioned about the digitalization related studies in Türkiye. In the research conducted by Tübitak in Türkiye in 2016, 1000 enterprises were examined. According to the results of the research, it has been found that 19% of the enterprises in Türkiye have no knowledge of smart production systems and technological-digital developments, 59% have general knowledge and 22% have comprehensive knowledge. The sectors with the highest awareness of digital innovations and technologies are software (93%), electronics (89%) and materials (84%) sectors. While 50% of enterprises have strategies to integrate smart automation systems and cyber-physical systems in the next 3-5 years, 30% do not have such a strategy. 20% of the enterprises also stated that they can integrate these systems in 5-10 years. Research findings show that the digital maturity level of the Turkish industry is between Industry 2.0 and Industry 3.0. Moreover as a result of another analyze, it is studied on 10.000 enterprises within the scope of Türkiye Productivity Development Map Project by the Ministry of Science, Industry and Technology in 2016, it was determined that the awareness of big data and internet of things technologies among enterprises in Türkiye is low (btk.gov.tr,2020).

Furthermore, in the "Digital Türkiye Roadmap" report prepared by the Ministry of Science, Industry and Technology in 2019; it is mentioned that the level of economic development and prosperity between Türkiye and other countries that can adapt the innovations brought by digital transformation to different areas is gradually increasing. For this reason, it has been clearly stated that we cannot have an option to stay behind this age (btk.gov.tr, 2020). So, it is possible to say that intensive efforts will be made to become a Smart State and reach the values of Society 5.0 with the projects and studies carried out under the coordination of the Digital Transformation Office.

EVOLUTION OF I4 TO I5 AND NEW TECHNOLOGIES

Industry 5.0 accelerated innovations in transportation, supply chain and logistics activities, and had an impact on the process from the procurement of resources to the production stage, from the production stage to the delivery of products and services to the customer. Increasing competition in today's business life, globalization, change and technological innovations force businesses to keep up with the systemic changes required by the era to be sustainable (Kırmaz & Sayın, 2022). In this context, Industry 4.0 and 5.0 are decisive on new business models and practices in the supply chain and logistics sector. In this process, in addition to operational practices, human resources management practices will also take their share from digital transformation and change will inevitably take place. Moreover leadership model that provides the integration of organizational and individual goals, which can lead processes and people independent of time and place, will be replaced by innovative, entrepreneurial, and digital leaders who support change, who are committed to the past and the conventional.

Behind the fourth industrial revolution and the development of Society 5.0, also called as the cyber revolution, there are many technological innovations that pioneered this revolution. Shortly these technologies are listed as follows (Özdogan,2019; Chang et al., 2019; Cited in Akca& Tepe Küçükoğlu, 2021):

- 3D printers

- Industrial robots and human-machine interfaces
- Big data management
- Cloud computing systems and data centers
- Data science and expertise
- Artificial intelligence and machine learning
- Internet of Things and machine-to-machine communication
- Blockchain
- Model Based Design and Digital Twin etc.

3D Printers: Three-dimensional printers or printing machines can be defined as CNC machines of Industry 4.0. It is a hardware technology that enables three-dimensional output of any product designed in virtual environments. It finds useage in many sectors. For example, today it is possible to produce indicators and end-use parts in aviation, detailed and smooth architectural models in the architectural field, low-number end-use parts in the automotive sector, and multi-material respirators with the possibility of mass production in the defense sector (Özdogan, 2019).

Industrial Robots and Human-Machine Interfaces: Robotics is a technology that involves the design, construction, operation, and use of robots. The goal of robotics is to design smart machines that can help people in their daily lives. Robotic technology aims to make machines that can replace humans or imitate human actions (btk.gov.tr, 2020). Autonomous robots are defined as robots that can act on their own, make decisions and solve problems, which are popularized in the manufacturing environment (Öztemel, 2018). Technological developments in industrial robot systems have led to advances in the field of robot-human interaction. New generation industrial robots work in active and passive cooperation with humans thanks to advanced technology sensors, actuators, and control systems. With the flexible robotic systems used in the human-robot interface, safety and sensitivity parameters have been enabled to comply with the standards (Dilibal & Şahin, 2018). In addition to unmanned factories, which are called dark smart factories, in many new applications, humans and machines work together in human-robot cooperation. While humans mostly do surveillance and follow-up tasks, robots perform physically strenuous and demanding jobs (Fırat & Fırat, 2017). Industrial robots increase not only quality but also efficiency in the systems used. Robotic systems are widely used because they eliminate human errors and have a high investment cost, as well as a system that pays for itself later and provides profitability (Çengelci & Çimen, 2005).

Cloud Computing Systems and Data Centers: Cloud Computing Systems have an approach that completely separates data, software and the devices required to access them (Klein, 2019). In addition to hosting services of cloud computing systems and software applications, many services such as data processing, file storage, database hosting have been started to be provided by many other businesses besides large enterprises such as Google and Amazon. The services performed vary from a single service to more than one service under the cloud title. While the concept of cloud refers to the externality of the services offered, it also refers to an infrastructure that companies with sufficient facilities can create within their own structure (Atan, 2020). Instead of allocating high budgets and purchasing new software as in the past, cloud computing technology and the possibilities of using both storage systems and software will be able to meet with very small costs (Öztemel, 2018).

Data Science and Expertise: While it was called data management in the beginning, the purpose of this concept, which is now called data science, is to produce information from data, that is, to make sense of it. The increase in data diversity, volume changes and increase in production speeds transform the field of data management from being a simple management field into a science (Ozdogan, 2019).

Artificial Intelligence: With the increasing data sources in today's world, many research topics have emerged in the way of obtaining meaningful information from this data. Many applications such as translation systems, mood analysis and sentence completion are made possible by machines' perception of natural language. Here are the language representation models that enable machines to understand and process natural language. With the development of generative models, artificial intelligence models that write stories and draw pictures continue to surprise with works that are not understood whether they were made by humans or not (Zeybel et al., 2020). Artificial intelligence is considered as the science and technology of making intelligent machines, especially intelligent computer programs. It is subdivided into artificial intelligence, natural language processing, robotics, expert systems, speech recognition and image recognition. Artificial intelligence is the use and development of machines to replace human intelligence to do complex tasks (Chang et al., 2019). In its most general definition, artificial intelligence is the ability of a computer or a computer-controlled robot to perform various activities in a similar way to intelligent living things (He is right, 2020). That is, by processing large amounts of data and recognizing patterns in data, machines, computers, and robots are capable of performing certain tasks, learning from their own experience, adapting to new inputs, and performing human-like tasks. Artificial Intelligence performs to extract valuable information from unstructured datasets. Speech, image and video recognition, intelligent automation, advanced simulation, and complex analytical predictions are among the capabilities of artificial intelligence (Grobotek, 2019).

Internet of Things and Machine-to-Machine Communication: The Internet of Things is one of the key elements of the Industry 4.0 trend. The Industry 4.0 approach is considered as a transformative force that will change not only production infrastructures, but also the development of products and services and customer relations. Internet of Things, big data, artificial intelligence and digital applications, cooperation, mobility and open innovation are among the main elements of the Industry 4.0 trend (European Commission, 2017).

Wireless Sensor: A wireless sensor network is defined as a group of spatially distributed sensors to monitor and record the physical conditions of the environment and organize the collected data in a central location. Temperature, noise, pollution levels, humidity, wind, etc. provides measurement of environmental conditions such as In Society 5.0, which is a Super Smart Society, people do not do things, but systems created using technologies offer suggestions or solutions to people by analyzing the data at hand (btk.gov.tr, 2020).

Blockchain: Blockchain, on the other hand, is a new mode of computer technology application such as distributed data storage, point-to-point transfer, consensus mechanism and encryption algorithm. Blockchain is an important part of Bitcoin. Blockchain is a decentralized database and consists of a series of data blocks generated by cryptography. It is possible to verify and exchange data automatically and securely in the system within the blockchain, but it is difficult to change the data. The feature of not being dependent on one party makes the system more reliable. On the other hand, information transfers can take place automatically (Chang et al., 2019; Nofer et al., 2017).

Model-Based Design and Digital Twin: Model-Based Design is a mathematical model that uses digital and visual methods to solve problems in complex system control algorithms and signal processing design. It is widely used in many motions control, industrial equipment, aerospace and automotive applications. In model-based design, what is transferred between the design and development processes is the model rather than the drawing, and the design document containing the calculations. Digital twins, on the other hand, are systems that can integrate supplier data into the platform when necessary to ensure the integration of value chain data. The Digital Twin helps companies optimize and test products in a virtual environment before they go into production. Thus, the activities in the production process are simultaneously optimized and efficiency, flexibility and innovation are supported. (Batty, 2018; Chang et al., 2019; Hartmann & Van der Auweraer, 2020).

Metaverse: The concept, which is formed by the combination of the words meta and verse, is called beyond the universe and although it is developing today, it is not completely known by most societies. The concept of Metaverse, which is important in the formation of a digital society, includes collaboration activities and innovations in virtual spaces as well as physical spaces. However, in the development of the Metaverse universe, the acceleration of digital transformation in the pandemic process and change on the name of Facebook INc. to Meta was effective (Duan et al, 2021; Kalkan, 2021; Rehm et al, 2015; cited in Özkahveci et al, 2022).

Wearable Technology: Wearable technology is an efficiency-based technological innovation that allows employees who are on the go to do more in less time. For example, when we consider a worker who aims to place the product boxes on the shelves and places in the warehouse in the logistics sector, this employee can not only detect the location of the product with a device he wears like a glove, but also process information about the product into the relevant inventory. In many sectors, the application area of similar innovation and technology-based devices is expanding (Çelik, 2020; cited in Kırmaz & Sayın, 2022).

On the other side, it is possible to say that in the human-robot cooperation philosophy of Industry 5.0 refers high quality and efficiency mechanisms that leads business processes can be monitored continuously. In this context, it is likely that daily and routine work will be given to machines and robots, and innovative, creative and entrepreneurial work and activities will be carried out by people. In addition, more skilled and qualified jobs are expected to be realized by people in Industry 5.0 (Maddikunta et al., 2021; cited in Calis Duman, 2022). For this reason, it is important to renew human resources practices to increase the competencies and skills of employees, whether it is Industry 5.0 or Society 5.0. At the same time, sustainability of organizational success with digital leaders who support the digital transition process and encourage the enrichment of employees' skills by directing change and transformation in today's post-information society will provide businesses with a competitive advantage.

Industry 5.0 and Society 5.0

The evolutions throughout history have been effective in reaching the present level of development of mankind. The stages of development that started with the hunter society continued with the agricultural society, the industrial society, and the information society. In this context, "Society 1.0" refers to the Hunter society, "Society 2.0" refers to the agricultural society that carries out agricultural activities, "Society 3.0" refers to the industrial society that started mass production with the industrial revolution, and "Society 4.0" refers to the information society with the invention of the computer and the emergence of information sharing. However, the rapid change in information and communication technologies has revealed new concepts related to digitalization at the end of the twentieth century. Emerging technological breakthroughs such as artificial intelligence (AI), robotics, internet of things (IoT), autonomous vehicles, 3D printers, nanotechnology, biotechnology, augmented reality, energy storage and quantum computing also affect the social structure and create a new form called "Society 5.0" had an impact on the formation of social structure. "Society 5.0" or also known as "Super Smart Society" is considered as an information society founded on Society 4.0, living in prosperity, and aiming for a human-centered approach. The concept of Society 5.0 was shared with the public for the first time at the CeBIT fair held in 2017. It laid the foundations of Society 5.0 to find solutions to the social problems facing Japan (aging population, declining birth rate, depopulation, and deteriorating infrastructure). Society 5.0 focuses on human and human happiness, quality of life, as well as carrying the traces of previous developmental stages. In this context, priority areas have been determined, particularly in cities and regions, energy, disaster prevention, health, agriculture and nutrients, logistics, products and services, finance, and public services (btk.gov.tr, 2020).

To transfer and develop international competition, it is seen that the Japanese Industry, where digitalization is encouraged, including all businesses, has recently been cooperated between companies and information sharing within the supply chain. In our developing world, the need to respond quickly to the labor problem in the supply chain and the problems in the environment has arisen. Likewise, infectious diseases such as Covid 19 or biological factors have also created the need for contactless or remote resolution. To meet these needs and to solve them within the supply process, remote and contactless transactions can be considered as the most reasonable solution (Keidanren, 2020; Kırmaz &Sayın, 2022). While observing that the transition to digital is increasing day by day due to the problems in the workforce, small and medium enterprises have encountered different problems in terms of human resources, lack of information and cost (Keidanren, 2020) In order to subsidize these problems, it is important to support digitalization for the private sector (Kırmaz & Sayın, 2022). The transition to digital for money transfers provides savings on materials used in money making, accelerating, and facilitating accounting transactions. At the same time, with the help of technology, the margin of error will be minimized, and more efficient reports will be generated. In this case, time and labor will be saved. It is seen that there are benefits to be provided in terms of production facilities. It is obvious that technology, product, and equipment data will also add value to cost optimization and quality control automation with data obtained from production areas. Again, in cases such as epidemics, the importance of data use will increase by supporting the supply chain rings. The development and rapid increase of E-Commerce around the world will affect the global industry 5.0 in the supply chain in different complex structures and will turn into new logistics activities. They will be able to be optimized in coordination with the use of artificial intelligence by simultaneously processing the data covering production, supply, transportation, and sales into digital fields (Kırmaz & Sayın, 2022).

Industry 5.0 provides benefits to humanity by considering technological developments more frequently with the concept of innovation. Each industry period has been revised from the previous one according to the requirements of technology and age. Industry 5.0 is also beneficial to businesses and humanity according to today's technology and requirements. With the experience of technology making our lives easier, the prejudices of businesses have completely come to an end. Enterprises still have prejudices against Industry 5.0, which includes revolutions such as artificial intelligence and robotic processes that we are not yet familiar with and are not widely used. The fact that different companies in the sector have implemented these practices at any stage of their supply chains has enabled other companies to view these practices positively (Bakırcı, 2020). In addition, other businesses that see the benefits of companies in areas such as reducing production costs, providing human resources and ensuring cost optimization will also want to benefit from the blessings of industry 5.0. In this way, the managers of the system, which includes robots as workers, will be humans. Again, when considered in this way, with the change of the worker group with robots, different professions will emerge and sub-sectors will also be formed (Bakırcı, 2020). As companies digitize their production, cost calculations and supply chains, the control mechanisms will be better thanks to the simultaneous data transfer, and the quality of the resulting products will increase at the same rate. Since they will replace the loss of time, which is one of the biggest problems of today, with savings, they will be able to provide customer satisfaction with product development and error-free production and simultaneously provide the highest quality service. Likewise, the existence of such a system will increase business reliability and increase the trust of business partners, customers, and employees in the system (Yacan, 2021).

Formation Phases of Industry 5.0

It is a generally accepted point that the world industrial revolution has developed in four stages. In these processes between revolutions, not only the previous technology has developed, but also innovations have occurred. These mentioned revolutions started as Industry 1.0 in the 18th century and came to the present as Industry 4.0 (Fırat & Fırat, 2017). Summarizing each of the building blocks of these phases will be useful in terms of increasing the dominance of the subject. In this context, these processes can be summarized as follows.

Industry 1.0: It covers the process in which mechanical workbenches working with steam and water-power are involved in production, rather than a production based on animal and human power or energy (Aksoy, 2017).

Industry 2.0: As a result of the use of electrical energy with production machines in the industry, the speed of mass production increased, and the industrial revolution took place. Although the machines operating using electrical power were used for the first time in the USA for slaughtering animals, in practice, it was realized by Ford's mass production line to produce cars (Batibay, 2022). Thus, Henry Ford laid one of the main foundations of the Industry 2.0 process.

Industry 3.0: To provide flexibility in production, numerically controlled machines and industrial robots that automate production have been invented. With the concepts of logistics management systems being technology-based, software such as TMS (Transport Management System), WMS (Warehouse Management System- Warehouse management system) became widespread in this period (Şekkeli & Bakan, 2018).

Industry 4.0: In this phase, which started with the rapid increase in the use of the internet in the 21st century, the importance of human power has been lost. Concepts such as the internet of things, big data, cloud technology, artificial intelligence have taken place in our daily lives (Gökten, 2018). First, this new process has created a production system that instantly adapts to the needs of the consumer by removing the production and consumption relations from the usual patterns, and an automation system that provides continuous coordination and communication with each other. Industry 4.0 consists of four parts: the physical environment where the devices are located, the big data and server systems embedded in the cloud system, the networks that enable the communication to be established in an integrated way, the smart factory showing the application level, the city, the services, and the users. As a matter of fact, devices communicate through networks and obtain the necessary information synchronously from the data in the cloud system, which enables smart consumers and factories mentioned at the application level (Alçın, 2016). In this context, with the fourth industrial revolution, communication between all actors in industrial production, access to instant data, and high added value can be created with these data (Özsoylu, 2017).

Industry 5.0: The fifth industrial revolution, which continues to be effective today, is expected that the need for human power will be eliminated by increasing the efficiency in production with the collaboration of robots. Digital factories created with digital data and software applications used in Industry 4.0 evolve as smart factories in Industry 5.0, and then the production systems are globalized with the applications of these developing smart technologies (Javaid, et al., 2020).

When all these formation phases of Industry 1.0, Industry 2.0 and Industry 3.0 are examined, it is seen that there is a process of approximately 100 years between them. Today, it can be clearly said that there is a much shorter time than the period between Industry 5.0, which is described as another industrial revolution, and Industry 4.0 (Özkahveci, Civek, & Ulusoy, 2022). In this context, it can be said that the concept of Industry 5.0, which came into our lives in 2016 and made a name for itself frequently in 2019 and afterwards, started to be emphasized only five years after the concept of Industry 4.0 (Sadıç, 2021).

Finally, when the industrial paradigms defined in general terms are examined, it is possible to express the transition process from Industry 4.0 to Industry 5.0 as the transition from digital production to digital society. This new era aims to increase the capacity of human resources by using artificial intelligence and to penetrate people's lives and argues that people will be the center of the universe (Yucebalkan, 2020). In this context, when all the industrial revolutions, with the focus on Industry 4.0, are examined, it is seen that Industry 5.0 offers more personalized products or services to consumers than any other. The fact that human and machine interaction has increased is the main factor at this point, but it should not be ignored that the participation of people in designing the product and service should also increase (Aslam, Aimin, Li, & Rehman, 2020).

HUMAN RESOURCE PRACTICES CHANGE IN THE DIGITAL REVOLUTION

Human resource management considers people as one of the most valuable resources of the enterprise to realize organizational activities and achieve organizational matches in a sustainable way. In this context, all efforts, and activities to attract human resources to the organization and to benefit from this valuable resource in the most effective way are included in the human resources management process today (Benligiray, 2013; cited in Oruçoğlu, 2022). Furthermore, in today's business life, where digital transformation is experienced rapidly, businesses need to invest in information and communication-based technologies, as well as increase the human resource qualifications to use these technologies. However, the emergence of new business areas will have an impact on human resource management activities such as job analysis and job descriptions (Kagermann et al., 2013). The development and growth in logistics and supply chain activities, especially with Covid-19, will show itself at every stage of the human resources management process of digitalization in the sector. Many activities, from recruitment processes to business organizations and training-professional development activities, will be able to be carried out through digital applications. For instance, supporting activities to increase employee competencies have started to be carried out interactively with Online Open Courses. On the other hand, one of the most important factors that determine the direction and power of the impact of the digitalization process on business policies is the leaders. In this context, it is necessary for leaders to have a high ability to persuade employees not to show resistance in change and transformation. In addition, it is important for human resources managers to show an inclusive approach to all employees in the digitalization of human resources management processes and the formation of e-human resources activities (Okumuşoğlu, 2022)

Moreover, the effects of digitization are likely to be felt in every industry and every business function. Similarly, the use of big data and artificial intelligence in the human resources management function of enterprises, creating a candidate pool in the recruitment processes, and profiling the candidates in the selection of candidates draws attention. It is also possible to say that Blockchain technologies are increasingly being used in recruitment techniques (Sivathanu &Pillai, 2018; Onik et al., 2018; cited in Oruçoğlu, 2022). For example, synchronous and asynchronous interviews on digital platforms, use of chatbots and social media applications are related to the impact of digitalization on the human resources recruitment process (Akduman, 2019; cited in Oruçoğlu, 2022).

On the other side, the increasing use of automation in production and supply chain processes and the sharing of information by internet-based expert systems within the supply chain have reduced the demand for unskilled labor in the sector and made it necessary to shape employment policies to renew the qualified workforce in the face of digital change (Türkel & Arıkan,2020; Sharma, 2021). In this context, developments are taking place in the direction of the most efficient management of human resources with the use of simulation in employment processes, the recruitment of personnel with the method of working groups, and distance and virtual training programs that support personal development based on creating value for employees (Walport & Lapthorne, 2013; Gentner, 2016 cited in Türkel & Arıkan,2020). Finally, with the influence of the business dynamics of the 21st century, innovation comes to the fore, digitalization is decisive on businesses, and customer expectations for products and services are changing. In this context, the activities of examining consumer habits and predicting customer expectations by using big data bring innovative employees to the fore and pave the way for the formation of new job descriptions, practices, requirements and qualifications (Mosterman & Zander, 2016).

CONCLUSION

Throughout human history, people have never had the chance to live in a social system that has been shaped before. All social life models were shaped within the framework of the needs and conditions of that time. For example, all the activities of the first humans, aiming only to find food and drink and survive, created a social structure and the mode of production of that social structure. Over time, these activities introduced people to private properties and then a restructuring took place (Canlıoğlu, 2008). With these formations, the internet and smart phones have spread rapidly and have led to the production of large amounts of data that always create new values around the world. Thus, civilization is a significant turning point for humanity, which has settled in the status of Information Society. At this stage, people have come to the point of reconciliation both with the environmental burdens and social inequalities created by traditional economic systems, and with digital transformations. In this context, although the ways of classification of societies vary, the 5th Basic Plan of Science and Technology defines the societies in which people live as Hunting Society (Society 1.0), Agricultural Society (Society 2.0), Industrial Society (Society 3.0), and Information Society (Society 4.0), and named the new society following these societies as "Society 5.0" (Keidanren, 2018).

Prime Minister of Japan, Shinzo Abe, stated that Industry 5.0, also known as Society 5.0, at the fair held in 2017, explained that societies should perceive this element not as a threat but as an auxiliary element (Yetkin & Coşkun, 2021). Prior to this introduction, the concept of Society 5.0 was used as a core concept in Japan's 5th Science and Technology Basic Plan. In this plan, the concept of Society 5.0 is described as fully integrating the Physical and Cyberspace with each other, and the ideal form of the future society as "Super Smart Society" (Science, Technology and Innovation Board, 2015).

The Society 5.0 phenomenon, put forward by the Japanese Government, was included in the 5th Science and Technology Basic Plan through the Japan Science, Technology and Innovation Council and was approved by the Japanese Council of Ministers in January 2016. In this context, Society 5.0 improves connectivity in the physical and virtual space, enabling people to carry out and support their work and adjustments as representatives. Hence, people will be freed from the cumbersome daily work. Moreover, human is at the center of this phenomenon. Therefore, many technologies such as Internet of Things (IoT), Big Data (Big Data), Robotics, Artificial Intelligence, Wireless Sensor Network are used together. As a matter of fact, the use of these technologies will eliminate various difficulties by affecting both industries and social life. Thus, people will live their lives in a more harmonious and sustainable society. In short, Society 5.0 stands for "Super Smart Society" (Information Technologies and Communications Authority, 2017).

The concept of Industry 5.0 is also considered as a philosophy that aims at the integration of industry and technology, and adopts to move beyond the Industry 4.0 model, in which production is carried out using cyber physical systems, and direct the focus and purpose of production systems to provide social contribution as well as gain profit and market share. The Industry 5.0 model aims to use technologies such as "internet of things", "cloud computing", "production cloud" and "augmented reality", which emerged as Industry 4.0 technologies, in line with sustainability and within the framework of human-machine cooperation (Sadıç, 2022).

Sustainability is defined as the art of meeting today's needs of mankind, while not compromising the capacity of future generations to meet their needs, and meeting today's needs without consuming the resources of the future. In this context, Industry 5.0 focuses on integration in the axis of economy-human-society and environment, as well as profit centralization at the center of its sustainability philosophy (Kamble et al, 2018; cited in Sadıç, 2022).

Furthermore, Industry 5.0 (introduced in the Japanese Science and Technology Plan in 2016), Industry 4.0 (introduced by the German Government in 2011) technologies such as the internet of things, big data, blockchain, etc. blends digital technologies to create a people-centered industry and society. In this context, Industry 4.0 focuses because of efficiency by combining concepts such as Smart Factories, automation, smart production with quality management and profitability, while Industry 5.0 focuses on solving human problems by aiming to strengthen automation with human factors, enrich mental competencies and maximize social contribution (Aslam et al., 2020; Fukuyama, 2018; cited in: Sadıç, 2022).

Society 5.0 includes the goal of transforming society and social life into a super smart society. To increase the level of social welfare, solve social problems, ensure cooperation, aim for a happy life, and establish an environment of trust, the obstacles in creating Society 5.0 should be removed with state supports (Sadıç, 2022).

Besides, some existing obstacles should be removed, systemic reliability should be increased, and the legal infrastructure should be established to enhance the usage and acceptance of Society 5.0. In this context, it is important to make human resources plans to eliminate obstacles in the legal system, resolve social and political obstacles, reduce technological obstacles, reduce resistance to change, strengthen social change-orientedness, and expand the employment of qualified human resources (Demirci Celep 2020; cited in Kırmaz & Sayin, 2022). In addition, approaches such as providing necessary government support, especially for small and medium-sized enterprises, empowering human resources, increasing social awareness, expanding cooperation working areas, strengthening public and private sector relations, encouraging digital transformation, have contributed to the development of Industry 5.0 and Society 5.0 concepts in Türkiye (Kırmaz & Sayın, 2022).

In addition with Supply Chain 5.0- Logistics 5.0, which will emerge within the scope of Industry 5.0, businesses will now offer 'Personalized Logistics Solutions' consisting of different scenarios for each customer with different demands. By using the smart warehouses and transportation systems developed in this context, where the studies are continued, information about where the products are, how they are produced, where they come from and where they go will be instantly accessible. It will be easier to create a self-working mechanism such as increasing customer satisfaction in the entire process within the supply chain, disseminating the philosophy of sustainability, protecting the environment, and executing recycling practices through automation in line with digitalization. In this process, there will be no need for people to carry out certain jobs, and competency and skill-based digital transformation-oriented human resources practices and leadership concepts will come to the fore for automation and jobs that need people (Globelink-Unimar, 2022). With the use of artificial intelligence and robots in a wider area within the scope of Industry 5.0, there is a risk that the need for employment demand will decrease. For this reason, in some sectors, there will be almost no need for human beings. On the other hand, the education system will need to be updated in the context of digitalization, and new business areas related to Society 5.0 will gain importance (Uysal Şahin, 2021).

Finally, it is also important to implement the following strategies to expand the application areas of Industry 5.0 and Society 5.0 (Keidanren, 2016; cited in: Uysal Şahin, 2021):

- Public institutions should plan national strategies for creating a technology-based Smart Society and a government incentive system should be established for these strategies.
- Legal ground should be established, and legal regulations should be prepared.
- Infrastructure should be established for the protection of personal data and cyber security, and activities supported by R&D should be carried out.
- To increase the quality of human resources, information technology literacy should be ensured, and intellectual capital should be equipped with numerical skills.
- For the formation of Society 5.0, it has a vital role to ensure social acceptance and the active participation of citizens in the new economic and social change-transformation that will emerge.

REFERENCES

Abdelkafi, N., & Pero, M. (2018). Supply Chain Innovation-Driven Business Models: Exploratory Analysis and Implications For Management. *Business Process Management Journal, 24*(2), 589–608. doi:10.1108/BPMJ-05-2016-0109

Akan Özkök, G., & Yardımcı Coşkun, İ. (2019). Knowledge Management In The Supply Chain And Effects Of Information Technologies And An Implementation In The Airline Company. *Proceedings of The International Congress On Business And Marketing.*

Akca, M., & Küçükoğlu, T. M. (2021). *Digital Transformation and Aviation Sector, Sectoral Analysis of Digital Transformation*, Nobel Academic Publication.

Aksoy, S. (2017). *Changing Technologies and Industry 4.0: An Introduction to Understand Industry 4.0.* Social Research Foundation Contribution Technology.

Alacadağlı, E. (2019). Information Age, Digitalization And Turkish Health System. *Electronic Turkish Studies, 14*(2), 67–86.

Alçin, S. (2016). A New Theme For Production: Industry 4.0. *Journal Of Life Economics*, *3*(2), 19–30.

Arlbjørn, J. S., De Haas, H., & Munksgaard, K. B. (2011). Exploring Supply Chain Innovation. *Logistics Research*, *3*(1), 3–18. doi:10.100712159-010-0044-3

Arlbjørn, J. S., & Paulraj, A. (2013). Special Topic Forum On Innovation in Business Networks From A Supply Chain Perspective: Current Status And Opportunities For Future Research. *The Journal of Supply Chain Management*, *49*(4), 3–11. doi:10.1111/jscm.12034

Arnold, C., Kiel, D., & Voigt, K. I. (2016). How the Industrial Internet of Things Changes Business Models In Different Manufacturing Industries. *International Journal of Innovation Management*, *20*(08), 1–20. doi:10.1142/S1363919616400156

Aslam, F., Aimin, W., Li, M., & Ur Rehman, K. (2020). Innovation in The Era of Iot and Industry 5.0: Absolute Innovation Management Framework. *Information (Basel)*, *11*(2), 124. doi:10.3390/info11020124

Atan, S. (2020). *Comparison of the Cloud Computing and the Traditional Alternatives: Advantages, Risks and Advices for Migration*. Afyon Kocatepe University Journal of Social Sciences.

Bakırcı, A., & Kocabıyık Çaşkurlu, Ş. (2020). Digitalized World Dynamics and The New Perspective of Vocational Education in Turkey. 9. *International Vocational Schools Symposium Book*, 41-42.

Batıbay, B. (2022). Electrical And Electronic Engineers Industry 4.0 Determining Awareness Levels. *Rahva Journal of Technical and Social Studies*, 131.

Batty, M. (2018). Digital Twins. *Environment and Planning. B, Urban Analytics and City Science*, *45*(5), 817–820. doi:10.1177/2399808318796416

Canlıoğlu, G. (2008). *Transformation Society For Changing Position Of Information*. Marmara University Institute of Turkic Studies.

Carrillo, J. E., Druehl, C., & Hsuan, J. (2015). Introduction to Innovation Within And Across Borders: A Review And Future Directions. *Decision Sciences*, *46*(2), 225–265. doi:10.1111/deci.12131

Çengelci, B., & Çimen, H. (2005). Industrial Robots. *The Electronic Journal of Mathematics & Technology*, *2*(2), 69–78.

Çetin Gürkan, G., & Çiftci, G. (2020). Developing A Supportive Culture in Digital Transformation. In U. Hacioglu (Ed.), *Digital Business Strategies in Blockchain Ecosystems. Contributions to Management Science*. Springer. doi:10.1007/978-3-030-29739-8_5

Chang, S., Wang, Z., Wang, Y., Tang, J., & Jiang, X. (2019). Enabling Technologies and Platforms To Aid Digitalization Of Commercial Aviation Support, Maintenance And Health Management. *International Conference on Quality, Reliability, Risk, Maintenance, And Safety Engineering*, 926-932. 10.1109/QR2MSE46217.2019.9021222

Chen, H., Chiang, R. H., & Storey, V. C. (2012). Business Intelligence and Analytics: From Big Data To Big Impact. *Management Information Systems Quarterly*, *36*(4), 1165–1188. doi:10.2307/41703503

Demetriou, G. A. (2011). Mobile Robotics in Education And Research. *Mobile Robots-Current Trends*, *27*, 48.

Digital Transformation Office. (2022). Cbddo.Gov.Tr/En/

Dilibal, S., & Şahin, H. (2018). Cooperative Industrial Robots And Digital Industry. *International Journal of 3D Printing Technologies and Digital Industry, 2*(1), 86-96.

Duman, M. Ç. (2022). Society 5.0: Human-Focused Digital Transformation. *Journal of Social Policy Conferences, 82*, 309-336.

Ehret, M., & Wirtz, J. (2017). Unlocking Value from Machines: Business Models and The Industrial Internet of Things. *Journal of Marketing Management, 33*(1-2), 111–130. doi:10.1080/0267257X.2016.1248041

European Commision. (2017). *Digital Transformation Monitor Industry 4.0 In Aeronautics: Iot Applications*. EU Commission Report.

Feldmann, K., Franke, J., & Schüßler, F. (2010). Development of Micro Assembly Processes for Further Miniaturization in Electronics Production. *CIRP Annals, 59*(1), 1–4. doi:10.1016/j.cirp.2010.03.005

Fırat, O. Z., & Fırat, S. Ü. (2017). Trends and Robots on the Industry 4.0 Journey. *Istanbul University Journal of the School of Business, 46*(2), 211–223.

Flint, D. J., & Larsson, E. (2007). Supply Chain Innovation. Handbook of Global Supply Chain Management, 49(4), 475-487.

Globelink-Unimar. (2022). *Logistics In The Supply Chain 5.0. Period*. Https://Globelink-Unimar.Com/Tedarik-Zincirinde-Lojistik-5-0-Donemi

Gökten, P. O. (2018). Manufacturing In The Dark: Scope Of The Cost In The New Age. *Journal of the World of Accounting Science, 20*(4), 880–897.

Grobotek, T. (2019). Intelligent Steps For The Future. *Skyway Magazine,* 42-44.

Gülseren, A., & Sağbaş, A. (2019). Evaluation of Digital Transformation and Digital Maturity Level in Industry from Industry 4.0 Perspective. *European Journal of Engineering And Applied Sciences, 2*(2), 1–5.

Haklıdır, M. (2020). Third Wave Artificial Intelligence Technologies. *Tübitak Bilgem*, (9).

Hartmann, D., & Van Der Auweraer, H. (2021). Digital Twins. In *Progess in Industrial Mathematics: Success Stories* (pp. 3–17). Springer. doi:10.1007/978-3-030-61844-5_1

Herbert, L. (2017). *Digital Transformation Build Your Organizations Future For The Innovation Age.* Bloomsbury Publishing Plc.

Hermann, M., Pentek, T., & Otto, B. (2015). Design Principles for Industrie 4.0 Scenarios: A Literature Review. *Technische Universität Dortmund, Dortmund, 45*, 1–15.

Hofmann, E., & Rüsch, M. (2017). Industry 4.0 and the Current Status As Well As Future Prospects On Logistics. *Computers in Industry, 89*, 23–34. doi:10.1016/j.compind.2017.04.002

Information Technologies and Communications Authority. (2017). Society 5.0. *Journal of Sectoral Research and Strategy Development*, 6-13.

Javaid, M., Haleem, A., Singh, R. P., Haq, M. I., Raina, A., & Suman, R. (2020). Industry 5.0: Potential Applications in Covıd-19. *Journal of Industrial Integration and Management*, 508-510.

Kagermann, H. (2015). Change Through Digitization—Value Creation in The Age Of Industry 4.0. In Management of Permanent Change (23-45). Springer Gabler.

Kagermann, H., Helbig, J., & Wahlster, W. (2013). *Securing the future of German manufacturing industry-Recommendations for implementing the strategic initiative Industrie 4.0-Final report of the Industry 4.0 Working Group*. Acatech – National Academy of Science and Engineering.

Karacan, S., & Bayram, G. (2019). Enterprice Resources Planning(Erp) Systems And Accounting Information System. *Journal Of International Social Research*, *12*(65), 1118–1123. doi:10.17719/jisr.2019.3521

Karli, H., & Tanyaş, M. (2020a). Suggestions For Supply Chain Risk Management In The Case Of Pandemic. *Istanbul Commerce University Journal of Social Sciences*, *19*(37), 174–190.

Karlı, H., & Tanyaş, M. (2020b). Digital Transformation of Logistics Management: A Systematic Literature Mapping on Smart Logistics. *Optimum Journal of Economics and Management Sciences*, *7*(2), 613–632.

Keçek, G., & Yildirim, E. (2009). Enterprise Resource Planning And The Importance For Company. *Electronic Journal of Social Sciences*, *8*(29), 240–258.

Keidanren. (2018). *Society 5.0 - Cocreating The Future.* Https://Www.Keidanren.Or.Jp/En/Policy/2018/095_Proposal.Pdf

Kiel, D., Arnold, C., & Voigt, K. I. (2017). The Influence of The Industrial Internet of Things on Business Models of Established Manufacturing Companies–A Business Level Perspective. *Technovation*, *68*, 4–19. doi:10.1016/j.technovation.2017.09.003

Kırmaz, M., & Sayın, A. A. (n.d.). *The Place of Industry 5.0 in Logistics and Supply Chain.* Kutlu Publisher.

Klein, M. (2019). Comprehensive Digital Transformation Approach – World 4.0. In E. S. B. Meydanoğlu, M. Klein, & D. Kurt (Eds.), *Digital Transformation Trends*. Filiz Bookstore.

Klein, M. (2020). Digital Transformation In Businesses And Its Drivers. *Journal Of Business In The Digital Age*, *3*(1), 24–35. doi:10.46238/jobda.729499

Liao, Y., Deschamps, F., Loures, E. D. F. R., & Ramos, L. F. P. (2017). Past, Present and Future of Industry 4.0-A Systematic Literature Review and Research Agenda Proposal. *International Journal of Production Research*, *55*(12), 3609–3629. doi:10.1080/00207543.2017.1308576

Liu, D. Y., Chen, S. W., & Chou, T. C. (2011). Resource Fit In Digital Transformation: Lessons Learned From The Cbc Bank Global E-Banking Project. *Management Decision*, *49*(10), 1728–1742. doi:10.1108/00251741111183852

Moeuf, A., Pellerin, R., Lamouri, S., Tamayo-Giraldo, S., & Barbaray, R. (2018). The Industrial Management of Smes in The Era Of Industry 4.0. *International Journal of Production Research*, *56*(3), 1118–1136. doi:10.1080/00207543.2017.1372647

Mosterman, P. J., & Zander, J. (2016). Industry 4.0 as a cyber-physical system study. *Software & Systems Modeling, 15*(1), 17–29. doi:10.100710270-015-0493-x

Nambisan, S., Lyytinen, K., Majchrzak, A., & Song, M. (2017). Digital Innovation Management: Reinventing Innovation Management Research İn A Digital World. *Management Information Systems Quarterly, 41*(1), 223–238. doi:10.25300/MISQ/2017/41:1.03

Nofer, M., Gomber, P., Hinz, O., & Schiereck, D. (2017). Blockchain. *Business & Information Systems Engineering, 59*(3), 183–187. doi:10.100712599-017-0467-3

Okumuşoğlu, N. T. (2022). The Impact of Digitalization on the Quality Performance in Supply Chain Management: An Application on Employees in Manufacturing Sector. *BNEJSS, 8*(03), 17–28.

Oruçoğlu, O. (2022). The Impacts Of Industry 4.0 On Recruitment From Human Resources Management Functions. *Aegean Journal of Strategic Studies, 13*(1), 57–84.

Özdemir, A. İ., & Doğan, N. Ö. (2010). Supply Chain Integration And Information Technologies. *Erciyes University Journal of Social Sciences Institute, 1*(28), 19–41.

Özdoğan, O. (2019). *Industry 4.0 The Fourth Industrial Revolution and Keys to Industrial Transformation* (3rd ed.). Pusula.

Özkahveci, E., Civek, F., & Ulusoy, G. (2022). The Place Of Metaverse (Fictional Universe) In The Period Of Industry 5.0. *The Sciences, 8*(50), 398–409.

Özsoylu, A. F. (2017). Industry 4.0. *Journal of Çukurova University Faculty of Economics and Administrative Sciences, 21*(1), 41–64.

Öztemel, E. (2018). Evaluation of New Trends in Education and Education 4.0. *Journal of University Research, 1*(1), 25–30.

Radziwon, A., Bilberg, A., Bogers, M., & Madsen, E. S. (2014). The Smart Factory: Exploring Adaptive and Flexible Manufacturing Solutions. *Procedia Engineering, 69*, 1184–1190. doi:10.1016/j.proeng.2014.03.108

Resch, A., & Blecker, T. (2012). Smart Logistics–A Literature Review. *Pioneering Supply Chain Design, 10*, 91–102.

Roy, S., Sivakumar, K., & Wilkinson, I. F. (2004). Innovation Generation In Supply Chain Relationships: A Conceptual Model and Research Propositions. *Journal of the Academy of Marketing Science, 32*(1), 61–79. doi:10.1177/0092070303255470

Rüßmann, M., Lorenz, M., Gerbert, P., Waldner, M., Justus, J., Engel, P., & Harnisch, M. (2015). *Industry 4.0: The Future of Productivity and Growth İn Manufacturing Industries.* Boston Consulting Group.

Sadıç, Ş. (2021). Industry 5.0 and Sustainability. In G.I. Bolatan (Ed.), Industry 5.0 Digital Society. Ekin Publishing House.

Şahin, U. Ö. (2021). Society 5.0 and public services: An assessment on Turkey. *Journal of Awareness, 6*(4), 229–246.

Science, Technology and Innovation Board. (2015). *Report On The 5th Science And Technology Basic.* Government of Japan: Https://Www8.Cao.Go.Jp/Cstp/Kihonkeikaku/5basicplan_En.Pdf Btk

Şekkeli, Z. H., & Bakan, İ. (2018). By The Effect Of The Industry 4.0 On Logistics 4.0. *Journal of Life Economics*, *5*(2), 17–36.

Tukker, A. (2004). Eight Types of Product–Service System: Eight Ways To Sustainability? Experiences From Suspronet. *Business Strategy and the Environment*, *13*(4), 246–260. doi:10.1002/bse.414

Türkel, S., & Arıkan, Ö. U. (2020). Strategic Human Resources Management and the Intersecting Ecosystem of Industry 4.0. *Toros University FEASS Journal of Social Sciences*, *7*(12), 115–139.

Ustundag, A., & Tanyas, M. (2009). The Impacts of Radio Frequency Identification (Rfıd) Technology On Supply Chain Costs. *Transportation Research Part E, Logistics and Transportation Review*, *45*(1), 29–38. doi:10.1016/j.tre.2008.09.001

Wagner, S. M., & Sutter, R. (2012). A Qualitative Investigation of Innovation Between Third--Party Logistics Providers and Customers. *International Journal of Production Economics*, *140*(2), 944–958. doi:10.1016/j.ijpe.2012.07.018

Waller, M. A., & Fawcett, S. E. (2013). Data Science, Predictive Analytics, And Big Data: A Revolution That Will Transform Supply Chain Design and Management. *Journal of Business Logistics*, *34*(2), 77–84. doi:10.1111/jbl.12010

Xu, L. D., Xu, E. L., & Li, L. (2018). Industry 4.0: State of The Art and Future Trends. *International Journal of Production Research*, *56*(8), 2941–2962. doi:10.1080/00207543.2018.1444806

Yacan, İ. (2021). Industry 4.0 Technologies and Society 5.0 Concept. *International Journal of Academic Research and Ideas*, *13*(27), 31–39.

Yetkin, E. G., & Coşkun, K. (2021). Industry 5.0 (Society 5.0) ve Architecture. *European Journal of Science and Technology*, (27), 347–353.

Yıldırım, M., & Bayraktar, C. (2014). Automation & Barcode System In Businesses And Contributions To Accounting Processes. *Business And Management Studies An International Journal*, *2*(1), 38–48. doi:10.15295/bmij.v2i1.57

Yin, Y., Stecke, K. E., & Li, D. (2018). The Evolution of Production Systems From Industry 2.0 Through Industry 4.0. *International Journal of Production Research*, *56*(1-2), 848–861. doi:10.1080/00207543.2017.1403664

Yücebalkan, B. (2021). Overview of The Transition From Industry 4.0 To Industry 5.0. *Pearson Journal Of Social Sciences & Humanities*, *5*(9), 241–250.

Zaus, R., & Choi, H. N. (2014). Evolving The Network For Machine-To-Machine Communication. *Intel Technology Journal*, *18*(1), 194–202.

Zeybel, M., Dervişoğlu, H., Eğriboz, E., Özbilen, M. L., & Bahadırlar, Y. (2020). New Trends in Artificial Intelligence. *Tubitak Bilgem,* (9).

Chapter 12
The Effect of Big Data Marketing and Human Resources Management on the Performance of Companies

Sahar Mesfar
https://orcid.org/0000-0001-8869-6644
Faculty of Economic Sciences and Management of Sfax, Tunisia

ABSTRACT

The objective of this chapter is to study the effect of big data marketing and human resources management on the performance of companies and to find in return a relevant solutions. This study is based on the selection of 22 recent articles. This literature search designates the causal relationship between marketing theory and big data, while indicating the specificities of big data marketing. Then, this study indicates the opportunities and constraints found with the following of this type of integration. After that, it indicates the importance of the correlation between big data and human resources and also the necessity of performance. Finally, this research specifies the effects of big data marketing and human resources management on the performance of companies. The contribution of this study is justified by previous studies that point to this gap based on the consideration of marketing and management literature.

INTRODUCTION

with the emergence of digital transformation and the technological development experienced, the need to a coherent organization of the expansion of data on information systems will have an asset, it is in this sense that the concept of Big data gives a new approach when using digital data, this concept which is defined as a set of voluminous data, and which are characterized by high speed, with the existence of data which are heterogeneous and which emerge with the increasing digitization of interactions, transactions, and in addition with the involvement in communications and daily experiences (McAfee et al.,, 2012; Cited by De Luca et al.,, 2021), this development has reached a stage of necessary transformation

DOI: 10.4018/978-1-6684-6745-9.ch012

in companies, some authors (for example: Chernova & Starostin, 2020) show that decades before big data was first mentioned, companies were analyzing collected data to gain insights and uncover trends. Through the data analysis and integration ability of big data, it is known that it has a great impact on the development of enterprises, and especially in the higher requirements, human resource management (Wang,2021), and among one of the essential factors to be able to optimize and improve the performance of the company is to make improvements to the human resources with regard to the human resource management (Lubis et al.,, 2022).Human resource performance is a combination of abilities, knowledge, and the idea of an employee in order to take responsibility (Pasamar et al.,, 2019; Cited by Kuncoro et al.,, 2022), the key to failure or success of an organization is the performance of human resources (Sudiantha et al.,, 2017; Cited by Kuncoro et al.,, 2022.), the performance of human resources can be optimized by the cooperation between the leader and the employee in each team of the organization (Zaenudin and Prasetyaninghayu, 2018; Cited by Kuncoro et al.,, 2022). Notably the research on the positive indication of HR performance that has been done as stated before (Muda et al.,, 2017; Cited by Kuncoro et al.,, 2022), HR performance is a capability of a human resource to accomplish the task supported by the training, education and experience he has (Zaenudin & Prasetyaninghayu, 2018; Cited by Kuncoro et al.,, 2022) .It is in this sense that, the business world is in a new situation which insists on the execution of big data, since the popularity of the digital living space is based on the integration of big data marketing, and whose total quantity of world information is known by an explosive increase. Based on this trend, there is a broad rise of a new concepts and paradigms such as big data and cloud computing, which undoubtedly lead to a new cycle of Internet trends (Quan, 2021). The importance of this study is justified by the results which show that research on the applications of Big Data in marketing is still at an embryonic stage, which makes it necessary to develop efforts to companies more directly, for Big Data to thrive in the field of marketing (Amado et al.,, 2018). In addition, these authors indicate that the adoption of Big Data within the industry is taking place nowadays, since there is a gap in research to clearly identify the advantages and disadvantages for organizations of investing in Big Data (Amado et al.,, 2018). This is why the integration of marketing with big data transforms the missions and services offered by companies, so it is essential to insist on the constraints experienced during the orientation towards the Big Data marketing, with indicating in return, the opportunities raised thanks to this transformation. The objective of this work is to present a review of the literature toward Big Data Marketing and human resources management and their effects on the performance of companies, with indicating the opportunities and problems experienced when performing the big data marketing, also our study precise the important role of human resources management with Big Data and the necessity of the performance. And to achieve a better understanding of this proposed problematic, the principal research questions are presented as follows:

1) What is the effect of the integration of Big Data on human resources?
2) What is the effect of big data marketing and human resources management on the performance of companies?

And to arrive to a better answers to these questions, This review study was conducted on the basis of 22 recent articles, the selection of these articles insist on the role of Big data marketing and human resources management and their effects on the performance of companies, while specifying the contribution of this study to the marketing and management literature in referring to the marketing theory on the one hand, and the importance of this study for the practitioners of human resources specifically with the field of Big data and marketing on the other hand. For these reasons, our chapter includes a presentation about the methods, the theoretical and conceptual framework about the big data and big data marketing, then, this study show a clarification about the role of human resources and human resources management with the integration of big data and it is insist about the importance of the performance with including the effect of the integration of big data marketing and human resources management on the performance of companies and finally our chapter focus on the discussion part, the theoretical and managerial contributions, and the limitations of our study and the future research .

METHODS

This review study was conducted through the selection of 22 articles (see Appendix) that are related to our research questions whose year of publication varies between the year 2018 and the year 2022, the choice of this specific period of publication is justified by our motivation towards the selection of the most recent articles to know the trends related to big data marketing by linking with companies, by accessing the Google Scholar search engine. After the selection of articles related to our topic, we show our research from which we begin firstly with the development of our problematic through the review literature which consists in the study of the integration of human resources management with the big data and the effect of big data marketing and human resources management on the performance of companies, then in indicating the theoretical and managerial implications, after that, we end with the presentation of the limits and future research paths (see figure1).

THEORETICAL AND CONCEPTUAL FRAMEWORK:

Big Data in the context of Marketing

The issue of big data has captured the attention of the academia world as has its importance in practice. Big Data is about the massive volume of information of zettabytes, and it is captured in different sources, in different formats and according to time. The concept of data ownership has been explored with respect to the information presented in big data (Nuseir, 2018). With its wide use in the economic society, big data has left more and more influence on the business world. The large or small company is forced to transform itself to adapt to the new market environment. On the one hand, it has to innovate its operational sections like marketing, production, design and sourcing, etc. on the other hand, it must base its innovation on market demand by fully exploiting big data (Li, 2021).

According to Nuseir (2018) the Big data are used in hospitality, telecommunications, government and entertainment, among other sectors. Various tools are deployed to collect data for better benefits. The study by Nuseir (2018) examined the importance of big data in advancing the marketing activities of firms. The concept and understanding of big data has been shaped by the seeking to examine complex sets of information necessary to make decisions that benefit the operating activities of a firm. It is clear that some of the big firms (in all industries) have realized the importance of big data to reach their clients (Nuseir, 2018)

Big Data is a recent informational phenomenon that has emerged as one of the considerable innovations in information systems, it is currently a new mode, both in academia and in industry, and it is used

Figure 1. (source: author 's preparation)

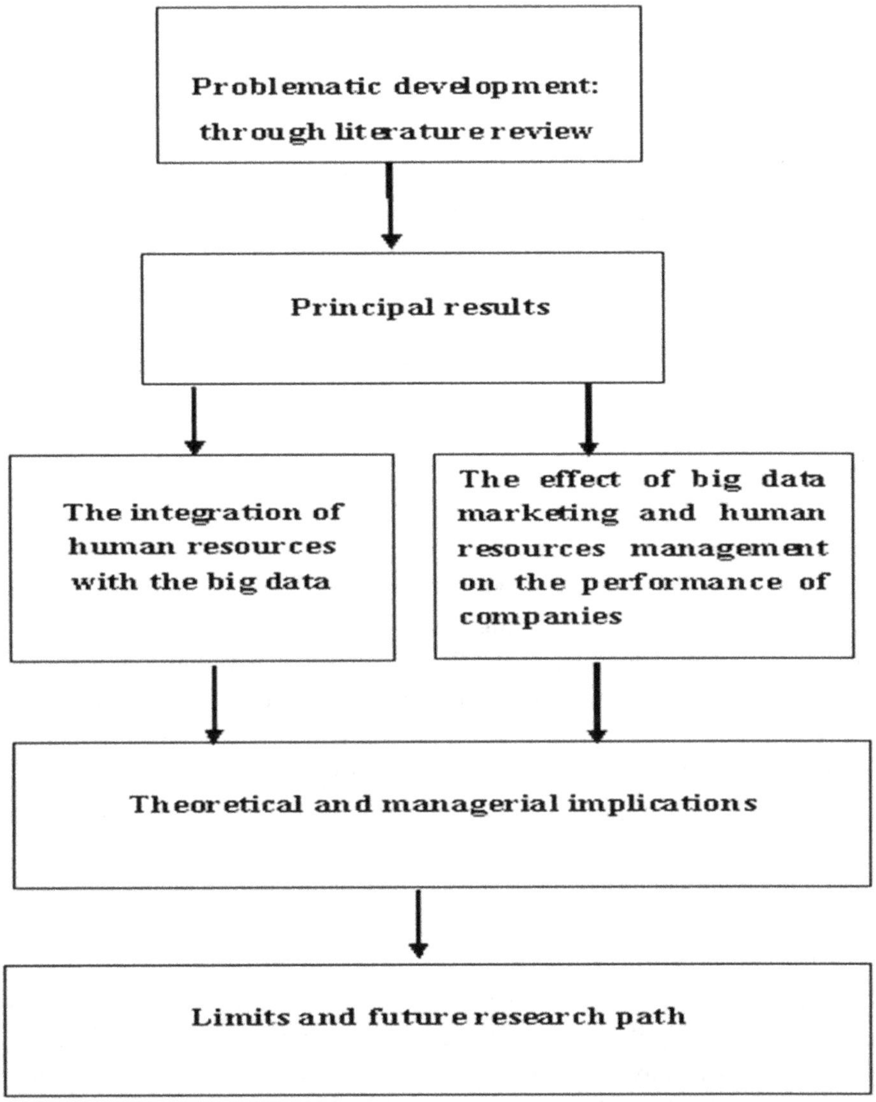

to describe a wide range of concepts, from extracting, storing and managing data, to processing and analyzing data using well-known schemas, for the purpose of extracting patterns in hidden relationships in order to make a better decisions and to gain a new insights when using analytical techniques and solutions. This technology which makes it possible to exploit the potential of big data is called: "Big Data Analytics", the important role of the analysis of big data is a major challenge which allows researchers, professional users, and analysts to make the better decisions will faster. Big Data has become an important element in marketing research and when executing marketing strategies also (Zineb et al.,, 2021). And also, big data creates a pool of knowledge that allows internal reorganization of activities so that goods, services and related information correspond to the perceived needs of customers. Obviously the reliance on marketing staff members to bring data to the "field" has been automated. Marketing personnel interpret data that has been sent by customers without their knowledge (Nuseir, 2018).

Chernova & Starostin (2020) indicate that we would probably generally agree that Big Data has become an important element in marketing strategies, for marketing planning and research and in all advertising and marketing processes of sale in the world, therefore, It is easy nowadays to understand why it is so important for consumers, it constitutes an easy way in the transmission of their preferences to the producers and sellers; that is why it represents an infinite source of data on each consumer, for producers and sellers, including tastes and many very sensitive information, and personal characteristics, since consumers, nowadays, do not don't even think about the data they provide online when registering or making purchases on the various online communities or social networks, in addition, internet shops are moving towards the collection and processing of data from customers, but very few of us think anything is wrong here. As a result, large retailers often know more about their customers than they know themselves.

Marketing theory and Big Data

Traditionally, marketing theories have emerged from the experience of academic and/or scholarly activity in marketing and related disciplines (for example: economics), which is why Big Data represents a complement to the source. Nevertheless, revealing research derived from big data requires knowledgeable industry experts and specialized computing capabilities, in addition to multidisciplinary research teams. This is why, big data is subject to biases that multidisciplinary specialists can considerably mitigate. Thus, marketers considering a contemporary ETT approach, which leverages Big Data-related data using analytical tools such as data mining, cognitive computing, artificial intelligence, and networking neurons and who need access to skills that go beyond traditional business graduate training (Lukosius & Hyman, 2019)

It is in this sense that over the past decade, practitioners who have collected and accessed big data have acted as gatekeepers protecting "the mine". Recently, academics have started to conceptualize the integration of Big Data with existing enterprise marketing systems (e.g. Bradlow et al.,, 2017; Cited by Lukosius & Hyman, 2019). Although complex, such integration can encourage the development of marketing theory, in addition, big data and marketing theory are mutually supportive, since marketing theory can suggest significant causal relationships and new trends, when application of big data, it is in this sense that the analysis of big data without theoretical foundation leads to regularity (that is to say: reifying spurious correlations and making type I errors). Conversely, big data can help refine and extend existing marketing theories by suggesting new, yet unexplored variables, for example: consumer behavior theories can be extended, such as finding non-sequential patterns in models AIDA to through geolocated data and consumer sentiment (Van Bommel et al.,, 2014; Cited by Lukosius & Hyman,2019). In addition, marketing theory may discourage endogeneity (i.e., treating non-random observations as random and committing Type II error) when identifying and evaluating models constructed with big data (Chung et al.,, 2017; Cited by Lukosius & Hyman,2019).

Big Data Marketing: Opportunities

"Big Data" has become an important part of the development of the times and has a direct impact on management companies in marketing. Since there are certain differences and peculiarities in the data, it is necessary to pay attention to the analysis, management and storage of the economy in the construction of the system (Jian & Zhenyi, 2020).

In the era of data-driven marketing, making good use of big data marketing technology and improving big data marketing effectiveness are the most important ways for improving a brand's goodwill. Specifically, companies are building the data analytics capabilities of marketers, who systematically use big data to understand, predict, shape and improve the customer experience, improving their brand perception, and shaping and differentiating services. what big data marketing brings to consumers, and by building brand awareness. The size of initial brand awareness does not prevent companies from using big data marketing to sell products. Under the big data, the products face the same tools of big data marketing, choosing the right business model and rationally using the advantage of big data marketing which is a way for companies to win (Ma & Hu, 2020).

And in the post-epidemic era, the development of big data marketing is still in the midst of continuous innovation of operation mode and improvement of management mode. Dynamic development and change are helping to improve the capabilities and quality requirements of big data marketing talent. Especially with the advent of the era of big data, data analysis plays an increasingly important role in the marketing process, and the teaching and talent training mode of the existing marketing course rarely integrates the big data marketing analysis (Quan,2021).

In addition Cao (2021) shows that with the development of big data, the traditional camps of great changes have taken place in the concepts, models and systems of marketing. According to the market analysis, STP and 4P are the basic theoretical systems of the basic marketing profession. This is why, in the context of the time, a refined reinterpretation is essential. Now big data is doing everything necessary like sales behavior and consumer behavior digitized, that's why companies put more emphasis on consumers a marketing concept, which is combined with visualization and accurate information data, to formulate accurate consumer marketing formulations and corresponding marketing strategy such as brand co-creation and digital consumer ecological value to improve enterprise marketing sales value. There is no doubt that the development of big data has brought the unprecedented development of enterprise marketing opportunities, but also the massive data processing technology, the effective use of data intelligence, data security, etc., and which pose a new problems for companies, that is why, the explanation of the opportunity of big data for marketing coexists with challenges (Cao, 2021).

The Challenges of Integrating Big Data in Marketing

With the advent of the era of Big Data, companies are faced with challenges such as development opportunities. It is because of the convenience of collecting and transmitting information, the commercial environment of enterprises tends to be more complex. Par examples: the information security and the cost of market are also issues to be paid attention to in the business development process. This is why, Big data technology characterized by both an advantages and disadvantages, and that is why, The era of big data is a rapid era of information sharing, it is in meaning that the Internet of Things, wearable devices, smart phones and other technical devices allow data to grow exponentially, which is why online activities and transactions are constantly increasing, this is why network security issues continue to emerge. Some unscrupulous people will do things against morality, and criminals will get it through the network like: viruses, web crawlers and system vulnerabilities for consumer data, using networks criminal or fraudulent, which entails great risks for consumer safety (Cao, 2021). This is why Chernova & Starostin (2020) indicate that Big Data opens a new era in marketing research. However, the pace at which it is taking place is far and too fast for the legislative and normative bases to adapt. Therefore, customers should be aware of how their data is collected and used and what it is used for. For those reasons, it is very important to create boundaries in marketing research that cannot be crossed without solid reasons.

BIG DATA AND HUMAN RESOURCES

According to Wang (2021) which is closely related to enterprise development. Therefore, in today's society, if you want to manage human resources better, cultivate more talents for enterprises, and improve the efficiency of enterprise employees, we must pay attention to innovative management methods. human resources, and realize that innovative methods of human resource management are the needs of the times. In this era of big data, human resources are taking up more and more space in new ideas and new technological environments. It can even be said that human resources are the strength and the pillar of the existence, development and participation of companies in social competition. The development of enterprises should attach importance to human resources, establish platforms, realize the value of employees, attach importance to human resources, improve employee efficiency, improve career promotion mechanism, respond to their personal ideals and aspirations and give them all their warmth and care, which will help to improve the cohesion of the core of the company. The company's human resource managers should understand the role, clarify the importance of innovation management concepts, ensure the integration effect of management and data human resource management, and then reform the management mode, improve the quality of management and convey more professional to achieve the development goals of each stage of the company. Incorporating big data thinking into the concept can analyze and plan management work from a holistic perspective, so as to optimize the management level and benefits of human resource departments in enterprises. Moreover, in practical work, HR managers can use information media to collect the data generated in the activities of employees (Wang, 2021).

Human Resources Management and Big Data

The study by Oge & Topaloglu (2018) is based on the development of an application that runs huge amounts of data integrated into a human resource management system to help in analysis and decision-making after having collected HR data that cannot be calculated exactly in a large data pool. The application accelerates the decision-making process of the human resource management system in a secure way with big data while improving performance by determining how well the personnel must improve for the future with the information obtained on the staff. The application offers solutions using big data for human resource management problems by doing analyzes for internal measures while doing the examination of external criteria at the same time. The departments of Human resource of organizations can also identify and remove blind spots by taking the necessary precautions, making the right decisions. Therefore, the organizations will be more successful in terms of management. In short, when the big data methods used in the study of (Oge & Topaloglu, 2018) are integrated with the right analytics methods, they can help companies for strategic decisions, risk management, and innovations to be made. As part of the study, two different disciplines were synthesized to improve the objectives and steps of the human resource management system using in the new application. Thus, Human resources managers will be able to list the right person(s) in a short time by processing a personnel information in using a big data solutions. Simply put, human resources is the set of processes between the employer and the employee. At the same time, it serves as a unit to provide the necessary human resources and to use these resources effectively. Human resource management aims to find and obtain the human resources that allow the organization to be competitive today and in the distant future and to achieve the objectives. For this reason, human resource management is the discipline that plans and implements the policies and strategies necessary to obtain and maintain human resources and to improve their representations (White 2012; Cited by Oge & Topaloglu, 2018) .

According to Rabhi et al.,, (2019) Big Data in human resource management refers to the large number of employees, customers and given transactions in organizations. By analyzing this Big data with specific tools, HR processes like Recruitment Process, Training Process, Employees Career Management Process, etc, that will become more relevant, which helps companies create greater benefits and make decisions.

For the recruitment process: sometimes the traditional recruitment process leads to bad hires Because most of the time the interviewer may not have correct information about the candidates which leads to false results. Combining great collected data and traditional recruiting process can help the recruiter to search for potential talents and everything he might want to know about them can be found on their profile (Couaillier and Project, 2016; Cited by Rabhi et al.,, 2019). The human resources manager can match the skills and the personal beliefs of the candidate and the needs of the company also . Therefore, the company can avoid investing in bad hires.

Regarding the Training Process: training talents can lead to increase the level of knowledge and skills of employees, it can also improve their performance at work. Through the traditional talent training organized by the company, professional trainers can be hired to provide training which requires a lot of material, human and financial resources. Usually, this training takes the traditional form of classroom instruction which cannot meet all employee needs. Using the Big Data context, any employee can easily search and access the information they need to know on the Internet anytime and anywhere (Zang and Ye, 2015; Cited by Rabhi et al.,, 2019). With respect to the employee career management process: by analyzing all information collected about employees, such as:

The interest in the position, professional experience, performance…, the HRD could find new ways to motivate employees and make them more committed. Companies can combine traditional career management with big data career management to make planning new talent retention programs more efficient and avoid employee turnover (Rabhi et al.,, 2019).

According to Nocker & Sena (2019) who have explored in their study the relationship between human resource management and big data. Their premise is that big data can provide for HR practitioners a number of opportunities. The HR teams produce a volumes of data as part of their routine activities; like any other organization, these data can be utilized for the development of standard HR metrics, but in actuality, they can be leveraged in sundry ways to provide information on how to make value through human resource management. The paper of this authors, its use in a number of organizations and has therefore provided a broad overview of talent analytics. One of their key insights is that, if used appropriately, talent analytics can help to align HR strategies to a value creation for an organization's senior management team. The essential contribution of talent analysis to the creation of value lies in the fact that it allows one to exploit data at the individual level and help to design measures that can assist employees in a personalized way.

THE IMPORTANCE OF THE PERFORMANCE

The performance is a very necessary element for companies, where they need a high performing employees to increase the productivity and to achieve the company's goals (Widyastuti and Hidayat, 2018; Cited by Rai et al.,, 2021). The three indicators (Widyastuti and Hidayat, 2018; Cited by Rai et al.,, 2021) are a person's ability to perform their duties, task performance, and the contextual performance that is behavior outside the work context for the purpose of improving the performance in the work environment, and regarding to the counterproductive behavior, it is a negative behavior of a worker in the exercise of his roles (Montowidlo, 2003; Cited by Rai et al.,, 2021).

Practitioners and researchers have been proposed different ways to define performance and to operationalize this concept while determining some characteristics or factors commonly used in measuring or describing organizational performance (Herciu and Şerban, 2018; De Waal, 2018; Apospori et al.,, 2008; Cited by Moustaghfir et al.,, 2020).

For example, Daft (2000); Cited by Moustaghfir et al.,, (2020) made clear how the performance of an organization is determined by its ability to achieve both operational and strategic objectives through the effective and efficient use of its resources.

Similarly, Barney (1991); Cited by Moustaghfir et al.,, (2020), a pioneer of resource-based theory, showed the basis on which most of practitioners and scholars came up with measures like profitability and they built their description of organizational performance (Gavrea et al.,, 2011; Cited by Moustaghfir et al.,, 2020).

THE EFFECT OF BIG DATA MARKETING ON THE PERFORMANCE OF COMPANIES:

Due to the wide use of information technology and the internet, big data is vital for marketing today. Big data marketing has left a lot of influence on business operation. To some extent, in the fierce competitive market, big data marketing determines whether the business operation succeeds or fails (Li, 2021).

Big data marketing is the product of science and technology. As an important part of business operation, it leaves far more effects on other parts of business operation than ever before. The company must coordinate them well so that they can function smoothly as an organic system as a whole. Various resources such as people, materials and finance etc. form this system. However, the people play a decisive role in it. Therefore, to successfully deploy the operational activities of the company, the company must develop the necessary people who can keep up with the evolution of Big Data technology (Li,2021).

Chernova & Starostin, (2020) show that retrieving big data takes time, while market research can be limited to a certain amount of time to get the information you need to make a business decision, Big data is characterized by providing several exciting opportunities for the business, and also presents challenges for the marketing of an industry (Trom and Cronje.2020; Cited by Miklosik & Evans, 2020). The volume of data is increasing rapidly with many types of data that are structured, untrusted and semi-structured and with data sources that are available (Cohn, 2015; Cited by Miklosik & Evans, 2020). This high and fast volume of data does not correspond to traditional database structures. It will also create challenges around privacy, management, security, and ethical issues in terms of collecting and tracking private data from customers, which must be addressed using information governance to obtain the real value of big data (Mathes, 2016, cited by Miklosik & Evans, 2020). This is why, Marketing organizations need to develop data governance structures to improve data quality and security, accuracy, meaning, value, etc. therefore, it is paramount to minimize such challenges and risks as the management of organizational structure information (Cohn, 2015; Cited by Miklosik & Evans, 2020). Data is seen as an asset that is important and if the organization fails to implement and maintain an effective governance structure, it can face huge losses in its data value (Trom and Cronje, 2020; Cited by Miklosik & Evans, 2020), that is why having a huge volume of data does not bring knowledge or value to the organization (Mathes, 2016 ; Cited by Miklosik & Evans, 2020).

According to Jian & Zhenyi (2020) an enterprise's marketing development cannot be separated from advertising, after a long period of development, a relatively stable advertising marketing system has gradually formed in the industry. But now there is the impact of the era of big data, that's why, many marketing agencies and consulting companies have started to create their own data and information systems, then, at the base of its own information that helps companies carry out advertising marketing activities.

In the traditional advertising marketing system, affiliated companies build advertising programs based on market information and then target the audience to achieve marketing goals. That's why, with big data marketing, companies can instantly get consumer feedback, track changes in their behaviors, and communicate the information to the product development team. Similarly, companies can gain insights into key product features and pricing policies of their competitors, which helps to optimize their pricing decisions (Xu et al.,, 2016; Cited by Wibowo et al.,, 2021). Some authors like: Chernova & Starostin (2020) indicate that fundamentally, modern big data analysis systems enable fast and efficient analysis methods. Meanwhile, businesses can work cheaply with big data analytics software. In today's modern business world and technological age, a company can easily capture all the customer data it needs. Therefore, a single big data analysis strategy is fundamentally needed to maximize the available data. And with a proper mechanism for analyzing customer data, a business can derive behavioral and critical insights that it needs to respond to in order to maintain customer base. Companies today lack big data mining specialists. Some suggest entrusting big data internally to a CAO directly attached to the management and capable of collecting and analyzing the data both from a technical point of view which is in collaboration with the IT directors and in marketing which is in collaboration with the CAO to understand marketing directors. Conversely, if the organization does not directly call on big data specialists, the appropriate institutions can position themselves as privileged specialists in the field and offer their expertise to both IT managers than marketing managers.

THE EFFECT OF HUMAN RESOURCES MANAGEMENT ON THE PERFORMANCE OF COMPANIES

The research of Moustaghfir et al.,, (2020) confirms the strategic role of HRM practices in promoting the entrepreneurial orientation and abilities of the company, while enriching, nourishing, and grouping the skills, knowledge, and distinctive skills of employees in the context of a company's innovation strategy. HRM practices, through strategic alignment with the company's business strategy, contribute to shaping behaviors, cultural determinants, and organizational attitudes which are, in turn, conducive to a better capacity for innovation, to decision-making initiative and risk appetite.

Huaming & Hang (2016); Cited by Roziq et al.,, (2021) conclude that enterprises performance is positively correlated with investment in human capital. The study shows the practical importance of research on companies' investment in human capital. And at the same time, the study shows that increasing investment in human capital is beneficial for increasing the level of human capital of the whole society.

And there are major investments in personnel in successful companies, in order to improve and increase the insight, experiences and abilities to compete in today's changing environment (Wang et al.,, 2011; Cited by Roziq et al.,, 2021). Experiments have shown that increasing staff capabilities and capabilities directly affect a company's financial results (Doong et al.,, 2011; Cited by Roziq et al.,, 2021). Boheme (2011); Cited by Roziq et al.,, (2021) studied the effects of human resource management skills on performance. One thousand (1000) employees were used as a simple sampling,in this case, the result indicated that there is a strong positive relationship between selection, performance, and employment.

DISCUSSION

Our review study add a multiples results: The Big Data is important in advancing the marketing activities of companies (Nuseir, 2018), in the marketing research and when executing marketing strategies (Zineb et al., 2021). In this sense, marketing theories have emerged from the experience of academic and/or scholarly activity in marketing and related disciplines, for example: economics, which is why Big Data represents a complement to the source (Lukosius & Hyman, 2019). In the post-epidemic era, the development of big data marketing is still in the midst of continuous innovation of operation mode and improvement of management mode. Dynamic development and change are helping to improve the capabilities and quality requirements of big data marketing talent (Quan,2021). With the advent of the era of Big Data, companies are faced with challenges such as development opportunities. It is because of the convenience of collecting and transmitting information, the commercial environment of enterprises tends to be more complex (Cao, 2021). In this era of big data, the human resources are taking up more and more space in new ideas and new technological environments. It can even be said that human resources are the strength and the pillar of the existence, development and participation of companies in social competition (Wang, 2021). Big Data in human resource management refers to the large number of employees, customers and given transactions in organizations. By analyzing this Big data with specific tools, HR processes (Recruitment Process, Training Process, Employees Career Management Process, etc.) become more relevant, which helps companies make decisions and create greater benefits (Rabhi et al.,, 2019). In addition, we conclude that performance is an important indicator for the development of corporate wealth. Big data marketing is the product of science and technology. As an important part of business operation, it leaves far more effects on other parts of business operation than ever before. The company must coordinate them well so that they can function smoothly as an organic system as a whole. Various resources such as people, materials and finance etc. form this system. However, the people play a decisive role in it. Therefore, to successfully deploy the operational activities of the company, the company must develop the necessary people who can keep up with the evolution of Big Data technology (Li,2021). In addition, our research indicates a strong correlation between investment in human resources and companies performance, which makes it necessary to value these sources.

Theoretical and Managerial Contributions

Our study contributes to the marketing and management literature by specifying the causal relationship between the marketing theory and the big data, the integration of human resources with the big data and in indicating, the principal role of big data marketing and its effect on companies development in return, it is for this reason, it is essential to find a relevant solutions in the face of these constraints of the adoption of big data marketing within companies, this is why the need to guide the employers and customers towards the familiarization with the digital component, and that it is will become one of the missions of marketing managers, and this state join the study of Chernova & Starostin (2020) also, these authors show that in the recent years, the Big Data has found its place in marketing strategies and in a large companies which they help to target and get many more customers compared to the using of traditional methods, hence the popularity of online content and access to social networks makes this task more difficult. It is in this sense that, it is clear that marketers want to know how they can monetize Big Data. In addition, it is essential that companies focus on trying to control personal data in order to guarantee the security of data related to these customers to gain their trust in the company and to improve its reputation. This is why the management of information and their governance are increasingly because controlling large amounts of data requires very efficient practices (Miklosik, & Evans, 2020), hence the association between the big data and marketing require a new strategy to improve the internal and external resources of each company so that it can adapt with this innovation. For these reasons, company directors must give great importance to human resources and try to provide the internal sources necessary for the adoption with the new technological trends in the time of the spread of big data. According to Wang (2021) as business managers, they must know how to use advanced science and technology tools to improve business management. Human resources are a top priority in business development.

In addition, we consider that it is interesting to give an importance toward the performance as it is an essential factor for better usage and management of human resources, which promotes the relevance of performance within the company and also an adoption with a new technological trends. So, integrating human resources management is an important element for a good quality returns.

Limitations and Future Research

Despite the contribution of this study on the theoretical and managerial context, our study is based on an narrative literature study which was conducted only on a limited number of articles and for a limited publication period, referring to a single database such as "Google Scholar", future research can integrate a quantitative research in order to develop a recent research model that is based on marketing theory and consist variables such Big Data and Human resources on the one hand, and to test the effect of Big data marketing and human resources management on the performance of companies and on consumer behavior, on the other hand, so it is important to test empirically the proposed variables of the model with the linear regression test, to explore the significant value of the variables . Future research can integrate a qualitative study to explore the challenges raised when companies adopt this innovation, and to know the attitude and the intention of employees towards the integration of big data marketing.

REFERENCES

Amado, A., Cortez, P., Rita, P., & Moro, S. (2018). Research trends on Big Data in Marketing: A text mining and topic modeling based literature analysis. *European Research on Management and Business Economics*, *24*(1), 1–7. doi:10.1016/j.iedeen.2017.06.002

Cao, S. (2021, March). Opportunities and Challenges of Marketing in the Context of Big Data. In *2021 Workshop on Algorithm and Big Data* (pp. 79-82). 10.1145/3456389.3456390

Chernova, V., & Starostin, V. (2020, January). Leading trends in marketing research: A case of big data. In *5th International Conference on Social, Economic, and Academic Leadership (ICSEALV 2019)* (pp. 210-215). Atlantis Press.

De Luca, L. M., Herhausen, D., Troilo, G., & Rossi, A. (2021). How and when do big data investments pay off? The role of marketing affordances and service innovation. *Journal of the Academy of Marketing Science*, *49*(4), 790–810. doi:10.100711747-020-00739-x

Jian, Z., & Zhenyi, Z. (2020, May). Deconstruction and Reconstruction of Marketing System under the Background of Big Data. *Journal of Physics: Conference Series*, *1550*(3), 032097. doi:10.1088/1742-6596/1550/3/032097

Kuncoro, W., Adi, F. N., & Santoso, B. (2022). The Model of Human Resources Performance Development on the Leader Organization of Regional Devices at Salatiga Government. *International Business Research*, *15*(7), 1–8. doi:10.5539/ibr.v15n7p8

Li, Z. (2021, February). Countermeasures and Effects of the Big Data Marketing on the Business Operational Management. In *6th International Conference on Economics, Management, Law and Education (EMLE 2020)* (pp. 369-372). Atlantis Press. 10.2991/aebmr.k.210210.060

Lubis, F. R. A., Syaifuddin, & Lubis, Y. (2022). Human Resources Performance Improvement Through Training During the Covid-19 Pandemic. *The International Journal of Science in Society*, *4*(1), 196–204. doi:10.54783/ijsoc.v4i1.429

Lukosius, V., & Hyman, M. R. (2019). Marketing theory and big data. *Journal of Developing Areas*, *53*(4). Advance online publication. doi:10.1353/jda.2018.0082

Ma, D., & Hu, J. (2020). Research on collaborative management strategies of closed-loop supply chain under the influence of big-data marketing and reference price effect. *Sustainability*, *12*(4), 1685. doi:10.3390u12041685

Miklosik, A., & Evans, N. (2020). Impact of big data and machine learning on digital transformation in marketing: A literature review. *IEEE Access: Practical Innovations, Open Solutions*, *8*, 101284–101292. doi:10.1109/ACCESS.2020.2998754

Moustaghfir, K., El Fatihi, S., & Benouarrek, M. (2020). Human resource management practices, entrepreneurial orientation and firm performance: What is the link? *Measuring Business Excellence*, *24*(2), 267–283. doi:10.1108/MBE-12-2019-0119

Nocker, M., & Sena, V. (2019). Big data and human resources management: The rise of talent analytics. *Social Sciences*, *8*(10), 273. doi:10.3390ocsci8100273

Nuseir, M. T. (2018). How big data is used in expanding marketing activities. *International Journal of Economics and Business Research*, *16*(4), 466–475. doi:10.1504/IJEBR.2018.095342

Oge, G., & Topaloglu, M. (2018). Using the Big Data in the human resources management systems. *Global Journal of Information Technology: Emerging Technologies*, *8*(3), 129–133. doi:10.18844/gjit.v8i3.4053

Quan, T. A. O. (2021). Research on Specialty Construction and Teaching Mode Reform of Big Data Marketing in the Post-Epidemic Era, 2021. *International Conference on Education, Humanities, Management and Information Technology (EHMIT 2021).*

Rabhi, L., Falih, N., Afraites, A., & Bouikhalene, B. (2019). Big data approach and its applications in various fields. *Procedia Computer Science*, *155*, 599–605. doi:10.1016/j.procs.2019.08.084

Rai, N. G. M., Silmina, N., Fitrananda, H., Hanoum, S., Sinansari, P., & Noor, B. A. (2021, December). The Effect of work Conflict and Job Stress on The Human Resources Performance (Case Study: Maintenance & Engineer Division at PT. Paiton Operation & Maintenance Indonesia). In *3rd International Conference on Business and Management of Technology (ICONBMT 2021)* (pp. 305-309). Atlantis Press.

Roziq, M., Reawaroe, H. P., & Rosyidi, A. I. (2021). Investment Perspectives in Human Resources Management and Its Contribution on Organizational Performance and Competitive Advantages. *Journal of Management and Leadership*, *4*(1), 1–13. doi:10.47970/jml.v4i1.207

Wang, F. (2021, April). Research on enterprise human resource management innovation in big data era. [). IOP Publishing.]. *Journal of Physics: Conference Series*, *1881*(4), 042038. doi:10.1088/1742-6596/1881/4/042038

Wibowo, S., Suryana, Y., & Kaltum, U. (2021). Value Creation with Big Data in Marketing: An Empirical Evidence on SMEs. *Asian Journal of Business and Accounting*, *14*(2), 173–196.

Zineb, E. F., Najat, R., & Jaafar, A. (2021). An Intelligent Approach for Data Analysis and Decision Making in Big Data: A Case Study on E-commerce Industry. *International Journal of Advanced Computer Science and Applications*, *12*(7). doi:10.14569/IJACSA.2021.0120783

APPENDIX

Table 1a. selected articles (N=22)

Author	Title	Year	Source of publication
Amado et al.,	Research trends on Big Data in Marketing: A text mining and topic modeling based literature analysis	2018	European Research on Management and Business Economics
Cao	Opportunities and Challenges of Marketing in the Context of Big Data	2021	In 2021 Workshop on Algorithm and Big Data
Chernova & Starostin,	Leading trends in marketing research: A case of big data	2020	5th International Conference on Social, Economic, and Academic Leadership (ICSEALV 2019) (pp. 210-215). Atlantis Press
De Luca et al.,	How and when do big data investments pay off? The role of marketing affordances and service innovation	2021	Journal of the Academy of Marketing Science
Jian & Zhenyi	Deconstruction and Reconstruction of Marketing System under the Background of Big Data.	2020	Journal of Physics

Table 1b. Continuous

Authors	Title	Year	Source of publication
Lukosius & Hyman	Marketing theory and big data	2019	Journal of Developing Areas
Ma & Hu	Research on collaborative management strategies of closed-loop supply chain under the influence of big-data marketing and reference price effect.	2020	Sustainability
Zineb et al.,	An Intelligent Approach for Data Analysis and Decision Making in Big Data: A Case Study on E-commerce Industry	2021	International Journal of Advanced Computer Science and Applications
Li	Countermeasures and Effects of the Big Data Marketing on the Business Operational Management	2021	6th International Conference on Economics, Management, Law and Education (EMLE 2020) (pp. 369-372). Atlantis Press.
Nuseir	How big data is used in expanding marketing activities	2018	International Journal of Economics and Business Research

Table 1c. Continuous

Authors	Title	Year	Source of publication
Miklosik & Evans	Impact of big data and machine learning on digital transformation in marketing: A literature review	2020	Ieee Access
Quan	Research on Specialty Construction and Teaching Mode Reform of Big Data Marketing in the Post-Epidemic Era	2021	International Conference on Education, Humanities, Management and Information Technology (EHMIT 2021).
Wibowo et al.,	Value Creation with Big Data in Marketing: An Empirical Evidence on SMEs.	2021	Asian Journal of Business and Accounting
Oge, G., & Topaloglu, M	Using the Big Data in the human resources management systems	2018	Global Journal of Information Technology: Emerging Technologies
Rabhi et al.,	Big data approach and its applications in various fields	2019	Procedia Computer Science
Nocker & Sena	Big data and human resources management: The rise of talent analytics. Social Sciences	2019	Social Sciences
Wang	Research on enterprise human resource management innovation in big data era	2021	Journal of Physics: Conference Series (Vol. 1881, No. 4, p. 042038). IOP Publishing.
Lubis et al.,	Human Resources Performance Improvement Through Training During the Covid-19 Pandemic	2022	International Journal of Science and Society, 4(1), 196-204.
Rai et al.,	The Effect of work Conflict and Job Stress on The Human Resources Performance (Case Study: Maintenance & Engineer Division at PT. Paiton Operation & Maintenance Indonesia)	2021	In 3rd International Conference on Business and Management of Technology (ICONBMT 2021) (pp. 305-309). Atlantis Press.
Moustaghfir et al.,	Human resource management practices, entrepreneurial orientation and firm performance: what is the link?	2020	Measuring Business Excellence.
Kuncoro et al.,	The Model of Human Resources Performance Development on the Leader Organization of Regional Devices at Salatiga Government	2022	International Business Research, 15(7), 1-8.
Roziq et al.,	Investment Perspectives in Human Resources Management and Its Contribution on Organizational Performance and Competitive Advantages	2021	Journal of Management and Leadership, 4(1), 1-13.

Chapter 13
How E-Working Is Effective in Education:
Observable Determinants and Challenges

Mudita Sinha
CHRIST University (Deemed), Bangalore, India

Radha Yadav
https://orcid.org/0000-0002-5772-0266
CHRIST University (Deemed), Bangalore, India

Minakshi Kishore
London School of Management, UK

ABSTRACT

The study focuses on the critical observable determinants reflecting the benefits of e-working for academicians. It highlights the four core constructs—work-life balance, job effectiveness or performance, flexibility, employee relationship—and trust with the organization, which is of prime importance for a fruitful remote working in the current scenario. Empirical testing of the proposed research model was done by collecting data through online questionnaires from 230 academicians involved in online teaching. The study showed that in an e-working scenario, there is indeed a healthier work-life balance, and increased e-working results in improved efficiency or work productivity. The e-working model is quite new for the education sector, and the current study will help colleges and universities to understand and support the well-being of academicians working remotely and will also help the stakeholders of the education sector to frame the strategies keeping in mind the requirement of academicians.

INTRODUCTION

E-working or remote working is a situation when a worker works beyond traditional protocols at anyplace which fits his requirement either from home, cyber spaces, or co-working places with the manager's

DOI: 10.4018/978-1-6684-6745-9.ch013

approval (Remote Year, 2020; Anscombe, 2020; Hilberath et al., 2020). Mutual trust between employee and the manger is particularly important in the case of e -working, as there are few expectations associated with each job profile that needs to be fulfilled when working remotely as well (Jarvenpaa & Staples, 2001). When working remotely or distantly, the representatives can encounter work environment separation that can withdraw them from their work and upset their performance and success (Collins et al., 2016; Marshall et al., 2007). Remote working can also be known as Telework, Telecommuting, Agnostic location, ROWE (Results only work environment, Home shored and Agile working (Grant et al., 2013; Howington, 2015). It has been reported that there are improved business results, retention of talents and better engaged employee through e working but the only difficulty is lack of supervision which is the major concern in e-working conditions (Nassazi, 2013) . Remote working has resulted in flexibility and productivity which has helped in reducing employers' expenditure and has increased employees' savings, enhanced employee job satisfaction etc. (Digneo, 2020). The period between 2005 and 2017 has seen 159 percent rise in remote working among US employees which intensified the job satisfaction among them (Wu, 2020). During Pandemic period currently it has been observed that 64 percent of US employees were working from home (Hirschhorn, 2020)(SHRM's COVID-19 Market Index) and 62 percent of American employees(Gallup, 2013) (Gallup 's research) and 88 percent of Indian employees prefer to work from home with flexibility (Business World, 2020). Compared to countries like Australia, New Zealand, South Korea, Malaysia and Thailand (Business World, 2020), 69 percent of Indian employees believe that telework/remote working has resulted in higher productivity which is higher in the APAC countries (Business World, 2020). Constructs like ambiguity of the role, working environment inside the organisation, job security and the management style considerably influences the psychological well-being and balancing work life of the employees (Chambel et al., 2017; Grant et al., 2013; Medhi, 2020; Sheppard, 2016; Yadav et al., 2021).

Pandemic on one side needs seclusion and social distancing but on the other side individuals must restart the system that was halted due to the pandemic. The immediate requirement of becoming digital due to the current pandemic COVID -19 which has completely changed the working pattern of almost all the sectors and has invariably increased the workload and related stress of the employees. Even the education sector is affected with this paradigm shift. The education sector is, expected to overcome challenges in meeting twenty first century global demands and expectations. Education sector is key to longterm maintenance of the nation's productivity and sustainability, the country's education sector has been going through continuous transition over the years. Working culture has been affected greatly in the higher education sector during pandemic. Teachers who were already struggling between teaching, administrative responsibilities and research for a better blended work life (Houston et al., 2006; Rapanta et al., 2020; Veletsianos & Houlden, 2020; Yadav et al., 2019; Yadav et al., 2022) are being burdened to prepare and take online classes. All academicians irrespective of the background and age have to formulate and execute their lectures notes or courses from home, handling all the pedagogic and technological issues they face without proper training and support (Hodges et al., 2020; Rapanta et al., 2020).

Post analysis of such world life situations, Governments are implementing necessary steps required for making rooms for students to continue learning through digital medium and adaptation required for this new teaching mode. Teaching faculties of all nations are trying to manage the communication with students though different virtual classroom platforms. Handling about 1.5 billion apprentices, who are affected because of the closure of educational institutions via remote teaching (UNESCO, 2020). Majority of the South Asian universities are not very prepared for remote or online teaching and the switch will take some time (Khan et al., 2020). This sudden change in the education industry is giving rise to technological stress to academicians with grave consequences to higher education institutions (Ahmed et al., 2020). To counter COVID-19 governments are implementing progressive surveillance technology that are triggering technostress among people (Bartoszko, 2020). It must be recognised that COVID-19 has altered the balance of personal and work life considerable and it is need of the hour that everyone indulging in remote working has *"to let go the mental model of thinking of work time and home-time being distinct and separate blocks"*(Wheeler & Gunasekara, 2020). Previous research suggests that the amount of time consumed in online teaching is two to three times of the actual time spent in face -to face teaching (Palloff & Pratt, 2007). This condition makes it difficult for the teaching staff to work from home where extra effort is needed for preparing lectures to tailor for the online requirement. The advanced technology however makes it easier for timely delivery of the teaching activities to the students without any compromise to the quality of lecture and student's learning experience (Li et al., 2014). On the other hand, academicians may be benefited in spending more time improving their research activities and performing other administrative duties from their home being safe from the virus. This study therefore focuses on the critical observable determinants reflecting the benefits of e-working (remote working) for academicians.

2.THEORETICAL BACKGROUND AND ASSOCIATE STUDIES:

2.1 E working and Bended work-life

Work life balance is invariably a precarious element to accomplish, which can be more challenging due to remote working (Grant et al., 2013). When home turns into a workplace, it becomes difficult to draw a line between the two. WLB is the mechanism in which staff aspire to combine their paying employment with compassionate obligation to build a balance between different role expectations (Bakker, 2017; Crompton & Lyonette, 2006; D. F. Parker & DeCotiis, 1983; Yuile et al., 2012). There are employees who can balance their work, and personal life by allocating their energy and time to the requirements they face, resulting in an enhanced well-being (D. F. Parker & DeCotiis, 1983; Whittington et al., 2011). However there are factors which affect work life balance such as Job requirements, Group and Organizational norms (Crompton & Lyonette, 2006; Voydanoff, 2005) employees' behaviors, attitudes, well-being, organizational effectiveness (Eby et al., 2005) absenteeism, dissatisfaction, and low productivity (Bakker, 2017; Edwards & Rothbard, 2000; Kort, 2017; D. F. Parker & DeCotiis, 1983; Rice et al., 1992; Whittington et al., 2011).

Work life balance theory which was set by Clark (2000), identifies an integration between work and family. As per spillover theory by Jacob (*Knowledge Spillover*, 2020) imbalanced work life affects both negatively and positively the work life balance of employees as they carry their work to private lives and vice versa (Bakker, 2017; Edwards & Rothbard, 2000; Kinnunen et al., 2014; Lambert, 1990; Michel et al., 2011; Molino et al., 2013; D. F. Parker & DeCotiis, 1983). This identifies the level of flexibility needed as a key constraint which positively influences work life balance (Bresman, 2015; Cowan & Hoffman, 2007; Hill et al., 2001; Mas-Machuca et al., 2016).

There has been a constant increase in shifting away from workplaces slowly from offices, ranging from 0.7 percent in 1980 to 3 percent in 2017 which has further increased due to the current pandemic (Schrotenboer, 2020). According to the Organisation for Economic Co-operation and Development (OECD better life index), Netherlands has been reported with the best WLB followed by Denmark, and Spain

(OECD, 2019), whereas India has an exceptionally low WLB when compared with other nations as per study conducted by Monster.com. 60 percent of the professionals in metro cities have terrible Work life balance, 70 percent of them prefer work from home due to long travel time (Basu, 2019). The agility has been adopted by the organization long back, which has changed the perception of the workplace from four boundaries to end less limits, resulting in accepting changes and flexibility according to industry requirements (Gillies, 2011). The home working concept was used earlier by employers for cost reduction like electricity bills or renting spaces for the organization and to hire people who are differently challenged, single parents etc. so that location cannot be a barrier (Baruch, 2000).

According to a survey by USA Today by (Schrotenboer, 2020), due to pandemic, employees have been asked to opt for long WFH option, which was taken positively by 54 percent of the professionals aged between 18-74, due to convenience like commuting, distraction from the peers and avoiding long meetings. However there are out-turn also of the employees working remotely for long term like limited communication with colleagues, problems in scheduling and following routine work life etc. (Schrotenboer, 2020).

According to (Bäck-Wiklund et al., 2011; IONOS, 2019) the concept of work life balance is associated with highly productive and happy employees. WFH has made management of work and home easy, flexible work patterns has also benefited individuals in ways like focusing on their hobbies / interests (Currie & Eveline, 2011). A healthy environment can be achieved by reducing ailments, balancing working hours, providing tangible and intangible rewards friendly facilities (Currie & Eveline, 2011; Kelliher et al., 2019).

WFH has provided employees more time with family and personal interest outside work. Still there are burnout symptoms experienced by 69 percent of the employees due to WFH (Wong, 2020). Human Resource has taken initiatives to narrow this gap by employee engagement programs like fun activity via video conferencing, Cash rewards on achieving targets, Webinars on Health and Fitness development. Furthermore, Charalampous et al.,(2019) and Grant et al., (2019) researched on the five well-being dimensions for E-working which are i) affective and social facets, ii) cognitive and social facets, iii) affective and professional facets, iv) professional and social facets and v) Psychosomatic and affective facets. All these dimensions focus on emotions, emotion exhaustion, satisfaction, isolation and organizational commitment. Virtual work has minimized mental and emotional depletion (Golden, 2006) as satisfaction and more family time increases the commitment towards organization. E-working has brought in existence new term workplace isolation (WI), organizations have to encourage interpersonal support and culture while away from workplace (Mulki & Jaramillo, 2011). Remote working needs to be adopted to build higher scaled teams and remain cost competitive, also taking measures like continuous communication with the talent pool to make the employees feel connected and cared for (Remote.Co, 2020).Therefore it can be concluded from the above literature that:

H_1: Work Life Balance is a significant observable determinant or indicator for e-working (remote working) of academicians. [More the e-working the greater is the work life Balance]

2.2 E- Working and Organizational Trust:

Organizational trust applies to those people who interact with the company and are prepared to develop strong and deep connection with the organisation (Robinson, 1996). Organisational trust includes trust in supervisors and within the organisation as a whole (Ashford et al., 1989). If employees trust their organisation, they are not only willing to share the associated organizational risks, but they are also able to recognize the risk associated with the Organisation (Costa, 2003). Human resource management has a huge effect on the well-being of workers at work (Baptiste, 2008; Cvenkel, 2020). Interpersonal trust (Guinot et al., 2014) also has a significant effect on job satisfaction.

To establish trust in organisations managers must put efforts by making their actions as constant, focused and transparent (Bandsuch et al., 2008). If the employees feel their managers are reliable and credible, their moral and commitment towards the organisation will escalate (Caldwell et al., 2008) in the form of dedication, happiness at work and effectiveness. (Bandsuch et al., 2008; Gillies, 2011) which will positively correlate to organizational efficiency, enhancing problem solving, interaction, conciliation, effectiveness, organizational engagement and turnover rates (Campione, 2015; Dirks & Ferrin, 2002; Gillespie & Mann, 2004).

During COVID - 19, Organisational trust among employees and vice-versa has played an especially important role. Employees working remotely showed a positive and stronger organisational commitment and trust (Taboroši et al., 2020). The certainty of clearly defined assignments and deadlines is highly valued by remote workers. Remote workers have greater confidence in their associates, than in management, and eventually, this leads to improved organizational recognition. Thus it can be inferred from above literature that:

H_2: Organisational Trust is a significant observable determinant or indicator for e-working (remote working) of academicians. [Higher the probability of e-working becoming more successful, the stronger is the trust of organisation towards the academicians]

2.3 E working and effectiveness/ productivity

In order to improve, individual performance organisation's have to reduce work life conflicts and implement effective work – life strategies, and legislation that support employees to meet their job and personal obligations (Baral & Bhargava, 2010; Beauregard & Henry, 2009; Gregory & Milner, 2009; D. F. Parker & DeCotiis, 1983). However, employees need to use, coping mechanisms, which can be defined as the, "individual's cognitive and behavioral efforts to manage specific external and/or internal demands, that are appraised as taxing or exceeding the resources of the individual "(Lazarus & Folkman, 1984). Researchers found that if employees can pursue the balance of work life, they can follow better job and overall satisfaction (Baltes et al., 1999; Kaiser et al., 2011; D. F. Parker & DeCotiis, 1983), higher level of commitment and responsibility towards the organisation. (Friedman & Greenhaus, 2000; Goldberg et al., 1989; Roehling et al., 2001), results in enhanced employer branding (Harrington & Ladge, 2009; Kort, 2017). When the eastern and western perspectives in WLB were compared it was found that gender socialization within Asian companies played a prominent role in one's cognition and thought process (Chandra, 2012).American multinational companies focus on flexible working arrangements whereas Indian companies concentrate on welfare programs. It is even found that the Western countries government initiatives focus on core hours and generous paternity leave as compared Indian companies (Chandra, 2012). As per sixth European working condition survey (EWCS) (Eurofound, 2015) in 2015 it was found that around 82 percent of workers feel that there is close fit between career and family in e working scenario (Eurofound, 2017). Thus, the above literature suggests that:

H_3: Effectiveness/productivity is a significant observable determinant or indicator for e-working (remote working) of academicians. [That is, more the e-working the higher is the effectiveness or work productivity]

2.4 E working and Flexibility:

According to studies, remote working is more flexible which brings positivity in the individual and reduces the work conflicts, bringing better relation between work and personal life (Grant et al., 2013; Roloff & Fonner, 2010). Factors "*such as flextime and compressed workweek*"(McNall et al., 2009) which are part of Flexible work arrangement helps employees to have greater enrichment from work to home, leads to greater staff satisfaction and slower turnover intentions (McNall et al., 2009; Sharma, 2021). The two factors "*work-to-family enrichment and family-to-work enrichment*"(Chan et al., 2016b) found "*positively related to self-efficacy*" which had beneficial effect on WLB, career and family satisfaction (Chan et al., 2016a). On contrary it is said that implementation and success of flexible working schedules depends on how it is supported by the management and how it fits in the work culture (Galea et al., 2014; Maestro et al., 2020). Maintaining social work opportunities and WLB are organisational leverage which reduces stress (Giauque et al., 2019). Qualitative study among Indian IT women employees, explores how social expectations affect their work life interface (WIL). As per study the women work life interface affects women (Shah & Barker, 2020).

A study conducted in Greek (Giannikis & Mihail, 2011), examined that in a flexible work scheme, the attitude towards advancement opportunities depends mainly on gender, employment sector and previous involvement. Balancing work life attributes are stronger predictors of flexible work advancements. Relevant obstacles should be overcome by employee centered organizations that perceive flexibility as a valuable management resource (Giannikis & Mihail, 2011). Flexible work allows workers a degree of flexibility, which will have a massive influence on their impressions of the perceived value of their jobs. Positive significant relationship between work flexibility and job quality expectations leads to perceived job quality, especially in relation to long term growth and advancement opportunities, indicating a more complex relationship (Kelliher & Anderson, 2008). Agarwala et al.,(2014) researched on work – family issues and related variables from a cross cultural perspective in three different countries (India, Peru and Spain) and the study depicted that for Spain and Peru, and even for Peru and India, the scale of the Work life conflict (WLC) faced by employees are quite close. High levels of transformational leadership also contribute to reduced innovation as micromanagement can reduce employee confidence and growth prospects (Agarwala et al., 2014). It can there

H_4: Work Flexibility is an observable determinant or indicator for e-working (remote working) of academicians. [That is, more the e-working result is more flexibility in work]

3.METHODOLOGY:

This study incorporates the reflective confirmatory analysis, as the researcher wanted to determine the critical observable determinants reflecting the benefits of e-working (remote working) for academicians during COVID-19 using the E-Work Life (EWL) Scale developed by Grant et al (2019). This research focuses on reflective constructs which are assumptions of classical test theory (Jarvis, C.B., MacKenzie, S.B. and Podsakoff, P.M., 2003) hence it is necessary to perform, construct validation through Confirmatory Factor Analysis (CFA) (i.e., convergent and discriminant validity) and reliability testing (i.e. Cronbach's Alpha)(Freeze, R. and Raschke, R.L., 2007).

3.1. Sample selection

The current study adopted convenience sampling strategy and the sample consisted of academicians teaching various subjects to graduates and postgraduate students in different Indian Universities. All the academicians were emailed an invitation to complete a structured questionnaire voluntarily, preliminary qualifying questions allowed only currently employed academicians who are taking classes through different online platforms like zoom, web ex meeting, web ex teams, google classrooms and Microsoft teams etc to complete the survey. Over 300 emails invitations were sent to academicians of different private and government universities in India out of which 230 respondents replied bringing the response rate to 76.6 percent, which is considered sufficient and adequate (Baruch & Holtom, 2008). A total of 230 collected responses made an adequate sample size for structural equation modelling (Rosseel, 2012) using SPSS AMOS version 24 software for statistical analysis. Table 1 provides the description of items considered for the research study.

3.2. Research instrument

Table 1 contains the element of the questionnaire which were implemented from E-Work Life (EWL) Scale developed by Grant et al. (2019). The EWL scale items comprises 28 items but only 16 items were considered for this research based on the previous literature.All the items were assessed on a five-point Likert scale ("from 1 strongly agree to 5 strongly disagree, with the choice 6 available for selection "not applicable"). The scale is divided into four sub-categories: (1) Job effectiveness that focuses on e-work success using abilities and skills, like self-management to be a productive e-worker and e-job success and also an e-worker, providing sufficient and consistent priorities and objectives to reach strive for greater degree of work performance (2) Relationship with the organisation or Management style or organisational trust is described by the e-worker in terms of how they interpret successful management skills, e.g. how an e-worker is handled by a line manager or supervisor using management methods and engaging with the team Confidence The degree of autonomy and transparency given to individuals during e-working (3) E-well-being flexibility which includes flexible working hours and autonomy to do the job the way employee wants to do (4)Work-life harmony or Work-life integration is the capacity to successfully incorporate work and non-work conditions efficiently. Poor integration of work life can lead to issues on other aspects such as e-well-being Task management / conflict to be able to transition in between various roles needed effectively.

The construct's validity was established by carrying out confirmatory factor analysis (CFA). For all the scale, validity tests were conducted on four key dimensions: content validity, convergent validity, discriminant validity, and validity related to criteria. The scales were tested for one-dimensionality and statistical reliability before performing construct validity analysis, (Table 2). Accordingly, the findings reveal that most of the constructs are showing higher than the required reliability. Hence it can be concluded that all the items grouped completely converge to its respective dimensions and consider all items for the analysis. Furthermore, the Cronbach alpha values across each of the dimensions depicted in the above table have more than 0.70 which states that there is a consistency in the data and questionnaire is addressed to relevant respondents.

Table 1. Structured Questionnaire adopted for the research study

Dimension	Item code	Item Description
Work/Life Interference	WLB_1	My social life is not bad when e-working remotely
	WLB_2	My e-working does not take up time that I would like to spend with my family/friends or on other non-work events
	WLB_3	When e-working remotely I do not often think about work related issues outside of my regularl working hours
	WLB_4	I am happy with my work-life balance when e-working remotely
	WLB_5	Constant access to work through e-working is not very tiring
	WLB_6	I do not feel that work demands are much higher when I am e-working remotely
Organisational Trust	ORT_1	My organisation provides training in e-working skills and behaviours
	ORT_2	I trust my organisation to provide good e-working facilities to allow me to e-work effectively
	ORT_3	My organisation trusts me to be effective in my role when I e-work remotely
Effectiveness/ Productivity	EFF_PRO_1	When e-working I can concentrate better on my work tasks
	EFF_PRO_2	E-working makes me more effective to deliver against my key objectives and deliverables
	EFF_PRO_3	If I am interrupted by family/other responsibilities whilst e-working from home, I still meet my line manager's quality expectations
	EFF_PRO_4	My overall job productivity has increased by my ability to e-work remotely/from home
Flexibility	FLEX_1	My work is so flexible I could easily take time off e-working remotely, if and when I want to
	FLEX_2	My line manager allows me to flex my hours to meet my needs, providing all the work is completed
	FLEX_3	My supervisor gives me total control over when and how I get my work completed when e-working

Table 3 Goodness-of-fit & Incremental Indices of Measurement model of dimensions reflecting E-working

	(χ2/df)	GFI	RMSEA	AGFI	NFI	CFI	IFI	RFI	PCFI	PNFI	
Accepted Value	< 5	> 0.90	< 0.10	> 0.80	> 0.90				> 0.50		
Model Value	3.118	0.901	0.086	0.802	0.891	0.923	0.924	0.901	0.792	0.765	

Results of analysis

The model relationships and indeed the fit measurements (Table 3) for the model are shown in Fig 1. In the table both accepted value and the model value is provided. The Goodness-of-fit & Incremental Indices for dimensions reflecting the E-working/remote working depicted in Table 2 indicates an overall acceptable fit and is an over identified model.

The maximum probability analytical results and t-values are shown on the model in Fig. 1. In this, the Organisational Trust dimension (set to one to define the unit of measurement for e-working dimen-

Table 2. Reliability and Item Loadings of dimensions reflecting E-working

Latent Variable	Indicators	Standardized loadings (b)	Composite Reliability	Cronbach Alpha	Average Variance Explained (AVE)
Work/Life Interference	WLB_1	0.831	0.910	0.911	0.631
	WLB_2	0.797			
	WLB_3	0.853			
	WLB_4	0.870			
	WLB_5	0.797			
	WLB_6	0.586			
Organisational Trust	ORT_1	0.851	0.901	0.901	0.752
	ORT_2	0.951			
	ORT_3	0.793			
Effectiveness/ Productivity	EFF_PRO_1	0.836	0.828	0.865	0.616
	EFF_PRO_2	0.879			
	EFF_PRO_3	0.761			
	EFF_PRO_4	0.826			
Flexibility	FLEX_1	0.838	0.802	0.858	0.669
	FLEX_2	0.880			
	FLEX_3	0.874			

sion. As indicated, (t=9.460) is 1.262 and is significant at the 0.01 level, demonstrating *Effectiveness/ Productivity* is the most observable indicator for e-working/remote working. In other words, 1.262 shows that e-working/remote working has important repercussions on effectiveness or productivity of teaching, with one unit in e-working leading to 1.26 times or units increase in effectiveness or productivity in teaching. On the other, *Work Life/interference* (and *Flexibility* (are observable indicators statistically for e-working/remote working but seems to be less important *[as are less than 1) than* Organisational Trust. *Yet, it has emerged from the measurement model (regression) result* all the four dimensions are the most observable determinant of e-working/remote working and thus statistically all the four defined hypotheses were accepted. In other words it can be accomplished that there is statistical evidence to determine that there is a better work life balance in an e-working scenario and increased e-working results in increased effectiveness or work productivity. Furthermore, in an e-working model enhanced effectiveness or work productivity is expected from academicians working remotely. Finally, as perceived by the sample respondents, e-working has resulted in increased flexibility in the education sector.

Discussion:

Remote or e-working models have been adopted by various sectors post the Government restrictions imposed to curb the spread of the COVID-19 and the education sector is one of them. Pre COVID-19

Figure 1. Measurement model along with path diagram result of dimensions reflecting E-working/ Remote Working

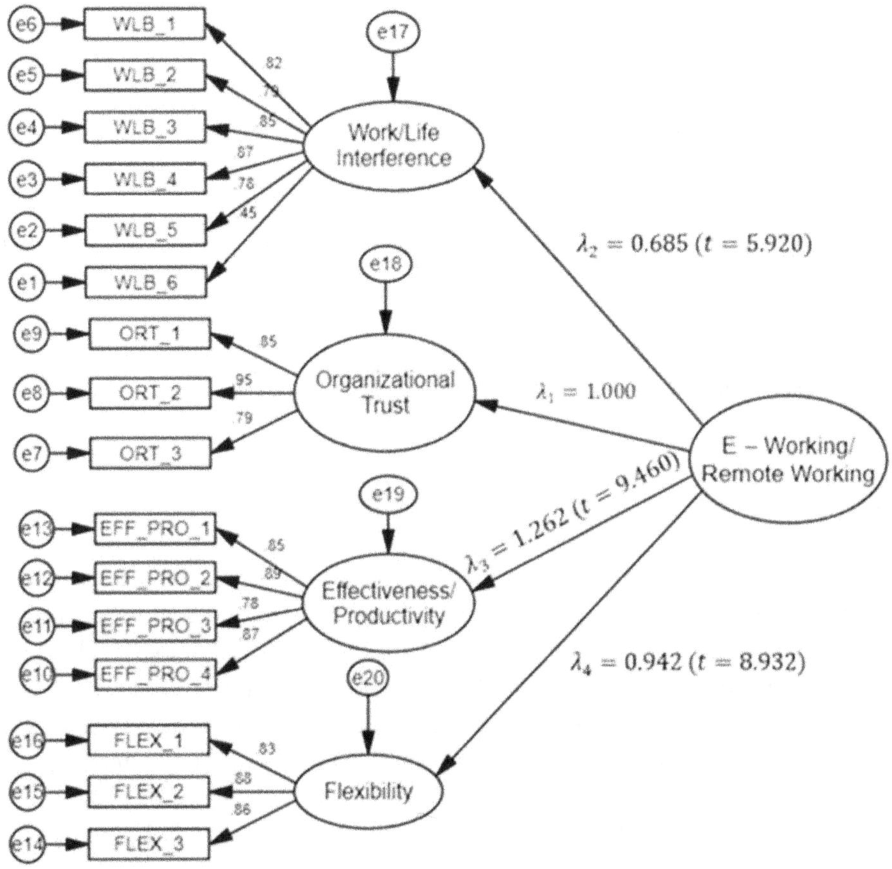

education industry was primarily defined by physical classes and workplace with extremely limited aspects of e-working but post COVID -19 the things have completely changed for the education sector with a major shift for the academicians going completely online. The current study focuses on the expectations and experience of the academicians on remote working and it was found that most of the academicians are quite comfortable and satisfied with the e-working model though there were few hurdles initially to understand and settle down with the new technology-based work model. E-working is associated with unpredicted expectations which must be considered when academicians are creating a workplace and few adjustments to be made to get amalgamated with this new normal. It becomes difficult to compartmentalize the personal place to ensure privacy during working hours while taking online classes, which is one major criteria of concern for the academicians.

The key for successful and smooth functioning of e-working is compassion and communication between the academicians and their front-line managers like Deans and Head of the departments. During the research it was analysed that the majority of the academicians said that they find it difficult to balance between work and life as the job requirements, like meeting schedules, training on adoption of new technologies etc were happening at any time. It was further analysed that ergonomics factors such as sitting posture, eye sight issues, body pains etc has emerged especially among academicians. Remote working without proper working infrastructure to work, may lead to slow pace towards health injuries. Employers need to provide employees with proper training and support them to create an ergonomic workplace.

Too much screen time may result in severe health issues like blurred vision and headaches, taking small breaks may help in minimising the impact. The energy and concentration can be regained by switching off from the technology for some time as the boundary between work and non-work timings is very blurred during e-working (Broadbridge, 2009). The unsaid norm of being always online adds to the pressure especially for female academicians who are already struggling to bring a balance between childcare, home schooling, rapid technical upskilling expected and health issues. Social isolation is another side effect of e working specially for people who are staying alone during a pandemic. Stress, depression, and anxiety is caused due to solitude which negatively affects the productivity of the academicians.

E working is an excellent alternative which has supported the education industry to a very great extent, but it requires few norms to be followed to maintain a work life balance and a healthy lifestyle.

CONCLUSION

Introducing virtual working by employers needs to be supported by three dimensions organization, manager and employees. Proper and timely training must be provided to employees while opting for remote working. There must be formal policy for proper functioning of remote working (Kowalski and Swanson, 2005). Other factors concerned with E-working are communication technologies related to three dimensions information overload, communication overload and system overload (Hung, Chen and Lin, 2015). Still many institutions have not adapted the technology and had a terrible experience, but institutions which were using ICT enabled classrooms were able to accept the change sooner (Lederman, 2020). The virtual working for academicians is a boon or bane is still a debatable question, but as per Sponaugle (2020) there was a positive response from the teachers as they stated that, 'they were able to focus more on teaching content', which does point on inner satisfaction. Teachers can bring in innovative modes of teaching in classes by using the features on conferencing platforms like zoom, google meet, WebEx etc. (Leon, 2020).Few factors contradict with the positivity of E-working like trust issues and micro management. Virtual classes have shown a great deal of flexibility where teachers are able to take classes at given schedules and then can manage households simultaneously, which can result in WLB (Noguchi, 2020). Various interactive features which can create effective learning and reducing technostress needed to be incorporated (Spataro, 2020). The change is supported by the organizations too, teachers are provided with required devices so that they can take classes from their homes in comfort and security (McHugh, 2020).This enables organizations to recruit talent without location constraints. It also gives comfort to teachers to avoid commuting and conducting classes in their comfort zone.

To sum up, E-working is disruption of technologies that offers benefits to employees and employers. During Pandemic remote working helped businesses to sustain. In the education sector, still debates are going on for virtual classes vs offline classes. The new work culture in academics has brought a new wave, which challenged teachers to cope up with accepting and sailing into a new platform of teaching experiences. This research illuminates the positivity of E-working which was possible only because technology was available but places where proper facilities are not there it will be challenging to do so.

REFERENCES

Agarwala, T., Arizkuren-Eleta, A., Del Castillo, E., Muñiz-Ferrer, M., & Gartzia, L. (2014). Influence of managerial support on work-life conflict and organizational commitment: An international comparison for India, Peru and Spain. *International Journal of Human Resource Management, 25*(10), 1460–1483. doi:10.1080/09585192.2013.870315

Ahmed, H., Allaf, M., & Elghazaly, H. (2020). COVID-19 and medical education. *The Lancet. Infectious Diseases, 20*(7), 777–778. doi:10.1016/S1473-3099(20)30226-7 PMID:32213335

Anscombe, T. (2020, March 16). *COVID-19 and the shift to remote work*. We Lives Security. https://www.welivesecurity.com/2020/03/16/covid19-forced-workplace-exodus/

Ashford, S. J., Lee, C., & Bobko, P. (1989). Content, Cause, and Consequences of Job Insecurity: A Theory-Based Measure and Substantive Test. *Academy of Management Journal, 32*(4), 803–829. doi:10.2307/256569

Bäck-Wiklund, M., Van der Lippe, T., Den Dulk, L., & Doorne-Huiskes, A. (2011). Quality of life and work in Europe: Theory, practice and policy. In Quality of Life and Work in Europe: Theory, Practice and Policy. Palgrave Macmillan. doi:10.1057/9780230299443

Bakker, K. (2017). *Role Overload and Job Stress: The Role of Perceived Organizational Support*. Tilburg University.

Baltes, B. B., Briggs, T. E., Huff, J. W., Wright, J. A., & Neuman, G. A. (1999). Flexible and Compressed Workweek Schedules: A Meta-Analysis of Their Effects on Work-Related Criteria Boris. *The Journal of Applied Psychology, 84*(4), 496–513. doi:10.1037/0021-9010.84.4.496

Baptiste, N. R. (2008). Tightening the link between employee wellbeing at work and performance: A new dimension for HRM. *Management Decision, 46*(2), 284–309. doi:10.1108/00251740810854168

Baral, R., & Bhargava, S. (2010). Work-family enrichment as a mediator between organizational interventions for work-life balance and job outcomes. *Journal of Managerial Psychology, 25*(3), 274–300. doi:10.1108/02683941011023749

Bartoszko, A. (2020). Accelerating Curve of Anxiousness. *Journal of Extreme Anthropology, 4*(1), E7–E17. doi:10.5617/jea.7861

Baruch, Y. (2000). Baruch-2000-New_Technology,_Work_and_Employment Qualis A1 muito importante. *New Technology. Work and Employment, 15*(1), 34–49. doi:10.1111/1468-005X.00063

Baruch, Y., & Holtom, B. C. (2008). Survey response rate levels and trends in organizational research. *Human Relations, 61*(8), 1139–1160. doi:10.1177/0018726708094863

Basu, D. S. (2019, February 27). Work-life: 60% working Indians rate work-life balance from average to terrible: Monster.com survey. *ET Bureau*. https://economictimes.indiatimes.com/magazines/panache/60-working-indians-rate-work-life-balance-from-average-to-terrible-monster-com-survey/articleshow/68183578.cms?from=mdr

Beauregard, T. A., & Henry, L. C. (2009). Making the link between work-life balance practices and organizational performance. *Human Resource Management Review, 19*(1), 9–22. doi:10.1016/j.hrmr.2008.09.001

Bresman, H. (2015, February 23). *What Millennials Want from Work, Charted Across the World*. HBR. https://hbr.org/2015/02/what-millennials-want-from-work-charted-across-the-world

Broadbridge, A. (2009). Sacrificing personal or professional life? A gender perspective on the accounts of retail managers. *International Review of Retail, Distribution and Consumer Research, 19*(3), 289–311. doi:10.1080/09593960903234226

Business World. (2020, July 30). *88 Of Indian Workforce Prefer To Have The Flexibility Of Working From Home SAP Concur Study*. BW Online Bureau. https://www.businessworld.in/article/88-Of-Indian-Workforce-Prefer-To-Have-The-Flexibility-Of-Working-From-Home-SAP-Concur-Study/30-07-2020-303132/

Caldwell, C., Hayes, L. A., Bernal, P., & Karri, R. (2008). Ethical stewardship - Implications for leadership and trust. *Journal of Business Ethics, 78*(1–2), 153–164. doi:10.100710551-006-9320-1

Campione, W. A. (2015). Corporate Offerings: Why Aren't Millennials Staying? *Journal of Applied Business and Economics, 17*(4), 60–75. http://t.www.na-businesspress.com/JABE/CampioneWA_Web17_4_.pdf

Chambel, M. J., Carvalho, V. S., Cesário, F., & Lopes, S. (2017). The work-to-life conflict mediation between job characteristics and well-being at work: Part-time vs full-time employees. *Career Development International, 22*(2), 142–164. doi:10.1108/CDI-06-2016-0096

Chan, X. W., Kalliath, T., Brough, P., Siu, O.-L., O'Driscoll, M. P., & Timms, C. (2016a). Work–family enrichment and satisfaction: The mediating role of self-efficacy and work–life balance. *International Journal of Human Resource Management, 27*(15), 1755–1776. doi:10.1080/09585192.2015.1075574

Chan, X. W., Kalliath, T., Brough, P., Siu, O. L., O'Driscoll, M. P., & Timms, C. (2016b). Work–family enrichment and satisfaction: The mediating role of self-efficacy and work–life balance. *International Journal of Human Resource Management, 27*(15), 1755–1776. doi:10.1080/09585192.2015.1075574

Chandra, V. (2012). Work-life balance: Eastern and western perspectives. *International Journal of Human Resource Management, 23*(5), 1040–1056. doi:10.1080/09585192.2012.651339

Clark, S. C. (2000). Work/family border theory: A new theory of work/family balance. *Human Relations, 53*(6), 747–770. doi:10.1177/0018726700536001

Collins, A. M., Hislop, D., & Cartwright, S. (2016). Social support in the workplace between teleworkers, office-based colleagues and supervisors. *New Technology, Work and Employment, 31*(2), 161–175. doi:10.1111/ntwe.12065

Costa, A. C. (2003). Work team trust and effectiveness. *Personnel Review, 32*(5), 605-622+672. doi:10.1108/00483480310488360

Cowan, R., & Hoffman, M. F. (2007). The flexible organization: How contemporary employees construct the work/life border. *Qualitative Research Reports in Communication*, *8*(1), 37–44. doi:10.1080/17459430701617895

Crompton, R., & Lyonette, C. (2006). Work-life "balance" in Europe. *Acta Sociologica*, *49*(4), 379–393. doi:10.1177/0001699306071680

Currie, J., & Eveline, J. (2011). E-technology and work/life balance for academics with young children. *Higher Education*, *62*(4), 533–550. doi:10.100710734-010-9404-9

Cvenkel, N. (2020). *Well-Being in the Workplace: Governance and Sustainability Insights to Promote Workplace Health*. Springer Singapore. doi:10.1007/978-981-15-3619-9

Digneo, G. (2020). *6 Important Remote Work Statistics To Know in 2020*. TimeDoctor. https://biz30.timedoctor.com/remote-work-statistics/

Dirks, K. T., & Ferrin, D. L. (2002). Trust in leadership: Meta-analytic findings and implications for research and practice. *The Journal of Applied Psychology*, *87*(4), 611–628. doi:10.1037/0021-9010.87.4.611 PMID:12184567

Eby, L. T., Casper, W. J., Lockwood, A., Bordeaux, C., & Brinley, A. (2005). Work and family research in IO/OB: Content analysis and review of the literature (1980-2002). *Journal of Vocational Behavior*, *66*(1), 124–197. doi:10.1016/j.jvb.2003.11.003

Edwards, J. R., & Rothbard, N. P. (2000). Mechanisms linking work and family: Clarifying the relationship between work and family constructs. *Academy of Management Review*, *25*(1), 178–199. doi:10.2307/259269

Eurofound. (2015). *Sixth European Working Conditions Survey: 2015*. https://www.eurofound.europa.eu/surveys/european-working-conditions-surveys/sixth-european-working-conditions-survey-201
5

Eurofound. (2017). *6th European Working Conditions Survey: 2017 update*. European Union.

Freeze, R., & Raschke, R.L. (2007). *An assessment of formative and reflective constructs in IS research*. Academic Press.

Friedman, S. D., & Greenhaus, J. H. (2000). *Work and Family—Allies or Enemies?: What Happens When Business Professionals Confront Life Choices - Oxford Scholarship* (1st ed.). Oxford University Press. doi:10.1093/acprof:oso/9780195112757.001.0001

Friedman, S. D., & Greenhaus, J. H. (2000). *Work and Family—Allies or Enemies?: What Happens When Business Professionals Confront Life Choices - Oxford Scholarship* (1st ed.). Oxford University Press. doi:10.1093/acprof:oso/9780195112757.001.0001

Galea, C., Houkes, I., & De Rijk, A. (2014). An insider's point of view: How a system of flexible working hours helps employees to strike a proper balance between work and personal life. *International Journal of Human Resource Management*, *25*(8), 1090–1111. doi:10.1080/09585192.2013.816862

Gallup. (2013). State of the Global Workplace. In Employee Engagement Insights for Business Leaders Worldwide. Gallup.

Giannikis, S. K., & Mihail, D. M. (2011). Flexible work arrangements in Greece: A study of employee perceptions. *International Journal of Human Resource Management, 22*(2), 417–432. doi:10.1080/09585192.2011.540163

Giauque, D., Anderfuhren-Biget, S., & Varone, F. (2019). Stress and turnover intents in international organizations: Social support and work–life balance as resources. *International Journal of Human Resource Management, 30*(5), 879–901. doi:10.1080/09585192.2016.1254105

Gillespie, N. A., & Mann, L. (2004). Transformational leadership and shared values: The building blocks of trust. *Journal of Managerial Psychology, 19*(6), 588–607. doi:10.1108/02683940410551507

Gillies, D. (2011). Agile bodies: A new imperative in neoliberal governance. Journal of Education Policy, 26(22). doi:10.1080/02680939.2010.508177

Goldberg, W. A., Greenberger, E., Koch-Jones, J., O'Neil, R., & Hamill, S. (1989). Attractiveness of child care and related employer-supported benefits and policies to married and single parents. *Child & Youth Care Quarterly, 18*(1), 23–37.

Golden, T. D. (2006). Avoiding depletion in virtual work: Telework and the intervening impact of work exhaustion on commitment and turnover intentions. *Journal of Vocational Behavior, 69*(1), 176–187. doi:10.1016/j.jvb.2006.02.003

Grant, C. A., Wallace, L. M., & Spurgeon, P. C. (2013). An exploration of the psychological factors affecting remote e-worker's job effectiveness, well-being and work-life balance. *Employee Relations, 35*(5), 527–546. doi:10.1108/ER-08-2012-0059

Grant, C. A., Wallace, L. M., Spurgeon, P. C., Tramontano, C., & Charalampous, M. (2019). Construction and initial validation of the E-Work Life Scale to measure remote e-working. *Employee Relations, 41*(1), 16–33. doi:10.1108/ER-09-2017-0229

Gregory, A., & Milner, S. (2009). Work-life balance: A matter of choice? *Gender, Work and Organization, 16*(1), 1–13. doi:10.1111/j.1468-0432.2008.00429.x

Guinot, J., Chiva, R., & Roca-Puig, V. (2014). Interpersonal trust, stress and satisfaction at work: An empirical study. *Personnel Review, 43*(1), 96–115. doi:10.1108/PR-02-2012-0043

Harrington, B., & Ladge, J. J. (2009). Work-Life Integration. Present Dynamics and Future Directions for Organizations. *Organizational Dynamics, 38*(2), 148–157. doi:10.1016/j.orgdyn.2009.02.003

Hilberath, C., Kilmann, J., Lovich, D., & Tzanetti, T. (2020, September 22). *Hybrid Work Is the New Remote Work*. BCG. https://www.bcg.com/en-in/publications/2020/managing-remote-work-and-optimizing-hybrid-working-models

Hill, E. J., Hawkins, A. J., Ferris, M., & Weitzman, M. (2001). Finding an extra day a week: The positive influence of perceived job flexibility on work and family life balance. *Family Relations, 50*(1), 49–58. doi:10.1111/j.1741-3729.2001.00049.x

Hirschhorn, J. (2020, May 5). *SHRM Releases COVID-19 U.S. Business Index*. Business Wire. https://www.businesswire.com/news/home/20200505005623/en/SHRM-Releases-COVID-19-U.S.-Business-Index

Hodges, C., Moore, S., Lockee, B., Trust, T., & Bond, A. (2020). *The difference between emergency remote teaching and online learning*. Educause. https://er.educause.edu/articles/2020/3/thedifference-between-emergency-remote-teaching-and-online-learning

Houston, D., Meyer, L. H., & Paewai, S. (2006). Academic staff workloads and job satisfaction: Expectations and values in academe. *Journal of Higher Education Policy and Management*, *28*(1), 17–30. doi:10.1080/13600800500283734

Howington, J. (2015, January 28). *Update: Want to Work from Home? 19 Ways to Say It*. Flexjobs. https://www.flexjobs.com/blog/post/want-to-work-from-home-17-ways-to-say-it

Hung, W. H., Chen, K., & Lin, C. P. (2015). Does the proactive personality mitigate the adverse effect of technostress on productivity in the mobile environment? *Telematics and Informatics*, *32*(1), 143–157. doi:10.1016/j.tele.2014.06.002

IONOS. (2019). *Work-life balance: harmony between work and personal life*. IONOS. https://www.ionos.com/startupguide/productivity/work-life-balance/

Jarvenpaa, S. L., & Staples, D. S. (2001). Exploring perceptions of organizational ownership of information and expertise. *Journal of Management Information Systems*, *18*(1), 151–183. doi:10.1080/07421222.2001.11045673

Jarvis, C. B., Mackenzie, S. B., Podsakoff, P. M., Giliatt, N., & Mee, J. F. (2003). A Critical Review of Construct Indicators and Measurement Model Misspecification in Marketing and Consumer Research. *The Journal of Consumer Research*, *30*(2), 199–218. doi:10.1086/376806

Kaiser, S., Ringlstetter, M. J., Eikhof, D. R., & Cunha, M. P. E. (2011). Creating balance? In *Springer-Verlag*. Springer Verlag. doi:10.1007/978-3-642-16199-5

Kelliher, C., & Anderson, D. (2008). For better or for worse? An analysis of how flexible working practices influence employees' perceptions of job quality. *International Journal of Human Resource Management*, *19*(3), 419–431. doi:10.1080/09585190801895502

Kelliher, C., Richardson, J., & Boiarintseva, G. (2019). All of work? All of life? Reconceptualising work-life balance for the 21st century. *Human Resource Management Journal*, *29*(2), 97–112. Advance online publication. doi:10.1111/1748-8583.12215

Khan, A. A., Niazi, S., & Saif, S. K. (2020, March 26). *Universities unprepared for switch to remote learning*. University World News. https://www.universityworldnews.com/post.php?story=20200326141547229

Kinnunen, U., Mäkikangas, A., Mauno, S., De Cuyper, N., & De Witte, H. (2014). Development of perceived job insecurity across two years: Associations with antecedents and employee outcomes. *Journal of Occupational Health Psychology, 19*(2), 243–258. doi:10.1037/a0035835 PMID:24730428

Knowledge spillover. (2020). In *Wikipedia*. https://en.wikipedia.org/wiki/Knowledge_spillover

Kort, de M. (2017). The relationship between work-life balance, work engagement and participation in employee development activities: A moderated mediation model. *Industrial Engineering Online, 13*(1). doi:10.20473/jmtt.v10i1.4805

Kowalski, K. B., & Swanson, J. A. (2005). Critical success factors in developing teleworking programs. *Benchmarking, 12*(3), 236–249. doi:10.1108/14635770510600357

Lambert, S. J. (1990). Processes Linking Work and Family: A Critical Review and Research Agenda. *Human Relations, 43*(3), 239–257. doi:10.1177/001872679004300303

Lazarus, R. S., & Folkman, S. (1984). *Stress, Appraisal, and Coping*. Springer Publishing Company, Inc. https://books.google.co.in/books?id=i-ySQQuUpr8C&printsec=frontcover#v=onepage&q&f=false

Lederman, D. (2020, March 18). *Most teaching is going remote. Will that help or hurt online learning?* Insidehighered.Com. https://www.insidehighered.com/digital-learning/article/2020/03/18/most-teaching-going-remote-will-help-or-hurt-online-learning

Leon, de J. (2020, March 20). *Best Practices for Positive and Productive Remote Work for Educators*. Education Elements. https://www.edelements.com/blog/best-practices-for-positive-and-productive-remote-work-for-educators

Li, F., Qi, J., Wang, G., & Wang, X. (2014). Traditional classroom VS e-learning in higher education: Difference between students' behavioral engagement. *International Journal of Emerging Technologies in Learning, 9*(2), 48–51. doi:10.3991/ijet.v9i2.3268

Maestro, M. las H., Albiol, N. C., & Grau Grau, M. (Eds.). (2020). The New Ideal Worker. Springer International Publishing. doi:10.1007/978-3-030-12477-9

Marshall, G. W., Michaels, C. E., & Mulki, J. P. (2007). Workplace Isolation: Exploring the Construct and Its Measurement. *Psychology and Marketing, 24*(3), 195–223. doi:10.1002/mar.20158

Mas-Machuca, M., Berbegal-Mirabent, J., & Alegre, I. (2016). Work-life balance and its relationship with organizational pride and job satisfaction. *Journal of Managerial Psychology, 31*(2), 586–602. doi:10.1108/JMP-09-2014-0272

McHugh, K. (2020). *Teachers Working From Home In Their Pajamas?* The Learning Counsel. https://thelearningcounsel.com/article/teachers-working-home-their-pajamas

McNall, L. A., Masuda, A. D., & Nicklin, J. M. (2009). Flexible work arrangements, job satisfaction, and turnover intentions: The mediating role of work-to-family enrichment. *The Journal of Psychology, 144*(1), 61–81. doi:10.1080/00223980903356073 PMID:20092070

Medhi, B. (2020, October 6). *5 Major Factors Affecting The Quality Of Work Life*. Vantage Circle. https://blog.vantagecircle.com/quality-of-work-life-qwl/

Michel, J. S., Kotrba, L. M., Mitchelson, J. K., Clark, M. A., & Baltes, B. B. (2011). Antecedents of work-family conflict: A meta-analytic review. *Journal of Organizational Behavior*, *32*(5), 689–725. doi:10.1002/job.695

Molino, M., Ghislieri, C., & Cortese, C. G. (2013). When work enriches family-life: The mediational role of professional development opportunities. *Journal of Workplace Learning*, *25*(2), 98–113. doi:10.1108/13665621311299780

Mulki, J. P., & Jaramillo, F. (2011). Workplace isolation: Salespeople and supervisors in USA. *International Journal of Human Resource Management*, *22*(4), 902–923. doi:10.1080/09585192.2011.555133

Nassazi, A. (2013). *Effects Of Training On Employee Performance*. Vaasan Ammattikorkeakoulu University. https://core.ac.uk/download/pdf/38098025.pdf

Noguchi, Y. (2020, March 17). *Coronavirus Triple Duty: Working, Parenting And Teaching From Home*. NPR. https://www.npr.org/2020/03/17/816631571/coronavirus-triple-duty-working-parenting-and-teaching-from-home

OECD. (2019). *Revealed: the countries with the best work-life balance*. OECD Better Life Index. https://www.oecdbetterlifeindex.org/topics/work-life-balance/

Palloff, R. M., & Pratt, K. (2007). *Building Online Learning Communities: Effective Strategies for the Virtual Classroom* (2nd ed.). Wiley. https://www.wiley.com/en-us/Building+Online+Learning+Communities%3A+Effective+Strategies+for+the+Virtual+Classroom%2C+2nd+Edition-p-9780787988258

Parker, D. F., & DeCotiis, T. A. (1983). Organizational determinants of job stress. *Organizational Behavior and Human Performance*, *32*(2), 160–177. doi:10.1016/0030-5073(83)90145-9

Rapanta, C., Botturi, L., Goodyear, P., Guàrdia, L., & Koole, M. (2020). Online University Teaching During and After the Covid-19 Crisis: Refocusing Teacher Presence and Learning Activity. *Postdigital Science and Education*, *2*(3), 923–945. doi:10.100742438-020-00155-y

Remote Year. (2020). *What the Future of Remote Work Means for You*. Remote Year. https://www.remoteyear.com/blog/remote-work-future

Remote.Co. (2020). *What are the keys to successful remote team relationships?* Remote.Co. https://remote.co/qa-leading-remote-companies/what-elements-are-key-to-successful-working-relationships-with-remote-teams/

Rice, R. W., Frone, M. R., & McFarlin, D. B. (1992). Work—Nonwork conflict and the perceived quality of life. *Journal of Organizational Behavior*, *13*(2), 155–168. doi:10.1002/job.4030130205

Robinson, S. L. (1996). Trust and breach of the psychological contract. *Administrative Science Quarterly*, *41*(4), 574–599. doi:10.2307/2393868

Roehling, P. V., Roehling, M. V., & Moen, P. (2001). The relationship between work-life policies and practices and employee loyalty: A life course perspective. *Journal of Family and Economic Issues*, *22*(2), 141–170. doi:10.1023/A:1016630229628

Roloff, M. E., & Fonner, K. L. (2010). Why teleworkers are more satisfied with their jobs than are office-based workers: When less contact is beneficial. *Journal of Applied Communication Research*, *38*(4), 336–361. doi:10.1080/00909882.2010.513998

Rosseel, Y. (2012). Lavaan: An R package for structural equation modeling. *Journal of Statistical Software*, *48*(1), 1–36. doi:10.18637/jss.v048.i02

Schrotenboer, B. (2020, May 4). Working at home had a positive effect on productivity during the pandemic. *USA Today*. https://www.usatoday.com/story/money/2020/05/04/coronavirus-pandemic-might-game-changer-working-home/3061862001/

Shah, D., & Barker, M. (2020). Work-life interface: Experiences of Indian IT women repatriates. *International Journal of Human Resource Management*. Advance online publication. doi:10.1080/09585192.2020.1737173

Sharma, N. (2021). Using positive deviance to enhance employee engagement: An interpretive structural modelling approach. *The International Journal of Organizational Analysis*, *30*(1), 84–98. doi:10.1108/IJOA-07-2020-2341

Sheppard, G. (2016). Work-life balance programs to improve employee performance. *Walden Dissertations and Doctoral Studies*, 1–329. http://ovidsp.ovid.com/ovidweb.cgi?T=JS&PAGE=reference&D=psyc13a&NEWS=N&AN=2016-47708-167%0Ahttps://search.proquest.com/docview/1765463932?accountid=12763%0Ahttp://primoa.library.unsw.edu.au/openurl/61UNSW_INST/UNSW_SERVICES_PAGE?url_ver=Z39.88-2004&rft_v

Spataro, J. (2020, March 11). *Helping teachers and students make the switch to remote learning*. Microsoft.Com. https://www.microsoft.com/en-us/microsoft-365/blog/2020/03/11/helping-teachers-students-switch-remote-learning/

Sponaugle, E. (2020, March 13). *Remote Teaching: 7 Positive Outcomes from My Experience*. Erinsponaugle.Com. https://www.erinsponaugle.com/post/remote-teaching-benefits

Taboroši, S., Strukan, E., Poštin, J., Konjikušić, M., & Nikolić, M. (2020). Organizational commitment and trust at work by remote employees. *Journal of Engineering Management and Competitiveness*, *10*(1), 48–60. doi:10.5937/jemc2001048T

UNESCO. (2020, March 30). *COVID-19 Webinar: A new world for teachers, education's frontline workers - COVID-19 education webinar #2*. UNESCO. https://en.unesco.org/news/covid-19-webinar-new-world-teachers-educations-frontline-workers-covid-19-education-webinar-2

Veletsianos, G., & Houlden, S. (2020, October 2). *An analysis of flexible learning and flexibility over the last 40 years of Distance Education*. Routledge. doi:10.1080/01587919.2019.1681893

Voydanoff, P. (2005). Toward a conceptualization of perceived work-family fit and balance: A demands and resources approach. *Journal of Marriage and Family*, *67*(4), 822–836. doi:10.1111/j.1741-3737.2005.00178.x

Wheeler, M. A., & Gunasekara, A. (2020, May 18). *Forget Work-Life Balance – It's All About Integration in the Age of COVID-19*. https://www.nextgov.com/ideas/2020/05/forget-work-life-balance-its-all-about-integration-age-covid-19/165473/

Whittington, R., Cailluet, L., & Yakis-Douglas, B. (2011). Opening strategy: Evolution of a precarious profession. *British Journal of Management*, *22*(3), 531–544. doi:10.1111/j.1467-8551.2011.00762.x

Wong, I. (2020). *Adjusting your employees to long-term remote work*. Fast Company. https://www.fastcompany.com/90539478/is-your-team-prepared-for-long-term-remote-work-ask-these-3-questions-to-determine-if-they-are

Wu, J. (2020, March 9). A Deep Dive Into Remote Work For Our Future Of Work. *Forbes*. https://www.forbes.com/sites/cognitiveworld/2020/03/09/a-deep-dive-into-remote-work-for-our-future-of-work/?sh=6b11177d1843

Yadav, R., Khanna, A., & Dasmohapatra, S. (2019). The effects of quality of work life on organisational commitment and job satisfaction: A study of academic professionals in higher education sector. *International Journal of Learning and Change*, *11*(2), 129–144.

Yadav, R., & Khanna, A., & Chenab. (2022). Quality of work life, emotional and physical well-being of police personnel in India. *International Journal of Police Science & Management*, *24*(1), 89–99.

Yuile, C., Chang, A., Gudmundsson, A., & Sawang, S. (2012). The role of life friendly policies on employees' work-life balance. *Journal of Management & Organization*, *18*(1), 53–63. doi:10.1017/S1833367200001061

Chapter 14
A Review on Diversity, Equality, and Inclusion Approach in Companies

Ayla Avci
https://orcid.org/0000-0002-1871-4090
Antalya AKEV University, Turkey & International Trade and Business, Turkey

ABSTRACT

The acceleration of globalization in the world as a result of the development of technology and transportation means in the process from the development of the industrial revolution to the present day has also led to an increase in international labor migration. Although labor migration is among the most criticized issues, it is actually an important criterion in providing the workforce to meet the change needs of companies in the process called the new normal after the COVİD-19 pandemic. Undoubtedly, different ideas and talents coming from the workforce from different countries come to the fore in the success of multinational companies that have increased in recent years. Under the title of diversity, equality, and inclusiveness practice, senior managers in companies should adopt the corporate culture that gathers employees of different races, languages, colors, religions, and beliefs under one roof and pay attention to ensuring equal rights.

INTRODUCTION

The covid-19 pandemic has had a unique impact on business and global economies. Along with epidemic international migration has increased as a result of the decrease in income due to workplace closure measures. Immigrants who have to work in temporary, insecure and bad conditions cause negativities in societies and economies (ilo.org, 2021). Today, especially in 2021 and beyond, many companies are trying to allocate and increase resources by paying more attention to the issues of diversity, equality and inclusion, which have a significant impact on their strategies (Romansky, 2021). With the onset of the coronavirus pandemic in the US in March 2020, more than 40 million Americans have applied for unemployment protection. The unemployment rate for whites in the USA has reduced from %14.2 to

DOI: 10.4018/978-1-6684-6745-9.ch014

% 12.4. Unemployment of black workers rose from % 16.7 to % 16.8. Women workers were also disproportionately affected in areas such as the hospitality sector that were most affected (Stevens, 2020). With the complexity brought by the Covid-19 pandemic to business life, the most important change has been the increasing pressure to prevent diversity, equality and inclusion in the workplace (Stahl, 2021). Now, companies have set their targets in his direction by paying more attention to the issues related to diversity, equality and inclusion.

Barriers to implementing diversity, equality and inclusion in institutions are overwhelming. Especially in SMEs, it difficult to create a perspective that all employees adopt and intersect in the workplace (Contini & Samardzic, 2021). However, the projects and innovations created as a result of the synergy created by the coming together of different talents of the institutions provide profit.

The reason why the issue of inequality and diversity in the workplace has been one of the most discussed topics in recent years is the cultural differences in multinational companies brought by globalization. It is an priority issue to adopt inclusive practices for employees in companies for inequality and diversity for problems arising from cultural adaptation and communuication difficulties.

DIVERSITY, EQUALITY, AND INCLUSION CONCEPTS

Diversity emerges with the participation of a group of people. Diversity in institutions means versatility with demographic characteristics such as age, ethnicity and disciplines (Bock, 2022). In the organizational literature, diversity has been used to describe the compositions of groups or workforces in businesses (Roberson, 2004:5). Employees are more flexible towards organizational changes when they perceive the existence of diversity, fair behavior and an environment of appreciation in the workplace (Chaudhry, 2021:20).

Although there are many changes all over the world and in companies the equality debate still maintains its place on the agenda (Frazer, 2021). The most widely known insidious phenomenon in affecting organizations is known as discrimination (Oswick & Noon, 2014:25).

Each employee in the institutions contributes with different perspectives, beliefs and thoughts about the business challenges or new business opportunities that are tried to be resisted by the employers. By defining the benefits brought by these differences in their institutions, employers practices of respecting and valuing each individual in order to create a better company culture with the experience of the employees are explained as inclusiveness. Inclusiveness in organizations is organizational efforts to make employees from different backgrounds feel welcomed and treated equally and fairly. Employees of institutions with an inclusive organizational culture have a high level of work commitment and motivation. Due to the existence of inclusiveness in institutions, employees feel valuable and important and when they focus on the success of the company, they work at full capacity with the awareness that their institutions are a part of the mission and core company values (Jouany & Martic, 2020).

DIVERSITY, EQUALITY, AND INCLUSION APPROACH IN COMPANIES

Diversity, and equality have been shaped by the effects of different cultures and beliefs with the emergence of globalization (Nyagadza, 2022:13). There are many advantages to diversity, equality and inclusion in institutions. There are many advantages to diversity, equality and inclusion in institutions. The benefits

Figure 1. Distribution of Institutional Employees And Race, Ethnicity

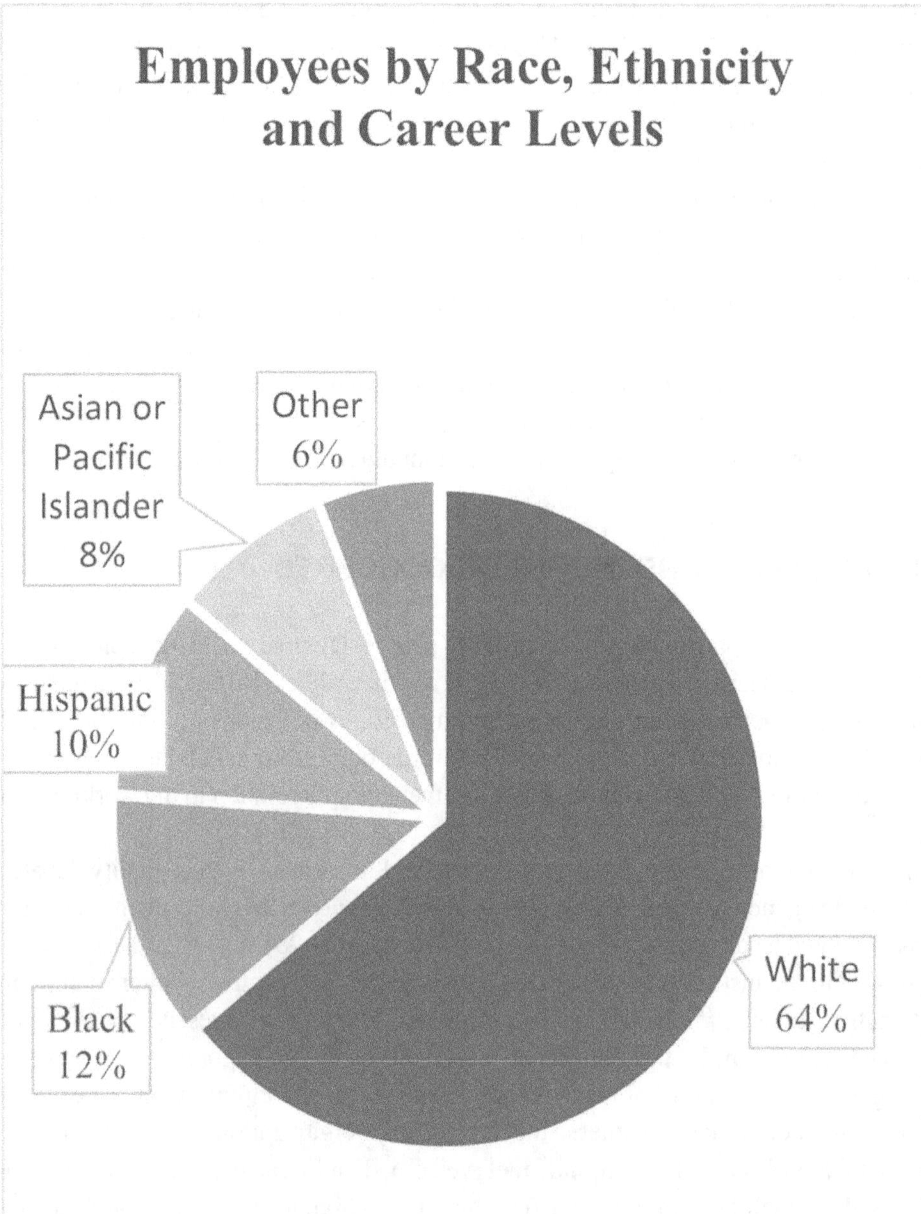

of teambuilding by individuals who provide different education, experience, knowledge, and skills are many. Diversity, equity, and inclusion are important criteria for effective problem-solving processes in addressing organizational issues, developing products for realistic needs (Bock, 2022). Effective diversity, equity, and inclusion succeeds through the participatory, cohesive and team-oriented approaches of institutions (Nyagadza, 2022:13).

Figure 1 and 2 show the data included in Mercer's research. In the research, it was determined that % 64 of the support personnel and operations level employees were white employees. Again it was deter-

Figure 2. Distribution of Female Managers
Source: Stevens, 2020. Mercer, cnbc.com.

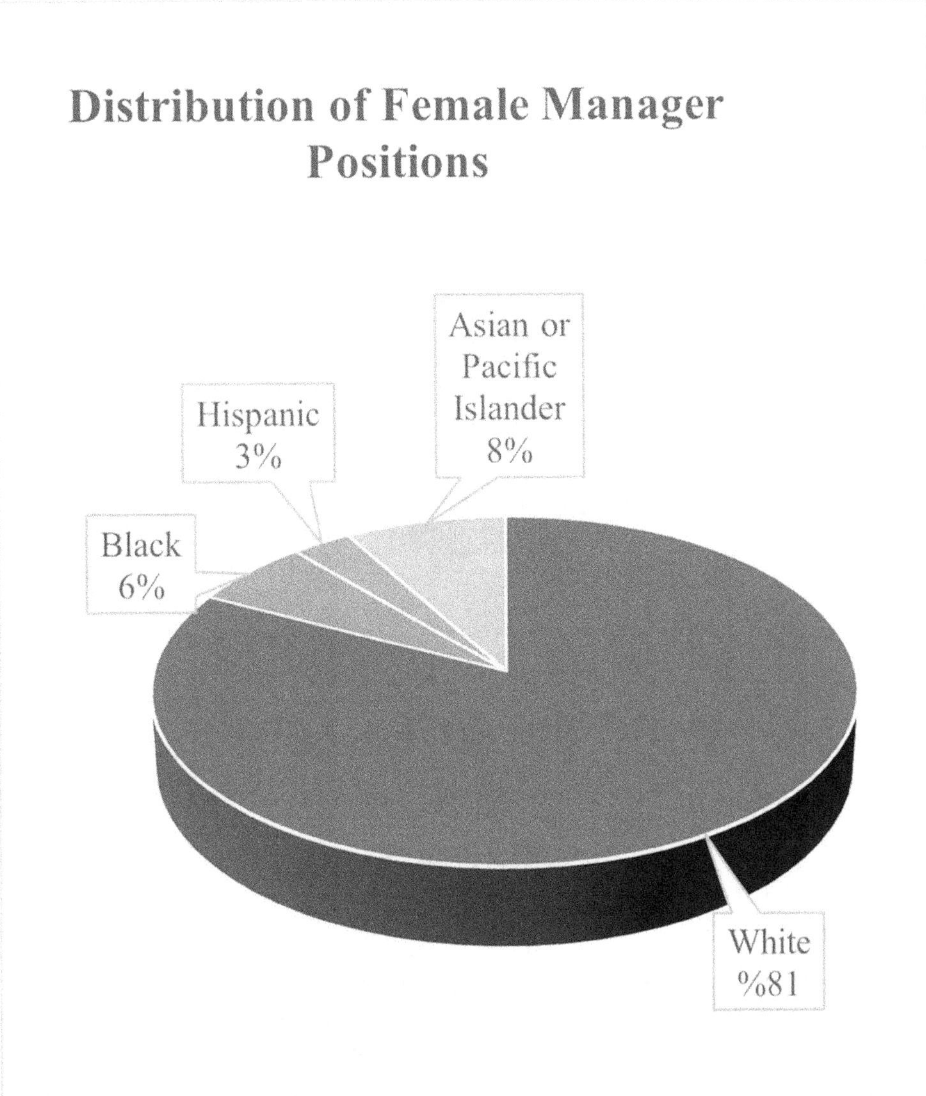

mined that %85 of employees in managerial positions were white employees. In the research, women in managerial positions consist of white employees with a ratio of % 81. This proportion is represented by % 6 black, % 3 Hispanic, and % 8, Asian and Pacific female executives. After the Covid-19 epidemic, according to the data of the International Labor Organization (ILO), international migrant workers are increasing in countries with high incomes. It is stated that 63.8 million of the 169 million international migrant workers work in Europe and Central Asia, 43.3 million in the Americas, 24 million in the Arab-Asia-Pacific region, and 13.7 million in Africa (Figure 3). Of these, 99 million are male workers and approximately 70 million are female workers. Therefore, women workers who have to migrate with their families have difficulty in balancing their work and life in the countries they migrate to due to social and economic difficulties as well as discrimination (www.ilo.org/ankara).

Figure 3. Distribution of International Migrant Worker. Source: ilo.org.

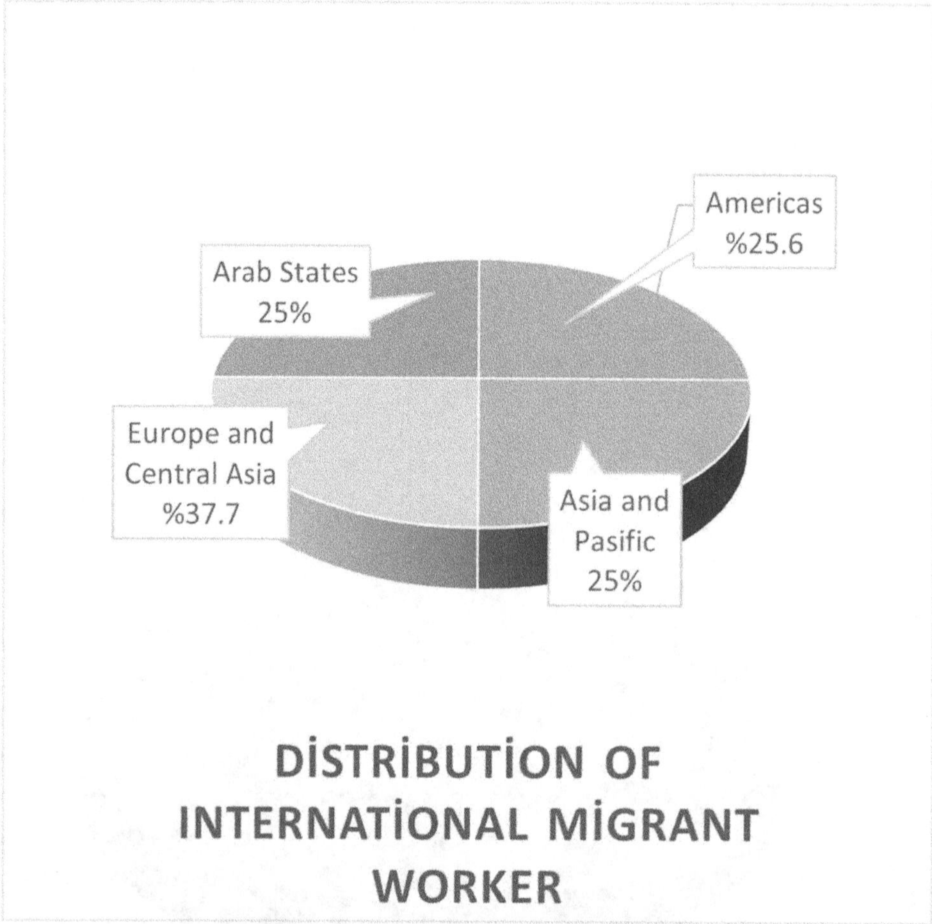

Increasing the level of institutional diversity, equality and inclusion is a factor that positively affects the realization of proactive actions, providing a productive and flexible working environment and increasing the quality of the work done (Karakhan, 2021). Discovering the qualities for diversity and inclusion in organizations based on diversity and knowing what the relationship between organizational variables are is an important factor (Roberson, 2004:27). According to Chaudhry et al (2021), diversity and inclusion practices in the workplace have a significant contribution to providing an innovative environment. It has benefits such as diversity and equality in the workplace, increasing financial performance, retention by providing employee loyalty (figure 4). An inclusive work environment plays an important role as it helps to achieve and encourage the best performances (Ayyala, Artunduaga, Morin, & Coley, 2022).

It is necessary to be conscious of social identities in order for institutions to create an inclusive workforce culture that is open to diversity. Instead of assuming that everyone is the same or thinking that everyone should be the same, trying to understand how the differences are is an important issue in achieving organizational success (Wong, 2019:28). In this context, it would be meaningful for managers o use their basic knowledge and abilities as a resource within the organization instead of considering individuals with different characteristics as problems (Çoban, 2022).

Figure 4. The Benefits of Diversity and Equality in The Workplace.
Source: Jouany and Martic (2020).

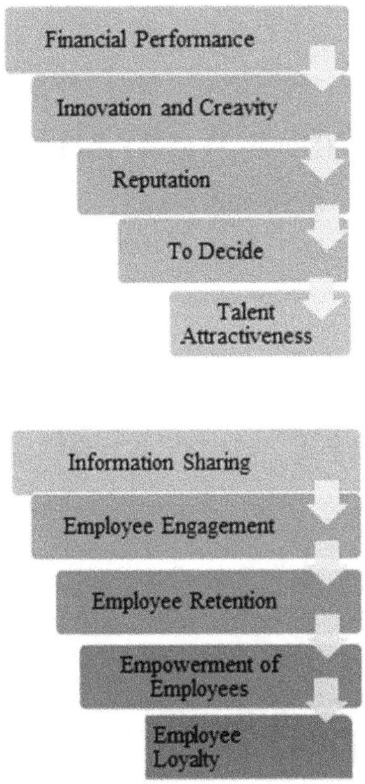

With the emergence of globalization, different beliefs and cultures have gained importance within the scope of diversity equality. Leaders of organizations, corporate human resources managers begun to questions how diversity and equality issues affect their companies (Nyagadza, Gwiza, & Hove, 2022:13). In recent years, racism and cultural oppresssion have become a threat to many minorities. Cultural diversity such as cultural values, traditions, national origin is racism classification (Gill, McNally, & Berman, 2018).

In order to understand the cause of the problem and bring a solution, organizations go through the following stages, respectively. Figure 5. It is known that racism is prevalent in the workplace. The first step can be taken by considering people's beliefs and prejudices. Organizations are required to include racist-free policies or pro-diversity statements (Livingston, 2020).

CONCLUSION

Financial crises, which have been experienced frequently in all countries of the world in the past years, have caused the deterioration of economic structures. The covid-19 pandemic, which is the most affecting of these crises, has had the most shocking effect on the economies of countries in the global sense. In this period, labor migration from underdeveloped countries to developed countries increased.

Figure 5. A Road Map for Racial Equity.
Source: Livingston (2020).

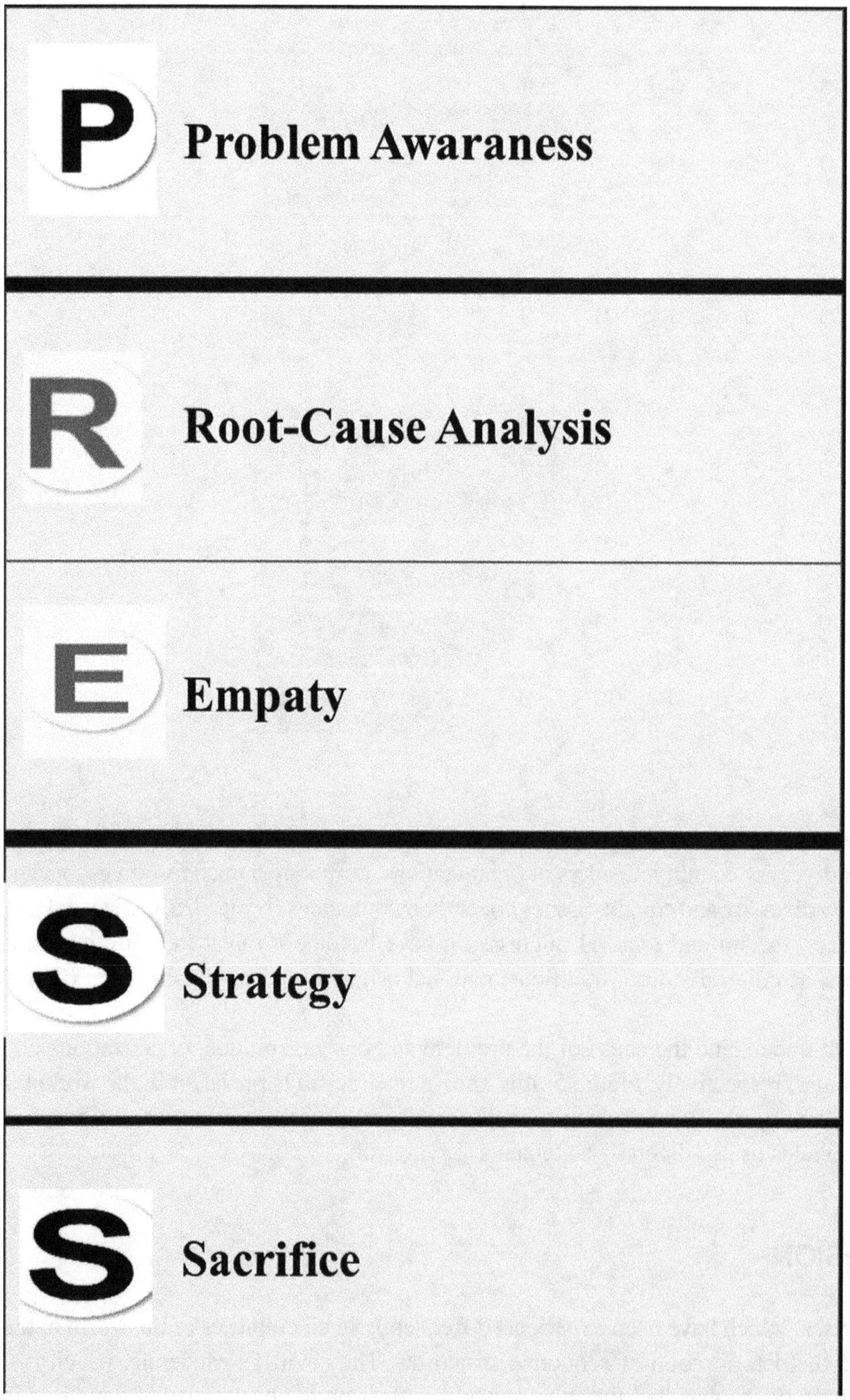

Due to these migrations, qualified labor migration contributes to the qualified workforce of countries and companies in terms of economies and therefore companies, on the other hand, it causes problems due to the socio-economic problems experienced by unskilled workers and the increase in the number of unemployment in the countries. At the beginning of these problems is the adaptation and cultural adaptation problem seen in companies. It is necessary to interpret and apply concepts such as diversity, equality and inclusiveness in companies in order to transform employees with different cultural structures into contribution and advantage to creativity and innovation.

Problems such as unemployment and poverty, which have increased due to the economic crises in recent years, fuel hostility towards non-native individuals in western societies. Therefore, when addressing discrimination issues, economic-based problems should not be ignored. In cases where discrimination is encountered, disclosing the events and raising awareness will be instrumental in the collective struggle against discrimination (Çevik, 2022). Therefore, instead of talking about the importance of diversity, inclusion and equality principles these statements should be revealed through effective actions (Chantarat, Rogers, Mitchell, & Ko, 2022).

There are still many gaps in diversity, equality and inclusion policies and practices in workplaces and institutions today (Contini & Samardzic, 2021). Diversity, equality and inclusion issues must become a priority in companies. Company managers and leaders need to reflect these issues by emphasizing their supportive attitudes. If it is insufficient support should be obtained from an expert in adapting to he change (Bağcan, 2021:147). Competencies to have in diversity management include developmental advantages such as relationship management and leadership skills, cultural intelligence analytical skills, flexibility and foreign language (Vatansever, Çalışkan, & Işık, 2015). Institutions and universities are also responsible for addressing the socio-economic inequalities that affect those with minority identities in their communities. In recent years, this responsibility has gained more importance (Parks, 2022). Societies and institutions need to accept that the world is a whole made up of differences and especially confront the issue of racial inequality (Kraus, 2022).

Although they have the necessary knowledge and equipment in terms of working conditions in companies, there are obstacles to women's seniority and promotion. Institutions and employers should take care to provide convenience in terms of employment so that women are more involved in business life (Bock, 2022).

Many businesses today operate in a global context. Therefore, companies must quickly adapt to this dynamic. To operate effectively, business leaders must provide competitive advantage by creating diverse, equitable and inclusive work environments It must accurately encode, understand and apply the benefits of these topics corporate values (Millo, Brown, & Harrington, 2021).

With globalization, the countries of the world have become a common market. Thanks to new technologies, communication between people has increased and distances have become closer. According to Erdur (2020), it was found that HR managers within the companies with domestic capital could not create a framework within the scope of diversity management in mental understanding, while the limited level of HR managers stated that diversity management and equality of opportunity are interconnected issues. Therefore, tastes and ideas have become common. For this reason, it attaches importance to the principles of diversity, equality and inclusiveness, which market he most contribution to the creation of synergy by bringing together different ideas with the same thought in companies In the recruitment processes in companies, the job evaluation of the individuals with different cultural structures of the human resources units will be beneficial in terms of the continuity of the enterprises.

REFERENCES

Ankara, I. L. O. (2021). *Küresel İşgücü Göçü 5 milyon Arttı*. https://www.ilo.org/ankara/areas-of-work/migration/WCMS_809374/lang--tr/index.htm

Ayyala, S. R., Artunduaga, M., Morin, C. E., & Coley, D. B. (2022). Leveraging Diversity, Equity And Inclusion For Promoting Wellness In The Radiology Workplace. *Pediatric Radiology, 52*(9), 1724–1729. doi:10.100700247-022-05292-z PMID:35088132

Bağcan, M. (2021). Ekonomi, Politik Ve Stratejik Yönetim Çerçevesinde Stratejik Halkla İlişkiler: Coca-Cola Afrika'ya İnanmak İçin Bir Milyar Neden Kampanyası Analizi. *İşletme Ve İktisadi Bilimler Araştırmaları*, 130.

Bock, C. (2022). Diversity, Equality, and Inclusion In Our Professions: A Thin and Leaky Pipeline. *The Electrochemical Society Interface, 31*(1), 31–41. doi:10.1149/2.F08221IF

Çevik, D. D. (2022). Çalışma Yaşamında Ayrımcılığın İzini Sürerken: Hollanda 'da Meslek Sahibi Türkiye Kökenliler [Tracing Discrimination at Work: Professionals from the Netherlands with Turkish Origin]. *Anadolu Üniversitesi İktisadi Ve İdari Bilimler Fakültesi, 23*(3).

Chantarat, T., Rogers, B. T., Mitchell, C. R., & Ko, J. M. (2022). Perceptions of Workplace Climate And Diversity, Equity And Inclusion Within Health Services And Policy Research. *Health Services Research.* DOI: doi:10.1111/1475-6773.14032

Chaudhry, I. S., Paquibut, Y. R. & Tunio, N. M. (2021). Do Workforce Diversity, Inclusion Practices & Organizational Charactersitics Contribute To Organizational Innovation? Evidence From The U. A. E. *Cogent Business & Management, 8*(1). doi:10.1080/23311975.2021.1947549

Çoban, R. (2022). Havayolu İşletmelerinde Farklılıkların Yönetimi Üzerine Bir Araştırma [A Study on the Management of Diversity in Airline Businesses]. 7th *International Entrepreneurship Social Sciences Congress, Proceeding Book,* 515.

Contini, M., & Samardzic, T. (2021). *Diversity, Equality And Inclusion Policies In Canadian Small-to-Medium Sized Enterprises Within Science, Tech, Engineering And Skilled Trades*. atrium.lib.uoguelph.ca

Erdur, D. A. (2020). İnsan Kaynakları Yöneticilerinin Gözünden Çeşitlilik, Kapsayıcılık ve Dışlayıcılık [Diversity, Inclusion and Exclusion from the Perspective of Human Resources Managers]. *Atatürk Üniversitesi İktisadi İdari Bilimler Dergisi. Journal of Economics And Administrative Sciences, 34*(1), 214–234.

Frazer, A., Frazer, A. N. B., & Frazer, F. G. (2021). Equity. In *The New Workplace: The Role of Diversity, Equality and Inclusion*. doi:10.2139srn.3864457

Gill, G. K., Mcnally, M. J., & Berman, V. (2018). Effective Diversity, Equity And Inclusion Practices. *Healthcare Management Forum, 31*(5), 196–199. doi:10.1177/0840470418773785 PMID:30114938

ILO. (2021). ILO Global Estimates on International Migrant Workers- Result and Methodology (3rd ed.). International Labor Office.

Jouany, V., & Martic, K. (2020). *Diversity and Inclusion Best Practices to Focus on in 2022.* https://haiilo.com/blog/diversity-and-inclusion-best-practices-focus-on-in-2020/

Karakhan, A. A., Gambatase, A. J., Simmons, R. D., & Al-Bayati, J. A. (2021). Identifying Pertinent Indicators for Assessing And Fostering Diversity, Equality And Inclusion of The Construction Workforce. *Journal of Management Engineering, 37*(2), 2. doi:10.1061/(ASCE)ME.1943-5479.0000885

Kraus, W. M., Torrez, B., & Hollie, L. (2022). How Narratives of Radical Progress Create Barriers to Diversity, Eqality And Inclusion In Organizations. *Current Opinion in Psychology, 43*, 108–113. doi:10.1016/j.copsyc.2021.06.022 PMID:34340144

Livinston, R. (2020, Sept.). How to Promote racial Equity In The Workplace. *Harvard Business Review.*

Millo, V., Brown, A., & Harrington, B. (2021). Addressing Race. In *The Workplace: Advancing Diversity, Equity And Inclusion. Boston College Center For Work & Family: Executive Briefing Series, UMB Digital Archive.* University of Maryland Baltimore.

Nyagadza, B., Gwiza, A., & Hove, K. P. (2022). Workplace Diversity, Equality And Inclusivity in Zimbabwean Labour Market. *Social Sciences, 8.* Advance online publication. doi:10.1080/23311886.2022.2033456

Oswick, C., & Noon, M. (2014). Discourses of diversity, equality and inclusion: Trenchant Formulations or transient fashions? *British Journal of Management, 25*(1), 23–39. doi:10.1111/j.1467-8551.2012.00830.x

Parks, M. A., Scott, G., Seijo, C., & Keys, T. (2022). *Anchored or Detached? A Student Commentary on Equity.* Diversity And Inclusion At Urban Institutions, Coalitions of Urban And Metropolitan Universities. doi:10.18060/26300

Roberson, M. Q. (2004). *Disentangling The Meanings of Diversity And Inclusion.* Center for Advanced Human Resource Studies, Working Paper 04-05. CAHRS/Cornel University.

Romansky, L., Garrod, M., Brown, K., & Deo, K. (2021). Organizational Culture How to Measure Inclusion in Workplace. *Harvard Business Review*, 27.

Stahl, A. (2021). *What's To Come In 2021 For Diversity, Equity And Inclusion In The Workplace.* https://www.forbes.com/sites/ashleystahl/2021/04/14/whats-to-come-in-2021-for-diversity-equity-and-inclusion-in-the-workplace/?sh=25efbbf57f26

Stevens, P. (2020). *Companies are making bold promises about greater diversity, but there's a long way to go.* https://www.cnbc.com/2020/06/11/companies-are-making-bold-promises-about-greater-diversity-theres-a-long-way-to-go.html

Vatansever, Ç., Çalışkan, S. & Işık, İ. (2015). Bir Dünya Şirketinin Türkiye'deki Çalışanlarına göre Çeşitliliklerin Yönetimi: Gömülü Kuram Analiziyle Modelleme [Diversity Management by Employees of a World Company in Turkey: Modeling with Embedded Theory Analysis]. *Yönetim Araştırmaları Dergisi, 2*(1-2), 29-61.

Wong, C. (2019). Changing Organizational From Embedded Bias to Equity And Inclusion. *Professional Safety Journal,* 26-30.

Compilation of References

Abdelkafi, N., & Pero, M. (2018). Supply Chain Innovation-Driven Business Models: Exploratory Analysis and Implications For Management. *Business Process Management Journal, 24*(2), 589–608. doi:10.1108/BPMJ-05-2016-0109

Accenture. (2019). *How we created a technology solution to enable Accenture's reimagined performance management approach.* WordPressBlog. https://www.accenture.com/us-en/blogs/how-accenture-does-it/how-we-created-a-technology-solution-to-enable-accentures-re imagined-performance-management-approach

Adel, A. (2022). Future of industry 5.0 in society: Human-centric solutions, challenges and prospective research areas. *Journal of Cloud Computing, 11*(1), 40. doi:10.118613677-022-00314-5 PMID:36101900

Agarwala, T., Arizkuren-Eleta, A., Del Castillo, E., Muñiz-Ferrer, M., & Gartzia, L. (2014). Influence of managerial support on work-life conflict and organizational commitment: An international comparison for India, Peru and Spain. *International Journal of Human Resource Management, 25*(10), 1460–1483. doi:10.1080/09585192.2013.870315

Ahmed, H., Allaf, M., & Elghazaly, H. (2020). COVID-19 and medical education. *The Lancet. Infectious Diseases, 20*(7), 777–778. doi:10.1016/S1473-3099(20)30226-7 PMID:32213335

Akan Özkök, G., & Yardımcı Coşkun, İ. (2019). Knowledge Management In The Supply Chain And Effects Of Information Technologies And An Implementation In The Airline Company. *Proceedings of The International Congress On Business And Marketing.*

Akca, M., & Küçükoğlu, T. M. (2021). *Digital Transformation and Aviation Sector, Sectoral Analysis of Digital Transformation,* Nobel Academic Publication.

Aksoy, S. (2017). *Changing Technologies and Industry 4.0: An Introduction to Understand Industry 4.0.* Social Research Foundation Contribution Technology.

Akundi, A., Euresti, D., Luna, S., Ankobiah, W., Lopes, A., & Edinbarough, I. (2022). State of Industry 5.0—Analysis and Identification of Current Research Trends. *Applied System Innovation, 5*(1), 27. doi:10.3390/asi5010027

Alacadağlı, E. (2019). Information Age, Digitalization And Turkish Health System. *Electronic Turkish Studies, 14*(2), 67–86.

Alçin, S. (2016). A New Theme For Production: Industry 4.0. *Journal Of Life Economics, 3*(2), 19–30.

Alessio, P., & Giustiniano, L. (2018). *Industry 4.0 and the emerging challenges to leadership.* Academic Press.

Aliger Augmented Reality. (n.d.). *Mixed Reality Glasses: work more efficiently thanks to AR visualisation.* Retrieved from https://alegerglobal.com/en/augmented-reality/smart-glasses/mixed-reality-glasses/

Altemeyer, B. (2019). Making the business case for AI in HR: Two case studies. *Strategic HR Review, 18*(2), 66–70. doi:10.1108/SHR-12-2018-0101

Altexsoft. (2019). *How to Successfully Implement HR Analytics and People Analytics in a Company*. https://www.altexsoft.com/blog/how-to-implement-hr-analytics/

Altynpara, E. (2021). *Integrating The Industrial Internet Of Things: The Benefits And Challenges*. Retrieved from https://www.forbes.com/sites/forbestechcouncil/2021/07/01/integrating-the-industrial-internet-of-things-the-benefits-and-challenges/?sh=41d9a95306f3

Amado, A., Cortez, P., Rita, P., & Moro, S. (2018). Research trends on Big Data in Marketing: A text mining and topic modeling based literature analysis. *European Research on Management and Business Economics, 24*(1), 1–7. doi:10.1016/j.iedeen.2017.06.002

Ancarani, A., Di Mauro, C., & Mascali, F. (2019). Backshoring strategy and the adoption of Industry 4.0: Evidence from Europe. *Journal of World Business, 54*(4), 360-371. doi:10.1016/j.jwb.2019.04.003

Ankara, I. L. O. (2021). *Küresel İşgücü Göçü 5 milyon Arttı*. https://www.ilo.org/ankara/areas-of-work/migration/WCMS_809374/lang--tr/index.htm

Ankum, M. (2022). People Analytics: 5 Real Case Studies. *Effectory*. https://www.effectory.com/knowledge/people-analytics-5-real-case-studies/

Anscombe, T. (2020, March 16). *COVID-19 and the shift to remote work.* We Lives Security. https://www.welivesecurity.com/2020/03/16/covid19-forced-workplace-exodus/

Arlbjørn, J. S., De Haas, H., & Munksgaard, K. B. (2011). Exploring Supply Chain Innovation. *Logistics Research, 3*(1), 3–18. doi:10.100712159-010-0044-3

Arlbjørn, J. S., & Paulraj, A. (2013). Special Topic Forum On Innovation in Business Networks From A Supply Chain Perspective: Current Status And Opportunities For Future Research. *The Journal of Supply Chain Management, 49*(4), 3–11. doi:10.1111/jscm.12034

Arnold, C., Kiel, D., & Voigt, K. I. (2016). How the Industrial Internet of Things Changes Business Models In Different Manufacturing Industries. *International Journal of Innovation Management, 20*(08), 1–20. doi:10.1142/S1363919616400156

Arslan, A., Ruman, A. N., & Tarba, S.Y. (2021). Human dynamics of automation and digitalisation of economies: discussion on the challenges and opportunities. In The Palgrave Handbook of Corporate Sustainability in the Digital Era. Palgrave Macmillan.

Arslan, A., Cooper, C., Khan, Z., Golgeci, I., & Ali, I. (2022). Artificial intelligence and human workers interaction at team level: A conceptual assessment of the challenges and potential HRM strategies. *International Journal of Manpower, 43*(1), 75–88. doi:10.1108/IJM-01-2021-0052

Ashford, S. J., Lee, C., & Bobko, P. (1989). Content, Cause, and Consequences of Job Insecurity: A Theory-Based Measure and Substantive Test. *Academy of Management Journal, 32*(4), 803–829. doi:10.2307/256569

Aslam, F., Aimin, W., Li, M., & Ur Rehman, K. (2020). Innovation in the era of IoT and industry 5.0: Absolute innovation management (AIM) framework. *Information (Basel), 11*(2), 124. doi:10.3390/info11020124

Atan, S. (2020). *Comparison of the Cloud Computing and the Traditional Alternatives: Advantages, Risks and Advices for Migration*. Afyon Kocatepe University Journal of Social Sciences.

Ayyala, S. R., Artunduaga, M., Morin, C. E., & Coley, D. B. (2022). Leveraging Diversity, Equity And Inclusion For Promoting Wellness In The Radiology Workplace. *Pediatric Radiology, 52*(9), 1724–1729. doi:10.100700247-022-05292-z PMID:35088132

Azizi, M. R., Atlasi, R., Ziapour, A., Abbas, J., & Naemi, R. (2021). Innovative human resource management strategies during the COVID-19 pandemic: A systematic narrative review approach. *Heliyon, 7*(6), e07233. Advance online publication. doi:10.1016/j.heliyon.2021.e07233 PMID:34124399

Bäck-Wiklund, M., Van der Lippe, T., Den Dulk, L., & Doorne-Huiskes, A. (2011). Quality of life and work in Europe: Theory, practice and policy. In Quality of Life and Work in Europe: Theory, Practice and Policy. Palgrave Macmillan. doi:10.1057/9780230299443

Baer, T. (2019). Bias in Human Decision-Making. *Understand, Manage, and Prevent Algorithmic Bias*, 9–20. doi:10.1007/978-1-4842-4885-0_2

Bağcan, M. (2021). Ekonomi, Politik Ve Stratejik Yönetim Çerçevesinde Stratejik Halkla İlişkiler: Coca-Cola Afrika'ya İnanmak İçin Bir Milyar Neden Kampanyası Analizi. *İşletme Ve İktisadi Bilimler Araştırmaları*, 130.

Bakırcı, A., & Kocabıyık Çaşkurlu, Ş. (2020). Digitalized World Dynamics and The New Perspective of Vocational Education in Turkey. 9. *International Vocational Schools Symposium Book*, 41-42.

Bakker, K. (2017). *Role Overload and Job Stress: The Role of Perceived Organizational Support*. Tilburg University.

Balducci, B., & Marinova, D. (2018). Unstructured data in marketing. *Journal of the Academy of Marketing Science, 46*(4), 557–590. doi:10.100711747-018-0581-x

Baltes, B. B., Briggs, T. E., Huff, J. W., Wright, J. A., & Neuman, G. A. (1999). Flexible and Compressed Workweek Schedules: A Meta-Analysis of Their Effects on Work-Related Criteria Boris. *The Journal of Applied Psychology, 84*(4), 496–513. doi:10.1037/0021-9010.84.4.496

Baltezarevic, V., Baltezarevic, R., & Jovanovic, D. (2016). *Challenges Of Modern Leadership*. Academic Press.

Baptiste, N. R. (2008). Tightening the link between employee wellbeing at work and performance: A new dimension for HRM. *Management Decision, 46*(2), 284–309. doi:10.1108/00251740810854168

Baral, R., & Bhargava, S. (2010). Work-family enrichment as a mediator between organizational interventions for work-life balance and job outcomes. *Journal of Managerial Psychology, 25*(3), 274–300. doi:10.1108/02683941011023749

Barbar, K., Choughri, R., & Soubjaki, M. (2019). Training and Development Strategy—Private Sector Case Study in Lebanon. *Journal of Management and Strategy, 10*(3), 27–36. doi:10.5430/jms.v10n3p27

Bartoszko, A. (2020). Accelerating Curve of Anxiousness. *Journal of Extreme Anthropology, 4*(1), E7–E17. doi:10.5617/jea.7861

Baruch, Y. (2000). Baruch-2000-New_Technology,_Work_and_Employment Qualis A1 muito importante. *New Technology. Work and Employment, 15*(1), 34–49. doi:10.1111/1468-005X.00063

Baruch, Y., & Holtom, B. C. (2008). Survey response rate levels and trends in organizational research. *Human Relations, 61*(8), 1139–1160. doi:10.1177/0018726708094863

Bass, B. M. (2000). The future of leadership in learning organizations. *The Journal of Leadership Studies, 7*(3), 18–40. doi:10.1177/107179190000700302

Basu, D. S. (2019, February 27). Work-life: 60% working Indians rate work-life balance from average to terrible: Monster.com survey. *ET Bureau*. https://economictimes.indiatimes.com/magazines/panache/60-working-indians-rate-work-life-balance-from-average-to-terribl e-monster-com-survey/articleshow/68183578.cms?from=mdr

Batıbay, B. (2022). Electrical And Electronic Engineers Industry 4.0 Determining Awareness Levels. *Rahva Journal of Technical and Social Studies*, 131.

Battini, D., Berti, N., Finco, S., Zennaro, I., & Das, A. (2022). Towards industry 5.0: A multi-objective job rotation model for an inclusive workforce. *International Journal of Production Economics*, *250*, 108619. doi:10.1016/j.ijpe.2022.108619

Batty, M. (2018). Digital Twins. *Environment and Planning. B, Urban Analytics and City Science*, *45*(5), 817–820. doi:10.1177/2399808318796416

Bauer, W., Schuler, S., Hornung, T., & Decker, J. (2019). Development of a procedure model for human-centered industry 4.0 projects. *Procedia Manufacturing*, *39*, 877–885. doi:10.1016/j.promfg.2020.01.402

Beauregard, T. A., & Henry, L. C. (2009). Making the link between work-life balance practices and organizational performance. *Human Resource Management Review*, *19*(1), 9–22. doi:10.1016/j.hrmr.2008.09.001

Beer, M., Spector, B., Lawrence, P. R., Quinn Mills, D., & Walton, R. E. (1984). *Managing Human Assets*. The Free Press.

Bendick, M. Jr, & Nunes, A. P. (2013). Developing the research basis for controlling bias in hiring. *The Journal of Social Issues*, *68*, 238–262.

Bennis, W., & Nanus, B. (1985). *The strategies for taking charge*. Harper. Row.

Berg-Beckhoff, G., Nielsen, G., & Ladekjær Larsen, E. (2017). Use of information communication technology and stress, burnout, and mental health in older, middle-aged, and younger workers—Results from a systematic review. *International Journal of Occupational and Environmental Health*, *23*(2), 160–171. doi:10.1080/10773525.2018.1436015 PMID:29460697

Berhil, S., Benlahmar, H., & Labani, N. (2020). A review paper on artificial intelligence at the service of human resources management. *Indonesian Journal of Electrical Engineering and Computer Science*, *18*(1), 32–40. doi:10.11591/ijeecs.v18.i1.pp32-40

Bhanumathi P. (2020). Unconscious Human Bias in HR Functions and Mitigation using Artificial Intelligence. *Journal of Arts, Humanities and Social Sciences, 7*(28).

Bhatt, P. (2022). AI adoption in the hiring process – important criteria and extent of AI adoption. *Foresight*. Advance online publication. doi:10.1108/FS-07-2021-0144

Bhatt, P., & Muduli, A. (2022). Artificial intelligence in learning and development: a systematic literature review. In *European Journal of Training and Development*. Emerald Group Holdings Ltd. doi:10.1108/EJTD-09-2021-0143

Bhave, D. P., Teo, L. H., & Dalal, R. S. (2020). Privacy at work: A review and a research agenda for a contested terrain. *Journal of Management*, *46*(1), 127–164. doi:10.1177/0149206319878254

Biriowu, C. S., & Kalio, N. L. (2020). Talent Analytics and Employee Retention in Nigeria Organizations. *International Journal of Human Resources Management, 9*(3), 1.12.

Birkel, H., & Müller, J. M. (2021). Potentials of industry 4.0 for supply chain management within the triple bottom line of sustainability–A systematic literature review. *Journal of Cleaner Production*, *289*, 125612. doi:10.1016/j.jclepro.2020.125612

Bishop, P. (2000). *Synchronicity and intellectual intuition in Kant, Swedenborg, and Jung*. The Edwin Mellen Press.

Biswas, S. (2019). *The Beginner's Guide to AI in HR*. Retrieved from https://www.hrtechnologist.com/articles/digital-transformation/the-beginners-guide-to-ai-in-hr/

Black, S. L., Washington, M. L., & Schmidt, G. B. (2016). *How to stay current in social media to be competitive in recruitment and selection. Social Media in Employee Selection and Recruitment*. Springer.

Blundell, R., Dearden, L., & Meghir, C. (1996). *The determinants and effects of work-related training in Britain*. doi:10.1920/re.ifs.1996.0050

Bock, C. (2022). Diversity, Equality, and Inclusion In Our Professions: A Thin and Leaky Pipeline. *The Electrochemical Society Interface*, *31*(1), 31–41. doi:10.1149/2.F08221IF

Bondarouk, T., Harms, R., & Lepak, D. (2017). Does e-HRM lead to better HRM service? *International Journal of Human Resource Management*, *28*(9), 1332–1362. doi:10.1080/09585192.2015.1118139

Borkakoty, K. (2017). *HR Analytics For Employee Engagement Strategy and More*. https://medium.com/@mynab247/hr-analytics-for-employee-engagement-strategy-and-more-659dd236d234

Bornet, P. (2022). *The Symbiosis of People and Technology*. Forbes Technology Council. Retrieve from https://www.forbes.com/sites/ forbes techcouncil /2022 /01/12 /the- symbiosis- of- people-and -technology /?sh= 42433dd71 fe4

Braun, V., & Clarke, V. (2006). Using thematic analysis in psychology. *Qualitative Research in Psychology*, *3*(2), 77–101. doi:10.1191/1478088706qp063oa

Breque, M., De Nul, L., & Petridis, A. (2021). *Industry 5.0: Towards a sustainable, human-centric and resilient European industry*. Publications Office. https://data.europa.eu/doi/10.2777/308407

Breque, M., Nul, L. de, & Petridis, A. (2021). Industry 5.0 Towards a sustainable human centric and resilient European Industry. doi:10.27777/308407

Bresman, H. (2015, February 23). *What Millennials Want from Work, Charted Across the World*. HBR. https://hbr.org/2015/02/what-millennials-want-from-work-charted-across-the-world

Brin, W. D. (2019, March 22). *Employers Embrace Artificial Intelligence for HR*. https://www.shrm.org/resourcesandtools/hr-topics/global-hr/pages/employers-embrace-artificial-intelligence-for-hr.aspx

Broadbridge, A. (2009). Sacrificing personal or professional life? A gender perspective on the accounts of retail managers. *International Review of Retail, Distribution and Consumer Research*, *19*(3), 289–311. doi:10.1080/09593960903234226

Brown, A. (2021). Artificial Intelligence Is Transforming Biotechnology, Especially When It Comes to Innovations In Nitric Oxide. *Forbes*. Retrieved on 02/09/2022 https://www.forbes.com/sites/anniebrown/2021/10/25/artificial-intelligence-is-transforming-biotechnology-especially-when-it-comes-to-innovations-in-nitric-oxide/?sh=d3e27797f00b

Brown, H. R., Meister, J., Styr, C., & Pring, B. (2020, June 25). *An Evolving Profession: 21 New HR Jobs to Watch For*. https://www.cognizant.com/us/en/latest-thinking/perspectives/an-evolving-profession-21-new-hr-jobs-to-watch-for

Bruce, D. (2022). *Human Augmentation Technology and its Real-Life Applications*. KnowledgeNile. https :// www. knowledgenile. com/ blogs/ human- augmentation- technology-and -its-real -life -applications/

Brynjolfsson, E., & McAfee, A. (2012). Winning the race with ever-smarter machines. *MIT Sloan Management Review, 53*(2), 53.

Büchi, G., Cugno, M., & Castagnoli, R. (2020). Smart factory performance and Industry 4.0. *Technological Forecasting and Social Change, 150*, 119790. doi:10.1016/j.techfore.2019.119790

Buckley, P., Minette, K., Joy, D., & Michaels, J. (2004). The use of an automated employment recruiting and screening system for temporary professional employees: A case study. *Human Resource Management, 43*(2-3), 233–241. doi:10.1002/hrm.20017

Buranyi, S. (2018). Dehumanising, impenetrable, frustrating": the grim reality of job hunting in the age of AI. *The Guardian*. Retrieved from https://www.theguardian.com/inequality/2018/mar/04/dehumanis ing-impenetrable-frustratingthe-grim-reality-of-job-hunting-
in-the-age-of-ai

Business World. (2020, July 30). *88 Of Indian Workforce Prefer To Have The Flexibility Of Working From Home SAP Concur Study*. BW Online Bureau. https://www.businessworld.in/article/88-Of-Indian-Workforce-Prefer-To-Have-The-Flexibility-Of-Working-From-Home-SAP-Conc
ur-Study/30-07-2020-303132/

Cahyadi, A., & Magda, R. (2021). Digital Leadership in the Economies of the G20 Countries: A Secondary. *Research in Economics, 9*(1), 32. doi:10.3390/economies9010032

Caldarola, E. G., Modoni, G. E., & Sacco, M. (2018). Enhancing the Workforce Skills and Competences by Leveraging a Human-Centered Knowledge-Based System in the Rise of Industry 4.0. *International Journal on Advances in Intelligent Systems, 11*(3&4), 309–324.

Caldwell, C., Hayes, L. A., Bernal, P., & Karri, R. (2008). Ethical stewardship - Implications for leadership and trust. *Journal of Business Ethics, 78*(1–2), 153–164. doi:10.100710551-006-9320-1

Calvard, T. S., & Jeske, D. (2018). Developing human resource data risk management in the age of big data. *International Journal of Information Management, 43*, 159–164. doi:10.1016/j.ijinfomgt.2018.07.011

Campione, W. A. (2015). Corporate Offerings: Why Aren't Millennials Staying? *Journal of Applied Business and Economics, 17*(4), 60–75. http://t.www.na-businesspress.com/JABE/CampioneWA_Web17_4_.p
df

Canlıoğlu, G. (2008). *Transformation Society For Changing Position Of Information*. Marmara University Institute of Turkic Studies.

Cano-Kollmann, M., Hannigan, T. J., & Mudambi, R. (2018). Global innovation networks–organizations and people. *Journal of International Management, 24*(2), 87–92. doi:10.1016/j.intman.2017.09.008

Cao, S. (2021, March). Opportunities and Challenges of Marketing in the Context of Big Data. In *2021 Workshop on Algorithm and Big Data* (pp. 79-82). 10.1145/3456389.3456390

Caputo, F., Greco, A., Fera, M., & Macchiaroli, R. (2019). Workplace design ergonomic validation based on multiple human factors assessment methods and simulation. *Production & Manufacturing Research, 7*(1), 195–222. doi:10.1080/21693277.2019.1616631

Carayannis, E. G., Campbell, D. F., & Grigoroudis, E. (2021). Helix trilogy: The triple, quadruple, and quintuple innovation helices from a theory, policy, and practice set of perspectives. *Journal of the Knowledge Economy*, 1–30.

Carayannis, E. G., Draper, J., & Bhaneja, B. (2021). Towards fusion energy in the Industry 5.0 and Society 5.0 context: Call for a global commission for urgent action on fusion energy. *Journal of the Knowledge Economy*, *12*(4), 1891–1904. doi:10.100713132-020-00695-5

Carrillo, J. E., Druehl, C., & Hsuan, J. (2015). Introduction to Innovation Within And Across Borders: A Review And Future Directions. *Decision Sciences*, *46*(2), 225–265. doi:10.1111/deci.12131

Carson, S. H., Peterson, J. B., & Higgins, D. M. (2003). Decreased latent inhibition is associated with increased creative achievement in high-functioning individuals. *Journal of Personality and Social Psychology*, *85*(3), 499–506. doi:10.1037/0022-3514.85.3.499 PMID:14498785

Castagnoli, R., Cugno, M., Maroncelli, S., & Cugno, A. (2022). Human-centric manufacturing: an interdisciplinary review of drivers and dark sides. *R&D Management Conference.*

Castellacci, F., & Viñas-Bardolet, C. (2019). Internet use and job satisfaction. *Computers in Human Behavior*, *90*, 141–152. doi:10.1016/j.chb.2018.09.001

Çengelci, B., & Çimen, H. (2005). Industrial Robots. *The Electronic Journal of Mathematics & Technology*, *2*(2), 69–78.

Çetin Gürkan, G., & Çiftci, G. (2020). Developing A Supportive Culture in Digital Transformation. In U. Hacioglu (Ed.), *Digital Business Strategies in Blockchain Ecosystems. Contributions to Management Science*. Springer. doi:10.1007/978-3-030-29739-8_5

Çevik, D. D. (2022). Çalışma Yaşamında Ayrımcılığın İzini Sürerken: Hollanda 'da Meslek Sahibi Türkiye Kökenliler [Tracing Discrimination at Work: Professionals from the Netherlands with Turkish Origin]. *Anadolu Üniversitesi İktisadi Ve İdari Bilimler Fakültesi, 23*(3).

Chakraborty, I., Kim, M., & Sudhir, K. (2019). Attribute Sentiment Scoring with Online Text Reviews: Accounting for Language Structure and Attribute Self-Selection. SSRN Electronic Journal, 2176. doi:10.2139/ssrn.3395012

Chambel, M. J., Carvalho, V. S., Cesário, F., & Lopes, S. (2017). The work-to-life conflict mediation between job characteristics and well-being at work: Part-time vs full-time employees. *Career Development International*, *22*(2), 142–164. doi:10.1108/CDI-06-2016-0096

Chander, B., Pal, S., De, D., & Buyya, R. (2022). Artificial intelligence-based internet of things for industry 5.0. In *Artificial Intelligence-based Internet of Things Systems* (pp. 3–45). Springer. doi:10.1007/978-3-030-87059-1_1

Chandola, V., Banerjee, A., & Kumar, V. (2009). Anomaly detection: A survey. *ACM Computing Surveys*, *41*(3), 1–58. doi:10.1145/1541880.1541882

Chandra, V. (2012). Work-life balance: Eastern and western perspectives. *International Journal of Human Resource Management*, *23*(5), 1040–1056. doi:10.1080/09585192.2012.651339

Chang, S., Wang, Z., Wang, Y., Tang, J., & Jiang, X. (2019). Enabling Technologies and Platforms To Aid Digitalization Of Commercial Aviation Support, Maintenance And Health Management. *International Conference on Quality, Reliability, Risk, Maintenance, And Safety Engineering*, 926-932. 10.1109/QR2MSE46217.2019.9021222

Chantarat, T., Rogers, B. T., Mitchell, C. R., & Ko, J. M. (2022). Perceptions of Workplace Climate And Diversity, Equity And Inclusion Within Health Services And Policy Research. *Health Services Research.* Doi:10.1111/1475-6773.14032

Chan, X. W., Kalliath, T., Brough, P., Siu, O.-L., O'Driscoll, M. P., & Timms, C. (2016a). Work–family enrichment and satisfaction: The mediating role of self-efficacy and work–life balance. *International Journal of Human Resource Management, 27*(15), 1755–1776. doi:10.1080/09585192.2015.1075574

Chaudhry, I. S., Paquibut, Y. R. & Tunio, N. M. (2021). Do Workforce Diversity, Inclusion Practices & Organizational Charactersitics Contribute To Organizational Innovation? Evidence From The U. A. E. *Cogent Business & Management, 8*(1). doi:10.1080/23311975.2021.1947549

Chelliah, J. (2017). Will artiðcial intelligence usurp white collar jobs? *Human Resource Management International Digest, 25*(3), 1–3. doi:10.1108/HRMID-11-2016-0152

Chen, H., Chiang, R. H., & Storey, V. C. (2012). Business Intelligence and Analytics: From Big Data To Big Impact. *Management Information Systems Quarterly, 36*(4), 1165–1188. doi:10.2307/41703503

Chen, J., Lim, C. P., Tan, K. H., Govindan, K., & Kumar, A. (2021). Artificial intelligence-based human-centric decision support framework: An application to predictive maintenance in asset management under pandemic environments. *Annals of Operations Research*, 1–24. doi:10.100710479-021-04373-w PMID:34785834

Chernova, V., & Starostin, V. (2020, January). Leading trends in marketing research: A case of big data. In *5th International Conference on Social, Economic, and Academic Leadership (ICSEALV 2019)* (pp. 210-215). Atlantis Press.

Chillakuri, B., & Attili, V. S. P. (2021). Role of blockchain in HR's response to new-normal. *The International Journal of Organizational Analysis*. Advance online publication. doi:10.1108/IJOA-08-2020-2363

Choudhury, P., Starr, E., & Agarwal, R. (2020). Machine learning and human capital complementarities: Experimental evidence on bias mitigation. *Strategic Management Journal*, 1381–1411.

Chowdhury, S., Dey, P., Joel-Edgar, S., Bhattacharya, S., Rodriguez-Espindola, O., Abadie, A., & Truong, L. (2022). Unlocking the value of artificial intelligence in human resource management through AI capability framework. *Human Resource Management Review*. Advance online publication. doi:10.1016/j.hrmr.2022.100899

Cillo, V., Gregori, G. L., Daniele, L. M., Caputo, F., & Bitbol-Saba, N. (2021). Rethinking companies' culture through knowledge management lens during Industry 5.0 transition. *Journal of Knowledge Management*.

Cirillo, V., Rinaldini, M., Staccioli, J., & Virgillito, M. E. (2021). Technology vs. workers: The case of Italy's Industry 4.0 factories. *Structural Change and Economic Dynamics, 56*, 166–183. doi:10.1016/j.strueco.2020.09.007

Clark, S. C. (2000). Work/family border theory: A new theory of work/family balance. *Human Relations, 53*(6), 747–770. doi:10.1177/0018726700536001

Çoban, R. (2022). Havayolu İşletmelerinde Farklılıkların Yönetimi Üzerine Bir Araştırma [A Study on the Management of Diversity in Airline Businesses]. *7th International Entrepreneurship Social Sciences Congress, Proceeding Book,* 515.

Coco, C. T., Jamison, F., & Black, H. (2011). Connecting people's Investments and Business Outcomes at Lowe's: Using Value Linkage Analytics to Link Employee Engagement with Business Performance. *People & Strategy, 34*(2), 28–33.

Coffey, J. W., Hoffman, R., & Cañas, A. (2006). Concept map-based knowledge modelling: Perspectives from information and knowledge visualization. *Information Visualization, 5*(3), 192–201. doi:10.1057/palgrave.ivs.9500129

Colbert, A., Yee, N., & George, G. (2016). The digital workforce and the workplace of the future. *Academy of Management Journal, 59*(3), 731–739. doi:10.5465/amj.2016.4003

Collings, D. G., Nyberg, A. J., Wright, P. M., & McMackin, J. (2021). Leading through paradox in a COVID-19 world: Human resources comes of age. *Human Resource Management Journal, 31*(4), 819–833. doi:10.1111/1748-8583.12343

Collins, A. M., Hislop, D., & Cartwright, S. (2016). Social support in the workplace between teleworkers, office-based colleagues and supervisors. *New Technology, Work and Employment*, *31*(2), 161–175. doi:10.1111/ntwe.12065

Contini, M., & Samardzic, T. (2021). *Diversity, Equality And Inclusion Policies In Canadian Small-to-Medium Sized Enterprises Within Science, Tech, Engineering And Skilled Trades.* atrium.lib.uoguelph.ca

Cooke, F. L., Liu, M., Liu, L. A., & Chen, C. C. (2019). Human resource management and industrial relations in multinational corporations in and from China: Challenges and new insights. *Human Resource Management*, *58*(5), 455–471. doi:10.1002/hrm.21986

Cornelissen, J. (2017). Editor's comments: Developing propositions, a process model, or a typology? Addressing the challenges of writing theory without a boilerplate. *Academy of Management Review*, *42*(1), 1–9. doi:10.5465/amr.2016.0196

Coron, C. (2022). Quantifying human resource management: a literature review. In Personnel Review (Vol. 51, Issue 4, pp. 1386–1409). Emerald Group Holdings Ltd. doi:10.1108/PR-05-2020-0322

Costa, A. C. (2003). Work team trust and effectiveness. *Personnel Review*, *32*(5), 605-622+672. doi:10.1108/00483480310488360

Cowan, R., & Hoffman, M. F. (2007). The flexible organization: How contemporary employees construct the work/life border. *Qualitative Research Reports in Communication*, *8*(1), 37–44. doi:10.1080/17459430701617895

Crompton, R., & Lyonette, C. (2006). Work-life "balance" in Europe. *Acta Sociologica*, *49*(4), 379–393. doi:10.1177/0001699306071680

Croskerry, P., Singhal, G., & Mamede, S. (2013). Cognitive debiasing 1: Origins of bias and theory of debiasing. *BMJ Quality & Safety*, *22*(Suppl 2), ii58–ii64.

Crowley, E., & Overton, L. (2021). *Learning and skills at work survey 2021.* Chartered Institute of Personnel and Development.

Cugno, M., Castagnoli, R., & Büchi, G. (2021). Openness to Industry 4.0 and performance: The impact of barriers and incentives. *Technological Forecasting and Social Change*, *168*, 120756. doi:10.1016/j.techfore.2021.120756

Cugno, M., Castagnoli, R., Büchi, G., & Pini, M. (2022). Industry 4.0 and production recovery in the covid era. *Technovation*, *114*, 102443. doi:10.1016/j.technovation.2021.102443

Currie, J., & Eveline, J. (2011). E-technology and work/life balance for academics with young children. *Higher Education*, *62*(4), 533–550. doi:10.100710734-010-9404-9

Cvenkel, N. (2020). *Well-Being in the Workplace: Governance and Sustainability Insights to Promote Workplace Health.* Springer Singapore. doi:10.1007/978-981-15-3619-9

Dahlbom, P., Siikanen, N., Sajasalo, P., & Jarvenpää, M. (2020). Big Data and HR Analytics in the Digital Era. *Baltic Journal of Management*, *15*(1), 120–138. doi:10.1108/BJM-11-2018-0393

Dalenogare, L. S., Benitez, G. B., Ayala, N. F., & Frank, A. G. (2018). The expected contribution of Industry 4.0 technologies for industrial performance. *International Journal of Production Economics*, *204*, 383–394. doi:10.1016/j.ijpe.2018.08.019

Dalton, S., & Villagran, M. (2018). Minimizing and addressing implicit bias in the workplace: Be proactive, part one. *College & Research Libraries News*, *79*(9), 478. doi:10.5860/crln.79.9.478

Das, D. (2022). Understanding the choice of human resource and the artificial intelligence: "strategic behavior" and the existence of industry equilibrium. *Journal of Economic Studies (Glasgow, Scotland)*. Advance online publication. doi:10.1108/JES-06-2021-0305

Davenport, T. H., & Bean, R. (2017). How P&G and American Express Are Approaching AI. *Harvard Business Review*. https://hbr.org/2017/03/how-pg-and-american-express-are-approaching-ai

Davenport, T., & Ronanki, R. (2018). Artificial intelligence for the real world. *Harvard Business Review*. Retrieved from https://hbr.org/2018/01/artificial-intelligence-for-the-real-world

Day One. (2021). *What is Human Augmentation? Will it become a mega-trend in the future?* Retrieved from https://www.day1tech.com/what-is-human-augmentation-will-it-become-a-megatrend-in-the-future/

Day, D. V. (2000). Leadership development: A review in context. *The Leadership Quarterly*, *11*(4), 581–613. doi:10.1016/S1048-9843(00)00061-8

De Goede, M. E. E., Van Vianen, A. E. M., & Klehe, U.-C. (2011). Attracting Applicants on the Web: PO fit, industry culture stereotypes, and website design. *International Journal of Selection and Assessment*, *19*(1), 51–61. doi:10.1111/j.1468-2389.2010.00534.x

De Luca, L. M., Herhausen, D., Troilo, G., & Rossi, A. (2021). How and when do big data investments pay off? The role of marketing affordances and service innovation. *Journal of the Academy of Marketing Science*, *49*(4), 790–810. doi:10.100711747-020-00739-x

del Giudice, M., Scuotto, V., Orlando, B., & Mustilli, M. (2021). Toward the human – Centered approach. A revised model of individual acceptance of AI. *Human Resource Management Review*. Advance online publication. doi:10.1016/j.hrmr.2021.100856

Deloitte. (2022). *Striving for balance, advocating for change. The Deloitte global 2022 gen Z & millenial survey*. https://www2.deloitte.com/content/dam/Deloitte/global/Documents/deloitte-2022-genz-millennial-survey.pdf

Demetriou, G. A. (2011). Mobile Robotics in Education And Research. *Mobile Robots-Current Trends*, *27*, 48.

Demir, K. A., Döven, G., & Sezen, B. (2019). Industry 5.0 and Human-Robot Co-working. *Procedia Computer Science*, *158*, 688–695. doi:10.1016/j.procs.2019.09.104

Desanctis, G., & Jackson, B. M. (1993). Coordination of information technology management: Team-based structures and computer-based communication systems. *Journal of Management Information Systems*, *10*(3), 85–110.

Dey, T. S., & De, P. (2015). *Predictive Analytics in HR: A Primer*. Tata Consultancy Services.

Dhanpat, N., Buthelezi, Z. P., Joe, M. R., & Maphela, T. v, & Shongwe, N. (2020). Industry 4.0: The role of human resource professionals. *SA Journal of Human Resource Management*. Advance online publication. doi:10.4102ajhrm

DiClaudio, M. (2019). People analytics and the rise of HR: How data, analytics and emerging technology can transform human resources (HR) into a profit center. *Strategic HR Review*, *18*(2), 42–46. doi:10.1108/SHR-11-2018-0096

Diebig, M., Müller, A., & Angerer, P. (2020). Impact of the Digitization in the Industry Sector on Work, Employment, and Health. In T. Theorell (Ed.), *Handbook of Socioeconomic Determinants of Occupational Health: From Macro-level to Micro-level Evidence* (pp. 305–319). Springer International Publishing. doi:10.1007/978-3-030-31438-5_10

Digital Transformation Office. (2022). Cbddo.Gov.Tr/En/

Digneo, G. (2020). *6 Important Remote Work Statistics To Know in 2020.* TimeDoctor. https://biz30.timedoctor.com/remote-work-statistics/

Dijk, R. (2022). 5 Advanced Data Analysis Techniques Applied to People Analytics. *Academy to Innovate HR.* https://www.aihr.com/blog/advanced-data-analysis-techniques-applied-to-people-analytics/.

Dilibal, S., & Şahin, H. (2018). Cooperative Industrial Robots And Digital Industry. *International Journal of 3D Printing Technologies and Digital Industry, 2*(1), 86-96.

Dirks, K. T., & Ferrin, D. L. (2002). Trust in leadership: Meta-analytic findings and implications for research and practice. *The Journal of Applied Psychology, 87*(4), 611–628. doi:10.1037/0021-9010.87.4.611 PMID:12184567

DiRomualdo, A., El-Khoury, D., & Girimonte, F. (2018). HR in the digital age: How digital technology will change HR's organization structure, processes and roles. *Strategic HR Review, 17*(5), 234–242. doi:10.1108/SHR-08-2018-0074

Drigas, A., & Papoutsi, C. (2019). Emotional Intelligence as an Important Asset for HR in Organizations: Leaders and Employees. *International Journal of Advanced Corporate Learning, 12*(1), 58–66. doi:10.3991/ijac.v12i1.9637

Druskat, V. U., & Wolff, S. B. (2001). Building the emotional intelligence of groups. *Harvard Business Review, 79*(3), 80–91. PMID:11246926

Duman, M. Ç. (2022). Society 5.0: Human-Focused Digital Transformation. *Journal of Social Policy Conferences, 82*, 309-336.

Dvorsky, G. (2013). The 12 cognitive biases that prevent you from being rational. *Gizmodo.*

Eby, L. T., Casper, W. J., Lockwood, A., Bordeaux, C., & Brinley, A. (2005). Work and family research in IO/OB: Content analysis and review of the literature (1980-2002). *Journal of Vocational Behavior, 66*(1), 124–197. doi:10.1016/j.jvb.2003.11.003

Edwards, M. R., Charlwood, A., Guenole, N., & Marler, J. (2021). HR Analytics: An Emerging Field Finding its Place in the World Alongside Simmering Ethical Challenges. *Human Resource Management Journal,* 1–11.

Edwards, J. R., & Rothbard, N. P. (2000). Mechanisms linking work and family: Clarifying the relationship between work and family constructs. *Academy of Management Review, 25*(1), 178–199. doi:10.2307/259269

Edwards, M. R., & Edwards, K. (2016). *Predictive HR Analytics: Mastering the HR Metric.* Kogan Page Limited.

Ehret, M., & Wirtz, J. (2017). Unlocking Value from Machines: Business Models and The Industrial Internet of Things. *Journal of Marketing Management, 33*(1-2), 111–130. doi:10.1080/0267257X.2016.1248041

Eimontaite, I., Gwilt, I., Cameron, D., Aitken, J. M., Rolph, J., Mokaram, S., & Law, J. (2019). Language-free graphical signage improves human performance and reduces anxiety when working collaboratively withe robots. *International Journal of Advanced Manufacturing Technology, 100*(1), 55–73. doi:10.100700170-018-2625-2

Ekka, S. (2021). HR Analytics: Why it Matters. *Journal of Contemporary Issues in Business and Government, 27*(2), 2283–2291.

ElMaraghy, H., Monostori, L., Schuh, G., & ElMaraghy, W. (2021). Evolution and future of manufacturing systems. *CIRP Annals, 70*(2), 635–658. doi:10.1016/j.cirp.2021.05.008

Enholm, I. M., Papagiannidis, E., Mikalef, P., & Krogstie, J. (2021). Artificial intelligence and business value: A literature review. *Information Systems Frontiers*, 1–26.

Erdur, D. A. (2020). İnsan Kaynakları Yöneticilerinin Gözünden Çeşitlilik, Kapsayıcılık ve Dışlayıcılık [Diversity, Inclusion and Exclusion from the Perspective of Human Resources Managers]. *Atatürk Üniversitesi İktisadi İdari Bilimler Dergisi. Journal of Economics And Administrative Sciences*, *34*(1), 214–234.

Eschbach, A. P. (2021). *These 9 sets of matching family Pajamas are on sale for Cyber Monday.* Retrieved August 28, 2022, from https://www.forbes.com/sites/forbes-personal-shopper/2021/11/29/matching-family-pajamas/?sh=b8665353ba84

Eurofound. (2015). *Sixth European Working Conditions Survey: 2015.* https://www.eurofound.europa.eu/surveys/european-working-conditions-surveys/sixth-european-working-conditions-survey-2015

Eurofound. (2017). *6th European Working Conditions Survey: 2017 update.* European Union.

Eurofound. (2020). *Living, working and COVID-19* (COVID-19 Series). Publications Office of the European Union.

European Commision. (2017). *Digital Transformation Monitor Industry 4.0 In Aeronautics: Iot Applications*. EU Commission Report.

Eurostat. (2020). *How usual is it to work from home?* https://ec.europa.eu/eurostat/web/products-eurostat-news/-/DDN-20180620-1

Eurostat. (2021). *Working from home across EU regions in 2020.* https://ec.europa.eu/eurostat/web/products-eurostat-news/-/ddn-20210923-1

Factories, A. C. E. (2019). *Human-Centred Factories from eory to Industrial Practice*. Lessons Learned And Recommendations.

Falletta, S. V., & Combs, W. L. (2021). The HR Analytics Cycle: A Seven-Step Process for Building Evidence-Based and Ethical HR Analytics Capabilities. *Journal of Work-Applied Management*, *13*(1), 51–68. doi:10.1108/JWAM-03-2020-0020

Fantini, P., Pinzone, M., & Taisch, M. (2020). Placing the operator at the centre of Industry 4.0 design: Modelling and assessing human activities within cyber-physical systems. *Computers & Industrial Engineering*, *139*, 105058. doi:10.1016/j.cie.2018.01.025

Farooq, U., & Grudin, J. (2019). *Human-Computer Integration. Microsoft Corporation Microsoft.* ACM.

Fast, K. (2021). The disconnection turn: Three facets of disconnective work in post-digital capitalism. *Convergence*, *27*(6), 1615–1630. doi:10.1177/13548565211033382

Fatima, Z., Tanveer, M. H., Zardari, S., Naz, L. F., Khadim, H., Ahmed, N., & Tahir, M. (2022). Production Plant and Warehouse Automation with IoT and Industry 5.0. *Applied Sciences (Basel, Switzerland)*, *12*(4), 2053. doi:10.3390/app12042053

Feldmann, K., Franke, J., & Schüßler, F. (2010). Development of Micro Assembly Processes for Further Miniaturization in Electronics Production. *CIRP Annals*, *59*(1), 1–4. doi:10.1016/j.cirp.2010.03.005

Fernandez, V., & Gallardo-Gallardo, E. (2020). Tackling the HR digitalization challenge: Key factors and barriers to HR analytics adoption. *Competitiveness Review*, *31*(1), 162–187. doi:10.1108/CR-12-2019-0163

Ferrar, J., & Green, D. (2021). *Excellence in People Analytics: How to Use Workforce Data to Create Business Value*. Kogan Page Limited.

Ferreira, A. M., & Filipe, J. A. (2022). *Nanotechnology Applications: The future arrived suddenly*. Retrieved from https://www. researchgate.net/ publication/357953395 _Nanotechnology _Applications _The_future_ arrived_suddenly

Fiasché, M., Pinzone, M., Fantini, P., Alexandru, A., & Taisch, M. (2016, September). Human-centric factories 4.0: A mathematical model for job allocation. In *2016 IEEE 2nd International Forum on Research and Technologies for Society and Industry Leveraging a better tomorrow (RTSI)* (pp. 1-4(. IEEE.

Fırat, O. Z., & Fırat, S. Ü. (2017). Trends and Robots on the Industry 4.0 Journey. *Istanbul University Journal of the School of Business*, *46*(2), 211–223.

Fischer, G., & Nakakoji, K. (1992). Beyond the macho approach of artificial intelligence: Empower human designers do not replace them. *Knowledge-Based Systems*, *5*(1), 15–30. doi:10.1016/0950-7051(92)90021-7

Fiss, P. C. (2011). Building better causal theories: A fuzzy set approach to typologies in organizational research. *Academy of Management Journal*, *54*(2), 393–420. doi:10.5465/amj.2011.60263120

Fleming, P. (2019). Robots and organization studies: Why robots might not want to steal your job. *Organization Studies*, *40*(1), 23–38. doi:10.1177/0170840618765568

Flemisch, F. O., Bengler, K., Bubb, H., Winner, H., & Bruder, R. (2014). Towards cooperative guidance and control of highly automated vehicles: H-Mode and Conduct-by-Wire. *Ergonomics*, *57*(3), 343–360. doi:10.1080/00140139.2013.869355 PMID:24559139

Flint, D. J., & Larsson, E. (2007). Supply Chain Innovation. Handbook of Global Supply Chain Management, 49(4), 475-487.

Fombrun, C., Tichy, N. M., & Devanna, M. A. (1984). *Strategic Huma Resource Management*. Wiley.

Frazer, A., Frazer, A. N. B., & Frazer, F. G. (2021). Equity. In *The New Workplace: The Role of Diversity, Equality and Inclusion*. doi:10.2139srn.3864457

Freeze, R., & Raschke, R.L. (2007). *An assessment of formative and reflective constructs in IS research*. Academic Press.

Friedman, S. D., & Greenhaus, J. H. (2000). *Work and Family—Allies or Enemies?: What Happens When Business Professionals Confront Life Choices - Oxford Scholarship* (1st ed.). Oxford University Press. doi:10.1093/acprof:oso/9780195112757.001.0001

Gaget, L. (2018). *3D bioprinting: What can we achieve today with a 3D bio-printer?* https:// www. sculpteo.com / blog/ 2018/ 02/21/3d- bioprinting -what-can-we-achieve-today-with-a-3d-bioprinter/

Galea, C., Houkes, I., & De Rijk, A. (2014). An insider's point of view: How a system of flexible working hours helps employees to strike a proper balance between work and personal life. *International Journal of Human Resource Management*, *25*(8), 1090–1111. doi:10.1080/09585192.2013.816862

Gallup. (2013). State of the Global Workplace. In Employee Engagement Insights for Business Leaders Worldwide. Gallup.

Gal, U., Jensen, T. B., & Stein, M.-K. (2020). Breaking the vicious cycle of algorithmic management: A virtue ethics approach to people analytics. *Information and Organization*, *30*(2), 100301. doi:10.1016/j.infoandorg.2020.100301

Garavan, T. N., Costine, P., & Heraty, N. (1995). The emergence of strategic human resource development. *Journal of European Industrial Training*, *19*(10), 4–10. doi:10.1108/03090599510095816

Garcia-Arroyo, J., & Osca, A. (2019). Big data contributions to human resource management: A systematic review. *International Journal of Human Resource Management*, 1–26. doi:10.1080/09585192.2019.1674357

Garg, S., Sinha, S., Kar, A. K., & Mani, M. (2022). A review of machine learning applications in human resource management. In International Journal of Productivity and Performance Management (Vol. 71, Issue 5, pp. 1590–1610). Emerald Group Holdings Ltd. doi:10.1108/IJPPM-08-2020-0427

Garret, G. (2021). How To Align Industry 5.0 Initiatives With Your Customer Experience Strategy. *Forbes*. Retrieved from, https://www.forbes.com/sites/forbesbusinesscouncil/2021/04/15/how-to-align-industry-50-initiatives-with-your-customer-experience-strategy/?sh=532095d657e9

Gartner. (2022). *Six Emerging HR Technology Trends.* Gartner. https://www.gartner.com/en/human-resources/trends/emerging-hr-technology

Gaur, B. (2020). *HR4.0: An Analytics Framework to Redefine Employee Engagement in the Fourth Industrial Revolution. 11th International Conference on Computing, Communication and Networking Technologies (ICCCNT)*, Kharagpur, India. 10.1109/ICCCNT49239.2020.9225456

Gautam, S. (2022, April 9). *Is our workforce ready for Industry 5.0?* https://hr.economictimes.indiatimes.com/news/workplace-4-0/learning-and-development/is-our-workforce-ready-for-industry-5-0/90737484

Georgiou, K., Gouras, A., & Nikolaou, I. (2019). Gamification in employee selection: The development of a gamified assessment. *International Journal of Selection and Assessment*, *27*(2), 91–103. doi:10.1111/ijsa.12240

Giannikis, S. K., & Mihail, D. M. (2011). Flexible work arrangements in Greece: A study of employee perceptions. *International Journal of Human Resource Management*, *22*(2), 417–432. doi:10.1080/09585192.2011.540163

Giauque, D., Anderfuhren-Biget, S., & Varone, F. (2019). Stress and turnover intents in international organizations: Social support and work–life balance as resources. *International Journal of Human Resource Management*, *30*(5), 879–901. doi:10.1080/09585192.2016.1254105

Giermindl, L. M., Strich, F., Christ, O., Leicht-Deobald, U., & Redzepi, A. (2022). The dark sides of people analytics: Reviewing the perils for organisations and employees. *European Journal of Information Systems*, *31*(3), 410–435. doi:10.1080/0960085X.2021.1927213

Gifford, J. (2022). Remote working: Unprecedented increase and a developing research agenda. *Human Resource Development International*, *25*(2), 105–113. doi:10.1080/13678868.2022.2049108

Gikopoulos, J. (2019). Alongside, not against: Balancing man with machine in the HR function. *Strategic HR Review*, *18*(2), 56–61. doi:10.1108/SHR-12-2018-0103

Gillenson, M. L., & Sanders, T. C. (2005). Employee relationship management: Applying the concept of personalization to U.S. Navy sailors. *Information Systems Research*, *22*(1), 45–50.

Gillespie, N. A., & Mann, L. (2004). Transformational leadership and shared values: The building blocks of trust. *Journal of Managerial Psychology*, *19*(6), 588–607. doi:10.1108/02683940410551507

Gill, G. K., Mcnally, M. J., & Berman, V. (2018). Effective Diversity, Equity And Inclusion Practices. *Healthcare Management Forum*, *31*(5), 196–199. doi:10.1177/0840470418773785 PMID:30114938

Gillies, D. (2011). Agile bodies: A new imperative in neoliberal governance. Journal of Education Policy, 26(22). doi: 10.1080/02680939.2010.508177

Glavas, C., Mathews, S., & Russell-Bennett, R. (2019). Knowledge acquisition via internet-enabled platforms: Examining incrementally and non-incrementally internationalizing SMEs. *International Marketing Review*, *36*(1), 74–107. doi:10.1108/IMR-02-2017-0041

Globelink-Unimar. (2022). *Logistics In The Supply Chain 5.0. Period.* Https://Globelink-Unimar.Com/Tedarik-Zincirinde-Lojistik-5-0-Donemi

Gökten, P. O. (2018). Manufacturing In The Dark: Scope Of The Cost In The New Age. *Journal of the World of Accounting Science*, *20*(4), 880–897.

Goldberg, W. A., Greenberger, E., Koch-Jones, J., O'Neil, R., & Hamill, S. (1989). Attractiveness of child care and related employer-supported benefits and policies to married and single parents. *Child & Youth Care Quarterly, 18*(1), 23–37.

Golden, T. D. (2006). Avoiding depletion in virtual work: Telework and the intervening impact of work exhaustion on commitment and turnover intentions. *Journal of Vocational Behavior*, *69*(1), 176–187. doi:10.1016/j.jvb.2006.02.003

Goleman, D. (1996). Emotional Intelligence. Why It Can Matter More than IQ. *Learning*, *24*(6), 49–50.

Gould-Williams, J. (2003). The importance of HR practices and workplace trust in achieving superior performance: A study of public-sector organizations. *International Journal of Human Resource Management*, *14*(1), 28–54.

Grandi, F., Peruzzini, M., Zanni, L., Campanella, C. E., & Pellicciari, M. (2018). Digital Manufacturing and Virtual Reality for Tractors' Human-Centred Design. In *Transdisciplinary Engineering Methods for Social Innovation of Industry 4.0*. IOS Press.

Grandi, F., Zanni, L., Peruzzini, M., Pellicciari, M., & Campanella, C. E. (2020). A Transdisciplinary digital approach for tractor's human-centred design. *International Journal of Computer Integrated Manufacturing*, *33*(4), 377–397. doi:10.1080/0951192X.2019.1599441

Grant, C. A., Wallace, L. M., & Spurgeon, P. C. (2013). An exploration of the psychological factors affecting remote e-worker's job effectiveness, well-being and work-life balance. *Employee Relations*, *35*(5), 527–546. doi:10.1108/ER-08-2012-0059

Grant, C. A., Wallace, L. M., Spurgeon, P. C., Tramontano, C., & Charalampous, M. (2019). Construction and initial validation of the E-Work Life Scale to measure remote e-working. *Employee Relations*, *41*(1), 16–33. doi:10.1108/ER-09-2017-0229

Green, M., Peters, R., & Young, J. (2020). *People Profession 2030: A collective view of future trends report.* CIPD. https://www.cipd.co.uk/Images/people-profession-2030-report-compressed_tcm18-86095.pdf

Green, B. N., Johnson, C. D., & Adams, A. (2006). Writing narrative literature reviews for peer-reviewed journals: Secrets of the trade. *Journal of Chiropractic Medicine*, *3*(3), 101–117. doi:10.1016/S0899-3467(07)60142-6 PMID:19674681

Gregory, A., & Milner, S. (2009). Work-life balance: A matter of choice? *Gender, Work and Organization*, *16*(1), 1–13. doi:10.1111/j.1468-0432.2008.00429.x

Griffin, R. W., Phillips, J. M., & Gully, S. M. (2019). *Organizational Behavior: Managing People and Organizations* (13th ed.). Cengage.

Grobotek, T. (2019). Intelligent Steps For The Future. *Skyway Magazine,* 42-44.

Gugerçin, S., & Gugerçin, U. (2021). How Employees Survive In The Industry 5.0 Era: In-Demand Skills Of The Near Future. *International Journal of Disciplines Economics & Administrative Sciences Studies, 7*(31), 524-533

Guinot, J., Chiva, R., & Roca-Puig, V. (2014). Interpersonal trust, stress and satisfaction at work: An empirical study. *Personnel Review, 43*(1), 96–115. doi:10.1108/PR-02-2012-0043

Gülseren, A., & Sağbaş, A. (2019). Evaluation of Digital Transformation and Digital Maturity Level in Industry from Industry 4.0 Perspective. *European Journal of Engineering And Applied Sciences, 2*(2), 1–5.

Gurusinghe, R. N., Arachchige, B. J. H., & Dayarathna, D. (2021). Predictive HR analytics and talent management: A conceptual framework. *Journal of Management Analytics, 8*(2), 195–221. doi:10.1080/23270012.2021.1899857

Guszcza, J., Lewis, H., & Evans-Greenwood, P. (2017). *Cognitive collaboration: Why humans and computers think better together.* Deloitte University Press.

Haenlein, M., & Kaplan, A. (2019). A brief history of artificial intelligence: On the past, present, and future of artificial intelligence. *California Management Review, 61*(4), 5–14. doi:10.1177/0008125619864925

Haklıdır, M. (2020). Third Wave Artificial Intelligence Technologies. *Tübitak Bilgem,* (9).

Harrington, B., & Ladge, J. J. (2009). Work-Life Integration. Present Dynamics and Future Directions for Organizations. *Organizational Dynamics, 38*(2), 148–157. doi:10.1016/j.orgdyn.2009.02.003

Hartmann, D., & Van Der Auweraer, H. (2021). Digital Twins. In *Progess in Industrial Mathematics: Success Stories* (pp. 3–17). Springer. doi:10.1007/978-3-030-61844-5_1

Haselton, M. G., Nettle, D., & Murray, D. R. (2015). The Evolution of Cognitive Bias, 1–20. The Handbook of Evolutionary Psychology. Wiley. doi:10.1002/9781119125563.evpsych241

Henfridsson, O., Mathiassen, L., & Svahn, F. (2014). Managing technological change in the digital age: The role of architectural frames. *Journal of Information Technology, 29*(1), 27–43. doi:10.1057/jit.2013.30

Herbert, L. (2017). *Digital Transformation Build Your Organizations Future For The Innovation Age.* Bloomsbury Publishing Plc.

Heric, M. (2018). *HR new digital mandate.* Bain & Company. Retrieved from https://www.bain.com/insights/hrs-new-digital-mandate/

Hermann, M., Pentek, T., & Otto, B. (2015). Design Principles for Industrie 4.0 Scenarios: A Literature Review. *Technische Universität Dortmund, Dortmund, 45,* 1–15.

Higginbotham, T., Weinberg, J., Aaker, J., & Fei, F. L. (2021). *Human - Centered Artificial Intelligence and workforce Displacement. Stanford Business.* Case Centre.

Hilberath, C., Kilmann, J., Lovich, D., & Tzanetti, T. (2020, September 22). *Hybrid Work Is the New Remote Work.* BCG. https://www.bcg.com/en-in/publications/2020/managing-remote-work-and-optimizing-hybrid-working-models

Hill, E. J., Hawkins, A. J., Ferris, M., & Weitzman, M. (2001). Finding an extra day a week: The positive influence of perceived job flexibility on work and family life balance. *Family Relations, 50*(1), 49–58. doi:10.1111/j.1741-3729.2001.00049.x

Hirschhorn, J. (2020, May 5). *SHRM Releases COVID-19 U.S. Business Index*. Business Wire. https://www.businesswire.com/news/home/20200505005623/en/SHRM-Releases-COVID-19-U.S.-Business-Index

Hodges, C., Moore, S., Lockee, B., Trust, T., & Bond, A. (2020). *The difference between emergency remote teaching and online learning*. Educause. https://er.educause.edu/articles/2020/3/thedifference-between-emergency-remote-teaching-and-online-learning

Hofmann, E., & Rüsch, M. (2017). Industry 4.0 and the Current Status As Well As Future Prospects On Logistics. *Computers in Industry*, *89*, 23–34. doi:10.1016/j.compind.2017.04.002

Houghton, E. (2015). *Evolution of HR Analytics: A Middle East Perspective*. Chartered Institute of Personnel and Development.

Houston, D., Meyer, L. H., & Paewai, S. (2006). Academic staff workloads and job satisfaction: Expectations and values in academe. *Journal of Higher Education Policy and Management*, *28*(1), 17–30. doi:10.1080/13600800500283734

Howington, J. (2015, January 28). *Update: Want to Work from Home? 19 Ways to Say It*. Flexjobs. https://www.flexjobs.com/blog/post/want-to-work-from-home-17-ways-to-say-it

HR Research Institute. (2021). *The State of HR Analytics in 2021*. HR.com. https://www.oracle.com/a/ocom/docs/applications/human-capital-management/hrt-talent-analytics-hrdotcom.pdf

Huang, M. H., & Rust, R. T. (2018). Artificial intelligence in service. *Journal of Service Research*, *21*(2), 155–172. doi:10.1177/1094670517752459

Human Augmentation Market. (2022). *Human Augmentation Market by Product Type (Wearable Devices, Virtual Reality Devices, Augmented Reality Devices, Exoskeletons, Intelligent Virtual Assistants), Functionality, Application, & Geography (2021-2026)*. https:// www. Market sand markets.com/Market-Reports/human-augmentation-market-177215310.html

Humayun, M., & Arabia, S. (2021). Industrial Revolution 5.0 and the Role of Cutting Edge Technologies. *International Journal of Advanced Computer Science and Applications*, *12*(12). doi:10.14569/IJACSA.2021.0121276

Hung, W. H., Chen, K., & Lin, C. P. (2015). Does the proactive personality mitigate the adverse effect of technostress on productivity in the mobile environment? *Telematics and Informatics*, *32*(1), 143–157. doi:10.1016/j.tele.2014.06.002

ILO. (2021). ILO Global Estimates on International Migrant Workers- Result and Methodology (3rd ed.). International Labor Office.

Inditex. (2021). *Collaborating with our people, the engine of that transformation*. https://static.inditex.com/annual_report_2021/en/documents/we-are-collaborating-our-people-engine-transformation.pdf

Information Technologies and Communications Authority. (2017). Society 5.0. *Journal of Sectoral Research and Strategy Development*, 6-13.

International Journal of Academic Research in Business and Social Sciences. (2017). *International Journal of Academic Research in Business and Social Sciences, 7*(3).

IONOS. (2019). *Work-life balance: harmony between work and personal life*. IONOS. https://www.ionos.com/startupguide/productivity/work-life-balance/

Ivanov, D. (2022). The Industry 5.0 framework: Viability-based integration of the resilience, sustainability, and human-centricity perspectives. *International Journal of Production Research*, 1–13. doi:10.1080/00207543.2022.2118892

Jaakkola, E. (2020). Designing conceptual articles: Four approaches. *AMS Review*, *10*(1-2), 18–26. doi:10.100713162-020-00161-0

Jain, P., & Jain, P. (2020). Understanding the Concept of HR Analytics. *International Journal on Emerging Technologies*, *11*(2), 644–652.

Jakubik, M., & Berazhny, I. (2018). *Rethinking leadership and its practices in the digital era*. Academic Press.

Jarrahi, M. H. (2018). Artificial Intelligence and the Future of Work: Human-AI Symbiosis in Organizational Decision Making. *Business Horizons*, *61*(4), 1–15. doi:10.1016/j.bushor.2018.03.007

Jarvenpaa, S. L., & Staples, D. S. (2001). Exploring perceptions of organizational ownership of information and expertise. *Journal of Management Information Systems*, *18*(1), 151–183. doi:10.1080/07421222.2001.11045673

Jarvis, C. B., Mackenzie, S. B., Podsakoff, P. M., Giliatt, N., & Mee, J. F. (2003). A Critical Review of Construct Indicators and Measurement Model Misspecification in Marketing and Consumer Research. *The Journal of Consumer Research*, *30*(2), 199–218. doi:10.1086/376806

Javaid, M., Haleem, A., Singh, R. P., Haq, M. I., Raina, A., & Suman, R. (2020). Industry 5.0: Potential Applications in Covıd-19. *Journal of Industrial Integration and Management*, 508-510.

Jian, Z., & Zhenyi, Z. (2020, May). Deconstruction and Reconstruction of Marketing System under the Background of Big Data. *Journal of Physics: Conference Series*, *1550*(3), 032097. doi:10.1088/1742-6596/1550/3/032097

Jibrail, W., Fry, R., & Liyana-Pathirana, R. (2001, August). A modified serial-search DS code-acquisition scheme. In *Proceedings of the Sixth International Symposium on Signal Processing and its Applications (Cat. No. 01EX467)* (Vol. 2, pp. 481-484). IEEE. 10.1109/ISSPA.2001.950185

Jin, Y. (2010). Emotional leadership as a key dimension of public relations leadership: A national survey of public relations leaders. *Journal of Public Relations Research*, *22*(2), 159–181. doi:10.1080/10627261003601622

Johansson, J., Abrahamsson, L., Kåreborn, B. B., Fältholm, Y., Grane, C., & Wykowska, A. (2017). Work and organization in a digital industrial context. *Management Review*, 281–297.

Jordan, I. M., & Mitchell, M. T. (2015). Machine learning:Trends, perspectives, and prospects. *Science*, *349*(6245), 255–260. doi:10.1126cience.aaa8415 PMID:26185243

Joseph, J., & Gaba, V. (2019). Organizational structure, information processing and decision making: A retrospective and roadmap for research. *The Academy of Management Annals*.

Joshi, N. (2019). *7 types of Artificial Intelligence*. Retrieved from https://www.forbes.com/sites/cognitiveworld/2019/06/19/7-types-of-artificial-intelligence/#3b31eefa233e

Jouany, V., & Martic, K. (2020). *Diversity and Inclusion Best Practices to Focus on in 2022*. https://haiilo.com/blog/diversity-and-inclusion-best-practices-focus-on-in-2020/

Kaasinen, E., Schmalfuß, F., Özturk, C., Aromaa, S., Boubekeur, M., Heilala, J., Heikkilä, P., Kuula, T., Liinasuo, M., Mach, S., Mehta, R., Petäjä, E., & Walter, T. (2020). Empowering and engaging industrial workers with Operator 4.0 solutions. *Computers & Industrial Engineering, 139*, 105678. doi:10.1016/j.cie.2019.01.052

Kadir, B. A., Broberg, O., & da Conceicao, C. S. (2019). Current research and future perspectives on human factors and ergonomics in Industry 4.0. *Computers & Industrial Engineering, 137*, 106004. doi:10.1016/j.cie.2019.106004

Kagermann, H. (2015). Change Through Digitization—Value Creation in The Age Of Industry 4.0. In Management of Permanent Change (23-45). Springer Gabler.

Kagermann, H., Helbig, J., & Wahlster, W. (2013). *Securing the future of German manufacturing industry-Recommendations for implementing the strategic initiative Industrie 4.0-Final report of the Industry 4.0 Working Group*. Acatech – National Academy of Science and Engineering.

Kahn, W. A. (1990). Psychological Conditions of Personal Engagement and Disengagement at Work. *Academy of Management Journal, 33*(4), 692–724. doi:10.2307/256287

Kaiser, S., Ringlstetter, M. J., Eikhof, D. R., & Cunha, M. P. E. (2011). Creating balance? In *Springer-Verlag*. Springer Verlag. doi:10.1007/978-3-642-16199-5

Kalev, L. (2016). Is Elon Musk Right and Will AI Replace Most Human Jobs? *Forbes*. https://www.forbes.com/sites/kalevleetaru/2016/11/08/is-elon-musk-right-and-will-ai-replace-most-human-jobs/#4d3e7add60f4

Kamar, E. (2016). *Directions in Hybrid Intelligence: Complementing AI Systems with Human Intelligence*. https://www.microsoft.com/en-us/research/wp-content/uploads/2016/11/hi.pdf

Kambur, E., & Akar, C. (2022). Human resource developments with the touch of artificial intelligence: A scale development study. *International Journal of Manpower, 43*(1), 168–205. doi:10.1108/IJM-04-2021-0216

Karacan, S., & Bayram, G. (2019). Enterprice Resources Planning(Erp) Systems And Accounting Information System. *Journal Of International Social Research, 12*(65), 1118–1123. doi:10.17719/jisr.2019.3521

Karakhan, A. A., Gambatase, A. J., Simmons, R. D., & Al-Bayati, J. A. (2021). Identifying Pertinent Indicators for Assessing And Fostering Diversity, Equality And Inclusion of The Construction Workforce. *Journal of Management Engineering, 37*(2), 2. doi:10.1061/(ASCE)ME.1943-5479.0000885

Karli, H., & Tanyaş, M. (2020a). Suggestions For Supply Chain Risk Management In The Case Of Pandemic. *Istanbul Commerce University Journal of Social Sciences, 19*(37), 174–190.

Karlı, H., & Tanyaş, M. (2020b). Digital Transformation of Logistics Management: A Systematic Literature Mapping on Smart Logistics. *Optimum Journal of Economics and Management Sciences*, *7*(2), 613–632.

Karmańska, A. (2020). The benefits of HR Analytics. *Research Papers of Wroclaw University of Economics and Business, 64*(8), 30–39.

Kazim, F. A. (2019). Digital transformation and leadership style: a multiple case study. *The ISM Journal of International Business, 3*(1), 24-33.

Keçek, G., & Yildirim, E. (2009). Enterprise Resource Planning And The Importance For Company. *Electronic Journal of Social Sciences*, *8*(29), 240–258.

Keenoy, T., & Anthony, P. (1994). HRM: metaphor, meaning and morality. In P. Blyton & P. Turnbull (Eds.), *Reassessing Human Resource Management* (pp. 233–255). Sage.

Keidanren. (2018). *Society 5.0 - Cocreating The Future.* Https://Www.Keidanren.Or.Jp/En/Policy/2018/095_Proposal.Pdf

Kelliher, C., & Anderson, D. (2008). For better or for worse? An analysis of how flexible working practices influence employees' perceptions of job quality. *International Journal of Human Resource Management, 19*(3), 419–431. doi:10.1080/09585190801895502

Kelliher, C., Richardson, J., & Boiarintseva, G. (2019). All of work? All of life? Reconceptualising work-life balance for the 21st century. *Human Resource Management Journal, 29*(2), 97–112. Advance online publication. doi:10.1111/1748-8583.12215

Khan, A. A., Niazi, S., & Saif, S. K. (2020, March 26). *Universities unprepared for switch to remote learning*. University World News. https://www.universityworldnews.com/post.php?story=20200326141547229

Khan, H. P., Sultana, A., & Reddy, T. N. (2017). Review on HR Analytics: An Emerging Scale for Evaluation of Human Assets. *International Journal of Management and Social Sciences, 5*(8), 140–145.

Kiel, D., Arnold, C., & Voigt, K. I. (2017). The Influence of The Industrial Internet of Things on Business Models of Established Manufacturing Companies–A Business Level Perspective. *Technovation, 68*, 4–19. doi:10.1016/j.technovation.2017.09.003

Kinnunen, U., Mäkikangas, A., Mauno, S., De Cuyper, N., & De Witte, H. (2014). Development of perceived job insecurity across two years: Associations with antecedents and employee outcomes. *Journal of Occupational Health Psychology, 19*(2), 243–258. doi:10.1037/a0035835 PMID:24730428

Kırmaz, M., & Sayın, A. A. (n.d.). *The Place of Industry 5.0 in Logistics and Supply Chain.* Kutlu Publisher.

Kitsios, F., & Kamariotou, M. (2021). Artificial intelligence and business strategy towards digital transformation: A research agenda. *Sustainability, 13*(4), 2025. doi:10.3390u13042025

Klein, M. (2019). Comprehensive Digital Transformation Approach – World 4.0. In E. S. B. Meydanoğlu, M. Klein, & D. Kurt (Eds.), *Digital Transformation Trends*. Filiz Bookstore.

Klein, M. (2020). Digital Transformation In Businesses And Its Drivers. *Journal Of Business In The Digital Age, 3*(1), 24–35. doi:10.46238/jobda.729499

Knowledge spillover. (2020). In *Wikipedia*. https://en.wikipedia.org/wiki/Knowledge_spillover

Kolot, A., Kozmenko, S., Herasymenko, O., & Štreimikienė, D. (2020). Development of a decent work institute as a social quality imperative: Lessons for Ukraine. *Economia e Sociologia, 13*(2), 70–85. doi:10.14254/2071-789X.2020/13-2/5

Kong, X. T., Luo, H., Huang, G. Q., & Yang, X. (2019). Industrial wearable system: The human-centric empowering technology in Industry 4.0. *Journal of Intelligent Manufacturing, 30*(8), 2853–2869. doi:10.100710845-018-1416-9

Konradt, U., Warszta, T., & Ellwart, T. (2013). Fairness Perceptions in Web-based Selection: Impact on applicants' pursuit intentions, recommendation intentions, and intentions to reapply. *International Journal of Selection and Assessment, 21*(2), 155–169. doi:10.1111/ijsa.12026

Korejan, M. M., & Shahbazi, H. (2016). An analysis of the transformational leadership theory. *Journal of Fundamental and Applied Sciences, 8*(3), 452–461. doi:10.4314/jfas.v8i3s.192

Kort, de M. (2017). The relationship between work-life balance, work engagement and participation in employee development activities: A moderated mediation model. *Industrial Engineering Online, 13*(1). doi:10.20473/jmtt.v10i1.4805

Kotera, Y., & Correa Vione, K. (2020). Psychological Impacts of the New Ways of Working (NWW): A Systematic Review. *International Journal of Environmental Research and Public Health, 17*(14), 5080. doi:10.3390/ijerph17145080 PMID:32674518

Kowalski, K. B., & Swanson, J. A. (2005). Critical success factors in developing teleworking programs. *Benchmarking, 12*(3), 236–249. doi:10.1108/14635770510600357

Kraaijenbrink, J. (2022). What Is Industry 5.0 And How It Will Radically Change Your Business Strategy? *Forbes*. Retrieved from https://www.forbes.com/sites/jeroenkraaijenbrink/2022/05/24/what-is-industry-50-and-how-it-will-radically-change-your-bu siness-strategy/?sh=2cc86f2220bd

Kraichy, D., & Chapman, D. S. (2014). Tailoring Web-Based Recruiting Messages: Individual Differences in the Persuasiveness of Affective and Cognitive Messages. *Journal of Business and Psychology, 29*(2), 253–268. doi:10.100710869-013-9311-z

Kraus, W. M., Torrez, B., & Hollie, L. (2022). How Narratives of Radical Progress Create Barriers to Diversity, Eqality And Inclusion In Organizations. *Current Opinion in Psychology, 43*, 108–113. doi:10.1016/j.copsyc.2021.06.022 PMID:34340144

Kruse, K. (2012). What is Employee Engagement. *Forbes*. https://www.forbes.com/sites/kevinkruse/2012/06/22/employee-engagement-what-and-why/

Kumar, P., Dwivedi, Y. K., & Anand, A. (2021). Responsible artificial intelligence (AI) for value formation and market performance in healthcare: The mediating role of patient's cognitive engagement. *Information Systems Frontiers*, 1–24. doi:10.100710796-021-10136-6 PMID:33948105

Kuncoro, W., Adi, F. N., & Santoso, B. (2022). The Model of Human Resources Performance Development on the Leader Organization of Regional Devices at Salatiga Government. *International Business Research, 15*(7), 1–8. doi:10.5539/ibr.v15n7p8

Lagorio, A., Cimini, C., Pirola, F., & Pinto, R. (2021). A Taxonomy of Technologies for Human-Centred Logistics 4.0. *Applied Sciences (Basel, Switzerland), 11*(20), 9661. doi:10.3390/app11209661

Lähteenmäki, S., Toivonen, J., & Mattila, M. (2001). Critical Aspects of Organizational Learning Research and Proposals for Its Measurement. *British Journal of Management, 12*(2), 113–129. doi:10.1111/1467-8551.00189

Lall, M., Torvatn, H., & Seim, E. A. (2017, September). Towards industry 4.0: increased need for situational awareness on the shop floor. In *IFIP international conference on advances in production management systems* (pp. 322–329). Springer. doi:10.1007/978-3-319-66923-6_38

Lambert, S. J. (1990). Processes Linking Work and Family: A Critical Review and Research Agenda. *Human Relations, 43*(3), 239–257. doi:10.1177/001872679004300303

Lam, S., & Hawkes, B. (2017). From Analytics to Action: How Shell Digitized Recruitment. *Strategic HR Review, 16*(2), 76–80. doi:10.1108/SHR-01-2017-0005

Lariviere, B., Bowen, D., Andreassen, T. W., Kunz, W., Sirianni, N. J., Voss, C., Wunderlich, N. V., & De Keyser, A. (2017). Service Encounter 2.0": An investigation into the roles of technology, employees and customers. *Journal of Business Research, 79*, 238–246. doi:10.1016/j.jbusres.2017.03.008

Lazarus, R. S., & Folkman, S. (1984). *Stress, Appraisal, and Coping*. Springer Publishing Company, Inc. https://books.google.co.in/books?id=i-ySQQuUpr8C&printsec=frontcover#v=onepage&q&f=false

Le Masson, P., Dorst, K., & Subrahmanian, E. (2013). Design theory: History, state of the art and advancements. *Research in Engineering Design, 24*(2), 97–103. doi:10.100700163-013-0154-4

Lederman, D. (2020, March 18). *Most teaching is going remote. Will that help or hurt online learning?* Insidehighered.Com. https://www.insidehighered.com/digital-learning/article/2020/03/18/most-teaching-going-remote-will-help-or-hurt-online-l
earning

Lee, J. (2021). *[3 stages + 8 steps] Model for HR Analytics Implementation*. https://www.linkedin.com/pulse/3-stages-8-steps-model-hr-analytics-implementation-jaejin-lee/

Lee, J., Davari, H., Singh, J., & Pandhare, V. (2018). Industrial Artificial Intelligence for industry 4.0-based manufacturing systems. *Manufacturing Letters, 18*, 20–23. doi:10.1016/j.mfglet.2018.09.002

Legge, K. (1995). *Human Resource Management: Rhetorics and Realities*. Macmillan. doi:10.1007/978-1-349-24156-9

Leon, de J. (2020, March 20). *Best Practices for Positive and Productive Remote Work for Educators*. Education Elements. https://www.edelements.com/blog/best-practices-for-positive-and-productive-remote-work-for-educators

Levenson, A., & Pillans, G. (2017). *Strategic Workforce Analytics*. Corporate Research Forum. https://www.orgvue.com/uploads/sites/2/2020/05/strategic-workforce-analytics-report.pdf

Levenson, A. (2011). Using Targeted Analytics to Improve Talent Decisions. *People & Strategy, 34*(2), 34–43.

Levy, P. E., Cavanaugh, C. M., Frantz, N. B., & Borden, L. A. (2015). The role of due process in performance appraisal: A 20-year retrospective. In *The Oxford handbook of justice in the workplace* (pp. 605–619). Oxford University Press. doi:10.1093/oxfordhb/9780199981410.013.29

Liao, Y., Deschamps, F., Loures, E. D. F. R., & Ramos, L. F. P. (2017). Past, Present and Future of Industry 4.0-A Systematic Literature Review and Research Agenda Proposal. *International Journal of Production Research, 55*(12), 3609–3629. doi:10.1080/00207543.2017.1308576

Li, D., Landström, A., Fast-Berglund, Å., & Almström, P. (2019). Human-centred dissemination of data, information and knowledge in industry 4.0. *Procedia CIRP, 84*, 380–386. doi:10.1016/j.procir.2019.04.261

Li, D., Paulin, D., Fast-Berglund, Å., Gullander, P., & Bligård, L. O. (2018, November). Supporting individual needs for intra-organizational knowledge sharing activities in pre-industry 4.0 SMEs. *15th International Conference on Intellectual Capital, Knowledge Management and Organisational Learning, ICICKM 2018*, 160-170.

Liddy, E. D. (2001). *Natural language processing*. Syracuse University.

Li, F., Qi, J., Wang, G., & Wang, X. (2014). Traditional classroom VS e-learning in higher education: Difference between students' behavioral engagement. *International Journal of Emerging Technologies in Learning, 9*(2), 48–51. doi:10.3991/ijet.v9i2.3268

Lindebaum, D., Vesa, M., & den Hond, F. (2020). Insights from The Machine Stops to better understand rational assumptions in algorithmic decision-making and its implications for organizations. *Academy of Management Review, 45*(1), 247–263. doi:10.5465/amr.2018.0181

Liu, D. Y., Chen, S. W., & Chou, T. C. (2011). Resource Fit In Digital Transformation: Lessons Learned From The Cbc Bank Global E-Banking Project. *Management Decision, 49*(10), 1728–1742. doi:10.1108/00251741111183852

Livinston, R. (2020, Sept.). How to Promote racial Equity In The Workplace. *Harvard Business Review.*

Li, Z. (2021, February). Countermeasures and Effects of the Big Data Marketing on the Business Operational Management. In *6th International Conference on Economics, Management, Law and Education (EMLE 2020)* (pp. 369-372). Atlantis Press. 10.2991/aebmr.k.210210.060

Logg, J. M., Minson, J. A., & Moore, D. A. (2019). Algorithm appreciation: People prefer algorithmic to human judgment. *Organizational Behavior and Human Decision Processes, 151*, 90–103. doi:10.1016/j.obhdp.2018.12.005

Longo, F., Nicoletti, L., & Padovano, A. (2019). Modeling workers' behavior: A human factors taxonomy and a fuzzy analysis in the case of industrial accidents. *International Journal of Industrial Ergonomics, 69*, 29–47. doi:10.1016/j.ergon.2018.09.002

Longo, F., Padovano, A., & Umbrello, S. (2020). Value-oriented and ethical technology engineering in industry 5.0: A human-centric perspective for the design of the factory of the future. *Applied Sciences (Basel, Switzerland), 10*(12), 4182. doi:10.3390/app10124182

Lubis, F. R. A., Syaifuddin, & Lubis, Y. (2022). Human Resources Performance Improvement Through Training During the Covid-19 Pandemic. *The International Journal of Science in Society, 4*(1), 196–204. doi:10.54783/ijsoc.v4i1.429

Lukosius, V., & Hyman, M. R. (2019). Marketing theory and big data. *Journal of Developing Areas, 53*(4). Advance online publication. doi:10.1353/jda.2018.0082

Luo, X., Tong, S., Fang, Z., & Qu, Z. (2019). Frontiers: Machines vs. humans: The impact of artificial intelligence chatbot disclosure on customer purchases. *Marketing Science, 38*(6), 937–947. doi:10.1287/mksc.2019.1192

Lu, Y., Zheng, H., Chand, S., Xia, W., Liu, Z., Xu, X., Wang, L., Qin, Z., & Bao, J. (2022). Outlook on human-centric manufacturing towards Industry 5.0. *Journal of Manufacturing Systems, 62*, 612–627. doi:10.1016/j.jmsy.2022.02.001

MacInnis, D. J. (2011). A framework for conceptual contributions in marketing. *Journal of Marketing, 75*(4), 136–154. doi:10.1509/jmkg.75.4.136

Ma, D., & Hu, J. (2020). Research on collaborative management strategies of closed-loop supply chain under the influence of big-data marketing and reference price effect. *Sustainability, 12*(4), 1685. doi:10.3390u12041685

Maddikunta, P. K. R., Pham, Q. V., Prabadevi, B., Deepa, N., Dev, K., Gadekallu, T. R., & Liyanage, M. (2022). Industry 5.0: A survey on enabling technologies and potential applications. *Journal of Industrial Information Integration, 26*, 100257.

Madsen, E. S., Bilberg, A., & Hansen, D. G. (2016, September). Industry 4.0 and digitalization call for vocational skills, applied industrial engineering, and less for pure academics. In *Proceedings of the 5th P&OM World Conference, Production and Operations Management, P&OM* (*Vol. 40*). Academic Press.

Maestro, M. las H., Albiol, N. C., & Grau Grau, M. (Eds.). (2020). The New Ideal Worker. Springer International Publishing. doi:10.1007/978-3-030-12477-9

Malik, A., Budhwar, P., Srikanth, N. R., & Varma, A. (2019). *May the Bots Be with You! Opportunities and Challenges of Artificial Intelligence for Rethinking Human Resource Management Practices.* Paper Accepted for presentation BAM 2019. https:// www.bam.ac.uk/sites/bam.ac.uk/files/contribution294_0.pdf

Mara, M., Meyer, K., Heiml, M., Pichler, H., Haring, R., Krenn, B., & Layer-Wagner, T. (2021). *CoBot studio VR: A virtual reality game environment for transdisciplinary research on interpretability and trust in human-robot collaboration.* Springer.

Marcucci, G., Antomarioni, S., Ciarapica, F. E., & Bevilacqua, M. (2021). The impact of Operations and IT-related Industry 4.0 key technologies on organizational resilience. *Production Planning and Control*, 1–15.

Marler, J. H., & Boudreau, J. W. (2017). An evidence-based review of HR Analytics. *International Journal of Human Resource Management, 28*(1), 3–26. doi:10.1080/09585192.2016.1244699

Marler, J. H., & Parry, E. (2016). Human resource management, strategic involvement and e-HRM technology. *International Journal of Human Resource Management, 27*(19), 2233–2253. doi:10.1080/09585192.2015.1091980

Maroncelli, S., & Castagnoli, R. (2022). Human-centred manufacturing: quale ruolo per la sociologia della persona? In *XXII incontro giovani Pontignano – Sociologia.* Persona e Sfera pubblica.

Marr, B. (2018). The amazing ways how Unilever uses artificial intelligence to recruit & train thousands of employees. *Forbes.* https://www.forbes.com/sites/bernardmarr/2018/12/14/the-amazing-ways-how-unileveruses-artificial-intelligence-to-recruit-train-thousands-of-employees

Marr, B. (2019). *The Future Of Work: 5 Important Ways Jobs Will Change In The 4th Industrial Revolution.* Retrieved from https://www.forbes.com/sites/bernardmarr/2019/07/15/the-future-of-work-5-important-ways-jobs-will-change-in-the-4th-industrial-revolution/?sh=5aa8d2a454c7

Marr, D. (1976). *Artificial Intelligence- A personal view.* Massachusetts Institute of Technology Artificial Intelligence Laboratory.

Marshall, G. W., Michaels, C. E., & Mulki, J. P. (2007). Workplace Isolation: Exploring the Construct and Its Measurement. *Psychology and Marketing, 24*(3), 195–223. doi:10.1002/mar.20158

Martin, W. (2018). *Leadership: Outdated theories and emerging non-traditional leadership* [Doctoral dissertation]. Northcentral University.

Martynov, V. V., Shavaleeva, D. N., & Zaytseva, A. A. (2019). Information Technology as the Basis for Transformation into a Digital Society and Industry 5.0. *Quality Management, Transport and Information Security, Information Technologies*, 23–29.

Marvin, G., Jackson, M., & Alam, Md. G. R. (2021). A Machine Learning Approach for Employee Retention Prediction. *2021 IEEE Region 10 Symposium (TENSYMP)*, 1–8.

Mas-Machuca, M., Berbegal-Mirabent, J., & Alegre, I. (2016). Work-life balance and its relationship with organizational pride and job satisfaction. *Journal of Managerial Psychology, 31*(2), 586–602. doi:10.1108/JMP-09-2014-0272

Maurer, R. (2020, April 20). *Virtual Onboarding of Remote Workers More Important Than Ever.* SHRM. https://www.shrm.org/resourcesandtools/hr-topics/talent-acquisition/pages/virtual-onboarding-remote-workers.aspx

May, G., Taisch, M., Bettoni, A., Maghazei, O., Matarazzo, A., & Stahl, B. (2015). A new human-centric factory model. *Procedia CIRP*, *26*, 103–108. doi:10.1016/j.procir.2014.07.112

Mazali, T. (2018). From industry 4.0 to society 4.0, there and back. *AI & Society*, *33*(3), 405–411. doi:10.100700146-017-0792-6

McCarthy, J. M., Bauer, T. N., Truxillo, D. M., Anderson, N. R., Costa, A. C., & Ahmed, S. M. (2017). Applicant Perspectives During Selection: A Review Addressing "So What?" "What's New?" and "Where to Next?". *Journal of Management*, *43*(6), 1693–1725. doi:10.1177/0149206316681846

McCartney, S., & Fu, N. (2022). Bridging the Gap: Why, How and When HR Analytics Can Impact Organizational Performance. *Management Decision*, *60*(13), 25–47. doi:10.1108/MD-12-2020-1581

McCormick, H. (2016). *The Real Effects of Unconscious Bias in the Workplace*. University of North Carolina Chapel Hill Executive Development.

McCracken, M., & Wallace, M. (2000). Towards a redefinition of strategic HRD. *Journal of European Industrial Training*, *24*(5), 281–290. doi:10.1108/03090590010372056

McGregor, D. (1960). *The Human side of Enterprise*. McGraw-Hill.

McHugh, K. (2020). *Teachers Working From Home In Their Pajamas?* The Learning Counsel. https://thelearningcounsel.com/article/teachers-working-home-their-pajamas

McNall, L. A., Masuda, A. D., & Nicklin, J. M. (2009). Flexible work arrangements, job satisfaction, and turnover intentions: The mediating role of work-to-family enrichment. *The Journal of Psychology*, *144*(1), 61–81. doi:10.1080/00223980903356073 PMID:20092070

Medhi, B. (2020, October 6). *5 Major Factors Affecting The Quality Of Work Life*. Vantage Circle. https://blog.vantagecircle.com/quality-of-work-life-qwl/

Michel, J. S., Kotrba, L. M., Mitchelson, J. K., Clark, M. A., & Baltes, B. B. (2011). Antecedents of work-family conflict: A meta-analytic review. *Journal of Organizational Behavior*, *32*(5), 689–725. doi:10.1002/job.695

Miklosik, A., & Evans, N. (2020). Impact of big data and machine learning on digital transformation in marketing: A literature review. *IEEE Access: Practical Innovations, Open Solutions*, *8*, 101284–101292. doi:10.1109/ACCESS.2020.2998754

Miller, J. S., & Cardy, R. L. (2000). Technology and managing people. *Journal of Labor Research*, *21*(3), 447–461.

Millo, V., Brown, A., & Harrington, B. (2021). Addressing Race. In *The Workplace: Advancing Diversity, Equity And Inclusion. Boston College Center For Work & Family: Executive Briefing Series, UMB Digital Archive*. University of Maryland Baltimore.

Mishra, S. N., Lama, D. R., & Pal, Y. (2016). Human Resource Predictive Analytics (HRPA) for HR management in organizations. *International Journal of Scientific & Technology Research*, *5*(5), 33–35.

Miskini, C. (2018). *Normal simulation models versus a digital twin-based simulation*. Challenge Advisory. https://www.challenge.org/insights/digital-twin-simulations/

Moencks, M., Roth, E., Bohné, T., Romero, D., & Stahre, J. (2022). Augmented Workforce Canvas: A management tool for guiding human-centric, value-driven human-technology integration in industry. *Computers & Industrial Engineering*, *163*, 107803. doi:10.1016/j.cie.2021.107803

Moeuf, A., Pellerin, R., Lamouri, S., Tamayo-Giraldo, S., & Barbaray, R. (2018). The Industrial Management of Smes in The Era Of Industry 4.0. *International Journal of Production Research, 56*(3), 1118–1136. doi:10.1080/00207543.2017.1372647

Mohammed, A. Q. (2019). HR Analytics: A Modern Tool in HR for Predictive Decision Making. *Journal of Management, 6*(3), 51–63. doi:10.34218/JOM.6.3.2019.007

Mohapatra, M., & Sahu, P. (2017). Optimizing the Recruitment Funnel in an ITES Company: An Analytics Approach. *5th International Conference on Information Technology and Quantitative Management, ITQM 2017, 122*, 706–714. 10.1016/j.procs.2017.11.427

Molino, M., Ghislieri, C., & Cortese, C. G. (2013). When work enriches family-life: The mediational role of professional development opportunities. *Journal of Workplace Learning, 25*(2), 98–113. doi:10.1108/13665621311299780

Momin, W. Y., & Mishra, K. (2015). HR Analytics as a Strategic Workforce Planning. *International Journal of Applied Research, 1*(4), 258–260.

Mondal, S. (2021). AI for Recruiting: News, Tips, and Trends- The 25 Top Recruiting Software Tools Of 02021. *Ideal.* https://ideal.com/top-recruiting-software/.

Moore, P. (2019). *OSH and the Future of Work: Benefits and risks of artificial intelligence tools in workplaces.* European Agency for Safety and Health at Work (EU-OSHA). https://osha.europa.eu/en/publications/osh-and-future-work-benefits-and-risks-artificial-intelligence-tools-workplaces

Moore, S. (2021). *An Overview of Nanobots and the Most Recent Developments.* https://www.azonano.com/article.aspx?ArticleID=5761

Moore, A. L., & Klein, J. D. (2020). Facilitating Informal Learning at Work. *TechTrends, 64*(2), 219–228. doi:10.100711528-019-00458-3

Mordor Intelligence. (2022). Workflow Automation Market – Growt, Trends, Covid-19 Impact, And Forecasts (2022 – 2027). Mordor Intelligence. https://www.mordorintelligence.com/industry-reports/workflow-automation-market.

Mosterman, P. J., & Zander, J. (2016). Industry 4.0 as a cyber-physical system study. *Software & Systems Modeling, 15*(1), 17–29. doi:10.100710270-015-0493-x

Moumita & Bhanumathi, P. (2021). A Study On Integration Of Artificial Intelligence In Human Resources Management. *Utkal Historical Research Journal, 34*(XXIII).

Moustaghfir, K., El Fatihi, S., & Benouarrek, M. (2020). Human resource management practices, entrepreneurial orientation and firm performance: What is the link? *Measuring Business Excellence, 24*(2), 267–283. doi:10.1108/MBE-12-2019-0119

Mueller, F., Lopes, P., Strohmeier, P., Wendy J., Seim, C., Weigel, M., Nanayakkara, S., Obrist M., … Maes, P. (2020). *Next Steps in Human-Computer Integration.* Association for Computing Machinery. doi:10.1145/3313831.3376242

Muhammad, G., & Naz, F. (2022). A Moderating Role of HR Analytics Between Employee Engagement, Retention and Organisational Performance. *International Journal of Business Environment, 13*(4), 345–357. doi:10.1504/IJBE.2022.126370

Mulki, J. P., & Jaramillo, F. (2011). Workplace isolation: Salespeople and supervisors in USA. *International Journal of Human Resource Management, 22*(4), 902–923. doi:10.1080/09585192.2011.555133

Mullen, K. M. (2011). Human-technology Integration. In A. A. Minai, D. Braha, & Y. Bar-Yam (Eds.), *Unifying Themes in Complex Systems*. Springer. doi:10.1007/978-3-642-17635-7_31

Müller, J. (2020). *Enabling Technologies for Industry 5.0: results of a workshop with Europe's technology leaders*. Publications Office. https://data.europa.eu/doi/10.2777/082634

Müller, J. (2020). *Enabling Technologies for Industry 5.0: Results of a workshop with Europe's technology leaders*. Publications Office of the European Union.

Müller, J. M., Kiel, D., & Voigt, K. I. (2018). What drives the implementation of Industry 4.0? The role of opportunities and challenges in the context of sustainability. *Sustainability*, *10*(1), 247. doi:10.3390u10010247

Nahavandi, S. (2019). Industry 5.0—A Human-Centric Solution. Institute for Intelligent Systems Research and Innovation, Deakin University.

Nahavandi, S. (2019). Industry 5.0-a human-centric solution. *Sustainability (Switzerland)*, *11*(16), 4371. Advance online publication. doi:10.3390u11164371

Nambisan, S., Lyytinen, K., Majchrzak, A., & Song, M. (2017). Digital Innovation Management: Reinventing Innovation Management Research İn A Digital World. *Management Information Systems Quarterly*, *41*(1), 223–238. doi:10.25300/MISQ/2017/41:1.03

Nassazi, A. (2013). *Effects Of Training On Employee Performance*. Vaasan Ammattikorkeakoulu University. https://core.ac.uk/download/pdf/38098025.pdf

Neumann, W. P., Winkelhaus, S., Grosse, E. H., & Glock, C. H. (2021). Industry 4.0 and the human factor – A systems framework and analysis methodology for successful development. *International Journal of Production Economics*, *233*, 107992. Advance online publication. doi:10.1016/j.ijpe.2020.107992

Newman, D. T., Fast, N. J., & Harmon, D. J. (2020). When eliminating bias isn't fair: Algorithmic reductionism and procedural justice in human resource decisions. *Organizational Behavior and Human Decision Processes*, *160*, 149–167. doi:10.1016/j.obhdp.2020.03.008

Ngai, E. W. T., & Wat, F. K. T. (2006). Human resource information systems: A review and empirical analysis. *Personnel Review*, *35*(3), 297–314. doi:10.1108/00483480610656702

Ngoc, H., Lasa, G., & Iriarte, I. (2022). Human-centred design in industry 4.0: Case study review and opportunities for future research. *Journal of Intelligent Manufacturing*, *33*(1), 35–76. doi:10.100710845-021-01796-x PMID:34149201

Niazi, B. A. S. (2011). Training and Development Strategy and Its Role in Organizational Performance. *Journal of Public Administration and Governance*, *1*(2), 42–57. doi:10.5296/jpag.v1i2.862

Niehueser, W., & Boak, G. (2020). Introducing artificial intelligence into a human resources function. *Industrial and Commercial Training*, *52*(2), 121–130. doi:10.1108/ICT-10-2019-0097

Nikolaou, I. (2021). What is the Role of Technology in Recruitment and Selection? *The Spanish Journal of Psychology*, *24*, e2. Advance online publication. doi:10.1017/SJP.2021.6 PMID:33536110

Nilles, J. M., Carlson, F. R., & Gray, P. (1976). *The Telecommunications-transportation Tradeoff: Options for Tomorrow*. Wiley.

Noack, B. (2019). Big data analytics in human resource management: Automated decision-making processes, predictive hiring algorithms, and cutting-edge workplace surveillance technologies. *Psychosociological Issues in Human Resource Management*, *7*(2), 37–42.

Nocker, M., & Sena, V. (2019). Big data and human resources management: The rise of talent analytics. *Social Sciences*, *8*(10), 273. doi:10.3390ocsci8100273

Nofer, M., Gomber, P., Hinz, O., & Schiereck, D. (2017). Blockchain. *Business & Information Systems Engineering*, *59*(3), 183–187. doi:10.100712599-017-0467-3

Noguchi, Y. (2020, March 17). *Coronavirus Triple Duty: Working, Parenting And Teaching From Home*. NPR. https://www.npr.org/2020/03/17/816631571/coronavirus-triple-duty-working-parenting-and-teaching-from-home

Nuseir, M. T. (2018). How big data is used in expanding marketing activities. *International Journal of Economics and Business Research*, *16*(4), 466–475. doi:10.1504/IJEBR.2018.095342

Nyagadza, B., Gwiza, A., & Hove, K. P. (2022). Workplace Diversity, Equality And Inclusivity in Zimbabwean Labour Market. *Social Sciences*, *8*. Advance online publication. doi:10.1080/23311886.2022.2033456

Oberai, H., & Anand, I. M. (2018). Unconscious bias: Thinking without thinking. *Human Resource Management International Digest*, *26*(6), 14–17. doi:10.1108/hrmid-05-2018-0102

OCI. (n.d.). What is AI? Learn about Artificial Intelligence. Oracle India.

OECD. (2019). *Revealed: the countries with the best work-life balance*. OECD Better Life Index. https://www.oecdbetterlifeindex.org/topics/work-life-balance/

Oge, G., & Topaloglu, M. (2018). Using the Big Data in the human resources management systems. *Global Journal of Information Technology: Emerging Technologies*, *8*(3), 129–133. doi:10.18844/gjit.v8i3.4053

Okumuşoğlu, N. T. (2022). The Impact of Digitalization on the Quality Performance in Supply Chain Management: An Application on Employees in Manufacturing Sector. *BNEJSS*, *8*(03), 17–28.

Oladipupo, O. O., & Olubusayo, F. H. (2020). Human Resource Analytics Dimensions and Employee Engagement in Manufacturing Industry in Nigeria: A Conceptual Review. *Journal of Management Information and Decision Sciences*, *23*(5), 629–637.

Olan, F., Arakpogun, E. O., Suklan, J., Nakpodia, F., Damij, N., & Jayawickrama, U. (2022). Artificial intelligence and knowledge sharing: Contributing factors to organizational performance. *Journal of Business Research*, *145*, 605–615. doi:10.1016/j.jbusres.2022.03.008

Oliveira, M., Arica, E., Pinzone, M., Fantini, P., & Taisch, M. (2019, July). Human-centered manufacturing challenges affecting European industry 4.0 enabling technologies. In *International Conference on Human-Computer Interaction*. Springer. 10.1007/978-3-030-30033-3_39

Opatha, H. H. D. P. J. (2020). HR Analytics: A Literature Review and New Conceptual Model. *International Journal of Scientific and Research Publications*, *10*(6), 130–141. doi:10.29322/IJSRP.10.06.2020.p10217

Oracle Taleo. (2012). *Oracle Taleo Recruiting Cloud Service*. https://www.oracle.com/a/ocom/docs/taleo-recruiting-cloud-service.pdf

Oracle Taleo. (n.d.). *Oracle Taleo*. Retrieved 30 July 2022, from https://www.oracle.com/es/human-capital-management/taleo/

Orso, V., Ziviani, R., Bacchiega, G., Bondani, G., Spagnolli, A., & Gamberini, L. (2022). Employee-centric innovation: Integrating participatory design and video-analysis to foster the transition to Industry 5.0. *Computers & Industrial Engineering, 173*, 108661. doi:10.1016/j.cie.2022.108661

Oruçoğlu, O. (2022). The Impacts Of Industry 4.0 On Recruitment From Human Resources Management Functions. *Aegean Journal of Strategic Studies, 13*(1), 57–84.

Østergaard, H. E. (2016, May 13). *Industry 5.0 – Return of the human touch*. https://www.universal-robots.com/blog/industry-50-return-of-the-human-touch/

Østergaard, H. E. (2017a, October 17). *Collaborative Robots ushering in Industry 5.0*. https://www.universal-robots.com/blog/collaborative-robots-ushering-in-industry-50/

Østergaard, H. E. (2017b, October 27). *Industry 5.0: The Factory of the Future*. https://www.universal-robots.com/blog/industry-50-the-factory-of-the-future/

Oswick, C., & Noon, M. (2014). Discourses of diversity, equality and inclusion: Trenchant Formulations or transient fashions? *British Journal of Management, 25*(1), 23–39. doi:10.1111/j.1467-8551.2012.00830.x

Overheid, A. (2022, April 15). *Understanding Fog Computing vs Edge Computing*. https://www.onlogic.com/company/io-hub/fog-computing-vs-edge-computing/#:~:text=In%20a%20nutshell%2C%20edge%20computing, purposes%2C%20such%20as%20data%20filtering

Özdemir, A. İ., & Doğan, N. Ö. (2010). Supply Chain Integration And Information Technologies. *Erciyes University Journal of Social Sciences Institute, 1*(28), 19–41.

Özdoğan, O. (2019). *Industry 4.0 The Fourth Industrial Revolution and Keys to Industrial Transformation* (3rd ed.). Pusula.

Özkahveci, E., Civek, F., & Ulusoy, G. (2022). The Place Of Metaverse (Fictional Universe) In The Period Of Industry 5.0. *The Sciences, 8*(50), 398–409.

Özsoylu, A. F. (2017). Industry 4.0. *Journal of Çukurova University Faculty of Economics and Administrative Sciences, 21*(1), 41–64.

Öztemel, E. (2018). Evaluation of New Trends in Education and Education 4.0. *Journal of University Research, 1*(1), 25–30.

Palloff, R. M., & Pratt, K. (2007). *Building Online Learning Communities: Effective Strategies for the Virtual Classroom* (2nd ed.). Wiley. https://www.wiley.com/en-us/Building+Online+Learning+Communities%3A+Effective+Strategies+for+the+Virtual+Classroom%2C+2nd+Edition-p-9780787988258

Pan, Y., Froese, F., Liu, N., Hu, Y., & Ye, M. (2022). The adoption of artificial intelligence in employee recruitment: The influence of contextual factors. *International Journal of Human Resource Management, 33*(6), 1125–1147. doi:10.1080/09585192.2021.1879206

Paredes-Astudillo, Y. A., Jimenez, J. F., Zambrano-Rey, G., & Trentesaux, D. (2019, October). Human-Machine Cooperation for the Distributed Control of a Hybrid Control Architecture. In *International Workshop on Service Orientation in Holonic and Multi-Agent Manufacturing* (pp. 98-110). Springer.

Parker, D. F., & DeCotiis, T. A. (1983). Organizational determinants of job stress. *Organizational Behavior and Human Performance, 32*(2), 160–177. doi:10.1016/0030-5073(83)90145-9

Parkhurst, C. A. L. (2017). *Presentation Design and Retention* [Doctoral dissertation, Old Dominion University].

Park, R. (2018). The roles of OCB and automation in the relationship between job autonomy and organizational performance: A moderated mediation model. *International Journal of Human Resource Management, 29*(6), 1139–1156. doi:10.1080/09585192.2016.1180315

Parks, M. A., Scott, G., Seijo, C., & Keys, T. (2022). *Anchored or Detached? A Student Commentary on Equity.* Diversity And Inclusion At Urban Institutions, Coalitions of Urban And Metropolitan Universities. doi:10.18060/26300

Park, Y., Woo, H., Oh, M.-R., & Park, S. (2020). The role and related variables of workplace learning in quantitative research. *Industrial and Commercial Training, 53*(1), 29–59. doi:10.1108/ICT-02-2020-0023

Partridge, D., & Hussain, K. M. (1992). Artificial Intelligence and Business Management. *International Journal of Management, 18*(3), 1–14.

Pautasso, M. (2019). The structure and conduct of a narrative literature review. A Guide to the Scientific Career. *Virtues, Communication, Research and Academic Writing*, 299-310.

Peeters, T., Paauwe, J., & Van De Voorde, K. (2020). People analytics effectiveness: Developing a framework. *Journal of Organizational Effectiveness: People and Performance, 7*(2), 203–219. doi:10.1108/JOEPP-04-2020-0071

Peruzzini, M., Grandi, F., & Pellicciari, M. (2018). How to analyse the workers' experience in integrated product-process design. *Journal of Industrial Information Integration, 12*, 31–46. doi:10.1016/j.jii.2018.06.002

Peruzzini, M., Grandi, F., & Pellicciari, M. (2020). Exploring the potential of Operator 4.0 interface and monitoring. *Computers & Industrial Engineering, 139*, 105600. doi:10.1016/j.cie.2018.12.047

Peruzzini, M., & Pellicciari, M. (2017). A framework to design a human-centred adaptive manufacturing system for aging workers. *Advanced Engineering Informatics, 33*, 330–349. doi:10.1016/j.aei.2017.02.003

Pessach, D., Singer, G., Avrahami, D., Chalutz Ben-Gal, H., Shmueli, E., & Ben-Gal, I. (2020). Employees recruitment: A Prescriptive Analytics Approach via Machine Learning and Mathematical Programming. *Decision Support Systems, 134*, 113290. doi:10.1016/j.dss.2020.113290 PMID:32501316

Petrie, N. (2011). Future trends in leadership development. *Center for Creative Leadership White Paper, 5*(5), 36.

Pinzone, M., Albè, F., Orlandelli, D., Barletta, I., Berlin, C., Johansson, B., & Taisch, M. (2020). A framework for operative and social sustainability functionalities in Human-Centric Cyber-Physical Production Systems. *Computers & Industrial Engineering, 139*, 105132. doi:10.1016/j.cie.2018.03.028

Piwowar-SULEJ, K. (2020). Human resource management in the context of Industry 4.0. *Organization & Management Scientific Quartely, 2020*(49). doi:10.29119/1899-6116.2020.49.7

Plastino, E., & Purdy, M. (2018). Game changing value from Artiðcial Intelligence: Eight strategies. *Strategy and Leadership, 46*(1), 16–22. doi:10.1108/SL-11-2017-0106

Poba-Nzaou, P., Galani, M., & Tchibozo, A. (2020). Transforming human resources management in the age of Industry 4.0: A matter of survival for HR professionals. *Strategic HR Review, 19*(6), 273–278. doi:10.1108/SHR-06-2020-0055

Poole, S. (2018). Elastic by Leonard Mlodinow review – unplug to think creatively. *The Guardian*. Retrieved from https://www.theguardian.com/books/2018/apr/18/elastic-flexiblethinking-leonard-mlodinow

Popomaronis, T. (2019). Here's How Many Google Interviews It Takes to Hire a Googler. *CNBC*. https://www.cnbc.com/2019/04/17/heres-how-many-google-job-interviews-it-takes-to-hire-a-googler.html

Prassida, G. F., & Asfari, U. (2021). A conceptual model for the acceptance of collaborative robots in industry 5.0. *Procedia Computer Science, 197*, 61–67. doi:10.1016/j.procs.2021.12.118

Praveen, S., & Karuppasamy, R. (2017). Competency-based compensation system: As a strategic HR technique with special reference to Coimbatore. *International Journal of Economic Policy in Emerging Economies, 10*(1), 116–128.

Purvis, J. (2016). Human Resources Marketing and Recruiting: Essentials of Digital Recruiting. In M. Zeuch (Ed.), *Handbook of Human Resources Management* (pp. 53–71). Springer. doi:10.1007/978-3-662-44152-7_3

Qamar, Y., Agrawal, R. K., Samad, T. A., & Chiappetta Jabbour, C. J. (2021). When technology meets people: The interplay of artificial intelligence and human resource management. *Journal of Enterprise Information Management, 34*(5), 1339–1370. doi:10.1108/JEIM-11-2020-0436

Quan, T. A. O. (2021). Research on Specialty Construction and Teaching Mode Reform of Big Data Marketing in the Post-Epidemic Era, 2021. *International Conference on Education, Humanities, Management and Information Technology (EHMIT 2021)*.

Rabhi, L., Falih, N., Afraites, A., & Bouikhalene, B. (2019). Big data approach and its applications in various fields. *Procedia Computer Science, 155*, 599–605. doi:10.1016/j.procs.2019.08.084

Rada, M. (2018). *Industry 5.0-from Virtual to Physical*. LinkedIn. Available online: https://www.linkedin.com/pulse/industry-50-from-virtual-physical-michael-rada

Radziwon, A., Bilberg, A., Bogers, M., & Madsen, E. S. (2014). The Smart Factory: Exploring Adaptive and Flexible Manufacturing Solutions. *Procedia Engineering, 69*, 1184–1190. doi:10.1016/j.proeng.2014.03.108

Rahwan, I., Cebrian, M., Obradovich, N., Bongard, J., Bonnefon, J.-F., Breazeal, C., Crandall, J. W., Christakis, N. A., Couzin, I. D., Jackson, M. O., Jennings, N. R., Kamar, E., Kloumann, I. M., Larochelle, H., Lazer, D., McElreath, R., Mislove, A., Parkes, D. C., Pentland, A., ... Wellman, M. (2019). Machine behaviour. *Nature, 568*(7753), 477–486. doi:10.103841586-019-1138-y PMID:31019318

Rai, N. G. M., Silmina, N., Fitrananda, H., Hanoum, S., Sinansari, P., & Noor, B. A. (2021, December). The Effect of work Conflict and Job Stress on The Human Resources Performance (Case Study: Maintenance & Engineer Division at PT. Paiton Operation & Maintenance Indonesia). In *3rd International Conference on Business and Management of Technology (ICONBMT 2021)* (pp. 305-309). Atlantis Press.

Raisamo, R., Rakkolainen, I., Majaranta, P., Salminen, K., Rantala, J., & Farooq, A. (2019). Human Augmentation: Past, present and future. *International Journal of Human-Computer Studies, 131*, 131–143. Advance online publication. doi:10.1016/j.ijhcs.2019.05.008

Raisch, S., & Krakowski, S. (in press). Artificial Intelligence and Management: The Automation-Augmentation Paradox. *Academy of Management Review*.

Rajamohan, S., & Dhanabalan, T. (2013). Rural development through ICT: Opportunities and challenges. *International Journal of Retailing & Rural Business Perspectives, 2*(2), 354.

Ranjan, P., & Basu, H. V. S. S. A. (2003). *Part of speech tagging and local word grouping techniques for natural language parsing in Hindi*. In Proceedings of the 1st International Conference on Natural Language Processing (ICON 2003). Semantic Scholar.

Rapanta, C., Botturi, L., Goodyear, P., Guàrdia, L., & Koole, M. (2020). Online University Teaching During and After the Covid-19 Crisis: Refocusing Teacher Presence and Learning Activity. *Postdigital Science and Education, 2*(3), 923–945. doi:10.100742438-020-00155-y

Rauch, E., Linder, C., & Dallasega, P. (2020). Anthropocentric perspective of production before and within Industry 4.0. *Computers & Industrial Engineering, 139*, 105644. doi:10.1016/j.cie.2019.01.018

Rayner, B., & Bolhuis, M. A. (2020). *The More the Merrier? A Machine Learning Algorithm for Optimal Pooling of Panel Data.* International Monetary Fund. doi:10.5089/9781513529974.001

Reilly, P. (2018). The impact of artificial intelligence on the HR function. *IES Perspectives on HR 2018.* Retrieved from https://www.employment-studies.co.uk/system/files/resources/files/mp142_The_impact_of_Artificial_Intelligence_on_the_HR_function-Peter_Reilly.pdf

Reiman, A., Kaivo-oja, J., Parviainen, E., Takala, E. P., & Lauraeus, T. (2021). Human factors and ergonomics in manufacturing in the industry 4.0 context–A scoping review. *Technology in Society, 65*, 101572. doi:10.1016/j.techsoc.2021.101572

Reitsma, T. (2022). Ten Best Employee Compensation Management Software In. *People Managing People.* https://peoplemanagingpeople.com/tools/best-compensation-management-software/.

Remote Year. (2020). *What the Future of Remote Work Means for You.* Remote Year. https://www.remoteyear.com/blog/remote-work-future

Remote.Co. (2020). *What are the keys to successful remote team relationships?* Remote.Co. https://remote.co/qa-leading-remote-companies/what-elements-are-key-to-successful-working-relationships-with-remote-teams/

Resch, A., & Blecker, T. (2012). Smart Logistics–A Literature Review. *Pioneering Supply Chain Design, 10*, 91–102.

Rice, R. W., Frone, M. R., & McFarlin, D. B. (1992). Work—Nonwork conflict and the perceived quality of life. *Journal of Organizational Behavior, 13*(2), 155–168. doi:10.1002/job.4030130205

Rich, B. L., LePine, J. A., & Crawford, E. R. (2010). Job Engagement: Antecedents and Effects on Job Performance. *Academy of Management Journal, 53*(3), 617–635. doi:10.5465/amj.2010.51468988

Ritz-Carlton. (n.d.). *Gold standards.* The Ritz-Carlton. Retrieved 2 August 2022, from https://www.ritzcarlton.com/en/about/gold-standards

Roberson, M. Q. (2004). *Disentangling The Meanings of Diversity And Inclusion.* Center for Advanced Human Resource Studies, Working Paper 04-05. CAHRS/Cornel University.

Robinson, S. L. (1996). Trust and breach of the psychological contract. *Administrative Science Quarterly, 41*(4), 574–599. doi:10.2307/2393868

Robotics Online Marketing Team. (2020). *The Role of Collaborative Robots in Industry 5.0.* https://www.automate.org/blogs/the-role-of-collaborative-robots-in-industry-5-0

Rodeghero, P., Zimmermann, T., Houck, B., & Ford, D. (2021). *Please Turn Your Cameras on: Remote Onboarding of Software Developers During a Pandemic.* https://ieeexplore.ieee.org/document/9402105

Rodrigues, J. (2019). *15 examples of human augmentation in everyday life.* https://www.freshconsulting.com/insights/blog/examples-of-human-augmentation/

Roehling, P. V., Roehling, M. V., & Moen, P. (2001). The relationship between work-life policies and practices and employee loyalty: A life course perspective. *Journal of Family and Economic Issues*, *22*(2), 141–170. doi:10.1023/A:1016630229628

Roloff, M. E., & Fonner, K. L. (2010). Why teleworkers are more satisfied with their jobs than are office-based workers: When less contact is beneficial. *Journal of Applied Communication Research*, *38*(4), 336–361. doi:10.1080/00909882.2010.513998

Romansky, L., Garrod, M., Brown, K., & Deo, K. (2021). Organizational Culture How to Measure Inclusion in Workplace. *Harvard Business Review*, 27.

Romero, D., Stahre, J., Wuest, T., Noran, O., Bernus, P., Fast-Berglund, Å., & Gorecky, D. (2016b, October). Towards an operator 4.0 typology: a human-centric perspective on the fourth industrial revolution technologies. *Proceedings of the international conference on computers and industrial engineering (CIE46),* 29-31.

Romero, D., Bernus, P., Noran, O., Stahre, J., & Fast-Berglund, Å. (2016a). The operator 4. 0: Human cyber-physical systems & adaptive automation towards human-automation symbiosis work systems. In *IFIP international conference on advances in production management system* (pp. 677–686). Springer. doi:10.1007/978-3-319-51133-7_80

Romero, D., Noran, O., Stahre, J., Bernus, P., & Fast-Berglund, Å. (2015, September). Towards a human-centred reference architecture for next generation balanced automation systems: human-automation symbiosis. In *IFIP international conference on advances in production management systems* (pp. 556–566). Springer. doi:10.1007/978-3-319-22759-7_64

Roquelaure, Y. (2021). *New forms of work in the digital era: Implications for psychosocial risks and musculoskeletal disorders.* https://osha.europa.eu/en/publications/digitalisation-work-psychosocial-risk-factors-and-work-related-musculoskeletal

Rosseel, Y. (2012). Lavaan: An R package for structural equation modeling. *Journal of Statistical Software*, *48*(1), 1–36. doi:10.18637/jss.v048.i02

Roy, S., Sivakumar, K., & Wilkinson, I. F. (2004). Innovation Generation In Supply Chain Relationships: A Conceptual Model and Research Propositions. *Journal of the Academy of Marketing Science*, *32*(1), 61–79. doi:10.1177/0092070303255470

Roziq, M., Reawaroe, H. P., & Rosyidi, A. I. (2021). Investment Perspectives in Human Resources Management and Its Contribution on Organizational Performance and Competitive Advantages. *Journal of Management and Leadership*, *4*(1), 1–13. doi:10.47970/jml.v4i1.207

Russell, S., Norvig, P., & Intelligence, A. (1995). *Artificial Intelligence: A modern approach.* Prentice-Hall.

Rüßmann, M., Lorenz, M., Gerbert, P., Waldner, M., Justus, J., Engel, P., & Harnisch, M. (2015). *Industry 4.0: The Future of Productivity and Growth İn Manufacturing Industries.* Boston Consulting Group.

Sadıç, Ş. (2021). Industry 5.0 and Sustainability. In G.I. Bolatan (Ed.), Industry 5.0 Digital Society. Ekin Publishing House.

Şahinel, D., Akpolat, C., Görür, O. C., Sivrikaya, F., & Albayrak, S. (2021). Human modeling and interaction in cyber-physical systems: A reference framework. *Journal of Manufacturing Systems*, *59*, 367–385. doi:10.1016/j.jmsy.2021.03.002

Şahin, U. Ö. (2021). Society 5.0 and public services: An assessment on Turkey. *Journal of Awareness*, *6*(4), 229–246.

Samek, W., & Müller, K.-R. (2019). *Towards explainable artificial intelligence.* doi:10.1007/978-3-030-28954-6_1

Samuel, O. W., Omisore, M. O., & Atajeromavwo, E. J. (2014). Online fuzzy based decision support system for human resource performance appraisal. *Measurement, 55*, 452–461. doi:10.1016/j.measurement.2014.05.024

Sanz de Miguel, P., Caprile, M., & Arasanz, J. (2021). *Regulating telework in a post-COVID-19 Europe.* Publications Office of the European Union. https://osha.europa.eu/es/publications/regulating-telework-post-covid-19-europe

Sarvesh, K. R., & Bhanumathi, P. (2022). A study on the Technology-driven employee monitoring trend during COVID-19. *Journal of Fundamental & Comparative Research, 12*(7).

Satyanarayanan, M., & Davies, N. (2019). Augmenting Cognition Through Edge Computing. *Augmenting Cognition Through Edge Computing. in Computer, 52*(7), 37–46. doi:10.1109/MC.2019.2911878

Saxena, A., Saxena, A., Sharma, R., & Parashar, M. (2021). *Emergence of Futuristic HRM in Perspective of Human-Cobot's Collaborative Functionality.* Research Gate.

Saxena, P., Charu, & Arora, R. (2022). Exploring the link between Innovativeness and Organizational Performance. *NMIMS Management Review, 30*(1), 68-89. doi:10.53908/NMMR.300104

Saxena, A., Saxena, A., Sharma, R., & Parashar, M. (2021). Emergence of Futuristic HRM in Perspective of Human - Cobot's Collaborative Functionality. *International Journal of Engineering and Advanced Technology, 10*(5), 292–296. doi:10.35940/ijeat.E2763.0610521

Schaufeli, W. B., & Bakker, A. B. (2003). *Utrecht Work Engagement Scale: Preliminary Manual.* Department of Psychology, Utrecht University.

Schaufeli, W. B., & Bakker, A. B. (2010). Defining and Measuring Work Engagement: Bringing Clarity to the Concept. In *Work Engagement: A Handbook of Essential Theory and Research.* Psychology Press.

Schick-Makaroff, K., MacDonald, M., Plummer, M., Burgess, J., & Neander, W. (2016). What Synthesis Methodology Should I Use? A Review and Analysis of Approaches to Research Synthesis. *AIMS Public Health, 3*(1), 172–175. doi:10.3934/publichealth.2016.1.172 PMID:29546155

Schiele, H., Bos-Nehles, A., Delke, V., Stegmaier, P., & Torn, R. J. (2022). Interpreting the industry 4.0 future: Technology, business, society and people. *The Journal of Business Strategy, 43*(3), 157–167. doi:10.1108/JBS-08-2020-0181

Schmidt, F. L., Oh, I. S., & Shaffer, J. A. (2016). The validity and utility of selection methods in personnel psychology: Practical and theoretical implications of 100 years. *Fox School of Business Research Paper*, 1-74.

Schrotenboer, B. (2020, May 4). Working at home had a positive effect on productivity during the pandemic. *USA Today.* https://www.usatoday.com/story/money/2020/05/04/coronavirus-pandemic-might-game-changer-working-home/3061862001/

Science, Technology and Innovation Board. (2015). *Report On The 5th Science And Technology Basic.* Government of Japan: Https://Www8.Cao.Go.Jp/Cstp/Kihonkeikaku/5basicplan_En.Pdf Btk

Şekkeli, Z. H., & Bakan, İ. (2018). By The Effect Of The Industry 4.0 On Logistics 4.0. *Journal of Life Economics, 5*(2), 17–36.

Selden, S., & Orenstein, J. (2011). Government e-recruiting web sites: The influence of e-recruitment content and usability on recruiting and hiring outcomes in US state governments. *International Journal of Selection and Assessment, 19*(1), 31–40. doi:10.1111/j.1468-2389.2011.00532.x

Senyucel, Z. (2009). *Managing the Human Resources in the 21st century.* Zorlu.

Shah, D., & Barker, M. (2020). Work-life interface: Experiences of Indian IT women repatriates. *International Journal of Human Resource Management*. Advance online publication. doi:10.1080/09585192.2020.1737173

Shankar, K. (2020). The Impact of COVID-19 on IT Services Industry—Expected Transformations. *British Journal of Management, 31*(3), 450–452. doi:10.1111/1467-8551.12423

Shannon, C. (1950). Programming a computer for playing chess. *Philosophical Magazine*, 41.

Sharma, N. (2021). Using positive deviance to enhance employee engagement: An interpretive structural modelling approach. *The International Journal of Organizational Analysis, 30*(1), 84–98. doi:10.1108/IJOA-07-2020-2341

Sharma, N. (Ed.). (2019). *Analyzing workplace deviance in modern organizations*. IGI Global.

Sharma, N., & Garg, P. (2017). Psychological contract and psychological empowerment as employee engagement drivers in Indian IT sector. *International Journal of Applied Business and Economic Research, 15*(1).

Sharma, N., & Singh, V. K. (2016). Effect of workplace incivility on job satisfaction and turnover intentions in India. *South Asian Journal of Global Business Research, 5*(2), 234–249. doi:10.1108/SAJGBR-02-2015-0020

Sharma, N., & Singh, V. K. (2018). Psychological empowerment and employee engagement: Testing the mediating effects of constructive deviance in Indian IT Sector. *International Journal of Human Capital and Information Technology Professionals, 9*(4), 44–55. doi:10.4018/IJHCITP.2018100103

Shaw, J. D., Gupta, N., & Delery, J. E. (2001). Congruence between technology and compensation systems: Implications for strategy implementation. *Strategic Management Journal, 22*(4), 379–386.

Sheppard, G. (2016). Work-life balance programs to improve employee performance. *Walden Dissertations and Doctoral Studies*, 1–329. http://ovidsp.ovid.com/ovidweb.cgi?T=JS&PAGE=reference&D=psyc13a&NEWS=N&AN=2016-47708-167%0Ahttps://search.proquest.com/docview/1765463932?accountid=12763%0Ahttp://primoa.library.unsw.edu.au/openurl/61UNSW_INST/UNSW_SERVICES_PAGE?url_ver=Z39.88-2004&rft_v

Shet, S., Poddar, T., Wamba Samuel, F., & Dwivedi, Y. K. (2021). Examining the determinants of successful adoption of data analytics in human resource management – A framework for implications. *Journal of Business Research, 131*, 311–326. doi:10.1016/j.jbusres.2021.03.054

Shinkarenko, A. (2020). *Internet of everything vs internet of things*. Retrieved from https:// www. Itransition.com/blog/internet-of- everything-vs- internet-of- things

Shrestha, Y. R., Ben-Menahem, S. M., & von Krogh, G. (2019). Organizational decision-making structures in the age of artificial intelligence. *California Management Review, 61*(4), 1–18. doi:10.1177/0008125619862257

Shrestha, Y. R., & Krishna, V. (forthcoming). Augmenting Organizational Decision-Making with Deep Learning Algorithms: Principles, Promises, and Challenges. *Journal of Business Research.*

Shrestha, Y. R., & Yang, Y. (2019). Fairness in algorithmic decision-making: Applications in multi-winner voting, machine learning, and recommender systems. *Algorithms, 12*(9), 199. doi:10.3390/a12090199

Shrivastava, S., & Dhaigude, A. S. (2022). Prime Data Tech Pvt. Ltd: Resolving Employee Recruitment Dilemma using HR Analytics. *Communications of the Association for Information Systems, 50*(27), 576–588. doi:10.17705/1CAIS.05027

Shuck, B., Twyford, D., Reio, T. G. Jr, & Shuck, A. (2014). Human Resource Development Practices and Employee Engagement: Examining the Connection With Employee Turnover Intentions. *Human Resource Development Quarterly*, *25*(2), 239–270. doi:10.1002/hrdq.21190

Singh, R., Sharma, P., Foropon, C., & Belal, H. M. (2022). The Role of Big Data and Predictive Analytics in the Employee Retention: A Resource-Based View. *International Journal of Manpower*, *43*(2), 411–447. doi:10.1108/IJM-03-2021-0197

Sinha, E. (2017). Emotional Intelligence: Proximal factor of Entrepreneurial Behaviour. *Twelfth Biennial Conference on Entrepreneurship*, *1*, 109-119.

Sinha, E. (2021). Towards an Integrative Framework of Intrapreneurship by Focusing on Individual Level Competencies. *Journal of Asia Entrepreneurship and Sustainability*, *17*(1), 106–163.

Sinha, E. (2022a). Managerial Intrapreneurship: Effect of Individual level Competencies and Mediating Role of Trait Emotional Intelligence. *Journal of Asia Entrepreneurship and Sustainability*, *18*(2), 3–51.

Sinha, E. (2022b). 'PREFACE' Leadership in Times of Crises: Evidence from Indian SME Sector. In L. P. Dana, N. Sharma, & V. Singh (Eds.), *Managing Human Resources in SMEs and Start-ups: International Challenges and Solutions*. World Scientific. doi:10.1142/9789811239212_0014

Sivathanu, B., & Pillai, R. (2020). Technology and Talent Analytics for Talent Management – A Game Changer for Organizational Performance. *The International Journal of Organizational Analysis*, *28*(2), 457–473. doi:10.1108/IJOA-01-2019-1634

Skobelev, P. O., & Borovik, S. Y. (2017). On the way from Industry 4.0 to Industry 5.0: From digital manufacturing to digital society. *Industry 4.0, 2*(6), 307-311.

Snell, A. (2011). Developing Talent Intelligence to Boost Business Performance. *Strategic HR Review*, *10*(2), 12–17. doi:10.1108/14754391111108301

Snyder, H. (2019). Literature review as a research methodology: An overview and guidelines. *Journal of Business Research*, *104*, 333–339. doi:10.1016/j.jbusres.2019.07.039

Sobot, R. (2019, November 30). Implantable Technology: History, Controversies, and Social Implications. *IEEE Technology and Society Magazine*. doi:10.1109/MTS.2018.2880167

Soll, J.B., Katherine, L.M., & Payne, J.W. (2015). Outsmart your own biases. *Harward Business Review*.

Song, S., Chen, Y., Ngai-Man, C., & Jay Kuo, C. (2018). *Defense against Adversarial Attacks with Saak Transform.* arXiv preprint, arXiv:1808.01785 [cs.CV].

Sotnikova, Y., Nazarova, G., Nazarov, N., & Bilokonenko, H. (2020). Digital technologies in HR management. *Management Theory and Studies for Rural Business and Infrastructure Development*, *42*(4), 527–535. doi:10.15544/mts.2020.54

Spataro, J. (2020, March 11). *Helping teachers and students make the switch to remote learning.* Microsoft.Com. https://www.microsoft.com/en-us/microsoft-365/blog/2020/03/11/helping-teachers-students-switch-remote-learning/

Specht, M. (n.d.). *2009-2010 HR Systems Survey*, (12th ed.). Cedar Crestone .

Sponaugle, E. (2020, March 13). *Remote Teaching: 7 Positive Outcomes from My Experience*. Erinsponaugle.Com. https://www.erinsponaugle.com/post/remote-teaching-benefits

Srinivasan, M. (2022). *Recent Trends in Compensation & Benefits.* LinkedIn. https://www.linkedin.com/pulse/recent-trends-compensation-benefits-mridhula-srinivasan

Srivastava, S. (2018). *Impact of Artificial Intelligence on strategic HR decision making.* Retrieved from https://www.peoplematters.in/article/technology/impact-of-artificial-intelligence-on-strategic-hr-decision-making-17935

Stahl, A. (2021). *What's To Come In 2021 For Diversity, Equity And Inclusion In The Workplace.* https://www.forbes.com/sites/ashleystahl/2021/04/14/whats-to-come-in-2021-for-diversity-equity-and-inclusion-in-the-work
place/?sh=25efbbf57f26

Stefan, T., & Nazarov, A. D. (2020, November). Challenges and competencies of leadership in Covid-19 Pandemic. In Research technologies of pandemic coronavirus impact (RTCOV 2020) (pp. 518-524). Atlantis Press. doi:10.2991/assehr.k.201105.092

Steimle, J. (2022). On-Skin Computing. *Communications of the Association for Computing Machinery (ACM).* https://cacm.acm.org/magazines/2022/4/259400-on-skin-computing/fulltext

Stevens, P. (2020). *Companies are making bold promises about greater diversity, but there's a long way to go.* https://www.cnbc.com/2020/06/11/companies-are-making-bold-promises-about-greater-diversity-theres-a-long-way-to-go.html

Storey, J. (1987). *Developments in the management of human resources: an interim report.* Warwick Papers in Industrial Relations, 17, IRRU, School of Industrial and Business Studies, University of Warwick.

Storey, J. (1992). *Developments in the Management of Human Resources: An Analytical Review.* Blackwell.

Strohmeier, S. (2013). Employee relationship management—Realizing competitive advantage through information technology? *Human Resource Management Review, 23*(1), 93–104.

Swift and efficient: Using artificial intelligence to enhance the talent acquisition process. (2021). In *Development and Learning in Organizations* (Vol. 35, Issue 5, pp. 43–45). Emerald Group Holdings Ltd. doi:10.1108/DLO-11-2020-0224

Taboroši, S., Strukan, E., Poštin, J., Konjikušić, M., & Nikolić, M. (2020). Organizational commitment and trust at work by remote employees. *Journal of Engineering Management and Competitiveness, 10*(1), 48–60. doi:10.5937/jemc2001048T

Taleo Research. (2010). *Talent Intelligent: The Key to Business Success.* Taleo.

Tamkin, P. (2005). *The Contribution of Skills to Business Performance.* Institute for Employment Studies (IES). https://www.employment-studies.co.uk/resource/contribution-skills-business-performance

Tange, K., De Donno, M., Fafoutis, X., & Dragoni, N. (2020). A Systematic Survey of Industrial Internet of Things Security: Requirements and Fog Computing Opportunities. *IEEE Communications Surveys and Tutorials, 22*(4), 2489–2520. doi:10.1109/COMST.2020.3011208

Taskan, B., Junça-Silva, A., & Caetano, A. (2022). Clarifying the conceptual map of VUCA: A systematic review. *International Journal of Organizational Analysis.*

Tata. (2018). *Cognitive Diversity: AI and The Future of Work.* Tata Communications.

Taylor, M. P., Boxall, P., Chen, J. J., Xu, X., Liew, A., & Adeniji, A. (2020). Operator 4.0 or Maker 1.0? Exploring the implications of Industrie 4.0 for innovation, safety and quality of work in small economies and enterprises. *Computers & Industrial Engineering, 139*, 105486. doi:10.1016/j.cie.2018.10.047

Thaler, R. H., & Sunstein, C. R. (2009). *Nudge: Improving decisions about health, wealth, and happiness*. HeinOnline.

Thoben, K. D., Wiesner, S., & Wuest, T. (2017). Industrie 4.0 and smart manufacturing-a review of research issues and application examples. *International Journal of automation technology, 11*(1), 4-16.

Thomas, O. (2018). Two decades of cognitive bias research in entrepreneurship: What do we know and where do we go from here? *Management Review Quarterly, 68*(2), 107–143. doi:10.100711301-018-0135-9

Tiwari, M. (2022, July 25). *An effective framework to prepare workplaces for digital transformation*. https://hr.economictimes.indiatimes.com/news/workplace-4-0/learning-and-development/an-effective-framework-to-prepare-workplaces-for-digital-transformation/93105433

Tomar, S., & Gaur, M. (2020). HR Analytics in Business: Role, Opportunities, and Challenges of Using It. *Journal of Xi'an University of Architecture & Technology, 12*(7), 1299–1306.

Toniolo, K., Masiero, E., Massaro, M., & Bagnoli, C. (2020). Sustainable business models and artificial intelligence: Opportunities and challenges. *Knowledge, People, and Digital Transformation*, 103-117.

Torraco, R. J. (2005). Writing integrative literature reviews: Guidelines and examples. *Human Resource Development Review, 4*(3), 356–367. doi:10.1177/1534484305278283

Torraco, R. J. (2016). Writing integrative reviews of the literature: Methods and purposes. *International Journal of Adult Vocational Education and Technology, 7*(3), 62–70. doi:10.4018/IJAVET.2016070106

Torrington, D., Hall, L., Taylor, S., & Atkinson, C. (2017). *Human Resource Management* (10th ed.). Pearson.

Truss, C., Gratton, L., Hope-Hailey, V., McGovern, P., & Stiles, P. (1997). Soft and hard models of human resource management: A reappraisal. *Journal of Management Studies, 34*(1), 53–73. doi:10.1111/1467-6486.00042

Tukker, A. (2004). Eight Types of Product–Service System: Eight Ways To Sustainability? Experiences From Suspronet. *Business Strategy and the Environment, 13*(4), 246–260. doi:10.1002/bse.414

Tulasi, D., Lukito, R., Wahyu, D., & Ellitan, L. (2019). *The Role of Leadership in Industrial Revolution 4.0*. Academic Press.

Turing, A. M. (1950). Computing machinery and intelligence. *Mind, 59*(236), 433–460. doi:10.1093/mind/LIX.236.433

Türkel, S., & Arıkan, Ö. U. (2020). Strategic Human Resources Management and the Intersecting Ecosystem of Industry 4.0. *Toros University FEASS Journal of Social Sciences, 7*(12), 115–139.

Ulrich, D. (2022). *How HR Innovation Is Driving The Future Of Work?* Sage.

UNESCO. (2020, March 30). *COVID-19 Webinar: A new world for teachers, education's frontline workers - COVID-19 education webinar #2*. UNESCO. https://en.unesco.org/news/covid-19-webinar-new-world-teachers-educations-frontline-workers-covid-19-education-webinar-2

Ustundag, A., & Tanyas, M. (2009). The Impacts of Radio Frequency Identification (Rfıd) Technology On Supply Chain Costs. *Transportation Research Part E, Logistics and Transportation Review, 45*(1), 29–38. doi:10.1016/j.tre.2008.09.001

Vatansever, Ç., Çalışkan, S. & Işık, İ. (2015). Bir Dünya Şirketinin Türkiye'deki Çalışanlarına göre Çeşitliliklerin Yönetimi: Gömülü Kuram Analiziyle Modelleme [Diversity Management by Employees of a World Company in Turkey: Modeling with Embedded Theory Analysis]. *Yönetim Araştırmaları Dergisi, 2*(1-2), 29-61.

Vaughan, K. (2008). Workplace Learning: A Literature Review. In *NZCER Press*. New Zealand Council for Educational Research.

Veena, V., & Bhanumathi, P. (2021). Inclusion of AI in improving employee retention among millennials: A case study of select IT firms. *PIMT Journal of Research UGC approved (Care List), 13*(4).

Veletsianos, G., & Houlden, S. (2020, October 2). *An analysis of flexible learning and flexibility over the last 40 years of Distance Education.* Routledge. doi:10.1080/01587919.2019.1681893

Verma, A., Bansal, M., & Verma, J. (2020). Industry 4.0: reshaping the future of HR. In Strategic Direction (Vol. 36, Issue 5, pp. 9–11). Emerald Group Holdings Ltd. doi:10.1108/SD-12-2019-0235

Verma, R., Bharti, U., & Tripathi, U. (2022). Digital Era And Its Impact On Leadership Transformation. *Sachetas, 1*(2), 36–41. doi:10.55955/120003

Victory, J. (2022). *Bone-anchored hearing systems.* https://www.healthyhearing.com/help/hearing-aids/bone-anchored

Villaronga, F. E., Kieseberg, P., & Li, T. (2018). Humans forget, machines remember: Artificial intelligence and the Right to Be Forgotten. *Computer Law & Security Review, 34*(2), 304–313. doi:10.1016/j.clsr.2017.08.007

Vinitha, K., Prabhu, R. A., Bhaskar, R., & Hariharan, R. (2020). Review on industrial mathematics and materials at Industry 1.0 to Industry 4.0. *Materials Today: Proceedings, 33*, 3956–3960. doi:10.1016/j.matpr.2020.06.331

Voydanoff, P. (2005). Toward a conceptualization of perceived work-family fit and balance: A demands and resources approach. *Journal of Marriage and Family, 67*(4), 822–836. doi:10.1111/j.1741-3737.2005.00178.x

Vrontis, D., Christofi, M., Pereira, V., Tarba, S., Makrides, A., & Trichina, E. (2022). Artificial intelligence, robotics, advanced technologies and human resource management: A systematic review. *International Journal of Human Resource Management, 33*(6), 1237–1266. doi:10.1080/09585192.2020.1871398

Wagner, S. M., & Sutter, R. (2012). A Qualitative Investigation of Innovation Between Third--Party Logistics Providers and Customers. *International Journal of Production Economics, 140*(2), 944–958. doi:10.1016/j.ijpe.2012.07.018

Walford-Wright, G., & Scott-Jackson, W. (2018). Talent Rising; People Analytics and Technology Driving Talent Acquisition Strategy. *Strategic HR Review, 17*(5), 226–233. doi:10.1108/SHR-08-2018-0071

Wallace, G., & Little, M. (2022). *Printing the future: 3D bioprinters and their uses.* Retrieved from https://www.science.org.au/curious/people-medicine/bioprinting#~:text= Bioprinting %20is% 20 an%20extension%20of,medical%20procedures%2C%20training%20and%20testing

Waller, M. A., & Fawcett, S. E. (2013). Data Science, Predictive Analytics, And Big Data: A Revolution That Will Transform Supply Chain Design and Management. *Journal of Business Logistics, 34*(2), 77–84. doi:10.1111/jbl.12010

Walton, R. E. (1985). From Control to Commitment in the Workplace. *Harvard Business Review, 63*(2), 77–84.

Wang, F. (2021, April). Research on enterprise human resource management innovation in big data era. []. IOP Publishing.]. *Journal of Physics: Conference Series, 1881*(4), 042038. doi:10.1088/1742-6596/1881/4/042038

Watkins, K. E., & Marsick, V. J. (2021). Informal and Incidental Learning in the time of COVID-19. *Advances in Developing Human Resources, 23*(1), 88–96. doi:10.1177/1523422320973656

Webster, J., & Watson, R. T. (2002). Analyzing the past to prepare for the future: Writing a literature review. *Management Information Systems Quarterly*, xiii–xxiii.

Welle, B. (Director). (2018). *Applied Perspective: Vol. Wharton People Analytics Conference 2018* [Video]. https://youtu.be/RyD2I0pUR1I

Wheeldon, J., & Faubert, J. (2009). Framing experience: Concept maps, mind maps, and data collection in qualitative research. *International Journal of Qualitative Methods*, *8*(3), 68–83. doi:10.1177/160940690900800307

Wheeler, M. A., & Gunasekara, A. (2020, May 18). *Forget Work-Life Balance – It's All About Integration in the Age of COVID-19.* https://www.nextgov.com/ideas/2020/05/forget-work-life-balance-its-all-about-integration-age-covid-19/165473/

Whittington, R., Cailluet, L., & Yakis-Douglas, B. (2011). Opening strategy: Evolution of a precarious profession. *British Journal of Management*, *22*(3), 531–544. doi:10.1111/j.1467-8551.2011.00762.x

Wiblen, S., & Marler, J. H. (2021). Digitalised talent management and automated talent decisions: The implications for HR professionals. *International Journal of Human Resource Management*, *32*(12), 2592–2621. doi:10.1080/09585192.2021.1886149

Wibowo, S., Suryana, Y., & Kaltum, U. (2021). Value Creation with Big Data in Marketing: An Empirical Evidence on SMEs. *Asian Journal of Business and Accounting*, *14*(2), 173–196.

Wilkinson, A., Dundon, T., & Redman, T. (2021). Contemporary Human Resource Management: Text and Cases. *Sage (Atlanta, Ga.)*.

Wilson, J. H., & Daugherty, R. P. (2018). Collaborative Intelligence: Humans and AI Are Joining Forces. *Harvard Business Review*, 2–11.

Wirges, F., & Neyer, A.-K. (2022). Towards a Process-Oriented Understanding of HR Analytics: Implementation and application. *Review of Managerial Science*. Advance online publication. doi:10.100711846-022-00574-0

Wong, C. (2019). Changing Organizational From Embedded Bias to Equity And Inclusion. *Professional Safety Journal,* 26-30.

Wong, I. (2020). *Adjusting your employees to long-term remote work.* Fast Company. https://www.fastcompany.com/90539478/is-your-team-prepared-for-long-term-remote-work-ask-these-3-questions-to-determine-if-they-are

Wontorczyk, A., & Rożnowski, B. (2022). Remote, Hybrid, and On-Site Work during the SARS-CoV-2 Pandemic and the Consequences for Stress and Work Engagement. *International Journal of Environmental Research and Public Health*, *19*(4), 2400. doi:10.3390/ijerph19042400 PMID:35206590

Wood, S. (1996). High Commitment Management and Unionization in the UK. *International Journal of Human Resource Management*, *7*(1), 41–58. doi:10.1080/09585199600000117

Work Management. (2022). 23 Remote Team Management Tools & Software. *Scoro.* https://www.scoro.com/blog/remote-employee-management-tools/.

World Economic Forum. (2019). https://www.weforum.org/agenda/2019/01/these-four-leadership-styles-are-key-to-success-in-the-fourth-industrial-revolution/

World Economic Forum. (2022). *Augmented Workforce: Empowering People, Transforming Manufacturing.* World Economic Forum and University of Cambridge.

Wu, J. (2020, March 9). A Deep Dive Into Remote Work For Our Future Of Work. *Forbes*. https://www.forbes.com/sites/cognitiveworld/2020/03/09/a-deep-dive-into-remote-work-for-our-future-of-work/?sh=6b11177d1
843

Xin, D. D., Ma, L. L., Liu, J. J., Macke, S. S., Song, S. S., & Parameswaran, A. A. (2018). Accelerating Human-in-the-loop Machine Learning: Challenges and opportunities. *Proceedings of the 2nd Workshop on Data Management for End-To-End Machine Learning, DEEM 2018 - In Conjunction with the 2018 ACM SIGMOD/PODS Conference*. 10.1145/3209889.3209897

Xing, B. (2016). Smart Robot Control via Novel Computational Intelligence Methods for Ambient Assisted Living. In Trends in Ambient Intelligent Systems: The Role of Computational Intelligence. Springer International Publishing. doi:10.1007/978-3-319-30184-6_2

Xu, L. D., Xu, E. L., & Li, L. (2018). Industry 4.0: State of The Art and Future Trends. *International Journal of Production Research*, *56*(8), 2941–2962. doi:10.1080/00207543.2018.1444806

Xu, X., Lu, Y., Vogel-Heuser, B., & Wang, L. (2021). Industry 4.0 and Industry 5.0—Inception, conception and perception. *Journal of Manufacturing Systems*, *61*, 530–535. doi:10.1016/j.jmsy.2021.10.006

Yacan, İ. (2021). Industry 4.0 Technologies and Society 5.0 Concept. *International Journal of Academic Research and Ideas*, *13*(27), 31–39.

Yadav, R., & Khanna, A., & Chenab. (2022). Quality of work life, emotional and physical well-being of police personnel in India. *International Journal of Police Science & Management*, *24*(1), 89–99.

Yadav, R., Khanna, A., & Dasmohapatra, S. (2019). The effects of quality of work life on organisational commitment and job satisfaction: A study of academic professionals in higher education sector. *International Journal of Learning and Change*, *11*(2), 129–144.

Yarberry, S., & Sims, C. (2021). The Impact of COVID-19-Prompted Virtual/Remote Work Environments on Employees' Career Development: Social Learning Theory, Belongingness, and Self-Empowerment. *Advances in Developing Human Resources*, *23*(3), 237–252. doi:10.1177/15234223211017850

Yetkin, E. G., & Coşkun, K. (2021). Industry 5.0 (Society 5.0) ve Architecture. *European Journal of Science and Technology*, (27), 347–353.

Yi, J., Nasukawa, T., Bunescu, R., & Niblack, W. (2003). Sentiment analyzer: Extracting sentiments about a given topic using natural language processing techniques. In *Third IEEE international conference on data mining* (pp. 427-434). IEEE.

Yıldırım, M., & Bayraktar, C. (2014). Automation & Barcode System In Businesses And Contributions To Accounting Processes. *Business And Management Studies An International Journal*, *2*(1), 38–48. doi:10.15295/bmij.v2i1.57

Yin, Y., Stecke, K. E., & Li, D. (2018). The Evolution of Production Systems From Industry 2.0 Through Industry 4.0. *International Journal of Production Research*, *56*(1-2), 848–861. doi:10.1080/00207543.2017.1403664

Yuan, C., Liu, W., Zhou, G., Shi, X., Long, S., Chen, Z., & Yan, X. (2022). Supply chain innovation announcements and shareholder value under industries 4.0 and 5.0: evidence from China. *Industrial Management & Data Systems*.

Yücebalkan, B. (2021). Overview of The Transition From Industry 4.0 To Industry 5.0. *Pearson Journal Of Social Sciences & Humanities*, *5*(9), 241–250.

Yuile, C., Chang, A., Gudmundsson, A., & Sawang, S. (2012). The role of life friendly policies on employees' work-life balance. *Journal of Management & Organization*, *18*(1), 53–63. doi:10.1017/S1833367200001061

Zamfirescu, C. B., Pirvu, B. C., Gorecky, D., & Chakravarthy, H. (2014). Human-centred assembly: A case study for an anthropocentric cyber-physical system. *Procedia Technology*, *15*, 90–98. doi:10.1016/j.protcy.2014.09.038

Zampetakis, L. A., & Moustakis, V. (2011). Managers' trait emotional intelligence and group outcomes: The case of group job satisfaction. *Small Group Research*, *42*(1), 77–102. doi:10.1177/1046496410373627

Zaus, R., & Choi, H. N. (2014). Evolving The Network For Machine-To-Machine Communication. *Intel Technology Journal*, *18*(1), 194–202.

Zehir, C., Karaboğa, T., & Başar, D. (2020). The transformation of human resource management and its impact on overall business performance: big data analytics and AI technologies in strategic HRM. In *Digital business strategies in blockchain ecosystems* (pp. 265–279). Springer. doi:10.1007/978-3-030-29739-8_12

Zeybel, M., Dervişoğlu, H., Eğriboz, E., Özbilen, M. L., & Bahadırlar, Y. (2020). New Trends in Artificial Intelligence. *Tubitak Bilgem,* (9).

Zhang, Y., Xu, S., Zhang, L., & Yang, M. (2021). Big data and human resource management research: An integrative review and new directions for future research. *Journal of Business Research*, *133*, 34–50. doi:10.1016/j.jbusres.2021.04.019

Zheng, L., Noroozi, V., & Yu, P. S. (2017). Joint deep modeling of users and items using reviews for recommendation. *WSDM 2017 - Proceedings of the 10th ACM International Conference on Web Search and Data Mining*, 425–433. 10.1145/3018661.3018665

Zhou, Y., Cheng, Y., Zou, Y., & Liu, G. (2021). e-HRM: A meta-analysis of the antecedents, consequences, and cross-national moderators. *Human Resource Management Review, 100862.* Advance online publication. doi:10.1016/j.hrmr.2021.100862

Zhuying, L., Brandmueller, F., Greuter, & Mueller, F. (2018). The Guts Game: Designing Playful Experiences for Ingestible Devices. In *Extended Abstracts of the 2018 CHI Conference on Human Factors in Computing Systems (CHI EA '18).* ACM. 10.1145/3170427.3186604

Zicong, L. (2021). Ethical Problems Concerning Human Augmentation Technology and Its Future Aspects. *Advances in Social Science, Education and Humanities Research,* vol. 554. *Proceedings of the 7th International Conference on Humanities and Social Science Research.*

Zineb, E. F., Najat, R., & Jaafar, A. (2021). An Intelligent Approach for Data Analysis and Decision Making in Big Data: A Case Study on E-commerce Industry. *International Journal of Advanced Computer Science and Applications*, *12*(7). doi:10.14569/IJACSA.2021.0120783

Zulkifli, S. L. A., Omar, S. S., Ariffin, Z. Z., Mahadi, N., & Yaakop, A. Y. (2021). A Review of Leadership Approaches in the Industrial Revolution of 4.0 Era. *Online Journal for TVET Practitioners*, *6*(2), 21–27.

About the Contributors

Naman Sharma is currently affiliated with the Indian Institute of Foreign Trade, Kolkata (India), as an Assistant Professor, and has nearly six years of academic experience in the field of Human resources, entrepreneurship, and strategic management. Before joining IIFT, Dr Sharma has worked with the Entrepreneurship Development Institute of India and was fortunate to be a part of the country's entrepreneurial ecosystem. He conducted several workshops for young entrepreneurs, sensitizing them about entrepreneurship and training them to get the best out of the country's ecosystem for their entrepreneurial journey. Dr Sharma also has substantial research experience. His research has been published in ABDC ranked/Scopus Indexed journals such as Journal of Organizational Change Management, International Journal of Organisational Analysis etc. and with reputable publishers such as the Emerald Publishing Group and Springer. He has also authored/edited books with various publishers of international repute such as IGI-Global and World Scientific. He is also serving as a guest editor for various reputed journals.

Kumar Shalender is a Post-Doctoral Fellow of the Global Institute of Flexible Systems Management and a Doctor of Philosophy in Strategic Management. He has more than 14-year experience in the domain of Business Policy, Strategic Management, and Business Model Development and a total of 70 Publications including presentations at international/national conferences and book chapters to his credit. His current research areas include the field of Metaverse, Blockchain Technology, and Sustainable Development with a special focus on sustainable cities and mobility ecosystems in India.

* * *

Pooja Agrawal currently working in Vishwakarma University as management faculty. Her area of expertise are competency mapping, leadership and Human resource management.

Meltem Akca works as the Deputy Dean of the Gazipaşa Aeronautics and Astronautics Faculty in Alanya Alaaddin Keykubat University, Türkiye. She has graduate degrees in Business Administration and Aviation Management. She also got a minor in Logistics management. Her master's degree in finance. In addition, she completed a second master's degree in civil aviation management. She holds a PhD in management and organization. Her associate professorship is in the field of management and strategy. In addition to her studies in business administration, she has multidisciplinary works in logistics and aviation management science.

Subhash Chander Arora is a PhD Research Scholar in Faculty of Management Studies, Gurukula Kangri (Deemed University), India. He is currently pursuing his Doctorate in Marketing titled as "Driving towards Sustainable Mobility: An analysis of factors influencing the adoption intention of electric vehicles among Indian Consumers. He has done his graduation/(B.Com Hons.) from Delhi College of Arts and Commerce (DCAC), University of Delhi and his Masters in Commerce from Shri Ram College of Commerce (SRCC), University of Delhi. He has one paper publication in Scopus indexed journal published by Springer. His interest areas include green marketing, sustainability, product and innovation management, consumer psychology and customer relationship management. Besides, he holds keen interest in International Business/Relations.

Ayla Avci graduated from Anadolu University, Department of Business Administration. She completed her master's thesis with her thesis on nepotism at Istanbul Sabahattin Zaim University. In 2021, she completed his doctoral thesis with her research on the workload and job boredom of employees. There are articles and book chapters in many national and international journals. Ayla Avci works as an assistant professor and head of department in the department of international trade and business at Antalya AKEV University.

Pramit Banerjee is a research scholar in Indian Institute of Foreign Trade (IIFT). He has done his Master of Business Administration (MBA) from Bharathidasan Institute of Management (BIM), Trichy and has around six years of experience in information technology sector. He has played different roles of Business Analysis, Product Specialist and Scrum Master while working in domains like Human Capital Management, E-commerce and Banking in reputed multi-national company as well as in startup company. His areas of interest include Strategic Management of Human Resources and Technology Management.

Sandeep Banger is acting as an Assistant Professor at University School of Applied Management, Punjabi University Patiala, Punjab, India. He is also acting as associate editor for International Journal of Technology Transfer and Commercialisation and editorial member of IJBG. He is qualified in diverse areas like LLB, MBA (HR) and Ph.D. in Management. He has more than ten years' experience in teaching and research. He is trainer of various software like SPSS, AMOS, Warp-PLS, Smart-PlS, ADANCO and JAMOVI.

Ece Boyacı graduated from the Department of International Trade at Alanya Alaaddin Keykubat University in 2021. In 2021, she started her master's degree in International Trade at Alanya Alaaddin Keykubat University. In order to contribute to social science in 2022, she published her first research article in the journal Alanya Akademik Bakış. Her areas of interest are international relations, logistics and the dynamics of international trade.

Smruti Bulsari is currently working as a Senior Research Officer in the ESRC Business and Local Government Data Research Centre, University of Essex. She has more than 17 years of teaching experience in Universities in India and possesses a strong research portfolio. Currently, she is pursuing research in the areas of vulnerable people and inequality, with special reference to healthcare. She also gives talks on Gender Sensitivity and Empowerment, and on data/statistics related topics. Dr Bulsari also delivers lectures in various national and international training programmes in quantitative techniques and data analysis.

Anna Cugno is associate professor at Department of Economics, Social Studies, Applied Mathematics and Statistics Department, University of Turin.

Monica Cugno is associate professor in Economics and Business Management at Management Department, University of Turin.

Minakshi Kishore holds a PhD in Business Administration and has 20 years of experience in Education and Teaching. Presently works as a lectures in London School of Management Education, London. She has a few research papers to her credit and keeps updating her knowledge and skills through attending International conferences and seminars.

Sahar Mesfar is a Ph.D student in Marketing at the Faculty of Economic Sciences and Management of Sfax, Tunisia. She was an author and co-author and she was a reviewer in IGI Global and European Journal of Marketing. Her research interests include Digital Marketing, Consumer Behaviour, Big Data Marketing, International Trade.

Ariadna Monje-Amor holds a Ph.D. in Economic Analysis and Business Strategy, a Master's in Human Resource Management, and a Bachelor's degree in Commerce. She is a lecturer at the University of A Coruña (Spain). Her research interests include organizational behaviour, human resource management, entrepreneurship, strategic employee relations, and organizational change.

David Egbe Ola is an experienced educator and currently a Doctoral candidate at the University of Port Harcourt, he has M Sc, B Sc in Computer Science and a Postgraduate Diploma in Education from the University of Port Harcourt Choba, Rivers State, Benue State University Makurdi and Usmanu Danfodiyo University Sokoto all in Nigeria respectively, he currently Lectures at the Department of Computer Science, Federal College of Education (Technical) Omoku Rivers State in Nigeria. His current research interest is blockchain technology.

Bhanumathi P. is an Associate Professor in the Human Resource Management Department at Ramaiah Institute of Management, Bangalore. She completed her Ph.D. in Knowledge management from the University of Mysore. She has qualified in UGC NET and AMT certification from AIMA and has over 18+ years of teaching and seven years of research experience. She is also a recognized Ph.D. guide at Ramaiah University of Applied Sciences. Her recent research works are on studying the applications of Artificial Intelligence in Human resource management functions, including recruitment, talent retention, and the impact of unconscious human bias in HR functions. Also, in stress management, workday analytics, and employee engagement. She has published research papers in peer-reviewed journals, including UGC-listed journals and a few reputed conferences. She has given talks on AI in HRM. She has served as coordinator of the PGDM-AICTE program of RIM since June 2016 and has attended many workshops. She has also served as one of the book's reviewers titled "Management Information System" (11th edition), authored by James O'Brien and published by Tata McGraw Hill in 2019. She has two patents on her credit.

Kiran Pandya has retired from the position of Provost of a large private University in Gujarat, India. He is also appointed as Member, National Statistical Commission under the Ministry of Statistics and

Programme Implementation, Government of India since 2019. He has more than 40 years of teaching experience and has a strong research portfolio. He was on the advisory panel of a research project funded by the British Academy; the host institution being Durham University. He has served as Professor & Head, Department of Human Resource Development, Veer Narmad South Gujarat University, Surat for nearly 15 years. Prof Pandya pursued his doctorate in economics from the University of Sussex; he was awarded the Commonwealth Scholarship for the same. But he decided to settle down in India with an objective to contribute his bit towards development of academic fraternity and cause of education, in which he was successful. The contribution of strengthening the base of research methodology, quantitative techniques and use of software / automation can be credited to him.

Jeevitha R. is an Assistant Professor at the Ramaiah Institute of Management. A postgraduate in MBA(Finance) from Mysore University. She has a sound academic record and has graduated as a topper in Bachelor's and Master's levels. She also cleared the UGC NET in June 2012. She is passionate about pursuing research in the area of Finance and is currently pursuing research in Hedge Funds in India from VTU.

Shraddha Rathod is a research scholar at Vishwakarma University. Her area of knowledge and learning is Leadership, Happiness, Mental being, and Human behavior. She is pursuing her Ph.D. under the guidance of Dr. Pooja Agrawal.

Gizem Şarlıoğlu graduated from Alanya Alaaddin Keykubat University, Department of International Trade in 2020 and started her master's degree in International Trade at Alanya Alaaddin Keykubat University in 2021. Her fields of interest include international marketing, economics and statistics.

Vinod Kumar Singh is Finance Officer of Gurukula Kangri (Deemed to be University). He is also Head and Dean at Faculty of Management Studies, of Gurukula Kangri (Deemed to be University). He has supervised more than 27 students in PhD program. He has published many books and research papers in reputed journal of ABDC, SCOPUS, Web of Science and UGC care listed journals. He has teaching experience of more than 25 years in academic world. He has also served as a reputed officer in Indian Airforce.

Rema V. has a demonstrated history of working in the education sector for 10+ years. She teaches Business Analytics courses such as R programming, Predictive Analytics, SPSS, Operations Research, Business Mathematics, Statistics, and Research Methodology to PG Management students. She is a gold medalist in M.Sc. Applied Mathematics from Christ University, Bengaluru and a first rank holder in B.Sc. in Statistics, Economics and Mathematics from Mount Carmel College, Bengaluru. She has submitted her Doctoral Thesis in the area of Stochastics and Healthcare Analytics. She has presented papers in several National and International Conferences of repute and her work is published in Scopus indexed, Springer and IEEE publications. She is passionate about writing and has co-authored a book titled "Business Mathematics" published by Cengage Learning and a book chapter for the edited book on Gender Equality & Women Empowerment. She dons multiple hats- a Guest speaker, avid researcher, Editorial board member of a peer reviewed International Journal, External examiner, and performs key administrative roles in the area of Accreditations & Rankings, Newsletter Editor, team member of the Japanese Centre, Content development, Media Team, Student Department club among several others.

Radha Yadav is working as an Assistant Professor with CHRIST (Deemed to be University) Bangalore in the School of Business and Management. She earned her PhD in HR/OB from IIT Roorkee. Her areas of expertise are HRM, and Organisation Behaviourt. She is a passionate researcher with great enthusiasm for teaching.

Index

I

K

L

M

O

P

R

S

T

V

W

www.ingramcontent.com/pod-product-compliance
Lightning Source LLC
LaVergne TN
LVHW062146300926
849161LV00010B/2639